T0136211

Blockchain for Information Security and Privacy

Blockchain for Information Security and Privacy

Edited by

Udai Pratap Rao
Piyush Kumar Shukla
Chandan Trivedi
Sweta Gupta
Zelalem Sintayehu Shibeshi

CRC Press
Taylor & Francis Group
Boca Raton London New York

CRC Press is an imprint of the
Taylor & Francis Group, an **informa** business

AN AUERBACH BOOK

First edition published 2022
by CRC Press
6000 Broken Sound Parkway NW, Suite 300, Boca Raton, FL 33487-2742

and by CRC Press
2 Park Square, Milton Park, Abingdon, Oxon, OX14 4RN

ISBN: 978-0-367-65448-1 (hbk)
ISBN: 978-1-032-14628-7 (pbk)
ISBN: 978-1-003-12948-6 (ebk)

DOI: 10.1201/9781003129486

Typeset in Garamond
by SPi Technologies India Pvt Ltd (Straive)

Contents

Preface

This book provides the reader with the most up-to-date knowledge of blockchain in mainstream areas of security, trust, and privacy in the decentralized domain, something which is both timely and essential. This is because the distributed and P2P applications are increasing on an almost daily basis, and the attackers adopt new mechanisms to threaten the security and privacy of the users in those environments. This book also provides technical information regarding blockchain-oriented software, applications, and tools required for the researcher and developer experts in both computing and software engineering to provide solutions and automated systems against current security, trust, and privacy issues in cyberspace.

Blockchain, a decentralized cryptographic-based technology, is promising for the Internet of Things (IoT) security, affecting many areas, including manufacturing, finance, healthcare, supply chain, identity management, e-governance, defence, education, banking, and trading. This book gives an overview of blockchain technology application domains in IoT, such as Vehicle Web, Power Web, Cloud Internet, Edge Computing, etc. This book also include categorization and side-by-side comparison of modern methods towards secure and privacy-preserving blockchain technology concerning specific safety objectives, efficiency, limitations, computational complexity, and communication overhead.

Trust is a crucial factor as cyber-physical systems need to depend on resources and assets controlled by various organizations, such as Edge, Fog, and Cloud computing. While numerous real-world frameworks attempt to assist such integration, they have platform independence, security, resource management, and multi-application execution limitations that provide insights to application based solutions. Decentralized digital ledger technology also allows people to create encrypted digital identities easily accessible via mobile applications and can verify identity as and when necessary. This book will discuss how blockchain can be used in various identity management applications and authentication in election voting.

In blockchain-based finance, security and privacy challenges can be solved at a more customized level with significantly less time. On the security aspect, it has distributed consensus, which reduces data theft by an intermediary. It showcases driving instruments to granular information security over each product stack layer, permitting certain information sharing in business systems. The expanding prominence of a keen, smart meter, smart home, smart city, and smart services applications has presented exceptional interest for improving the hidden data innovation framework to guarantee the straightforwardness, security, and protection of client information. Blockchain is a promising innovation fit for tending to such requests. This book will also focus on the security and privacy concerns of various smart applications, present existing issues and challenges with case studies related to these applications.

The rising blockchain innovation demonstrates the promising potential to upgrade modern frameworks and IoT by giving applications with repetition, changeless capacity, and encryption. In this book, we address the combination of blockchain and IoT from concerning industrial perspective. This book presents blockchain empowered IoT structure that included basic methods, principles, applications, and critical difficulties. This book also explore the various blockchain-based systems such as the Internet of Vehicles (IoV), Electronic Healthcare Records (EHR), Copyrights Management, and Domain Name Broker services for ensuring security, protection, and high accessibility.

Editors

Udai Pratap Rao is an Assistant Professor in the Department of Computer Engineering at Sardar Vallabhbhai National Institute of Technology, Surat. In 2014, he earned a PhD in Computer Engineering at Sardar Vallabhbhai National Institute of Technology, Surat. His research interests include Information security and privacy, Location-based privacy, Security in IoT and Cyber Physical Systems, Big Data analytics, distributed computing, and methodologies that promote interdisciplinary education.

Piyush Kumar Shukla is an Associate Professor in the Department of Computer Science and Engineering at the University Institute of Technology – Rajiv Gandhi Proudyogiki Vishwavidyalaya (Technological University of Madhya Pradesh), Bhopal, India. He has 15 years' experience in teaching and research. He completed a postdoctoral fellowship (PDF), Information Security Education and Awareness Project Phase II.

Chandan Trivedi is an Assistant Professor in the Computer Science and Engineering Department at Nirma University. He has more than six years' teaching experience. He earned a BTech in Computer Science Engineering at Rajasthan Technical University, Kota, and MTech in Computer Engineering at Sardar Vallabhbhai National Institute of Technology, Surat.

Sweta Gupta is an Assistant Professor in the Department of Computer Science and Engineering at JLU School of Engineering and Technology. She has a 10+ years of academic as well as industrial experience.

Zelalem Sintayehu Shibeshi is a Senior Lecturer at Rhodes University, South Africa. He earned a PhD at Rhodes University (2016) and a BSc in physics (1989), an associate degree in computer science (1999), and MSc in information science (2001) at Addis Ababa University, Ethiopia.

Contributors

L. Javid Ali
Department of Information
Technology
St. Joseph's Institute of Technology
Chennai, India

Bhavna Bajpai
Department of Information Technology
Dr. C.V. Raman University
Khandwa, India

Ankur Bang
Sardar Vallabhbhai National Institute of
Technology
Surat, India

Smita Bansod
Information Technology Department
Shah & Anchor Kutchhi Engineering
College
Mumbai, India

Pronaya Bhattacharya
Department of Computer Science and
Engineering
Institute of Technology
Nirma University
Ahmedabad, India

Madhuri Bhavsar
Department of Computer Science and
Engineering
Institute of Technology
Nirma University
Ahmedabad, India

Umesh Bodkhe
Department of Computer Science and
Engineering
Institute of Technology
Nirma University
Ahmedabad, India

Preeti Chandrakar
Department of Computer Science and
Engineering
National Institute of Technology
Raipur, India

S. Chandraprabha
Department of Electrical
and Computer Engineering
KPR Institute of Engineering and
Technology
Coimbatore, India

Subrata Chowdhury
Sri Venkateswara College of
Engineering and Technology
(Autonomous)
Chittoor, India

Narendra Kumar Dewangan
Department of Computer Science and
Engineering
National Institute of Technology
Raipur, India

Ram Kishan Dewangan
Department of Computer Science and
  Engineering
Thapar Institute of Engineering and
  Technology
Patiala, India

Ayushi Dwivedi
Amity Institute of Forensic Sciences
Faculty of Science and Technology
Amity University
Noida, India

Bhavesh N. Gohil
Department of Computer Science and
  Engineering
Sardar Vallabhbhai National Institute
  of Technology
Surat, India

S. Gomathi
UK International Qualifications, Ltd.
Sharjah, UAE

Nirmal Kumar Gupta
Manipal University Jaipur
Jaipur, India

Rajeev Kumar Gupta
Pandit Deendayal Energy University
Gujarat, India

Shubham Gupta
Department of Computer Science and
  Engineering
Sardar Vallabhbhai National Institute
  of Technology
Surat, India

Sweta Gupta
Jagran Lakecity University
Bhopal, India

Aanchal Handa
HSBC Technology
India

Aditya Hirapara
Department of Computer Science and
  Engineering
Sardar Vallabhbhai National Institute
  of Technology
Surat, India

Aakanksha Jain
Department of Computer Science
  Engineering
Poornima University
Jaipur, Rajasthan, India

Ashish Jain
Manipal University Jaipur
Jaipur, India

Avinash Jaiswal
Department of Computer Science and
  Engineering
Sardar Vallabhbhai National Institute
  of Technology
Surat, India

Dhaval Jha
Department of Computer Science and
  Engineering
Institute of Technology
Nirma University
Ahmedabad, India

Atharva Kalsekar
Department of Computer Science and
  Engineering
Sardar Vallabhbhai National Institute
  of Technology
Surat, India

S. Usha Kiruthika
School of Computer Science and
    Engineering
Vellore Institute of Technology
Chennai, India

Rogin Koshy
Department of Computer Science and
    Engineering
Sardar Vallabhbhai National Institute of
    Technology
Surat, India

Rishabh Kumar
Department of Computer Science and
    Engineering
Sardar Vallabhbhai National Institute of
    Technology
Surat, India

S.A. Siva Kumar
Department of Electrical and
    Computer Engineering
Ashoka Women's Engineering
    College
Kurnool, India

S. Gokul Kumar
Department of Technical Supply
    Chain
Ros Tech (A&D)
Bangalore, India

S. Satheesh Kumar
Department of Electrical and
    Computer Engineering
KPR Institute of Engineering and
    Technology
Coimbatore, India

Sarvesh Kumar
Babu Banarasi Das University
Lucknow, India

Ujjwal Kumar
Department of Computer Science and
    Engineering
Sardar Vallabhbhai National Institute of
    Technology
Surat, India

Sameer Mandloi
Department of Computer Science and
    Engineering
Sardar Vallabhbhai National Institute of
    Technology
Surat, India

Nisha Mansoori
EZDI Solutions and Healthcare
India

Abhishek Mehta
Parul Institute of Computer
    Application
Parul University
Vadodara, Gujarat, India

Amarnath Mishra
Amity Institute of Forensic Sciences
Faculty of Science and Technology
Amity University
Noida, India

Deep Mistry
Department of Computer Science
    Engineering
Sardar Vallabhbhai National Institute of
    Technology
Surat, India

Amruta Mulay
Department of Computer Science
    Engineering
Sardar Vallabhbhai National Institute of
    Technology
Surat, India

Rajit Nair
Inurture Education Solutions Private
    Limited
Bengaluru, India

Utkarsh Nigam
Department of Civil Engineering
L.D. College of Engineering
Ahmedabad, India

Nihal Parsania
Parul Institute of Computer Application
Parul University
Vadodara, India

Sankita Patel
Department of Computer Science and
    Engineering
Sardar Vallabhbhai National Institute
    of Technology
Surat, India

Vivek Kumar Prasad
Department of Computer Science and
    Engineering
Institute of Technology
Nirma University
Ahmedabad, India

Lata L. Ragha
Department of Computer Engineering
Fr. C. Rodrigues Institute of
    Technology
Navi Mumbai, India

S. Kanaga Suba Raja
Department of Information
    Technology
Easwari Engineering College
Chennai, India

C.J. Raman
Department of Information
    Technology
St. Joseph's College of Engineering
Chennai, India

Nikhil Ranjan
Department of Computer Science
    Engineering
Chandigarh University
Punjab, India

Udai Pratap Rao
Department of Computer Science and
    Engineering
Sardar Vallabhbhai National Institute
    of Technology
Surat, India

Paresh Rawat
S.N. Technology
Bhopal, India

Kevin Shah
Sardar Vallabhbhai National Institute
    of Technology
Surat, India

B. Maruthi Shankar
Department of Electrical and
    Computer Engineering
Sri Krishna College of Engineering and
    Technology
Coimbatore, India

Hrishabh Sharma
Department of Computer Engineering
Sardar Vallabhbhai National Institute
    of Technology
Surat, India

Piyush Kumar Shukla
Department of Computer Science and
Engineering
University Institute of Technology
Rajiv Gandhi Prodyogiki
Vishwavidyalaya
Bhopal, India

Debabrata Singh
Department of Computer
Application
ITER
SOA University
Bhubaneswar, India

Khushi Solanki
Parul Institute of Computer
Application
Parul University
Vadodara, India

Mukesh Soni
Department of Computer Science and
Engineering
Jagran Lackecity University
Bhopal, India

Priya Swaminarayan
Parul Institute of Computer
Application
Parul University
Vadodara, India

Shivangi Tanwar
John Deere Technology Centre
Pune, India

Chandan Trivedi
Department of Computer Science and
Engineering
Institute of Technology
Nirma University
Ahmedabad, India

Ashwin Verma
Department of Computer Science and
Engineering
Institute of Technology
Nirma University
Ahmedabad, India

Mehak Wadhwani
Monash University
Melbourne, Australia

Anil Kumar Yadav
IES College of Technology
Bhopal, India

Mohd Zuhair
Department of Computer Science and
Engineering
Institute of Technology
Nirma University
Ahmedabad, India

Chapter 1

Blockchain Impact in Education and Society

S. Gomathi
UK International Qualifications, Ltd., UAE

Mukesh Soni
Jagran Lackecity University, India

Utkarsh Nigam
L.D. College of Engineering, India

Bhavna Bajpai
Dr. C.V. Raman University, India

Subrata Chowdhury
Sri Venkateswara College of Engineering and Technology (Autonomous), India

Contents

DOI: 10.1201/9781003129486-1

1.1 Introduction

Blockchain was launched in 2008 as an emerging technology. The first time the transactions were registered in Bitcoin cryptocurrency [1] was used as a peer-to-peer ledger. The goal was to remove any intermediary (or third) parties and to allow users to transact directly. Blockchain has been developed to achieve this as a decentralized peer-node network. Every network node: (1) contains a copy of the transaction records; (2) writes an entry into the network's own record when it receives consensus from other network nodes; (3) broadcasts any transaction that the network user transmits to other nodes on the network; and (4) verifies periodically that the network's records are similar to those in the entire web [2]. As Bitcoin is continuing to grow in popularity, the tremendous potential of its underlying technology is realized by both researchers and practitioners [3]. Blockchain is used as a service in many other areas, not only in cryptocurrencies, since it has several key advantages: immutability, transparency, and trustworthiness.

Consequently, a growing number of Blockchain-based applications in various fields were developed [4]. The development of Blockchain-based applications, according to Gatteschi et al. [5], can be split into three key stages: 1.0, 2.0, and 3.0. Initially, it was used to allow single cash transactions, with Blockchain 1.0 for cryptocurrencies. Blockchain 2.0 for properties and smart contracts was eventually launched. These intelligent contracts enforce specific requirements and standards to be satisfied before being registered in the Blockchain. Registration happens without a third party's involvement. Many applications in different sectors, such as government [6], education [7], health [8], and science[9], were built in to Blockchain 3.0.

Blockchain remains in its early stages in its application for education. A small number of educational institutions rely entirely upon Blockchain technology. Most of these institutions use it to validate and share their students' academic and learning outcomes. However, field researchers believe Blockchain technology has a lot more to offer and will revolutionize the field. Blockchain may be able to undermine the critical position played by educational institutions as certification officers, according to Nespor [10]. While the literature on Blockchain application has increased in recent years, there is currently no systematic analysis of the topic. Such a study is beneficial for an up-to-date analysis of the subject and informs evidence-based practices. Through research into how Blockchain technologies are used in education, this chapter provides an original and timely contribution to the literature on education technology. The primary target audiences are administrators, leaders, researchers, and scientists who want to protect their expertise and how it can have a profound effect on the field of education.

1.2 Topics Covered in This Section

1. How education can take benefit with Blockchain – Blockchain technology could provide significant educational benefits, including high-security, low-cost, improved evaluations of students, improved data access monitoring, improved accountability and transparency, identification authentication, increased confidence, and better data record performance, support of career decisions for learners and enhancement of interactivity between students.
2. Challenges in education – While Blockchain has shown its promise in an educational context, many challenges remain when using Blockchain technology. In this post, we have summed up these challenges in some main categories.
3. Blockchain applications in education – While an increasing number of Blockchain-based apps for education have been created, to date few have been released publicly. Such conditions can be divided into major categories, as described in the previous section. Every type deals with a problem of confidence, privacy, or protection in the field of education.
4. Student records and credentialing – Some institutions find Blockchain to be an excellent platform for storing, tracking, and using student credentials. A Blockchain diploma enables students to view their records quickly and efficiently and share this information with future employers. Employers would then have no need to contact universities and colleges directly to inquire about their achievements.
5. Copyright and digital rights protection – Academic plagiarism is a serious problem. Blockchain systems can be used to control the distribution of copyrighted material over the Internet. The technology's primary function is the secure storage of data recorded in a chain. Therefore, data in the Blockchain cannot be altered manually because advanced encryption measures protect it.

The following paragraphs explain how these five measures were carried out in this systematic review. The following research questions were formulated based on the intent of this report.

1. Which applications were developed for educational purposes with Blockchain technology?
2. What advantages could technology Blockchain bring to training?
3. What are the challenges of Blockchain education technology?

1.2.1 Finding the Relevant Article

A number of academic databases, such as the ACM Digital Library, IEEE Xplore and Taylor and Francis, were searched online to compile articles related to a systematic review of the work. These included SAGE Papers, ProQuest, Springer, and the Web of Science. The databases were chosen on the Monash University Library website [6]. This website is compiled by one of the world's leading universities, which is recognized for its excellence in teaching and science. This platform provides the largest number of critical databases. The nine databases are known for their high-impact, high-quality papers in education, and information technology. The last of these searches was carried out in April 2019. The quest was performed using the terms "Blockchain AND Education,". "Blockchain AND Learning," and "Blockchain AND Teaching" As each database uses a search syntax separately, every query string was set (see Table 1.1).

Google Scholar was also searched for more papers during the subsequent completion of the report. The aim was to find other articles of quality not identified

Table 1.1 Used Strings for Query Purpose

Strings	Source
Blockchain AND education, Blockchain AND learning, Blockchain AND teaching	Sciencedirect
((Blockchain) AND education), ((Blockchain) AND teaching), ((Blockchain) AND learning)	IEEE Xplore
[All Blockchain] AND [All education], [All Blockchain] AND [All teaching], [All Blockchain] AND [All learning]	SAGE Journals
digital library (Blockchain + education), (Blockchain + learning), (Blockchain + teaching)	ACM
[All: Blockchain] AND [All: education], [All: Blockchain] AND [All: teaching],[All: Blockchain] AND [All: learning]	Taylor & Francis online
Blockchain AND education, Blockchain AND teaching, Blockchain AND learning	Springer
(Blockchain) AND TITLE-ABS-KEY (teaching)), (TITLE-ABS-KEY (Blockchain) AND TITLE-ABS-KEY (learning))	Scopus
TOPIC: (Blockchain) AND TOPIC: (education),	Web of Science
Blockchain AND education, Blockchain AND teaching, Blockchain AND learning	ProQuest

during the initial quest for databases. But, since the search requires references not checked by peers, Google Scholar has been limited to articles by well-known publishers, e.g., the AACE, the Australasian Society for the Advancement of Education Computers, the Canadian Education Innovation Network, Consortia Academia Publishing, and Distance Editorial. Google Scholar's Advanced Search page has been used to limit the search to specific editors. The publishers' names were entered in the field "Return published objects," while the question stings were entered into the field "with all the words" using the following query strings for this search.

1. The researchers reviewed the titles and abstracts for the papers searched with the pre-defined requirements of inclusion and exclusion after the conclusion of their search. The search was completed.
   a. An essay was omitted where the complete text was not accessible online.
   b. Blockchain technology did not apply in education.
   c. The application being tabled was not practical; i.e., opinion.
      The application was not submitted. EndNote has inserted the remaining products and duplicates have been excluded. Finally, the full text of every document has been read to ensure that all the details relevant to this systematic analysis are included. There has been no consistency evaluation. Through using empirical bases as a main source for finding the related papers, the accuracy of this analysis has been assured. Only peer-reviewed papers written by leading publishers have then been deemed to be part of this analysis for the search on Google Scholar. We were thus able to include high-quality papers.
2. Data Extraction – For the extraction of data from the studies included, a data extraction form was used. The type was specifically developed for this review and was piloted on a sample of documents.
3. Data Analysis – Data analysis was carried out after extracting the data from documents. The extracted information was analysed on four key themes which emerged from the questions of study. The topics included: application, advantages, threats, and the future. Several sub-topics arose from data analyses for each of these key themes.

1.3 Blockchain in Education

Several Blockchain applications for educational purposes have been developed, as shown in Section 2.2. Such applications can be grouped into 12 distinct categories: management of qualifications, competence management, and learning results management, assessment of students' abilities, the security of learning objects, safeguarding of shared learning environment, transferring fees and credits, gaining digital custodial consent, management of competitions, copyright management, enhancing interactions between students.

1.3.1 Categories of Application

1. Certification Management – Full virtual schools problematize what is meant by the term 'school attendance'. Does it require the child to log in (regardless of the amount of work done) to the school's software system, or should it alternatively be measured by how much work has been submitted (irrespective of the duration of time for login)? How do you understand how many teachers do when students work at home? Using documents and interviews with 22 teachers of 10 US VPNs Virtual Private Networks (VPNs), this article looks at schools in terms of time savings, animated by two temporary accumulation circuits: one that generates students' academic records; a second one that measures the amount of times schools work with pupils. Cyber education reconfigures and connects these chains with impacts on school finance, student certification, and teachers' employment [10]. Xu et al. [11] has introduced an educational certificate Blockchain (ECBC) that supports high performance and low latency and provides speeding-up queries. The ECBC consensus mechanism uses co-operation between peers to build competitive blocks to minimize latency and increase performance. ECBC provides an MPT (MPT-Chain) tree structure that cannot only include an effective transaction request, but also support a historical account transaction query. MPT-Chain requires only a short update period and can accelerate block verification. ECBC is also designed to protect user privacy via transaction format. The experiment shows that ECBC has better throughput and latency efficiency to accommodate rapid queries. Like this, there are many articles based on certificate management [12–16].

2. Competencies and learning outcomes management – Farah et al. [17] presented a framework for a Blockchain-tech architecture stored in a distributed repository network without diminishing its authenticity by signing and validating learning traces. The proposal puts online study participants at the center of the design process, enabling them to store traces of learning in a place of their choice. Employing intelligent contracts, stakeholders can retrieve the data and share it securely and with third parties, ensuring that it is unaltered. However, a preliminary assessment showed that only 56 percent of studied teachers considered a tamper-evident depository to be a useful feature [18]. These results encourage further examination of data used in their practice with other end-users, such as learning analytics researchers.

Duan et al. [19] introduced a Blockchain education technology based on a study results index, including professional certification and automatic tools for determining university graduation requirements. The achievement results of courses are reported in a block based on the quantitative and qualitative combination of qualifications, method and facts, name of courses, name of the study results (diploma criteria indicator), the courses' weight, etc. The transition from the assessment of students' achievement to the post-jobs assessment results is completed, and counterparts from the evaluation of student skills are sent to the program, in which the curriculum is continually improved. Some more articles based on Competencies and learning outcomes management are given in three articles [20–22].

1.3.2 Benefits

Blockchain could bring education to seven different types of benefits. Blockchain could bring to education were highlighted in the checked papers. Security is the first advantage [23, 24]. Seventeen articles (55%) defined protection as an essential advantage of incorporating Blockchain education technology. Data protection, privacy, and dignity are all part of security. A second significant advantage of using Blockchain in education is greater control over how and by whom student data are accessed. Twelve papers (39%) highlighted this gain. Increased accountability and openness is the third benefits highlighted in 11 articles (36%). The fourth advantage of Blockchain technology in education is increasing trust. Blockchain can create trust between all parties involved and promote contact with them, according to 10 articles (32%). A fifth advantage of using Blockchain in education lowers costs. Nine reports (29%) documented this gain. The type of Blockchain technology, according to these papers, can help reduce the unnecessary costs of transactions and data storage. Authentication is the sixth advantage. Nine studies (29%) indicate that Blockchain technology will identify students and render digital certificates authenticated. The seventh benefit is correlated with the tests of students. Eight papers (26%) suggested that Blockchain technology might change how student performance and learning results are evaluated [25].

Figures 1.1 and 1.2 represents the number of articles related to challenges and benefits, respectively.

1.3.3 Challenges Faced during the Adoption of Blockchain Technology in Education

Six different types of problems were illustrated in the reviewed papers (see Figure 1.1).

I. The first concern is the scalability of the Blockchain. Ten papers (32%) note that the number of Blockchain network transactions contributes to block size growth. Ultimately, the transaction latency will be increased.

II. The second issue relates to Blockchain privacy and security. Nine (29 percent) papers discussed several concerns related to protection and privacy, for example, malicious attacks and data leaks, by using Blockchain technology.

III. The cost of using this technology poses the third significant barrier to Blockchain in education. Nine papers (29 percent) approached this problem

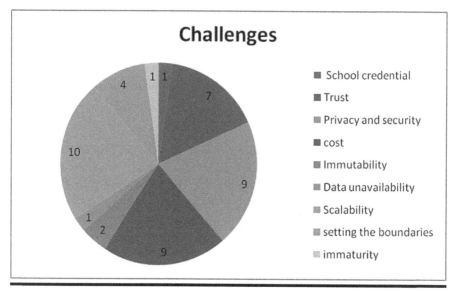

Figure 1.1   Number of articles related to challenges

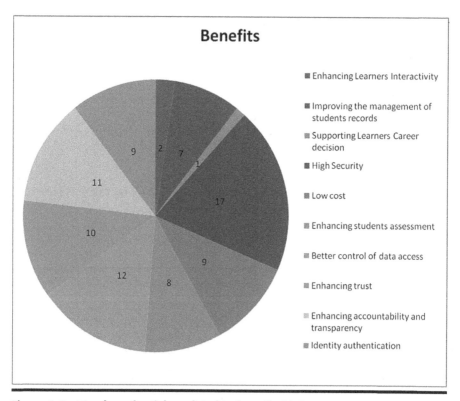

Figure 1.2   Number of articles related to benefits [25]

from different angles: power computation costs [26]; changing the current infrastructure; slow transaction time; and large-scale data management costs.

IV. Trust is related to the fourth obstacle. Seven articles (23%) find that schools are still unwilling to share their data in a Blockchain network.

V. A fifth challenge seen in four papers (13%) sets limits on the adoption of Blockchain technology. These four posts make it difficult for educational institutions to decide which data and services should be delivered across the Blockchain network. Two articles (6%) showed that immutability, a significant characteristic of Blockchain, could challenge the implementation of Blockchain technology for education. These papers explained that immutability would make it impossible for educational institutions to enforce new information storage rules or correct inaccurate data.

VI. The sixth problem concerns the immature existence of Blockchain technology. One article (3%) stated that Blockchain still has immaturity problems, such as weak usability and complicated setups. Data unavailability is also a problem mentioned in one article (3%). This post will become inaccessible if data management is put in the user's hands itself, and applications relying on this data could impact. One final obstacle that has been illustrated in one of the papers discussed (3%) is to weaken the importance of conventional school diplomas. According to this report, Blockchain may allow students to serve as their lifetime education records, which may undermine education institutions' central position as certification agents.

1.4 Discussion

The publication trend shows that the use of Blockchain technology in education is increasing worldwide because of the relatively limited number of studies found. However, further research in this field is required. Overall, our three study questionnaires were supported by this systematic analysis of the 31 reports.

1.4.1 What Applications Have You Developed for Educational Purposes with Blockchain Technology?

Although more and more Blockchain-based applications for educational purposes are being developed, to date only a few have been released to the public. These applications, discussed in the previous section, can be grouped into 12 major categories. Each category deals with a trust, privacy, or safety problem in the educational setting. Specific applications relating to certificates management were concentrated in the first group. This group deals with all kinds of university credentials, transcripts, qualifications for students, or other achievement styles. Many implementations have been using Blockchain for digital certificates in the field of education. Much of the performances of these certificates benefitted from the great faith and protection that Blockchain technology offers.

Bdiwi et al. [27] introduced the Ubiquitous Learning Framework (ULS), which uses Blockchain technology to ensure a high degree of safety when students work together. U-learning (Ubiquitous learning), therefore, include an immersive multimedia environment to facilitate better teacher–student contact. Similarly, Bore et al. [28] stressed the need to enhance schools' educational climate by using Blockchain as a School Information Platform (SIH). Such a framework may compile, evaluate, and report information about school systems to improve decision-making. The fifth category involves the transfer of charges and credit. It includes applications with similar functions for the transfer of credentials or fees between institutions, organizations, and even universities because of Blockchain's high level of protection and confidence. Educational institutions typically rely on a third party to manage and authorize credit or fee transfer. Fortunately, the Blockchain can be used to share information and remove the necessity for a high level of protection of certain third parties or intermediaries. The tokens used to demonstrate the transfer process were used in the EduCTX method [29]. These tokens can be in any digital format for learning units, including diplomas, certificates, and training. Each school has its EduCTX address for safe transferring processes. Some demands related to the acquisition of digital guard consent were addressed in category six. Blockchain helped to improve the conventional method of obtaining consent from parents instead of electronically. The confidence Blockchain technology can bring great reflection. The decentralized design of Blockchain helps speed up the consent process without affecting its privacy. Through the adoption of this technology the selection and switching process between several students, parents, and educational institutions would be facilitated greatly. The mechanism for allowing public schools, which want to meet their students without parents' permission for every single occasion, is suggested by Gilda and Mehrotra [30].

Nespor [10] suggested a certification platform that would offset the school's use as a certification agent for the project. This request would allow higher education providers or employers to provide students with a high degree of information privacy with official certificates. Students could thus explicitly share it with someone asking for their official documents. Similarly, Han et al. [31] use Blockchain technology's decentralized existence to supply new Blockchain-based educational records to search and issue official transcripts or certificates. Individually, their data can be accessed. However, the access and alteration of saved data in the system under certain limited conditions and regulations are only allowable to accredited businesses. Competencies and learning results management were based in the second group. More focus has been given to developing Blockchain applications to boost learning goals and enhance their skills. This will lead to better preparation and enrich the field of education in a wide variety.

Farah et al. [17] have developed a framework for monitoring students' success in their multi-learning work. For each particular operation, it adds into a block independently of all traces. This learning block may also be viewed as self-describing, as all metadata on several activities is included. This application contributes to a high degree of self-efficiency.

Another Williams application [32] suggested a student learning environment. Fast and direct support and constructive feedback are given. The application aims to strengthen the learning process by integrating a broad range of skills, promoting critical thinking, and problem-solving through improved teamwork and communication. Since Blockchain offers a decentralized network, open to all parties, including students, faculty members, and public authorities, it builds a collaborative climate with high protection and honesty.

Blockchain contributed to creating a nested permission mechanism that speeds up the entire process and maintains privacy and consent control. Another category is the management of competition, using Blockchain technology to help control and improve competitive transactions' quality and transparency. Wu and Li [33] have introduced an e-commerce operating sandbox competition model, a decision framework that tests students' technical skills and expertise. This framework was built for an assessment system that tests and manages the operational skills of students.

Blockchain application software was built to assess students' technical skills based on their academic performance and achievement, which could then be given to the interested industry. This method was developed to evaluate and analyze the capabilities of students based on the Blockchain clustering algorithm [34]. Another system, known as the management of copyrights, covers ownership rights when the Blockchain is used. To enhance learning engagement, this application was created. It provides top learners with virtual currencies based on predefined policies in the Blockchain network. It offers incentives. Another group of applications listed in this analysis is the review examination. The protection of auditing examinations papers can be greatly improved by using a licensed Blockchain technique.

A decentralized analysis application called dAppER was created by Mitchell, Hara, and Sheriff [35], which was built in line with quality assurance principles when disrupting inspections by external examiners. DAppER was useful to monitor the quality assurance processes based on their findings. Finally, it is the last application group to promote lifelong learning. In enhancing lifelong learning dimensions, such as improving skills, information, and productivity, Blockchain technologies have played an important role.

1.4.2 What Benefits Will the Technology of Blockchain Bring to Education?

Technology from Blockchain could offer significant advantages in education, including high safety, low cost, better evaluations of the student, better data control, enhanced accountability and transparency, authentication of identities, confidence-building, better management of student records, promoting career choices for learners and enhancing interactivities among the learners. The use of Blockchain guarantees data/transactions shared between the intended parties for authentication and privacy. The design of peer topology in the Blockchain reduces the potential for protection in the education sector. The consensus protocol was used in Comparison to preserve the order of Application [27].

The ledger contents are checked, 12 of the 18 transactions, and there are decrease in the risk of non-secured transactions. The security of transactions is ensured through the use of cryptographical hatches and signatures. The beauty of the Blockchain system depends on the data themselves being protected and on whether or not they are not damaged. To demonstrate this, Blockchain traces, and records of learning were signed and authenticated [17]. There are different types of data related to a learning activity in each learning block. To secure these data before sending it to other participants, an encryption algorithm was implemented [36]. Furthermore, the field of education will benefit greatly from the Blockchain for cost reduction. The costs include storage, transaction costs, and the handling and preservation of educational documents. Costs are included. The cost of conventional cloud-based storage is significantly reduced through using a public/private distributed network which is accessible from anywhere. In general, it needs extra costs to check and process academic certificates, while Blockchain reduces these costs [29]. The use of Blockchain technology can also increase the evaluation of students. The Blockchain was introduced with regard to calculating the learning output based on the results. One of the significant characteristics and advantages of Blockchain is to restrict/control access to stored documents. Transcripts, diplomas, or personal students/teachers' documents are included in educational records.

Arenas [37] demonstrated an excellent example in which a licensed Blockchain platform was used to restrict access to academic credentials and limit them solely to the intended participants. Only accredited organizations can access and change stored data according to relevant regulations on the Blockchain platform. In addition, improving accountability and transparency are two benefits that Blockchain technology has accomplished. Saving all educational and school information at one readily available location [38] would make the use of these records more accountable and transparent.

Bore et al. [28]establishes the framework for gathering and storing school reports and records in the School Information Hub (SIH) based on Blockchain. This framework helped make shared data more accessible and increase the flexibility to interpret, compare, or distribute data. Blockchain also guarantees the validity and identification of digital certificates. A digital curriculum was held in a Blockchain in comparison [39]. The approved university signs this with a private key when blocks have been formed. A cryptographic hash will then be provided to ensure that nobody can interrupt the material. The university verifies these data's validity, and use the initial institution's key to confirm them. Trust is another benefit of Blockchain technology. Only responsible parties can either add blocks to the network, or access it. When engaging with authorities from various regions, trust is a significant concern. Introducing stable and efficient systems based on Blockchain, universities, or educational institutions can create a dedicated group. EduCTX was launched in relation [40], which is a credit and grading Blockchain network. Tokens are passed to responsible parties. These tokens depend on the credits that are collected in the records of students. This contributed to the establishment of higher education organizations of an internationally trusted and cohesive structure.

Moreover, the enhancement of the quality of student record management is one significant advantage of Blockchain technology. Using Blockchain in education, the probability of trade errors between intended parties may theoretically be minimized. It uses a ledger to share data quicker and more effectively. Because of its simplicity and accountability, digital records and certificates can be best handled by Blockchain. The "UZHBC," a Blockchain system operated at the University of Zurich, and taking into account multiple stakeholder criteria, was implemented by Gresch et al. [13]. Also, the Application will achieve productivity and accountability. The Blockchain Framework for Advisory Advice is shared in 2019 with 13 of 18 institutions, students, and job agencies. [21]. Another benefit of using Blockchain technology is helping learners' career choices.

For the engagement in learning events, they used a learning incentive scheme. The study tools in the peer-to-peer network can be shared across all nodes. All learning records are compiled into a block and can easily be tracked to track the learners' interactivity and interoperability progress. What are Blockchain Technology's problems in education? While Blockchain has demonstrated its value in an educational environment, there are many challenges to overcome when using such technology in education. In this review paper we have outlined these problems in some fundamental categories. While protection is the key feature of Blockchain technology, it is impossible to eliminate the possibility of malicious attacks. It is a challenge to provide both security and confidentiality at the same time, and when an individual is at risk (through the online authorization of educational qualifications and certificates), the problem becomes more critical [31]. Many systems use private and public keys to ensure privacy. However, since each public key's available details are publicly accessible, Blockchain cannot guarantee transactional privacy, and user transactions can therefore be attached to disclose information for users.

Many studies have been carried out in attempts to address this problem. Several researchers have suggested concepts, including Zilliqa [41], a new Blockchain framework focused on a shared mechanism for disconnecting the large Blockchain network through multi-shard transactions. However, before the Blockchain can be implemented on a large scale, scalability problems must be addressed effectively. Blockchain is an evolving technology that must be incorporated into the existing framework. But it can cost so much for adoption and execution. In addition to this deployment expense, many Blockchain technologies are often costly for transactions or computations [17]. The cost would increase as the block size increases with users' rise to handle and store such large student data. This approach would be difficult to use in conventional education systems without handling this growth and running costs. To verify credentials, all entities must agree to share their records. But how are all organizations prepared to share their data? The question remains. In some cases, whether or not a DLT/Blockchain solution improves over a more conventional, centralized directory is unclear. In addition, inadequate evidence exists for business profits for educational institutions. There can be a considerable risk of changing current educational practices, which affect both current systems and the economy. How can accredited organizations take the risk of offering certificates to their students? If approved organizations do not consent to provide such data, further difficulties may be generated in the authorization phase [40]. Policymakers for higher education or other policymakers must determine how long, and indeed whether, the Blockchain can be trusted. The borders of all legal entities are also absent from clarification. Some companies do not wish, for all of their business processes, to embrace Blockchain technology. Without identifying the potential benefits of Blockchain in conventional systems, a major challenge will be established. It's also important to respond to who will identify the limits that this organization needs to pass technology and how many Blockchain technology processes it can adopt.

The pace of Blockchain implementation in the education sector can be set in early collaborations among the government or higher schools with the private sector in regulatory compliance. The poor usability of its products, especially the earliest, is another key problem with Blockchain technology. The language and perceived immaturity of the technology are also lacking in clarification. In addition to this, for security purposes, including the main key, public key, and recovery seeds, there are several complicated settings that users will have to store. Blockchain has completely different terminology, which is confusing for consumers in the area of education. The usability must be enhanced through the simple interfaces of Blockchain products so that the framework is readily understood and used by persons without technological expertise. Further studies would also be required in field usability testing. Effective design and simple terminology in the education sector will lead to Blockchain adaptation. Through further data protection checks, the data are inaccessible for sites based on the data of users. There is a balance between privacy and data access.

Consequently, access to such data is more complicated as users handle their data in Blockchain technology. Blockchain's immutability makes it harder to edit data until everyone decides to alter the ledger's contents. This immutability can create a dilemma for government entities needing data from their people for law and order. Furthermore, Blockchain's immutability function would not allow for modifications to any framework already specified policies. Due to decentralized Blockchain technology, the centralized structure of any educational system can be affected. The availability of a constantly aggregated directory will affect the value of the traditional school credentials as in Blockchain. One of the best breakthroughs in recent times is Blockchain technology. It will probably take a long time before the technology is embraced widely. Since Blockchain implementation is related to many obstacles, it must be tackled before using the technology in the education sector.

1.5 Future Research Areas

Blockchain has a lot more to offer and can offer significant benefits in other fields of education. Collaboration and collaboration between educational institutions are the prominent places where Blockchain can be very successful. As already mentioned, Blockchain is proving itself to be a safe and secure technology for tracking the academic accomplishments of its students. This includes the certificates of students and their different learning results and abilities. A future study will explore how Blockchain could promote collaboration and partnership between educational establishments. It would also assist educational institutions with mutual facilities, services, and academic programs to reduce their operating costs. Job-driven training is another field for the use of Blockchain technology. Work-oriented education is primarily aimed at delivering training courses that fulfill current and potential recruitment needs and contribute to participating students' jobs. In promoting this form of education, Blockchain may play a crucial role. Businesses will share the expertise and skills needed by Blockchain. This knowledge, and the design of training programs that respond to business needs, can be checked periodically by educational institutions. Students may also use Blockchain to consolidate their skills. Agencies for recruitment may study the Blockchain, and assess and recommend particular training programs to students based on their abilities.

Blockchain technology to accredit and enhance online education quality is also a required field for future study. Although there are many benefits to online education, including lower costs, accessibility, and versatility, several disadvantages are also present. The accreditation and low quality are the greatest of these disadvantages. Many educational institutions demand accreditation and deliver high-quality online courses. Blockchain could solve this problem. It can be used as a decentralized forum for the safe and accurate exchange of information between students, educational institutions, and accrediting agencies. Electronic Data Interchanges (EDIs) can store information about their online classes, online programs, teachers, and accreditation programs. After completing the course, students will share their evaluations of both the framework and their teachers.

1.6 Conclusion

Taken as a whole, Blockchain will strengthen the education system in several ways. The technology is ideal for the safe storage, sharing, and networking of information. This advanced device will make many processes quicker, simpler, and safer. It bridges the gap in credentials, security of copyright, and effective communication. The Blockchain will soon benefit from these regular processes. New technology joins our lives, and we can use it wisely to make progress in the right direction. Today's students are the ones living in a whole new world! We should help them, accept the changes, and learn how to improve things.

References

[1] C. S. Wright, "Bitcoin: A peer-to-peer electronic cash system," *SSRN Electron. J.*, 2019.

[2] S. Chowdhury, R. Govindaraj, S. S. Nath, and K. Solomon, "Analysis of the IoT sensors and networks with big data and sharing the data through cloud platform," *Int. J. Innov. Technol. Explor. Eng.*, 8, 405–408, 2019.

[3] R. Collins, "Blockchain: A new architecture for digital content," *Econtent*, 39, 22–23, 2016.

[4] Y. J. Lee, and K. M. Lee, "Blockchain-based multi-purpose authentication method for anonymity and privacy," *Int. J. Recent Technol. Eng.*, 8, 409–414, 2019.

[5] V. Gatteschi, F. Lamberti, C. Demartini, C. Pranteda, and V. Santamaria, "To Blockchain or not to Blockchain: That Is the question," *IT Prof.*, 20, 62–74, 2018.

[6] S. Ølnes, J. Ubacht, and M. Janssen, "Blockchain in government: Benefits and implications of distributed ledger technology for information sharing," *Gov. Inf. Q.*, 34, 355–364, 2017.

[7] Chen, G., Xu, B., Lu, M. et al. "Exploring Blockchain technology and its potential applications for education," *Smart Learn. Environ.*, 5, 1, 2018.

[8] R. J. Krawiecet al., "Blockchain: Opportunities for health care," *ComputerWeekly.com*, 2016.

[9] A. Kamilaris, A. Fonts, and F. X. Prenafeta-Boldú, "The rise of Blockchain technology in agriculture and food supply chains," *Trends Food Sci. Technol.*, 91, 640–652, 2019.

[10] J. Nespor, "Cyber schooling and the accumulation of school time," *Pedagog. Cult. Soc.*, 27, 325–341, 2019.

[11] Y. Xu, S. Zhao, L. Kong, Y. Zheng, S. Zhang, and Q. Li, "ECBC: A high performance educational certificate Blockchain with efficient query," in *Lecture Notes in Computer Science (including subseries Lecture Notes in Artificial Intelligence and Lecture Notes in Bioinformatics)*, 2017.

[12] M. Hori, and M. Ohashi, "Adaptive Identity authentication of Blockchain system-the collaborative cloud educational system," in *EdMedia+ InnovateLearning*, 2018.

[13] J. Gresch, B. Rodrigues, E. Scheid, S. S. Kanhere, and B. Stiller, "The proposal of a Blockchain-based architecture for transparent certificate handling," in *Lecture Notes in Business Information Processing*, 2019.

[14] D. Lizcano, J. A. Lara, B. White, and S. Aljawarneh, "Blockchain-based approach to create a model of trust in open and ubiquitous higher education," *J. Comput. High. Educ.*, 32, 109–134, 2020.

[15] E. Funk, J. Riddell, F. Ankel, and D. Cabrera, "Blockchain technology: A data framework to improve validity, trust, and accountability of information exchange in health professions education," *Acad. Med.*, 93, 1791–1794, 2018.

[16] N. Satheesh, G. R. K. Rao, S. Chowdhury, K. B. Prakash, and S. Sengan, "Blockchain-facilitated iot built cleverer home with unrestricted validation arrangement," *Int. J. Adv. Trends Comput. Sci. Eng.*, 9, 5398–5405, 2020.

[17] J. C. Farah, A. Vozniuk, M. J. Rodriguez-Triana, and D. Gillet, "A blueprint for a Blockchain-based architecture to power a distributed network of tamper-evident learning trace repositories," in *Proceedings – IEEE 18th International Conference on Advanced Learning Technologies, ICALT 2018*, 2018.

[18] R. Nair, and A. Bhagat, "Feature selection method to improve the accuracy of classification algorithm," *Int. J. Innov. Technol. Explor. Eng.*, 8, 124–127, 2019.

[19] B. Duan, Y. Zhong, and D. Liu, "Education application of Blockchain technology: Learning outcome and meta-diploma," in *Proceedings of the International Conference on Parallel and Distributed Systems – ICPADS*, 2018.

[20] W. Zhao, K. Liu, and K. Ma, "Design of student capability evaluation system merging Blockchain technology," *J. Phys. Conf. Ser.*, 1168, 032123, 2019.

[21] Q. Liu, Q. Guan, X. Yang, H. Zhu, G. Green, and S. Yin, "Education-industry cooperative system based on Blockchain," in *Proceedings of 2018 1st IEEE International Conference on Hot Information-Centric Networking, HotICN 2018*, 2019.

[22] S. Chowdhury, P. Mayilvahanan, and R. Govindaraj, "Optimal feature extraction and classification-oriented medical insurance prediction model: machine learning integrated with the internet of things," *Int. J. Comput. Appl.*, 1–13, 2020.

[23] G. Arora, P. L. Pavani, R. Kohli, and V. Bibhu, "Multimodal biometrics for improvised security," in *2016 1st International Conference on Innovation and Challenges in Cyber Security, ICICCS 2016*, 2016.

[24] S. Chowdhury, and P. Mayilvahanan, "A survey on internet of things: Privacy with security of sensors and wearable network ip/protocols," *Int. J. Eng. Technol.*, 7, 200–205, 2018.

[25] A. Alammary, S. Alhazmi, M. Almasri, and S. Gillani, "Blockchain-based applications in education: A systematic review," *Appl. Sci. (Switzerland)*, 9, 240, 2019.

[26] P. Sharma, R. Nair, and V. K. Dwivedi, "Power consumption reduction in iot devices through field-programmable gate array with nanobridge switch," in *Lecture Notes in Networks and Systems*, 2021.

[27] R. Bdiwi, C. DeRunz, S. Faiz, and A. A. Cherif, "A Blockchain based decentralized platform for ubiquitous learning environment," in *Proceedings – IEEE 18th International Conference on Advanced Learning Technologies, ICALT 2018*, 2018.

[28] N. Bore, S. Karumba, J. Mutahi, S. S. Darnell, C. Wayua, and K. Weldemariam, "Towards Blockchain-enabled school information hub," in *ACM International Conference Proceeding Series*, 2017.

[29] M. Holbl, A. Kamisalic, M. Turkanovic, M. Kompara, B. Podgorelec, and M. Hericko, "EduCTX: An ecosystem for managing digital micro-credentials," in *2018 28th EAEEIE Annual Conference, EAEEIE 2018*, 2018.

[30] S. Gilda, and M. Mehrotra, "Blockchain for student data privacy and consent," in *2018 International Conference on Computer Communication and Informatics, ICCCI 2018*, 2018.

[31] M. Han, D. Wu, Z. Li, Y. Xie, J. S. He, and A. Baba, "A novel Blockchain-based education records verification solution," in *SIGITE 2018 – Proceedings of the 19th Annual SIG Conference on Information Technology Education*, 2018.

[32] P. Williams, "Does competency-based education with Blockchain signal a new mission for universities?," *J. High. Educ. Policy Manag.*, 41, 104–117, 2019.

[33] B. Wu, and Y. Li, "Design of evaluation system for digital education operational skill competition based on Blockchain," in *Proceedings – 2018 IEEE 15th International Conference on e-Business Engineering, ICEBE 2018*, 2018.

[34] R. Nair, and A. Bhagat, "An Introduction to clustering algorithms in big data," 559–576, 2020.

[35] I. Mitchell, S. Hara, and M. Sheriff, "DAppER: Decentralised application for examination review," in *Proceedings of 12th International Conference on Global Security, Safety and Sustainability, ICGS3 2019*, 2019.

[36] A. Anand, A. Raj, R. Kohli, and V. Bibhu, "Proposed symmetric key cryptography algorithm for data security," in *2016 1st International Conference on Innovation and Challenges in Cyber Security, ICICCS 2016*, 2016.

[37] R. Arenas, and P. Fernandez, "CredenceLedger: A permissioned Blockchain for verifiable academic credentials," in *2018 IEEE International Conference on Engineering, Technology and Innovation, ICE/ITMC 2018 – Proceedings*, 2018.

[38] S. Saibabavali, B. Manikanta, S. N. Siddhu, and S. Chowdhury, "Application for searching product nearby location," *Int. Res. J. Eng. Technol.*, 4, 2751–2755, 2017.

[39] I. Bandara, F. Ioras, and M. P. Arraiza, "The emerging trend of Blockchain for validating degree apprenticeship certification in cybersecurity education," in *INTED2018 Proceedings*, 2018.

[40] M. Turkanović, M. Hölbl, K. Košič, M. Heričko, and A. Kamišalić, "EduCTX: A Blockchain-based higher education credit platform," *IEEE Access*, 6, 5112–5127, 2018.

[41] M. Sharples, and J. Domingue, "The Blockchain and kudos: A distributed system for educational record, reputation and reward," in *Lecture Notes in Computer Science (including subseries Lecture Notes in Artificial Intelligence and Lecture Notes in Bioinformatics)*, 9891, 490–496, 2016.

Chapter 2

Apply and Analyse Several Blockchain Techniques in IoT and Big Data Sector

Nikhil Ranjan
Chandigarh University, Punjab, India

Sarvesh Kumar
Babu Banarasi Das University, Lucknow, India

Aakanksha Jain
Poornima University, India

Contents

DOI: 10.1201/9781003129486-2

19

2.1 ■ Blockchain Technology

Blockchain innovation became a worldwide innovation in 2008 when it was utilized for the Bitcoin digital currency. A Blockchain is a far-off object in information base for taking care of a dynamical rundown of records called blocks. A square chain is recreated in a decentralized design, where each center stores a copy of the entire article or item. The geography of an advanced record is a chain of article since each item, except for the principal object, the alleged Genesis Block or Object, contains a connection to the former article realized as a hash of the past thing. Each square in a Blockchain is likewise carefully time bound. The fundamental construction of the Blockchain is shown in Figure 2.1.

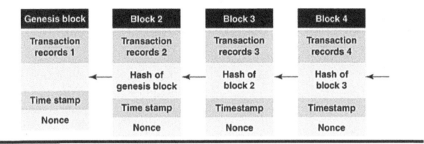

Figure 2.1   Blockchain Structure

2.1.1 *Centralized, Decentralized and Distributed*

Let's try to understand them further with an example. Suppose Phil is an entrepreneur who starts a business selling household furniture. In order to do this, he set up various showrooms in the city to sell the furniture. He created a warehouse to store all the furniture there and supply it according to the demands from the showrooms. You can map this scenario to the centralised database system. Just as the single warehouse stores all of the furniture, a central database stores all the data.

As Phil's business expanded, he ventured out to multiple cities by setting up various showrooms. Now Phil realised that having one warehouse will not suffice his requirements, so he set up warehouses in all the cities. He created one warehouse in each of the cities he ventured into. All of his furniture was stored there and distributed from there to the showroom in one city. Here this can be mapped to the decentralised database system. Multiple warehouses hold the merchandise. Similarly, in a decentralised database system all of the information is stored not in one place but in multiple places or databases.

Listed below are the critical points of differences between the three types of system we have encountered to date.

Feature	Centralized	Decentralized	Distributed
Security	Low; Most vulnerable to data security issues	Moderate; Data can be rebuilt from parallel servers if backed up	Highest; Very difficult to lose data completely
Response Speed (**Applicable in* *case the networks* *having large* *amounts of data*)	Bottlenecks can cause response speed to reduce significantly	Quick response speed depending on the distribution of data	Fastest response rates

(Continued)

Feature	Centralized	Decentralized	Distributed
Overheads and Costs	Low; Redundancy is minimized	Substantial processing overheads to ensure proper coordination among servers	Massive overheads to ensure appropriate coordination among multiple nodes
Points of Failure / Maintenance	Single point of failure; Easy to maintain	A limited number of points of failure; Maintenance more complex than centralised systems	Multiple points of failure; Difficult to maintain
Stability	Highly unstable; if the central server fails, entire network collapses	Stability better than centralised systems; the network can continue to operate at a reduced level if any one server fails	The highest level of stability; single node failure doesn't affect the network
Scalability	Low scalability	Moderately scalable	Infinitely scalable
Ease of Setup	Easy to set up	Difficult to set up	Difficult to set up

2.1.2 Types of Blockchain

A major transformation is taking place in the Indian banking system, with all of the banks coming together to form a common lending platform—the India Lending Blockchain, under the leadership of the Reserve Bank of India (RBI). In addition to the banks, this platform will also incorporate credit bureaus, risk departments, legal and technical panels and other stakeholders in the banking industry. Can this Blockchain platform be purely democratic, such as the bitcoin network, or heavily regulated, such as the SWIFT network?

A **public permissionless Blockchain** is free for anyone to join or leave. Bitcoin Blockchain is the best example of a public permissionless network. This type of network provides **anonymity**, **immutability**, and **transparency**, but compromises on efficiency.

A **public permissioned Blockchain** is an intermediary between private and public networks. It values **efficiency** and **immutability** over transparency and anonymity, where every participating member is aware of the identities of the other members in the network. For example, the Goods and Services Tax (GST) network in India will be most suitable for a permissioned Blockchain since it is operated by known entities, and all participants are verified before they join the network.

However, the above-mentioned Blockchains will not be appropriate for the India Lending Blockchain network. Permissionless Blockchains do not provide the identity of the participants and are lacking in efficiency; by contrast, public permissioned Blockchains, although they restrict access, are still exposed to the public at large. This can raise concerns over the security of the network since they do not provide anonymity for the participants. So, for example, in the case of a GST network, you wouldn't want other taxpayers in the country to know the details of your tax returns.

A private Blockchain is one which is operated and managed by a single entity. These types of Blockchains are generally applicable in the case of a conglomerate where the parent company runs the network for the underlying group of companies. In such a situation, they value efficiency over anonymity, transparency, and immutability. If we consider the India Lending Blockchain, the RBI could be considered as the entity which has supreme authority over the entire network. However, this raises the question of concentrating too much power in the hands of a single entity.

A consortium Blockchain is largely similar to a private Blockchain, but it differs in terms of who controls or manages the network. Instead of concentrating all of the power into one entity, authority is distributed across two or more participants. This scenario is also suitable for the India Lending Blockchain, where authority can be distributed between RBI and a few of the major banks to ensure benefits for all of its members.

Let us summarize the key differences between the types of Blockchains:

Type	Ano-nymity	Trans-parency	Immu-tability	Effi-ciency	Confi-dentiality	Through-put	Finality Turnaround time (TAT)
Public	Yes	Yes	Yes	No	Low	Low	High
Permissioned	No	No	Yes	Yes	Medium	Low/ Medium	Medium/ High
Private	No	No	No	Yes	Very high	High	Very Low
Consortium	No	Partial	Yes	Yes	High	High	Low

2.2 Blockchains and IoT Systems

The traditional Internet of Things (IoT) framework is reliant on a shared engineering. Data are sent from the machine to the cloud where the information is ionized utilizing methodical methodology and afterwards sent back to the IoT machine

(Rosenstock, Rohrbach, Nowak, & Girvetz, 2018). With billions of machines set to join the IoT network in the future, this kind of united system has extremely restricted ascendable, revealed billions of industry centers that unapproved meshwork security, and will turn out to be amazingly unbalanced and moderate if outsiders need to, more than once, check and affirm each miniature exchange between machines.

2.3 Blockchain IoT Platforms

There are numerous Blockchain standards focus on IoT are arising as the business gets greater. One of the first Blockchain IOT standards is IOTA (Yuan & Wang, 2018).

2.4 Need of IOTA

   i Authenticity
  ii Integrity
 iii Confidentiality
 iv Micropayments

     a. **Authenticity:** Authentication is a type of mechanism that organizations use to protect their crucial asset or resources (Modha et al., 2011, pp. 62–71). While enabling the authentication organization to keep its network or resource secure by permitting only authenticated users. Here IOTA used the same concept for data exchange with help of token; if you do not have no token then you are not able to be authenticated successfully. You should prove that you sent the data or your own IOTA token.

     b. **Integrity:** When the user exchanges their data they have to insure about data unchanged. For the purity of data block organization enable one more mechanism that is called integrity these all are cover in one principle who is name is the Confidentiality, Integrity, Availability (CIA) triad or triangle. Here Integrity is directly proportional to Confidentiality, which means that if your data is not properly protected then this will offer a chance to breach the data or lose Integrity (Kaelbling, Littman, & Moore, 1996, pp. 237–285).

     c. **Confidentiality:** In this mechanism, you should use the concept of data hiding using encryption methodologies (Xu et al., 2017, pp. 243–252). In this method data should be completely changed or laymen language data is coded, why we need this coding because our crucial data is freely traveling in the public network only. Here is the chance of losing Confidentiality that's why we need to encryption method (Glaser, 2017, pp. 1543–1552).

     d. **Micropayments:** It is a type of mechanism was we used a small amount of IOTA token without paying any fees.

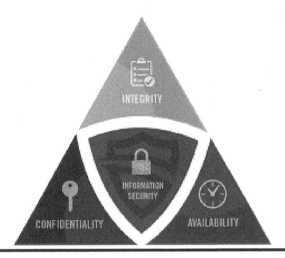

Figure 2.2 CIA Tringle

2.5 Challenges to Address the Integration of Blockchain in IoT

Extraordinary steps being developed have been made around there, yet Blockchain methodology in IoT is a new trend and a few key difficulties should be defeated before we will see the total advantage of Blockchain in IoT be figured it out.

1. Scalability
2. Security
3. Interoperability
4. Legal, compliance, and regulation

2.5.1 Scalability

Could Blockchain networks adapt to the sheer volume of information that is relied upon to be created by IoT gadgets in the following 5–10 years without hindering exchange speeds or the progression of information? Particle tends to this issue explicitly by not utilizing a Blockchain-based suburbanized organization, rather choosing their Tangle stage. Yet this is only one project (Georgeff, Pell, Pollack, & Wooldridge, 1998, pp. 1–10). All the more notable cryptographic record like Ethereum and Bitcoin have for quite some time been experiencing versatility issues and are not appropriate for the measure of information IoT gadgets are delivering.

2.5.2 Security

Urbanized advanced record networks give an undeniable degree yet what level of shortcoming (assuming any) do the IoT gadgets make at where they interface with the organization? Gadgets themselves should be secured in order to keep programmers from messing with them (Lotti, 2016 pp. 96–110).

2.5.3 Interoperability

Cross-fasten interoperability should be addressed and improved in the event that we genuinely need to use the advantages of interconnected brilliant gadgets. If not, we can end up with a circumstance in which we are associated with various secluded decentralized organizations that function admirably for their motivation, yet cannot really converse with different gadgets for which they were not explicitly planned (Dika, 2017).

2.5.4 Legal, Compliance, and Regulation

The issuance of obligation should be investigated intensively. How brilliant responsibility plan of activities are managed on the planet outside of cryptographic record. We have to be stipulated (Alharby & Moorsel, 2017, pp. 125–140). For instance, who assumes liability if an IoT-associated clinical gadget embedded in a patient makes a move dependent on certain keen agreement administers yet ultimately causes harm to the patient? Is this the obligation of the maker or the IoT stage? In the event that the IoT stage is cryptographic record-based, it will be suburbanized without a concentrated element, so centering a responsible gathering may introduce an issue.

2.6 Blockchain in IoT: Real-World Applications and Solutions

2.6.1 Supply Chain Logistics

A production network includes various partners, and this is fundamentally the motivation behind why conveyance delay gets probably the greatest test in the inventory network and coordination industry. This is the place at which Blockchain and IoT enter. While IoT-empowered gadgets will permit organizations to follow shipment development at each stage, Blockchain will make the whole exchange more straightforward. IoT sensors (for instance, movement sensors, GPS, temperature sensors, and so forth) can offer insights regarding the shipment status.

2.6.2 Automotive Industry

Digitization has covered across all areas of the business, and the auto business is no exemption. Today, auto organizations are utilizing IoT-enabled sensors to develop totally automated vehicles. The auto business is additionally disposed to interfacing IoT-empowered vehicles with Blockchain tech to permit different clients to trade urgent data effectively and rapidly.

2.6.3 Smart Homes Industry

In the conventional concentrated methodology, trading data produced by IoT gadgets come up short on the security principles. Be that as it may, on account of Blockchain IoT permits mortgage holders to deal with the home security framework distantly from the cell phone Blockchain could raise the level of Smart Home security by disposing of the constraints of brought together foundation.

2.6.4 Pharmacy Industry

Probably the greatest test of the drug area is the proliferation of fake medication. Because of Blockchain IoT, the drug store industry is presently fit for countering this issue. Blockchain IoT permits every one of the partners engaged in the medication-producing cycle to be dependable and update the Blockchain network with pertinent data progressively.

2.6.5 Mediledger

This is one interesting Blockchain IoT applications that can track the legal change of ownership of prescription medicines.

2.7 Instances of Blockchain-Based Security Mix for IoT Systems

The suburbanized and self-choosing features of a cryptographic record make it an essentially ideal part in IoT dependability emulsion. Blockchain use can empower an IoT security level, which, in any case, would be troublesome or even difficult to accomplish. This part presents a portion of the recently proposed IoT security arrangements that depend on Blockchain innovation.

2.7.1 Secure Management of IoT Devices

The administration of an IoT gadget incorporates the control of design settings and activity modes just as guaranteeing continuous activity. Blockchain-based control of setup settings and activity modes can forestall unapproved access endeavors and furthermore ensure against disavowal of-administration assaults.

In Huh et al. (2017), the creators proposed the control and setup of IoT gadgets utilizing Ethereum as a Blockchain stage. A recognizable proof accreditation for an IoT gadget can be actualized by an interesting key pair (i.e., a private key and a public key) in broad daylight key cryptography. The private key is embedded in the IoT device, while the open key is selected as a trade record in an Ethereum block. An IoT gadget would then be able to be attended to on Ethernet through its public key. Ethereum was picked as the Blockchain stage since its savvy contracts empower the execution of projects on the Blockchain. IoT gadget conduct can, in this manner, be customized in brilliant agreements. For a proof of the proposed idea, a re-enactments was constructed on a framework consisting of three IoT gadgets: a power meter, a LED light, and a constrained air framework. An approach requiring the air framework and the light to change to an energy-saving mode if the meter estimation surpasses 150 kW was set up by a cell phone. For the meter, a virtual Assistant contract was customized for sending estimation and personality accreditations (i.e., its public key and mark) to Ethereum. Keen agreements were additionally modified for the climate control system and the light. These agreements recovered estimation esteems with related personality qualifications from Ethereum.

2.7.2 Secure Firmware Updates in IoT Devices

IoT gadget merchants distantly update the firmware of conveyed gadgets to insert new usefulness and remove found weaknesses. These updates are normally downloaded dependent on customer demands from a store worker containing precompiled firmware pairs got by open key framework public key infrastructure (PKI)-marked message digests. The marked message digest and the public marking key are joined to a downloaded firmware record. The firmware update on an IoT gadget begins only if a security check with the downloaded public key succeeds. Nonetheless, this customer worker firmware update convention makes an excess of organization traffic if a large number of IoT gadgets at the same time demand refreshes.

A solution using blockchains has been proposed for secure firmware updates in IoT devices where the worldwide organization traffic to a server is replaced by generally neighborhood distributed correspondence between Blockchain network hubs (Lee and Lee, 2016). In this arrangement, an IoT gadget producer stores the hashes of delivered firmware forms on a Blockchain that is available to all conveyed IoT gadgets. Christidis and Devetsikiotis (2016) proposed that utilizing a preinstalled virtual Assistant contract with a condition to over and check after a preset time stretch has slipped by in the event that another firmware discharge is accessible, an IoT gadget can independently get some answers concerning new firmware discharges

2.7.3 Trust Evaluation of a Trusted Computing Base in IoT Devices

A Thought Computing Base (TCB) is the executing, firmware, or potentially programming parts that guarantee the security of a PC framework. This implies that to break the security, an aggressor should undercut at least one of these parts. A TCB can, hence, be a piece of an IoT gadget, which is a little PC framework. A TCB is reliable if all TCB parts are unaltered by issues and not tampered with by enemies. A TCB estimation, which makes hashes of all TCB segments, is completed to assess the reliability of a TCB. On the off-chance that these hashes are safely put away, they can be used subsequently to check the TCB. TCB estimations are done when an IoT gadget is associated with the Internet and each time its TCB is refreshed. Reliability has been undermined if a TCB estimation cannot be confirmed. A verifier performs far-off verification by giving a cryptographic nonce and marking the connection of a confirmed TCB estimation and the nonce to guarantee that the TCB of an IoT gadget is dependable.

2.7.4 IoT Device Identity Validation

A safe character of an IoT gadget can be actualized as a private key in an implanted public key cryptography chip. The relating public key is secreted in a Blockchain block created by the IoT gadget (Lombardo, 2016). An organization hub begins getting to an IoT gadget with an arbitrary test message, which is returned by the IoT gadget with a mark. The getting to arrange block from that point approves the IoT gadget personality with the public key that can be recovered from the Blockchain. An IoT gadget character that is approved utilizing a Blockchain empowers the entirely secure confirmation of an IoT, makes personality spoofed almost inconceivable, and guarantees the uprightness of information caught from IoT gadgets in view of the flexibility of a Blockchain.

An IoT gadget character that is approved utilizing a Blockchain has been proposed to be utilized to make a Blockchain-based character log catching the gadget ID, its creation, the arrangements of available firmware invigorates, and realized security issues (Manning, 2017). The historical backdrop of a gadget with a safely approved personality can likewise be followed by a Blockchain. The set of experiences begins when the maker stores the character—the public key—of a produced IoT gadget in a Blockchain block. Personalities that are approved utilizing a Blockchain are being created for IoT gadgets like reconnaissance cameras.

2.7.5 Secure Data Store System for Access Control Information

Current standard answers for access control to arrange associated gadgets depend on access control records (ACLs). Nonetheless, it is difficult to keep an ACL for each IoT gadget and to depend on unified admittance control workers when the IoT scales to billions of gadgets and a large number of gadget proprietors. To put these IoT gadget proprietors in charge of the information created by their gadgets, Blockchain organization is a potential arrangement that bars reliance on concentrated outsiders.

A Blockchain-based secure information stockpiling framework for access control data has been presented as a segment in a proposed answer for the assurance of IoT gadget proprietors' entrance control to information produced by their IoT gadgets (Hashemi et al., 2016). Different segments are an information the board convention and an informing administration. The proposed arrangement actualizes job- and capacity-based admittance control. At the point when a gathering with a characterized job sends an entrance control message to another gathering likewise with a characterized job, at that point the message is conveyed to the informing administration. The informing administration sends the message to the data storage structure, where it becomes a trade record in a Blockchain square. After that, the receiving party gets the message from the Blockchain block in the data-amassing structure through the advising organization.

2.7.6 Blockchain-Based Security Architecture for IoT Devices in Smart Homes

A Blockchain-based design has been proposed for neighborhood networks in smart homes (or some other nearby conditions) with a few associated IoT gadgets like smart home regulators, brilliant bulbs, and IP cameras (Dorri et al., 2016).

The engineering has three levels, specifically, the nearby organizations in brilliant homes, an overlay organization, and distributed storage. In every level, substances use Blockchain exchanges to communicate with one another. The exchange types incorporate beginning exchanges, store exchanges, access exchanges, and screen exchanges. The engineering, which is represented in Figure 2.4.

A solid assurance against disavowal of administration assaults, adjustment assaults, dropping assaults, mining assaults, affixing assaults, and connecting assaults. In the neighborhood organization, there is a private nearby Blockchain, which is put away, mined, and overseen by in any event one gadget. At the point when another IoT gadget is associated with the nearby organization, a beginning exchange record is placed in a neighborhood Blockchain block. At the point when a current IoT gadget is eliminated, its record is erased from the neighborhood Blockchain. This nearby Blockchain has an arrangement header containing an entrance control list, which empowers a neighborhood network proprietor's control of all Blockchain exchanges in the neighborhood organization. Correspondence between IoT gadgets is scrambled by pre-shared Diffie-Hellman 8 key. The neighborhood organization can have proximate capacity for information. The digger gadget keeps a rundown of public keys addressing the advanced characters of elements, which can be offered consents to get to nearby arrange information from outside.

2.7.7 Improved Reliability of Medical IoT Devices

Clinical IoT gadgets are dependent upon a number of security worries similar to those associated with other IoT gadgets. Client security in clinical IoT-based frameworks

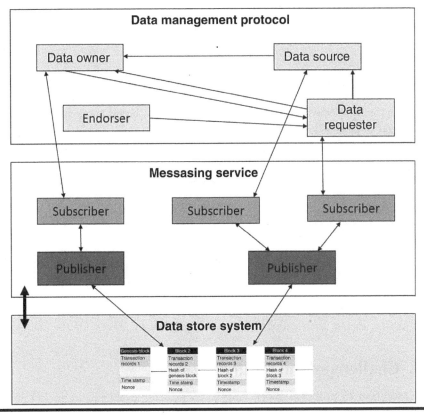

Figure 2.3 An overview of the proposed solution for a secure access control message

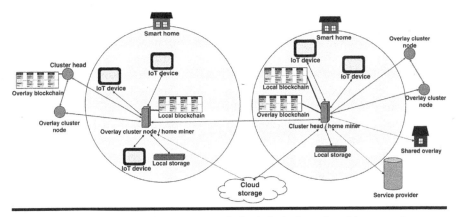

Figure 2.4 An overview of the proposed Blockchain-based architecture for smart homes

is a first concern (D. Siegel Sep. 19, 2018). A customer should be protected from any system breakdown achieved by a contraption issue or security event. A clinical IoT gadget should work dependably and oppose security assaults. Additionally, the uprightness and client security of information produced by clinical IoT frameworks should be conceded. Blockchain use in the administration of clinical IoT gadgets can ensure against the noxious alteration of gadget settings and methods of activity. An unchanging Blockchain record of records from the board occasions can relieve the danger of gadget breakdown.

Nichol and Brandt (2016) proposed the use of blockchain advancement for device the heads to improve the immovable nature of clinical IoT gadgets. At the point when a clinical IoT gadget is made, a hash of a fascinating contraption identifier along with other huge information, for instance, association name, is put away in a Blockchain block. At that point, this information can be refreshed with patient information, clinic, specialist, crisis contacts, and patient consideration mandates. Consequently, the patient and the guardians can be told about gadget administration needs, moving toward battery lapse, and distinguished patient wellbeing anomalies through a bunch of brilliant agreements. The danger of disastrous gadget disappointment is, hence, diminished by virtual contracts sending preventive upkeep data to the patient and guardian (Tsankov et al., 2018).

2.8 Challenges and Future Research

The execution of proposed Blockchain-based security arrangements in IoT is an exceptionally significant theme for future exploration. To start with, IoT applications possibly profiting by Blockchain security highlights ought to be thoroughly studied. One illustration of an important area is medical care IoT applications, where the altering of wellbeing-related estimation information could be heartbreaking. At the point when the applications and their security necessities have been set up, the following stage is to assess how Blockchain innovation could be executed. Basic reenactments and test assessments of the security and execution of Blockchain-based security arrangements are required before these arrangements can be actualized in genuine applications (Dickerson, Gazzillo, Herlihy, & Koskinen, 2017, pp. 303–312). Simultaneously, new alteration-safe Blockchain-based security arrangements giving definite legal sciences about security assaults are required. Much work is additionally required in the advance of norms for the plan of IoT equipment, IoT firmware, and other IoT programming supporting executed and checked Blockchain-based security arrangements (Atzei, Bartoletti, & Cimoli, 2017).

One critical issue with utilizing Blockchain arrangements in IoT frameworks is the restricted of the preparation capacities of a large portion of the pre-owned gadgets. As Blockchain innovation utilizes cryptography in a broad manner for hashing, computerized marking, and encryption, more exploration on lightweight cryptographic calculations is required for the down-to-earth usage of Blockchain-based security arrangements (R. Qin, Y. Yuan, and F.-Y. Wang, pp. 748–757, September 2018).

2.8.1 Conclusion

Whether or not IoT frameworks have been involved in different plans for quite a while, security blends appear and will continue to arise in the unpredictable future. General IT security techniques and devices do not satisfy all particular requirements for secure IoT sending. Hence, the ID of eminent techniques appropriate for IoT security arrangements is significant. Blockchain innovation may improve the capacity of programmed reaction to a security episode. This is particularly significant for IoT frameworks since reallocated IoT networks are expected to work constantly and securely without human administration.

A pertinent security hazard for all IT frameworks, and hence likewise for IoT frameworks, is the chance of aggressors altering the product and also the information relating to a security arrangement. Blockchain-based IoT security arrangements alleviate this danger since they are "practically" alteration-safe and on account of their capacity to perform ongoing reviews on exchanges, despite the fact that there are additionally downsides and inadequacies with regard to computerized record use in the security coordination of IoT frameworks. The critical drawback for resource of IoT machines are the creating change power should have of PoW mining and the growing amassing necessities in cutting-edge record center points when the size of a Blockchain record creates. Blockchain development is the reaction to a segment of the fundamental troubles of IoT, including its versatility, security, and enduring quality. Blockchain tech can be a wonderful method to track and screen billions of related contraptions, thereby engaging in the sharing and treatment of trades between related devices. Moreover, being decentralized, it would remove single reasons for frustration, making a more grounded climate for contraptions to run on. Blockchain IoT enable secure and solid effort between related gadgets in an IoT setup.

2.9 Blockchain in Big Data

In current years, the high-level record is at the center of PC robotization. It is a guaranteed circled information base mechanics for taking care of and give the information. Every segment in the information base is known as a block and implants nuances related to the agreement date and associated with the main square. The rule benefit of the cryptographical record is that it is scattered. No one controls the data dispatch into or their decency. In spite of the way that, these gander at are taken consistently by the various PCs on the system. These particular instruments pass on comparative data. Control information on one PC cannot enter the chain since it will not facilitate the indistinguishable data held by various machines. To spread it out obviously, if the framework exists, the information stays in a comparable state.

Because of cryptographic cash, for instance, Bitcoin, Ethereum, the high-level record can reinforce such a digitized information. This is the clarification it is feasible to utilize it in the field of Big Data, particularly to amass the security or the possibility of the information For example, a crisis center can use it to attest that

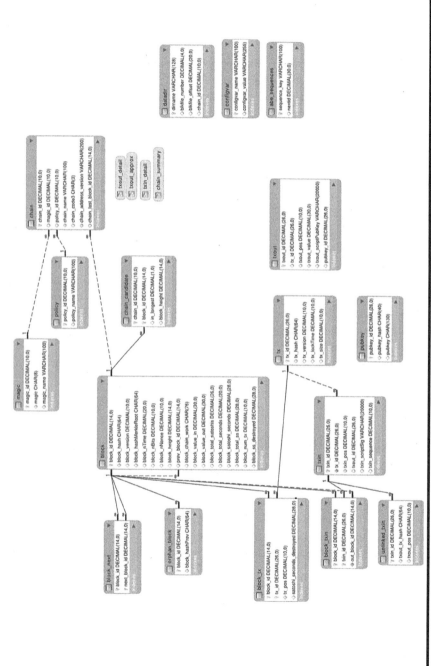

Figure 2.5 Cryptocurrency and big data to secure information Quality

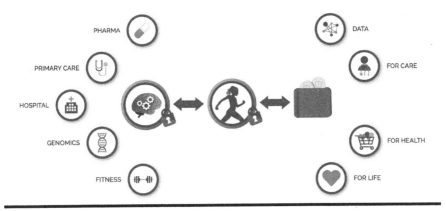

Figure 2.6   Source of statistics in digital ledger with big data analysis

calm data stays cautious, ground-breaking, and that its make-up is totally manage. By putting flourishing information bases on the high-level record, the clinical facility avow that all of its agents will have approach to manage a solitary, invariant wellspring of information.

Doubtless, defenceless estimations control in the force keep natural factors and face a test that the patient might be ruined, curved, or the continuation of their tests may either be lost or pay off. Likewise, two specialists who have similar patients may have way to deal with two distinct arrangements of information. The advanced record prevents this.

2.9.1 Digital Ledger as Fulfilling Career Chances

Given that best in class record motorization is a creating industry, an incredible request of Blockchain consultation can help you with getting the spots of Cryptocurrency Analyst, Cryptocurrency Developer, Full Battery Developer, Bitcoin, and various others (F. Knirsch, A. Unterweger, and D. Engel, pp. 71–79, 2018). As we are presumably mindful, cryptographic cash is a subset of the Blockchain; it can essentially be used by new organizations and money-related foundations. The informational gathering of this certification course gave to the control of computerized monetary standards, for instance, Bitcoin and Ethereum will be involved modelers and IT fashioners, similarly as market investigators, socio-anthropologists, lawful consultants and representatives, all invested huge energy in Blockchain development and linked it with future monetary changes. Various universities, and electronic learning platforms such as Udemy, Simplilearn, Blockchain Council, etc. offer affirmation courses. You can even find discount codes for these stages, such as a 10% off Blockchain Council coupon (Q. Xia et al., pp. 14757–14767, 2017).

This advance similarly hinders potential data spills. At the point when the information is taken care of on the channel, even the most well-positioned chiefs in an association will require various assents from various concentrations in the framework

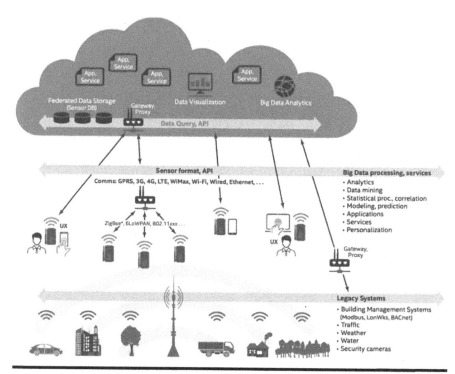

Figure 2.7 Blockchain in Big Data

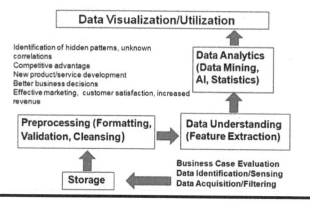

Figure 2.8 Blockchain in Big Data Analysis

to get to the data (Yuan and Wang, pp. 2663–2668, 2016). It is thus impossible for a cybercriminal to grasp it. Through its expansion, the Blockchain grants sharing data even more calmly. To use the instance of the facility, a foundation may have to give prosperity data to the courts, with protection organizations, or with the organizations of a patient. Regardless, without the Blockchain, this technique can present dangers (The Energy Web Foundation, September 2, 2018).

2.9.2 Blockchain and Big Data Advancements for Information Investigation

The Blockchain moreover supplements data examination progressions. For example, in 2017, a consortium of 47 Japanese banks combined with the startup Ripple to develop the trading of money between records by methods for the Blockchain (S. Amani, M. Bégel, M. Bortin, and M. Staples, pp. 66–77, 2018). Regularly, continuous trades are exorbitant, especially because of the peril of twofold spending blackmail (giving two trades using a comparable asset). The chain of squares removes this danger (Y. Hirai pp. 520–535, 2017). Similarly, Big Data separates perceive unsafe trades. Even more importantly, the Blockchain allows banking establishments to constantly recognize deception attempts. Granted that the Blockchain holds records for each trade, this system grants banks the opportunity to explore data searching for plans in a logical manner. The Blockchain and the Big Data therefore make it possible to fortify the security of the monetary trades as much as possible (S. Amani, M. Bégel, M. Bortin, and M. Staples, pp. 66–77, 2018).

2.9.3 Blockchain and Big Data: Protection Concerns

Nonetheless, this utilization of the Blockchain likewise raises issues of privacy, in direct logical inconsistency to why this innovation initially became well known (G. Roşu and T. F. Şerbănuţă, 2010). A few specialists are worried that exchange

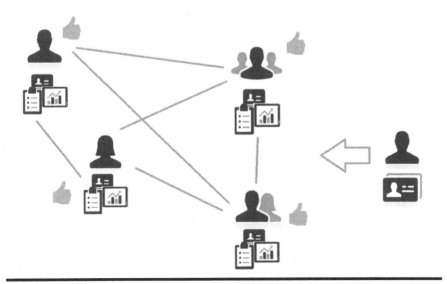

Figure 2.9 Blockchain Protection Concern

records might be abused to fabricate purchaser profiles or to promote different abuses (E. Hildenbrandt et al., 2018).

Notwithstanding, Blockchain improves the straightforwardness of information examination. On the off-chance that a section cannot be checked, it is naturally dismissed. In this manner, the information is entirely straightforward. Different specialists are additionally worried about the effect of Blockchain and Big Data on nature (Poon & Buterin, 2017).

2.9.4 Blockchain and Big Data: Community-Based Data to Forecast the Price of Bitcoin

The information from interpersonal organizations (Social Data) can be helpful in foreseeing customer conduct. Be that as it may, incidentally, clients of Bitcoin and interpersonal organizations have numerous segment likenesses, just as shared traits as far as feelings and mentalities (Zhang et al., pp. 829–840, September 2018b).

2.9.5 Blockchain Use Cases in Big Data

1. **Ensuring Trust (Data Integrity)**

   Data recorded on the Blockchain are trustworthy, given the way in which the check technique ensures its quality. It furthermore obliges straightforwardness, since activities and trades that occur on the Blockchain framework can be followed. Five years ago, Lenovo showed this use of Blockchain development to recognize counterfeit records and constructions. They used Blockchain development to support actual records that were encoded with cutting-edge marks. The modernized imprints are set up by PCs and the validity of the report is affirmed through a Blockchain record.

2. **Preventing Malicious Activities**

   Since Blockchain uses an understanding count to check trades, a single unit cannot address a danger to the data organization. A center (or unit) that begins to act in an abnormal manner can easily be perceived and eradicated from the framework. Since the organization is so dispersed, it is almost impossible for a solitary gathering to produce sufficient computational ability to change the approval rules and permit undesirable information in the framework. To change the Blockchain rules, a dominant part of hubs should be pooled together to make an agreement. This will be impossible for a solitary agitator to accomplish.

3. **Making Predictions (Predictive Analysis)**

   Blockchain data, similar to various kinds of data, can be desperate down to uncover gigantic experiences into the practices, designs and as such can be used to anticipate future outcomes. Furthermore, Blockchain gives coordinated data gathered from individuals or individual contraptions. In an insightful examination, data specialists' base on enormous courses of action of data to choose with incredible precision the consequence of social gatherings like customer tendencies, customer lifetime regard, dynamic expenses, and mix rates as it relates to associations. This is, nevertheless, not confined to business pieces of information as essentially any event can be anticipated with the right data assessment whether it is social conclusions or hypothesis markers. Furthermore, in light of the scattered thought of Blockchain and the enormous computational power available through it, data specialists, even in smaller affiliations, can accept expansive insightful assessment tasks. These data analysts can use the computational power of two or three thousand PCs related on a Blockchain orchestrate as a cloud-based help of inspect social outcomes on a scale that would not have been otherwise possible (R. Qin, Y. Yuan, and F.-Y. Wang, 748–757, Sep. Qin et al., 2018).

4. **Real-Time Data Analysis**

   As has been shown, in real money-related and divide structures, Blockchain makes for consistent cross-edge exchanges. A few banks and fintech trailblazers are currently investigating Blockchain in light of the fact that it manages the cost of quick — essentially, instant — settlement of immense entireties regardless of geographic boundaries. Likewise, affiliations that require the ceaseless assessment of data for a huge degree can move toward a Blockchain-engaged structure to achieve. With Blockchain, banks and various affiliations can watch changes in data dynamically, making it possible to make smart decisions — whether or not it is to deter a questionable trade or track unusual patterns of activity (P. Tsankov et al., 2018; T. Dickerson, P. Gazzillo, M. Herlihy, and E. Koskinen, pp. 303–312, 2017).

5. **Oversee Data Sharing**

   In such manner, information received from information studies can be dealt within a Blockchain sort out. Accordingly, adventure bunches don't reiterate data assessment recently did by various gatherings or misguidedly reuse data that is as of now been used. Moreover, a Blockchain stage can help data specialists adjust their work; in all likelihood, by trading examination results set aside on the stage (G. Greenspan Sep. 30, 2018).

2.10 Conclusion

Blockchain, as has been noted, is in its earlies phases, even if this may not appear so on account of the advances the development has achieved in such a short period. One would expect that as the technology develops, progressively stronger use cases will be recognized and examined — information science being one zone that will profit by this. That being said, a couple of difficulties have been brought about its effect with regard to information science, particularly in terms of the enormous amount of information which is required to be dealt with. One concern is that the

Blockchain application in such a manner will be extravagant to seek after. This is on the grounds that information stockpiling on a Blockchain is costly when compared with conventional methods. Squares manage moderately limited quantities of information contrasted with the huge volumes of information gathered each second for enormous information and other information investigation assignments. How Blockchain develops to address these worries and continues to disturb the information science space will be especially intriguing on the grounds that, as we have seen, the innovation can possibly entirely change how we oversee and use information.

References

Alharby, M., and A. V. Moorsel, "Blockchain-based smart contracts: Asystematic mapping study," in *Proc. Int. Conf. Artif. Intell. Soft Comput.*, 2017, pp. 125–140.

Amani, S., M. Bégel, M. Bortin, and M. Staples, "Towards verifying Ethereum smart contract bytecode in Isabelle/HOL," in *Proc. 7th ACM SIGPLAN Int. Conf. Certified Progr. Proofs (CPP)*, Los Angeles, CA, USA, Jan. 2018, pp. 66–77.

Atzei, N., M. Bartoletti, and T. Cimoli, "A survey of attacks on Ethereum smart contracts," in *Principles of Security and Trust.* Heidelberg, Germany: Springer, 2017, pp. 164–186.

Australian Securities Exchange. *CHESS Replacement.* Accessed: Oct. 15, 2018. [Online]. Available: https://www.asx.com.au/services/chess-replacement.htm.

Ayed, A. B., "A conceptual secure blockchain-based electronic voting system," *Int. J. Netw. Security Appl.*, vol. 9, no. 3, pp. 1–9, 2017.

Bhargavan, K. et al., "Formal verification of smart contracts: Short paper," in *Proc. ACM Workshop Program. Lang. Anal. Security (PLAS)*, Vienna, Austria, Oct. 2016, pp. 91–96.

Bliss, R. R., and R. S. Steigerwald, "Derivatives clearing and settlement: A comparison of central counterparties and alternative structures," *Econ. Perspectives*, vol. 30, no. 4, pp. 22–29, 2006.

Caytas, J., "Blockchain in the U.S. regulatory setting: Evidentiary use in Vermont, Delaware, and elsewhere," in *Columbia Science and Technology Law Review*, 2017. [Online]. Available: https://ssrn.com/abstract=2988363.

Chang, T.-H., and D. Svetinovic, "Improving bitcoin ownership identification using transaction patterns analysis," *IEEE Trans. Syst., Man, Cybern., Syst.*, n.d. doi: 10.1109/TSMC.2018.2867497.

Christidis, K. and M. Devetsikiotis, "Blockchains and smart contracts for the Internet of Things," *IEEE Access*, vol. 4, pp. 2292–2303, 2016.

Delmolino, K. et al., "Step by step towards creating a safe smart contract: Lessons and insights from a cryptocurrency lab," in *Proc. Int. Conf. Financ. Cryptography Data Security*, 2016, pp. 79–94.

Dickerson, T., P. Gazzillo, M. Herlihy, and E. Koskinen, "Adding concurrency to smart contracts," in *Proc. ACM Symp. Principles Distrib. Comput.*, 2017, pp. 303–312.

Dika, A., "Ethereum smart contracts: Security vulnerabilities and security tools," M.S. thesis, Dept. Comput. Sci., Norwegian Univ. Sci. Technol., Trondheim, Norway, 2017.

Dorri, A., S. S. Kanhere, and R. Jurdak, "Towards an optimized blockchain for IoT," in *Proc. ACM 2nd Int. Conf. Internet Things Design Implement*, 2017, pp. 173–178.

Dorri, A., S. S. Kanhere, R. Jurdak, and P. Gauravaram, "Blockchain for IoT security and privacy: The case study of a smart home," in *Proc. IEEE Int. Conf. Pervasive Comput. Commun. Workshops (Per Com Workshops)*, 2017, pp. 618–623.

Ethereum Yellow Paper. (2018). [Online]. Available: https://ethereum.github.io/yellowpaper/paper.pdf

Gatteschi, V., F. Lamberti, C. Demartini, C. Pranteda, and V. Santamaria, "Blockchain and smart contracts for insurance: Is the technology mature enough?" *Future Internet*, vol. 10, no. 2, p. 20, 2018.

Georgeff, B., Pell, M. Pollack, M. Tambe, and M. Wooldridge, "The belief-desire-intention model of agency," in *Proc. Int. Workshop Agent Theories Archit. Lang.*, 1998, pp. 1–10.

Glaser, F., "Pervasive decentralisation of digital infrastructures: A framework for blockchain enabled system and use case analysis," in *Proc. 50th Hawaii Int. Conf. Syst. Sci.*, 2017, pp. 1543–1552.

Greenspan, G. *Why Many Smart Contract Use Cases Are Simply Impossible.* Accessed: Sep. 30, 2018. [Online]. Available: https://www.coindesk.com/three-smart-contract-misconceptions/

Hansen, J. D., and C. L. Reyes, "Legal aspects of smart contract applications," in *Legal aspects of smart contract applications*, Perkins Coie's Blockchain Ind. Group, Seattle, WA, USA, White Paper, May 2017.

Hildenbrandt, E. et al., "KEVM: A complete formal semantics of the Ethereum virtual machine," in *Proc. IEEE 31st Comput. Security Found. Symp. (CSF)*, 2018, pp. 204–217.

Hirai, Y., "Defining the Ethereum virtual machine for interactive theorem provers," in *Proc. Int. Conf. Financ. Cryptography Data Security*, Sliema, Malta, 2017, pp. 520–535.

Hou, H., "The application of blockchain technology in E-government in China," in *Proc. 26th Int. Conf. Comput. Commun. Netw. (ICCCN)*, Vancouver, Canada, 2017, pp. 1–4.

de la Rosa, J. L. et al., "On intellectual property in online open innovation for SME by means of blockchain and smart contracts," in *Proc. 3rd Annu. World Open Innov. Conf. (WOIC)*, Barcelona, Spain, Dec. 2016, pp. 1–16.

Juels, A., A. Kosba, and E. Shi, "The ring of Gyges: Investigating the future of criminal smart contracts," in *Proc. ACM SIGSAC Conf. Comput. Commun. Security (CCS)*, Vienna, Austria, Oct. 2016, pp. 283–295.

Kaelbling, L. P., M. L. Littman, and A. W. Moore, "Reinforcement learning: A survey," *J. Artif. Intell. Res.*, vol. 4, pp. 237–285, May 1996.

Knirsch, F., A. Unterweger, and D. Engel, "Privacy-preserving blockchain-based electric vehicle charging with dynamic tariff decisions," *Comput. Sci. Res. Develop.*, vol. 33, nos. 1–2, pp. 71–79, 2018.

Kosba, A., A. Miller, E. Shi, Z. K. Wen, and C. Papamanthou, "Hawk: The blockchain model of cryptography and privacy-preserving smart contracts," in *Proc. IEEE Symp. Security Privacy (SP)*, San Jose, CA, USA, May 2016, pp. 839–858.

Lotti, L., "Contemporary art, capitalization and the blockchain: On the autonomy and automation of art's value," *Finance Soc.*, vol. 2, no. 2, pp. 96–110, 2016.

Luu, L., D. H. Chu, H. Olickel, P. Saxena, and A. Hobor, "Making smart contracts smarter," in *Proc. ACM SIGSAC Conf. Comput. Commun. Security (CCS)*, Vienna, Austria, Oct. 2016, pp. 254–269.

Marino, B., and A. Juels, "Setting standards for altering and undoing smart contracts," in *Proc. Int. Symp. Rules Rule Markup Lang. Semantic Web*, 2016, pp. 151–166.

McCorry, P., S. F. Shahandashti, and F. Hao, "A smart contract for boardroom voting with maximum voter privacy," in *Proc. Int. Conf. Financ. Cryptography Data Security*, 2017, pp. 357–375.

Modha, D. S. et al., "Cognitive computing," *Commun. ACM*, vol. 54, no. 8, pp. 62–71, 2011.

Ojetunde, B., N. Shibata, and J. Gao, "Secure payment system utilizing MANET for disaster areas," *IEEE Trans. Syst., Man, Cybern., Syst.*, n.d. doi: 10.1109/TSMC.2017.2752203.

Peyton, A. (2017). *Mizuho Trials Australia–Japan Trade Transaction on Blockchain.* [Online]. Available: https://www.bankingtech.com/2017/07/mizuho-trials-australia-japan-trade-transaction-on-blockchain/

Poon, J., and V. Buterin. (2017). *Plasma: Scalable Autonomous Smart Contracts.* [Online]. Available: https://plasma.io/plasma.pdf

Qin, R., Y. Yuan, and F.-Y. Wang, "Research on the selection strategies of blockchain mining pools," *IEEE Trans. Comput. Soc. Syst.*, vol. 5, no. 3, pp. 748–757, Sep. 2018.

Risius, M. and K. Spohrer, "A blockchain research framework: What we (don't) know, where we go from here, and how we will get there," *Bus. Inf. Syst. Eng.*, vol. 59, no. 6, pp. 385–409, 2017.

Rosenstock, T. S., Rohrbach, D., Nowak, A., & Girvetz, E., An introduction to the climate-smart agriculture papers. *The Climate-Smart Agriculture Papers*, pp. 1–12, 2018. doi: 10.1007/978-3-319-92798-5_1.

Siegel, D. *Understanding the DAO Attack.* Accessed: Sep. 19, 2018. [Online]. Available: https://www.coindesk.com/understanding-dao-hackjournalists/

The Energy Web Foundation. *Promising Blockchain Applications for Energy: Separating the Signal From the Noise.* Accessed: Sep. 2, 2018. [Online]. Available: http://www.coinsay.com/wp-content/uploads/2018/07/Energy-Futures-Initiative-Promising-Blockchain-Applications-for-Energy.pdf

Tsankov, P. et al., "Securify: Practical security analysis of smart contracts," *arXiv preprint arXiv:1806.01143v2*, 2018.

U.S. Securities and Exchange Commission. *Investor Bulletin: Initial Coin Offerings.* Accessed: Nov. 3, 2018. [Online]. Available: https://www.sec.gov/oiea/investor-alerts-and-bulletins/ib_coinofferings

Wang, S. et al., "A preliminary research of prediction markets based on blockchain powered smart contracts," in *Proc. IEEE Int. Conf. Blockchain (Blockchain)*, Jul./Aug. 2018, pp. 1287–1293.

Watanabe, H. et al., "Blockchain contract: A complete consensus using blockchain," in *Proc. IEEE 4th Glob. Conf. Consum. Electron. (GCCE)*, 2015, pp. 577–578.

Xia, Q. et al., "MeDShare: Trust-less medical data sharing among cloud service providers via blockchain," *IEEE Access*, vol. 5, pp. 14757–14767, 2017. doi: 10.1109/ACCESS.2017.2730843.

Xu, X. et al., "The blockchain as a software connector," in *Proc. 13th Working IEEE/IFIP Conf. Softw. Archit. (WICSA)*, 2016, pp. 182–191.

Xu, X. et al., "A taxonomy of blockchain-based systems for architecture design," in *Proc. IEEE Int. Conf. Softw. Archit. (ICSA)*, 2017, pp. 243–252.

Yua, Y., & F.-Y. Wang, "Blockchain and cryptocurrencies: Model, techniques, and applications," *IEEE Trans. Syst., Man, Cybern., Syst.*, vol. 48, no. 9, pp. 1421–1428, Sep. 2018.

Yuan, Y., and F.-Y. Wang, "Towards blockchain-based intelligent transportation systems," in *Proc. IEEE 19th Int. Conf. Intell. Trans. Syst. (ITSC)*, Rio de Janeiro, Brazil, 2016, pp. 2663–2668.

Zhang, F., E. Cecchetti, K. Croman, A. Juels, and E. Shi, "Town crier: An authenticated data feed for smart contracts," in *Proc. ACM SIGSAC Conf. Comput. Commun. Security (CCS)*, Vienna, Austria, Oct. 2016, pp. 270–282.

Zhang, J. J. et al., "Cyber-physical-social systems: The state of the art and perspectives," *IEEE Trans. Comput. Soc. Syst.*, vol. 5, no. 3, pp. 829–840, Sep. 2018b.

Zhang, Y. et al., "Smart contract-based access control for the Internet of Things," *arXiv preprint arXiv:1802.04410*, 2018a.

Chapter 3

Blockchain: Trends, Role and Future Prospects

Priya Swaminarayan, Abhishek Mehta, Nihal Parsania, and Khushi Solanki
Parul University, India

Contents

DOI: 10.1201/9781003129486-3

3.1 Introduction to Cryptocurrency

The notion of cryptocash implies it takes into account the creation and the preparation of advanced monetary forms and their exchange across decentralized frameworks. This cycle of exchange is the essential component of the Bitcoin Blockchain. Exchanges are approved and communicated. Numerous exchanges structure a square. Each square experiences a cycle to choose the following square that will be added to the chain. Furthermore, this cycle is conveyed by the exceptional companions known as "miners". Digital currencies are constantly intended to be liberated from the control of the public authority, and as they have become a more mainstream system this fundamental part of the business has experienced harsh criticism. There are numerous sorts of cryptographic forms of money, yet these monetary standards are simpler to mine than Bitcoin. They are compromises, including more serious danger by lower levels of liquidity, acknowledgment and worth maintenance. As of January 2020, there are more than 2,000 digital currencies, and a considerable number of these tokens and coins have become infamous among a network of patrons, speculators and others. A cryptocurrency is a digital or virtual currency that is secured by cryptography, making it nearly impossible to counterfeit or double-spend. Many cryptocurrencies are decentralized networks based on Blockchain technology— a distributed ledger which is enforced by a disparate network of computers. One defining feature of cryptocurrencies is that they are generally not issued by any central authority, rendering them theoretically immune to government interference or manipulation.

- A cryptocurrency is a new form of digital asset based on a network that is distributed across a large number of computers. This decentralized structure allows them to exist outside the control of governments and central authorities.
- The word "cryptocurrency" is derived from the encryption techniques which are used to secure the network.
- Blockchains, which are organizational methods for ensuring the integrity of transactional data, are an essential component of many cryptocurrencies.
- Many experts believe that Blockchain and related technology will disrupt many industries, including finance and law.
- Cryptocurrencies face criticism for a number of reasons, including their use for illegal activities, the volatility of their exchange rates, and the vulnerabilities of the infrastructure underlying them. However, they also have been praised for their portability, divisibility, inflation resistance, and transparency.

Cryptocurrencies are systems that allow for secure online payments. These are denominated in terms of virtual "tokens," which are represented by ledger entries internal to the system. "Crypto" refers to the various encryption algorithms and cryptographic techniques that safeguard these entries, such as elliptical curve encryption, public–private key pairs, and hashing functions.

3.1.1 Advantages of Cryptocurrency

Cryptocurrencies hold the promise of making it easier to transfer funds directly between two parties, without the need for a trusted third party such as a bank or a credit card company. These transfers are instead secured by the use of public keys and private keys and different forms of incentive systems, such as proof of work or proof of stake.

In modern cryptocurrency systems, a user's "wallet", or account address, has a public key, while the private key is known only to the owner and is used to sign transactions. Fund transfers are completed with minimal processing fees, allowing users to avoid the steep fees charged by banks and financial institutions for wire transfers.

3.1.2 Disadvantages of Cryptocurrency

The semi-anonymous nature of cryptocurrency transactions makes them well suited to a host of illegal activities, such as money laundering and tax evasion. However, cryptocurrency advocates often value their anonymity highly, citing benefits of privacy such as protection for whistleblowers or activists living under repressive governments. Some cryptocurrencies are more private than others.

Bitcoin, for instance, is a relatively poor choice for conducting illegal business online, since the forensic analysis of the Bitcoin Blockchain has helped authorities to arrest and prosecute criminals. More privacy-oriented coins do exist, however, such as Dash, Monero, or ZCash, which are far more difficult to trace.

3.1.3 Criticisms of Cryptocurrency

Since market prices for cryptocurrencies are based on supply and demand, the rate at which a cryptocurrency can be exchanged for another currency can fluctuate widely, since the design of many cryptocurrencies ensures a high degree of scarcity.

Bitcoin has experienced some rapid surges and collapses in value, climbing as high as $19,000 per Bitcoin in December of 2017 before dropping to around $7,000 in the month of February [2]. Cryptocurrencies are thus considered by some economists to be a short-lived fad or speculative bubble.

There is concern that cryptocurrencies such as Bitcoin are not rooted in any material goods. Some research, however, has identified that the cost of producing a Bitcoin, which requires an increasingly large amount of energy, is directly related to its market price.

Cryptocurrency Blockchains are highly secure, but other aspects of a cryptocurrency ecosystem, including exchanges and wallets, are not immune to the threat of hacking. In Bitcoin's history of more than a decade, several online exchanges have been the subject of hacking and theft, sometimes with millions of dollars' worth of "coins" stolen [5].

Nonetheless, many observers see potential advantages in cryptocurrencies, such as the possibility of preserving value against inflation and facilitating exchange while at the same time being more easy to transport and divide than precious metals and existing outside the influence of central banks and governments.

3.1.4 Types of Cryptocurrency

1. Ethereum (ETH): From this innovation the idea of reasonable agreement was presented along with decentralized platform and Daps (Decentralized Application) to strengthen the run with time-frame, control, extortion and most fundamental is impedance from an outsider. As of 8 January 2020, ETH had a market of $15.6 billion and each has a symbolic worth of $142.54.

2. Litecoin (LTC): This was launched in 2011, and has been described as "Silver to Bitcoin's gold". it's a partner open inventory universally installment network that is not constrained by any focal position and uses "script" as a "Proof of work". As of 8 January 2020, LTC had a market of $3.0 billion and each coin has a symbolic worth of $46.92, making it the 6th-largest digital currency in the world.

3. Ripple (XRP): This was launched in 2012. It permits the banks to settle the cross-fringe installments progressively, with the top to complete straightforwardness

at a lower esteem. The most important factor with respect to XRP is the shared trait of the record is selective and there is no need for mining. As of 8 January 2020, XRP had a market of $9.2 billion and a per-token worth $0.21.

4. Bitcoin money (BCH): This was launched in 2017. It experienced issues with the issue of versatility; the bitcoin network includes a severe breaking point on the elements of squares: 1MB. BCH will expand the square size from 1MB to 8MB, with the idea being that bigger squares can give more rapid management times. As of 8 January 2020, BCH had a market of $4.4 billion and a value for each badge of $240.80.

5. Libra: In the case of this currency, rumors emerged that Facebook was building up its own digital currencies. What's more, along these lines, the brief dispatch date is inside the year 2020.

6. Tether (USDT): Tether was launched in 2014. Tie was one in all the chief norm of a gaggle known as stablecoin, which intends to achieve their market cost of the money or distinctive marker on cutting back unpredictability, low worth variances in order to attract clients. It will allow individuals to use a Blockchain organization and innovation to collaborate in antiquated monetary standards, thereby limiting the quality and instability. As of 8 January, 2020, USDT had a market of $4.6 billion and a per-token worth of $1.00.

7. Monero (XMR): This had begun in 2017. BCB token grants Binance clients the ability to change many different digital currencies speedily on their foundation. As of 8 January 2020, the currency had a market of $2.3 billion and a per-token worth of $14.71.

8. Binance Coin (BNB): This was launched in 2017. A Binance Coin permits Binance users to change dozens of various cryptocurrencies expeditiously on their platform. As of 8 January 2020, this had a market of $2.3 billion and a per-token worth of $14.71.

9. Bitcoin SV (BSV): Here SV means "Santoshi Vision", and this is a unique Bitcoin Network. The designers of BSV asked that this cash re-establishes on Santoshi Nakamoto's convention, and allows for new improvements to expand dependability and simultaneously improve security and speed up management time. As of 8 January 2020, BSV had a market of $2.1 billion and a symbolic worth of $114.43 per token.

10. EOS: it had been dispatched in the Gregorian schedule month of 2018, and made by Dan Larimer. Greek god gives a designated verification of-stake component that it wants to be prepared to offer quantifiability on the most distant side of its rivals. Furthermore, it's conjointly progressive inferable from its absence of a mining system to make the coin. As of 8 January 2020, EOS had a market of $2.7 billion and a per-token worth is $2.85.

3.2 Introduction to Blockchain Technology and Structure

Blockchain grants friends the ability to transfer advanced resources without the need for any trusted intermediaries. It had been an innovation initially made to help the eminent digital money, Bitcoin. The Blockchain, without any further developments, has taken its very own long period and infiltrates a wide fluctuation of utilizations across a few enterprises, including accounting, medical care, government, creation, and dispersion. We will regard Blockchain as a circulated framework because it keeps a shared rundown of each record and manages each of them. Furthermore, this record is known as a "square", and each one these squares region unit encoded and these squares contain the historical backdrop of each square that goes before it with timestamped managing data. The Blockchain is ready to present and modify a decent shift of utilizations, just as product move, for example, give chain. Advanced media move, for example, the offer of workmanship. Far off Services Delivery, for instance, travel, and business ventures. A stage for limited business rationale, for example, moving registering to data sources. Furthermore, appropriated insight, for instance, instruction credentialing. Additional utilizations of Blockchain exemplify dispersed assets, for example, power age and circulation. Blockchain will adjust a thorough economy. It will allow a person in an extremely distant corner of the planet to participate in a majority rule strategy during this field open doors for inventive applications region unit unending. Also, most indispensable consider the Blockchain is it made up with two essential parts: (a) a confined organization for encouraging and corroborative exchanges; (b) changeless record Blockchain seems complicated, and it definitely can be, but its core concept is really quite simple. A Blockchain is a type of database. To be able to understand Blockchain, it helps to first understand the actual nature of a database.

A database is a collection of information that is stored electronically on a computer system. Information, or data, in databases is typically structured in table format to allow for easier searching and filtering for specific information. This poses the question: What is the difference between someone using a spreadsheet to store information rather than a database?

Spreadsheets are designed for one person, or a small group of people, to store and access limited amounts of information. In contrast, a database is designed to house significantly larger amounts of information that can be accessed, filtered, and manipulated quickly and easily by any number of users at once.

Large databases achieve this by storing data on servers that are made up of powerful computers. These servers can sometimes be built using hundreds or thousands of computers in order to have the computational power and storage capacity necessary for many users to access the database simultaneously. While a spreadsheet or database may be accessible to any number of people, it is often owned by a business and managed by an appointed individual who has complete control over both how it works and the data within it.

One key difference between a typical database and a Blockchain is the way in which the data are structured. A Blockchain collects information together in groups, also known as blocks, that hold sets of information. Blocks have certain storage capacities and, when filled, are chained onto the previously filled block, forming a chain of data known as the "Blockchain." All new information that follows that freshly added block is compiled into a newly formed block that will then also be added to the chain once filled.

A database structures its data into tables whereas a Blockchain, as its name implies, structures its data into chunks (blocks) that are chained together. This means that all Blockchains are databases, but not all databases are Blockchains. This system also inherently makes an irreversible timeline of data when implemented in a decentralized nature. When a block is filled it is set in stone and becomes a part of this timeline. Each block in the chain is given an exact timestamp when it is added to the chain.

Blockchain became famous as an underlying technology of Bitcoin. It was first introduced in 2008, and it becoming increasingly popular since then. At first it was used only for cryptocurrencies, but then people realized that Blockchain could be used for other purposes. And now the application range of Blockchain is very wide-ranging. Blockchain can be regarded as a public append-only ledger, in which every transaction is stored in a block-like structure. These blocks are connected with each other using cryptographic links, with every block being connected with its previous block. Every participant on the network holds the same copy of Blockchain. That provides many benefits, such as there being no single point of failure, equal rights for all participants, and detection of malicious activities. Every transaction in Blockchain is done on a peer-to-peer basis. There is no intermediary involved. Those participants who validate transactions and update the ledger are known as miners. Miners compete to solve a difficult mathematical problem based on cryptographic hash functions and whoever wins gets to append the block. The miner who appends the valid block is rewarded with cryptocurrency. Many applications are there, which can be made more efficient, secure and reduce the costs using Blockchain. These application domains include healthcare, supply chains, government records, cloud, financial etc. As there is no intermediary involved in regulations, there are consensus mechanisms available to overcome that. Some of these consensus algorithms include proof of work, proof of stake, byzantine fault tolerance, and many more. One more feature that Blockchain provided is that of enabling use of smart contracts securely. Smart contract is a piece of code which is run automatically when certain conditions are met. These conditions are set prior the deploying the contract and with the signature of both of the parties. So no party can deny of the terms they agreed upon. With the help of smart contracts, the applications of Blockchain sky-rocketed. Many sectors implemented these smart contracts to avoid various kinds of problems.

3.2.1 Decentralization in Blockchain

For the purpose of understanding Blockchain, it is instructive to view it in terms of how it has been implemented by Bitcoin. Like a database, Bitcoin needs a collection of computers to store its Blockchain. For Bitcoin, this Blockchain is just a specific type of database that stores every Bitcoin transaction ever made. In Bitcoin's case, and in contrast to most databases, these computers are not all housed under the same roof, and each computer or group of computers is operated by a unique individual or group of individuals.

Imagine that a company owns a server comprised of 10,000 computers with a database holding all of its client's account information. This company has a warehouse containing all of these computers under one roof. It also has full control of each of these computers and all the information contained within them. Similarly, Bitcoin consists of thousands of computers, but each computer or group of computers that hold its Blockchain is in a different geographic location and they are all operated by separate individuals or groups of people. The computers, which make up Bitcoin's network, are called nodes.

In this model, Bitcoin's Blockchain is used in a decentralized way. However, private, centralized Blockchains, where the computers that make up its network are owned and operated by a single entity, also exist.

In a Blockchain, each node has a full record of the data that has been stored on the Blockchain since its inception. For Bitcoin, the data are the entire history of all Bitcoin transactions. If one node has an error in its data, it can use the thousands of other nodes as a reference point to correct itself. This means that no one node within the network can alter the information held within it. Because of this, the history of transactions in each block that make up Bitcoin's Blockchain is irreversible.

If one user tampers with Bitcoin's record of transactions, all other nodes would cross-reference each other and easily pinpoint the node with the incorrect information. This system helps to establish an exact and transparent order of events. For Bitcoin, this information is a list of transactions, but it is also possible for a Blockchain to hold a variety of information, such as legal contracts, state identifications, or a company's product inventory.

In order to change how that system works, or the information stored within it, a majority of the decentralized network's computing power would need to agree on said changes. This ensures that whatever changes do occur are in the best interests of the majority.

3.2.2 Transparency in Blockchain

Because of the decentralized nature of Bitcoin's Blockchain, all of the transactions can be transparently viewed by either having a personal node or by using Blockchain explorers that allow anyone to see transactions occurring live. Each node has its own copy of the chain that gets updated as fresh blocks are confirmed and added. This means that if you wanted to, you could track Bitcoin wherever it goes.

For example, exchanges have been hacked in the past, where those who held Bitcoin on the exchange lost everything. While the hacker may be entirely anonymous, the Bitcoins that they extracted are easily traceable. If the Bitcoins that were stolen in some of these hacks were to be moved or spent somewhere, it would be known.

3.2.3 Types of Blockchain

a. **Public Blockchain:** This is an open source. This allows everyone to be the part of their processes like miners, users, developers and other community members. Whatever transaction has been done under this they all are transparent, means everyone is able to examine the transaction details.

b. **Private Blockchain:** This is also called a permissioned Blockchain. To carry out a transaction on a private Blockchain the participant needs to join the networks. All the transactions are private. And it is more centralized than a public network.

c. **Hybrid Blockchain:** This combines the privacy benefits of a permissioned and private Blockchain with the security and transparency benefits of a public Blockchain.

3.2.4 Need for Blockchain Technology

There three main reasons why Blockchain is becoming an increasingly significant technology: (a) a radical increase in the quantity of cybercrimes; (b) increased advanced handling force; and (c) the rise of bitcoin and cryptographic money. These are very much the main advantages of Blockchain. In addition, you get a past filled with action, there is no essential issue of assault and there is no brought together control.

3.2.5 How Does Blockchain Technology Work?

Activities inside the suburbanized organization zone unit the duty of the friendly members and their few-cycle hubs, for example, PC, work area, and worker racks. These tasks grasp approval exchanges, assembling the exchanges for a square, communicating the polling form exchanges inside the square, and concession to succeeding square creation, related anchoring the squares to make a constant record. Members that start an exchange of imports by making a managing, further members alluded to as diggers, United Nations office settle on worth-added work or calculation to check exchanges, communicated managing, the battle to state the right to shape a square, chip away at agreeing by corroboratory the square, communicating the newly made square, and affirming exchanges. You may wonder why members would assault further work. Indeed, the digger's zone unit boosted with bitcoins for the endeavors in dealing with the Blockchain, as we'll decide. Managing approval is dispensed severally by all diggers. The strategy includes approval of very twenty standards, just as size, language structure, and so forth. Among these models are: reported Input unexpended managing Output, UTXOs region unit legitimate, review, UTXO is very much characterized before in exercise 2, reference yield UTXOs region unit right, reference input amount and yield amount coordinated adequately, invalid exchanges zone unit dismissed and can't be the transmission. All the legitimate exchanges region unit esteem added to a pool of exchanges. Excavators pick an assortment of managing from this pool to shape a square. This makes a test. On the off-chance that each jack adds the square to the chain, there'll be a few branches to the chain, prompting a conflicting state. Review, the Blockchain could be a solitary steady associated chain of transition. We'd like a framework to beat this test, the appropriate response. Excavators fight to goal a riddle to see the United Nations office acquire the right to frame the succeeding square. Inside the instance of the bitcoin Blockchain, this package could be a calculation of bundle and furthermore, the focal cycle unit or processor escalated. When a jack tackles the riddle, the declaration is communicated to the organization and, furthermore, the square is also communicated to the organization. At that point, another member confirms the new square. Members agree to highlight a substitution square to the chain. This new square is esteem added to their local duplicate of the Blockchain. Consequently, a substitution set of exchanges zone units recorded and affirmed. The equation for understanding is named the evidence of-work convention since it includes a work cycle capacity to unwind the riddle and to state the right to make the succeeding square. Managing zero, list zero of the affirmed block is framed by the jack of the square. It's an exceptional UTXO and doesn't have any info UTXO. It's alluded to as the coin-base managing that produces a miner's expenses for the square creation. Right now, the miner's charges region unit twelve [5]. BTC for a bitcoin. This can be anyway new coin is kept up in bitcoin. To sum up, most activities during a Blockchain region unit managing approval and square creation with the arrangement of the members.

3.2.6 Advantages and Disadvantages

■ Integrity, security, quick preparation, and discernibility you can consider to be among the upsides of Blockchain.
■ Power use, and cost of the arrangement, are the hindrance of the Blockchain.

3.2.7 How to Secure Blockchain

■ Integrity of the square is overseen by confirming that the square header substance doesn't appear to be altered, the exchanges don't appear to have been tempered with, the state advances square measure with productivity registered, hashed, and checked. Blockchain is intended to be Associate in the Nursing unchanging record. All the climate inside the square header, just as the managing root and state root hashes. We need an Associate in Nursing efficient gratitude to locate the change of state and approve the managing effectiveness.

- If any member hub messes with the square, its hash worth changes, prompting the twin of the hash esteems Associate in Nursing delivering the local chain of the hub in an invalid state. Any future squares started by the hub would be dismissed by various diggers on account of hash twins. This establishes the unchangeability of the chain. A combination of hashing and cryptography square measure utilized for making sure about the different parts of the Blockchain.

3.2.8 What Is Ledger and Proof of Work in Blockchain?

- Proof of Work (PoW) implies that whatever means have been used to affirm the exchange and create the square, it will go under PoW. It is exceptionally hard to make; however, once done it is easy for buyers to approve the exchange subtleties.
- Ledger implies whatever the exchange has been finished within two shoppers the two of them have their information passage for similar exchange; however, in parallel those customers who are at the top of it they all make a section of that exchange which is done between those two purchasers. The primary advantage of it is that nobody can enter some unacceptable detail of the exchange. In the wake of checking the exchange subtleties by others then the lone exchanges will be finished.

3.2.9 Smart Contract (Blockchain 2.0)?

- Ethereum upholds reasonable agreements and of a virtual machine on that reasonable agreements execute. Furthermore, this reasonable agreement plan was presented inside the Blockchain a couple of 2.0.
- Smart contracts progressively change decentralized applications that achieve over exchange significance.
- A reasonable agreement could be a bit of code sent inside the Blockchain hub. The execution of a shrewd agreement begins with a message installed inside the dealings. The moving of computerized money demands simple expansion and deduction. Ethereum grants dealings that will do a large number of refined tasks. For example, managing may require a restrictive exchange: it will require some examination, it will need more than one mark for the move of resources, or it will include anticipating a chosen time or date.

3.3 Methods of Blockchain

Discussing the strategies for Blockchain, let us state that the different sorts of methods that remember enhancements for the Blockchain procedures which are required, some of them are Blockchain's online security, and the energy fitness of verification-of-work public Blockchains which was discovered glaringly poor. To date, strategies are deprived to create study plans which distinguish threat and dangers. Here, there are various essential strategies for significant Blockchain issues: (a) diffused registering methods with basic Blockchain organizations, for example, CAP hypothesis, FLP difficulty hypothesis, ACID standard, and Paxos/Raft; And (b) particularized procedures for Blockchain networks, similar to agreement instrument, Byzantine issues, and calculations, secure multi-party calculation; (c) explicit strategies for Blockchain information systems, for example, decentralized capacity, Blockchain information structure, trait based encryption, zero-information evidence. With ad libbed Blockchain venture, demand-driven Blockchain procedures have been developed to meet explicit business thoughts, and a variety of expert-level strategies for Blockchain-based applications have been conveyed. The business-level techniques further amplify and enhance the essential Blockchain strategies to make supreme framework answers for the Blockchain entreaties. To hold up extremely proficient and complex exchanging plots, the Blockchain base is moved up to find interlinked Blockchain networks with multi-layer and essential optional connections, to clarify result situated square information structure, for the motivation to return the Blockchain-layer evidence of-work with business-layer impetuses, and to create Blockchain passages and internetwork agreement systems to relate various Blockchain networks. For cluttered exchanging, keen agreement strategies for firm confirmation and equal models are to be extended. Additionally, uncommon information changing strategies are created to amalgamate information from outside just as inside the Blockchains and mark the information lack and deficiency immerged without anyone else administrative Blockchain information.

3.3.1 Application Methods for Blockchains

There exist different harsh issues to be set apart for executing an apparent and efficient Blockchain application in the biological system. By seeing a product structure, an exemplary Blockchain environment has four coats which incorporate the Blockchain, brilliant agreements, utilities, and UIs. The basic execution issues, for an environment, incorporate the arranging network model, the engineering of the biological system, patrons and affirmation arrangements, hubs and surveying instrument, motivation component, and clients. Furthermore, information assortment and information change calculations are required to address the significant issues identified with Blockchain applications.

The Blockchain network model is demonstrated to be a test for the majority of the continuous activities. The Blockchain strategies are developing rapidly, and no all-around endorsed viable ID has been delivered. A few activities patronaging Bitcoin lack acknowledged due to their inadequacy and organizing cost. Numerous individuals just take Blockchain as a type of a diffused information base structure. A conventional Blockchain environment is an assortment of a Blockchain framework, the partakers' data frameworks with a mix of programming interfaces, and a gathering of shrewd agreements for activity. In them, the Blockchain concocts a communicated and automatic information system wherein a few information and procedures are put away. The patrons' data frameworks are to be created to be Blockchain customers and are in a condition to recuperate or transfer business information on the Blockchains. Information-gathering techniques are basic to holding up Blockchain-based organizations and is analyzed that the information are close to home and self-constrained by the members in a Blockchain, which raises a few supported issues at gathering information, some of them are including information deficiency, shortage, and repetition. It is imperative to grow all-around clarified pay calculations for lost information, ascribes, and unimportant or irrelevant information. Basically, a large number of Blockchain improvement conditions have been advanced for extraordinary situations such as store network money, monetary leeway, business guideline, and oversight.

3.4 Blockchain Application 3.0

3.4.1 Blockchain in E-governance

Blockchain is known as an authorized arrangement of the disseminated information base or to be a particular record, since arbitrary data can be reserved into the metadata of the procedures. The indigenous Bitcoin Blockchain just upheld eighty bytes of metadata; however, other Blockchain executions uphold bigger sizes. Going to the possibility of nonfinancial applications for the local and other Blockchain advancements. Quite recently, the idea of Blockchain 3.0 has been raised up to address the nonfinancial uses of the scattered record technique. These applications are executed as assentless or as agreed Blockchain networks.

3.4.2 Blockchain 3.0 When Used as Discrete Office

Blockchain is known as an authorized setup of the appropriated information base or to be a particular record, since arbitrary data can be stored in the metadata of the procedures. The original Bitcoin Blockchain just contained just 80 bytes of metadata; however, other Blockchain executions can deal with more capacity. Going to the possibility of nonfinancial applications for the local and other Blockchain advances. In the not so distant past, the idea of Blockchain 3.0 has been suggested as a solution to the problem of addressing nonfinancial uses of the scattered record strategy. These applications are executed as assentless or as agreed Blockchain networks.

3.4.3 Blockchain 3.0 Technology for Health Care

In medical services applications, the one most featured is associated with the securing of Blockchains as a fundamental structure for Health Information Exchange (HIE) or for the very reason for wellbeing procedures between emotionless, providers, payers, and other appropriate gatherings. These applications can later be separated dependent on their essential objectives to utilize the Blockchain-gathered information, and are described in clinical records.

3.5 Comparisons Table of Blockchain Platforms

Blockchain innovation has the ability to place us in a predicament and essentially changes the monetary society. With the headway of Bitcoin as another type of monetary forms and ICOs rising to the pinnacle of billions of dollars, the Blockchain world has been in the top-most mode throughout the previous few years. Yet, more than digital forms of money, endeavor selection of Blockchain has created solid premium from significant players here is a short correlation.

Table 3.1 Comparisons Table of Blockchain Platforms

Sr.	Features	Bitcoin	Ethereum	Hyperledger fabric	Status
1	Completely developed	Yes	Yes	Yes	Ongoing
2	Miner involvement	Type: public	Public, private and hybrid	Private	public
3	Deceitful operation	Yes	Yes	Yes	yes
4	Multi-application	Financial	Yes	Yes	At present financial only
5	Consensus	poW	poW, poS	PBFT	Presently a coordinator approves the TXs through a Tip selection algorithm
6	Consensus conclusiveness	No	No	Yes	No

(Continued)

Table 3.1 (Continued) Comparisons Table of Blockchain Platforms

Sr.	Features	Bitcoin	Ethereum	Hyperledger fabric	Status
7	Blockchain forks	Yes	Yes	No	Not exactly forks although a tangle might be fade out later
8	Fees less	No	No	Optional	Yes
9	Able to run smart contracts	No	Yes	Yes	No
10	TX probity and authenticity	Yes	Yes	Yes	Yes
11	Is data confidential	No	No	Yes	No
12	ID management	No	No	Yes	No
13	Key management	No	No	Yes	No
14	User authenticity	Digitalised signature	Digitalised signature	Based on enrolment of certificates	Digitalised signatures
15	Device authenticity	No	No	No	No
16	Vulnerability to attacks	51% linking attacks	51%	One third part faulty nodes	34% attack
17	TX throughput	7/TPS	8–9/TPS	Can get thousand TPS	Presently, the coordinator being the bottleneck, the through put varies between 7–12 TPS
18	Latency for single confirmation for TX	10 mins	15–20 seconds	Less than enthereum and bitcoin	Right now in transition phase the TX confirmation time varies from period of minutes to hours
19	Scalable	No	No	No	Yes

3.6 Future Trends in Blockchain Technology

As indicated by the ongoing improvement of Bitcoin innovation applications, the Blockchain ought to speak to one of the most fundamental segments that might be applied in heaps of areas at a future date. This is on the grounds that the substance material of the Blockchain is realities and its utilization is more flexible than the cryptographic forms of money. Kell et al. check that this advance seems to represent a promising impetus for accomplishing worldwide supportable improvement targets. For example, Blockchain innovation can likewise make commitments to building a keen city through the advancement of shared financial contributions. Indeed, to place in power trust-detached sharing contributions in a savvy city, it's extremely fundamental to recall assurance factors (which incorporate classification, accessibility, and uprightness) which speak to one of the basic qualities of the Blockchain-based period. This is on the grounds that a Blockchain is a decentralized convention where all insights are secret and the accessibility of realities does presently don't depend on any 1/3 gatherings. In addition, uprightness is guaranteed because of the way that this innovation can be viewed as a circulated report gadget, where members save duplicates of documents and consent to changes through agreement. Faber and Hadders have underlined the capacity of the Blockchain time to make a framework to actualize "new implicit agreements for manageability", adding to the advance of the change to the reasonable turn of events. They realm that Blockchains offer foundation for data exchanges that don't need incorporated capacities supporting genuine associations and connections among individuals to take care of issues. Hence, this innovation beats the forefront venture model, which is mostly overseen through vintage standard regulatory and power establishments such as ideological groups, banks, close by governments, and so on

Blockchain period can likewise be applied inside the decentralization of the DNS (space name gadget) control called "block-stack", another, DNS-like machine that replaces DNS root workers with Blockchain time for planning areas to DNS records. DNS resembles the phonebook of the web, as when composing a net adapt to a DNS worker deciphers that address and returns an IP (net convention) manage. DNS workers are constrained by governments and gigantic organizations and this unified control may likewise cultivate maltreatments of energy in controlling exercises, capturing, spying, and programmer assaults. The Blockchain period may also encourage the decentralization, insurance, control opposition, protection, and movement of specific added substances of the net's foundation, including DNS workers. Given that currently Blockchains do not have focal variables of trust, a Blockchain-essentially based DNS is a lot harder to edit. Additionally, the Blockchain age may likewise be utilized to decentralize TLS (transport layer insurance) testament approval, sponsored through Blockchain agreement. TLS is a cryptographic convention that offers correspondences insurance over a PC organization. A few varieties of the convention have been dispatched and it very widely broadly utilized in web perusing, email, web fax, prompt informing, and voice-over-IP (VoIP). At the end of the day, TLS will support all interchanges among workers and web programs on a PC. Document marks, casting a ballot, bonds/stocks/shares, the net of trust, public accountant contributions, and confirmation of presence are energizing and modern projects of Blockchains, and open-source trial applications are developing on the web. Intriguing examinations are being progressed in profoundly digitalized nations, including Estonia, wherein the arrival of virtual citizenship (e-residency), a virtual ID for non-Estonians that offers admittance to administrations like banking, value preparing, and tax collection, and of a pristine government-supported cryptographic money (Estcoin) with no chance of duplicating and use for unlawful purposes, will presumably cultivate the change toward a genuinely advanced, without outskirts society. The Blockchain has demonstrated its potential in both industrial and educational settings. We talk about conceivable future bearings concerning a number of territories: Blockchain testing, stopping the propensity to centralization, the investigation of large information, and computerized reasoning.

3.6.1 Blockchain Testing

As of late, particular types of Blockchains appear and more than 700 digital currencies are recorded in agrees (2020) as much as now. Nonetheless, a couple of developers would perhaps misrepresent their Blockchain execution to draw purchasers passed through the huge benefit. In addition, while clients need to consolidate Blockchain into a business endeavor, they need to acknowledge which Blockchain suits their prerequisites. So Blockchain testing instrument wishes to be set up to test exceptional Blockchains. The consideration of Blockchain can be isolated into just two phases: the normalization area and the testing segment. In the normalization stage, all measures should be made and settled upon. At the point when a Blockchain is conceived, it can be tried with the concurred norms to approve if the Blockchain works as efficiently as the designers guarantee. Concerning the evaluating stage, Blockchain evaluating should be done with phenomenal guidelines. For instance, an individual who is in the cost of an online retail endeavor thinks about the throughput of the Blockchain, so the test needs to test the basic time from a purchaser sending an exchange to the exchange being stuffed into the Blockchain, the potential for a Blockchain block and so on.

3.6.2 Stop the Tendency to Centralization

Blockchain is planned as a decentralized framework. Nonetheless, there's a style that diggers are unified inside the mining pool. To date, the five largest mining pools together own more than 51% of the full hash power in the Bitcoin network (bitcoin around the world, n.d.). Apart from that, the egotistical mining procedure (Eyal and Since, 2014) indicated that pools with over 25% of general registering strength ought to get more income than a decent amount. Balanced diggers could be pulled into the egocentric pool lastly, the pool ought to without trouble surpass 51% of the absolute power. As the Blockchain is not intended to serve a few associations, a couple of techniques should be proposed to cure this issue

3.6.3 Big Data Analytics

Blockchain can be pleasantly blended in with enormous measurements. Here we pretty much arranged the mix into types: data on the board and information investigation. Concerning information control, Blockchain may be utilized to keep significant data as it's miles apportioned and secure. Blockchain ought to likewise ensure the realities is unique. For instance, if Blockchain is utilized to shop patients' wellbeing data, the realities couldn't have altered and it is hard to acquire that private information. With regards to information investigation, exchanges at the Blockchain may be utilized for large information examination. For instance, individual purchasing and selling examples may be separated. Clients can expect their capacity accomplices' exchanging practices with the examination.

3.6.4 Artificial Intelligence

Late qualities in the Blockchain age are developing new open doors for man-made consciousness (AI) applications (Omohundro, 2019). Man-made intelligence advances should help to resolve numerous Blockchain challenges. For example, there is ceaselessly a profit who's chargeable for deciding if the arrangement condition is fulfilled. By and large, this profit is reliant on an outsider. Computer-based intelligence strategies may help build an astute prophet. It isn't constantly constrained by any gathering; it just gains from an external perspective and educates itself. In that manner, there may be no contentions inside the astute agreement and the sharp understanding can come to be more intelligent. Then again, AI is now infiltrating into our lives. Blockchain and smart contracts should help to limiting mischievous activities completed by methods for AI items. For example, laws written in an astute agreement should help to limit mischievous activities finished by driverless vehicles.

3.7 Integration of Machine Learning in Blockchain-Based Application

The learning abilities of machine learning (ML) can be executed to Blockchains based absolutely bundles to lead them to more astute. Through the use of ML, wellbeing of the dispensed record can be improved. ML can likewise be utilized to enhance the time taken to accomplish agreement by means of building better records-sharing courses. Further, it makes an occasion to assemble higher models

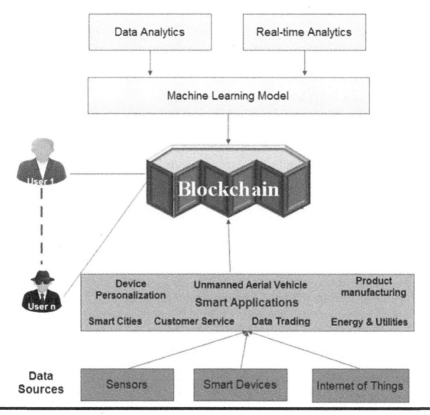

Figure 3.1   Planned architecture for Machine Learning acceptance in Blockchain-based applications

via taking the increase of the decentralized structure of BT. We proposed the design for ML appropriation in BT-based absolutely keen programming, as appeared in Figure 3.1.

Here, the smart utility gathers data from remarkable insights sources which incorporate sensors, smart gadgets, and Internet of Things (IoT) devices. Information amassed from these gadgets become viewed as all of a piece of smart bundles. The Blockchain works of art as a vital piece of these brilliant projects. At that point, ML might be actualized to these product's realities for investigation (Data examination and ongoing investigation) and expectation. The record sets used by ML models will be saved money on a Blockchain network. This reduces mistakes inside the information comprising of duplication, missing records worth, blunders, and clamor. Blockchains are focused on the measurements, and henceforth data-related issues in ML styles can be wiped out. ML-designs might be basically founded on specific portions of the chain instead of the whole insights set. This could give custom models for various bundles, for example, extortion discovery and character burglary location. A couple of the preferred position is recorded underneath while ML is applied:

■ User verification as a legitimate client for mentioning or playing out any exchange inside the Blockchain network.
■ BT gives a high phase of security and trust.
■ Blockchain coordinates public ML models into sharp agreements to guarantee that the circumstances and expressions which were earlier concurred are continued.
■ BT helps inside the solid usage of a motivation-based framework; accordingly, it empowers clients/clients to contribute data. This monstrous measurement will assist with improving ML model execution.
■ ML models can be exceptional on-chain climate of BT with a little charge and off-chain, locally on a person's device with none expenses.
■ Good information commitments can happen from clients/customers, these data continually calculated, and rewards might be given to the clients.
■ Tamper-evidence brilliant agreements can be assessed with the guide of unique machines (having explicit equipment setup), ML models will presently don't separate from their ability and pass on outcomes unequivocally as it is intended to do.
■ Payments prepared continuously, with accept on a Blockchain climate.

3.8 What Research Subjects Have Been Addressed in the Present Research on Blockchain?

The results of this planning study indicated that a lion's share of the cutting-edge research on Blockchain is centred around finding and sorting out enhancements to the present-day difficulties and impediments in Blockchain [1]. One major aspect of the examination focuses on security and protection inconveniences in Blockchain. The security weakness of the Blockchain network and the developing interest in Bitcoin have expanded the financial misfortunes of every miner and end-clients. The perceived weaknesses incorporate calculation energy-based assaults, for example, the 51% assault, narrow-minded mine assault, exchange data pliability issues, and deanonymization by methods for exchange connecting. Although a few responses to address these difficulties have been introduced, many of them are essentially sortterm, ad hoc recommendations, which lack any solid assessment of their viability.

The examination of various subjects in requesting circumstances and restrictions characterized by utilizing Swan [1], along with squandered sources and ease of use, changed into an elective restricted. We noticed a few investigations executed on computational strength and squandered assets in Bitcoin mining and overhauls at the ease of use of Bitcoin. Notwithstanding, the scope of papers in this area is relatively smaller than those focused on the subjects of security and protection.

Computational strength is one of the critical qualities in Blockchain, and it requires careful consideration. At the point when Blockchain develops additional unpredictability, it likewise requires extra computational energy to affirm more squares. The Proof-of-Work idea is as an option ground-breaking thought; that is the reason why it should be concentrated extra, to verify that it might work in large scope Blockchain conditions.

Curiously, at this point we have found no trace of any exploration of the difficulties and constraints in inertness, length, and transmission capacity, throughput, forming, extreme forks, and a few chains. It is astonishing that the consideration paid to and examined is accomplished on other requesting circumstances and impediments than security and protection were as an elective low. We accepted that, in particular, subjects such as idleness, length and data transmission, and squandered sources may have received additional consideration in the general examinations map. At the point when the components of Blockchain builds, it directly affects a large portion of these difficulties and limits versatility. It is practical that these difficulties have now not been examined because of the reality that thought around Blockchain thought is still new.

Notwithstanding the recognized exploration points, the discoveries on this planning study affirmed that a greater part of the examination transformed into led in the Bitcoin environmental factors. This transformed into additionally the genuine presumption of the creators, taking into account that Bitcoin is, by and by, the most ordinarily utilized and basic innovation the use of Blockchain, with the biggest purchaser base. In any case, we were pretty amazed that the scope of different answers than Bitcoin for the utilization of Blockchain is currently so low. The outcomes demonstrated that the investigations outside the Bitcoin environmental factors become generally centred around astute agreements and other digital forms of money, yet the examinations on Bitcoin and its assurance issues designed the larger part.

3.9 What Are the Present Research Holes in Blockchain Research?

We have attempted to acknowledge some significant investigation holes. The principal opening is that the investigations on subjects comprising of dormancy, throughput, length and transmission capacity, forming, hard forks, and more than one forks do at this point don't exist in the present-day writing. This is a significant exploration hole, which requires more noteworthy examination inside what's to come. These subjects are not necessarily the most intriguing subjects for scientists right now, because of the reality the extents of the current Blockchain bundles are profoundly small. Bitcoin is currently the most important arrangement with Blockchain. The current quantity of exchanges in Bitcoin is considerably more modest than, for example, in VISA. However, it is likely that if Blockchain arrangements are utilized by several countless people and the wide assortment of exchanges expands radically, more prominent exploration on, for example, inertness, length and data transfer capacity, and squandered resources is likely to occur in order to guarantee adaptability.

The subsequent examination opening is the deficiency of studies on the ease of use. We recognized the most available papers to reference ease of use from the buyer viewpoint, no longer from the engineer point of view, as directed through Swan [1]. For example, to date the issue of the utilization of Bitcoin API has not yet been handled. This longing to be contemplated and improved inside what's to come. This should start additional projects and answers for the Bitcoin climate.

The third gap in the analysis is that most of the current exploration is directed in the Bitcoin climate, instead of aloof Blockchain conditions. Examination on, e.g., smart agreements should be done to expand the understanding of entryways digital currencies. Indeed, even despite the fact that Blockchain transformed into first presented in the cryptographic money climate, the indistinguishable thought can be utilized in various conditions. Accordingly, it's very imperative to lead research on the conceivable outcomes of utilizing Blockchain in different conditions, since it can screen and create better models and opportunities for doing exchanges in extraordinary ventures.

The fourth investigation opening can be found in the low scope of top-notch guides in diary-level digital book channels. At present, the vast majority of the exploration is posted in meetings, discussions, and workshops. There is a requirement for amazingly great diaries where the point of convergence is on Blockchain.

3.10 What Are the Forthcoming Research Guidelines for Blockchain?

The future exploration directions for Blockchain are unsatisfactory, and it's very intriguing to look where it is going. Then again, Bitcoin has received a wide range of interest as cryptographic money, and more individuals are exchanging and purchasing Bitcoins consistently. Thus, it's exceedingly possible that Bitcoin is indispensable as one in everything about future examination points, and it'll pull in industry and the scholarly world to direct more prominent investigations from both business endeavor and specialized viewpoints.

Bitcoin is simply a single arrangement utilizing Blockchain innovation. There are additionally various other cryptographic forms of money in the interim, contending with Bitcoin to be the world's main digital currency. We concur that predetermination examination will likewise incorporate investigations did on other cryptographic forms of money. In any case, in the intervening time, it gives the idea that clearly Bitcoin has by methods for far the biggest piece of the overall industry, and it will be an endeavor for other cryptographic forms of money to rival it.

In any case, we consider that future investigations won't focus exclusively on Bitcoin and other digital forms of money; they will look instead at various possible applications utilizing Blockchain as an answer. We previously found a couple of papers that contemplated the chance of the utilization of smart contracts, authorizing, IoT, and smart properties in the Blockchain climate. We concur that this sort of exploration will have an assortment of effect inside the future, and can almost certainly be significantly more noteworthy intriguing than digital currencies. To utilize decentralized environmental factors in e.g., sharing a virtual property may be an answer that upsets the manner in which organizations can sell their items. Mulling this over, we emphatically believe that when Blockchain innovation gets received extra via both endeavor and the scholarly world, it will create an enormous number of new investigations.

At the point when extra Blockchain answers are being employed by huge quantities of clients, it will likewise affect the investigations finished on specialized limits and difficulties. In fate, extended sizes and individual bases in various Blockchains will create the need to conduct more examinations on the requesting circumstances and boundaries in subjects identified with versatility. Moreover, the security and protection of Blockchain will be normally a subject for research, while new methodologies are created to upset and attack Blockchain. Despite the fact that Blockchain is an entirely new innovation, there exists effectively significant examination in each issue territory, including security and assigned machine writing (for instance, staggered verification procedure, energy-productive asset the board for disseminated frameworks, and so forth). A closer examination and the appropriation of demonstrated answers would support up defeating current requesting circumstances and limits of Blockchain innovation.

3.11 Conclusion

The Blockchain is exceptionally assessed and embraced for its decentralized foundation and distributed nature. Nonetheless, numerous kinds of examination about the Blockchain are protected by Bitcoin. Be that as it may, Blockchain could be applied to an assortment of fields a long way past Bitcoin. Blockchain has demonstrated its potential for changing the customary business with its key qualities: decentralization, persistency, secrecy, and discernibility. In this chapter, we present a far-reaching review on the Blockchain. We first give an outline of the Blockchain advances, including Blockchain engineering, favourable circumstances, and necessities of the Blockchain. At that point we talk about the average agreement strategies utilized in the Blockchain. We examine and analyse these techniques in various regards. We additionally research commonplace Blockchain applications. In addition, we show a few difficulties and issues that would prevent Blockchain improvement and sum up some current methodologies for taking care of these issues. Some conceivable future bearings are additionally examined. These days brilliant agreement is growing quick and many shrewd agreement applications are proposed. Notwithstanding, as there are as yet numerous imperfections and cut-off points in smart agreement dialects, numerous inventive applications are difficult to execute right now. We intend to take a top-to-bottom examination of keen agreements later on. Blockchain technology runs the Bitcoin cryptocurrency. It is a decentralized environment for transactions, where all the transactions are recorded to a public ledger, visible to everyone. The goal of Blockchain is to provide anonymity, security, privacy, and transparency to all its users. However, these attributes set up a lot of technical challenges and limitations that need to be addressed. To understand where the current research on Blockchain technology positions itself, we decided to map all relevant research by using the systematic mapping study process [2]. The goal of this systematic mapping study was to examine the current status and research topics of Blockchain technology. We excluded the economic, law, business, and regulation perspectives, and included only the technical perspective. We extracted and analysed 41 primary papers from scientific databases. We provide the following recommendations on future research directions of Blockchain technology based on the current research status:

■ *Continue to identify more issues and propose solutions to overcome challenges and limitations of Blockchain technology.* The interest on Blockchain technology has been increased drastically since 2013. The cumulative number of papers has increased from 2 in 2013 to 41 in 2015. The majority of the studies has been focused on addressing the challenges and limitations, but there still exist many issues without proper solutions.

■ *Conduct more studies on scalability issues of Blockchain.* Most of the current research on the Blockchain technology is focused on security and privacy issues. To be ready for the pervasive use of Blockchain technology, scalability issues such as performance and latency have to be addressed.

■ *Develop more Blockchain-based applications beyond Bitcoin and other cryptocurrency systems.* The current research is focused on the Bitcoin system. However, the research also shows that Blockchain technology is applicable for other solutions such as smart contracts, property licensing, voting etc.

■ *Evaluate the effectiveness of the proposed solutions with an objective evaluation criteria.* Although several solutions to challenges and limitations have been presented, many of them are just brief idea suggestions and lack concrete evaluation on their effectiveness.

References

[1] OECD. Health spending. 2018. doi: 10.1787/8643de7e-en. URL https://www.oecdilibrary.org/content/data/8643de7e-en.

[2] Elizabeth A. Bell, Lucila Ohno-Machado, and M. Adela Grando. Sharing my health data: a survey of data sharing preferences of healthy individuals. In *AMIA Annual*

Symposium Proceedings, volume 2014, page 1699. American Medical Informatics Association, 2014. https://pubmed.ncbi.nlm.nih.gov/25954442/.

[3] Fabian Wahl Peter Behner, and Marie-Lyn Hecht. *Fighting counterfeit pharmaceuticals*, 2018 (accessed Nov 15, 2018). https://www.strategyand.pwc.com/reports/counterfeit-pharmaceuticals.

[4] Tsung-Ting Kuo, Hyeon-Eui Kim, and Lucila Ohno-Machado. Blockchain distributed ledger technologies for biomedical and health care applications. *Journal of the American Medical Informatics Association*, 24(6): 1211–1220, 2017. doi: 10.1093/jamia/ocx068. URL http://dx.doi.org/10.1093/jamia/ocx068.

[5] Vikram Dhillon, David Metcalf, and Max Hooper. *Blockchain in Health Care*, pages 125–138. Apress, Berkeley, CA, 2017. ISBN 978-1-4842-3081-7. doi: 10.1007/978-1-4842-3081-7_9 URL https://doi.org/10.1007/978-1-4842-3081-7_9.

[6] Mark A Engelhardt, and Diego Espinosa. Hitching healthcare to the chain: An introduction to blockchain technology in the healthcare sector *An Introduction to Blockchain Technology in the Healthcare Sector*. 7(10): 22–35, 2017.

[7] Al-Debei, M. M., and Avison, D. (2017). Developing a unified framework of the business model concept developing a unified framework of the business model concept. *European Journal of Information Systems*, 9344. doi: 10.1057/ejis.2010.21

[8] Anjum, A., Sporny, M., and Sill, A. (2017). Blockchain Standards for Compliance and Trust. *IEEE Cloud Computing*, 4(4), 84–90. doi: 10.1109/MCC.2017.3791019

[9] Arnott, D., and Pervan, G. (2012). Design science in decision support systems research: An assessment using the hevner, march, park, and ram guidelines. *Journal of the Association for Information Systems*, 13(11), 923–949.

[10] Benchoufi, M. (2017). *Blockchain technology for improving clinical research quality*, 1–5. doi: 10.1186/s13063-017-2035-z

[11] Casino, F., Dasaklis, T. K., and Patsakis, C. (2019). A systematic literature review of blockchain-based applications: Current status, classification and open issues. *Telematics and Informatics*, 36(May 2018), 55–81. doi: 10.1016/j.tele.2018.11.006

[12] Chan, Y. Y. Y., and Ngai, E. W. T. (2011). Conceptualising electronic word of mouth activity: An input-process-output perspective. *Marketing Intelligence and Planning*, 29(5), 488–516. doi: 10.1108/02634501111153692

[13] China Daily. (2019). Nation leads world in blockchain projects. Retrieved May 21, 2019, from http://www.china.org.cn/business/2019-04/02/content_74636929_2.htm

Chapter 4

Cybersecurity and Privacy Issues of Blockchain Technology

Ayushi Dwivedi and Amarnath Mishra
Amity University, Noida, India

Debabrata Singh
SOA University, India

Contents

DOI: 10.1201/9781003129486-4

69

4.1 Introduction

At this point, we can move standard non-automated cash, but this is not really the same as the exceptional kind of money mechanics. When the mechanized type of money becomes the norm, the decision to offer cash electronically is similar to those found with standard currency standards. Nevertheless, it is the technological progress behind this technology that separates the automated kind of money. It's in my wallet! The problem is that the world's current cash structures have a lot of problems, including the following.

The segment structure, the fee card and the transfer are outdated, at the same time, make the exchanges become excessive and moderate. Money-related mismatch is growing all over the world. About three billion individuals cannot make money for related associations. It's the majority of everyone on the planet! Advanced kinds of money, such as cryptocurrencies, want to address some of these issues.

4.1.1 The Basics of Cryptomonetary Forms

At the time of writing, among the most common cryptomonetary forms are: Ethereum, Ripple, Litecoin and Bitcoin. Recently, Bitcoin (invented in 2008) operates mainly through Blockchain technology and it is set to disrupt the currency market. Do you need to do it or move to another person by Blockchain technology? Undoubtedly, modernized money-related principles may give you the option of disposing of money in the light of banks and other unified judges, the encrypted kind of money is decentralized. Each PC belonging to it is affirmed because it relies on an improvement called Blockchain called transaction [1].

4.1.2 The Significance of Money

Prior to getting into the service of cutting-edge financial structures, there needs to be some appreciation of the centrality of cash in the modern economy. The viewpoint behind cash is somewhat similar to the entire question of "Which came first: the chicken or the egg?" With a definitive goal for cash to be huge, it ought to have various properties, for example:

- Enough individuals ought to have it.
- Sellers ought to remember it as a sort of bit.
- Society ought to acknowledge that it's huge and that it will remain in broadly the same form in future.

Plainly, under previous trading systems, when someone exchanged their sheep for clothes, the appraisals of the traded goods were normal to their tendency. Regardless, when money was transformed into a crucial factor, the significance of money and, significantly and more basically, the model of money changed significantly over time [2].

Another factor in real cash is the exchange. The activity of transporting a huge stack of gold bars from one country to another, with the differences between the prices in each of the two, was one of the main ways to make money. At that point, when the individual became very lazy, other means of payment were created. In any event, Mastercard transmits the target your society manages. As the world is becoming increasingly interconnected and more concerned with experts who may have unavoidable favorable circumstances as a primary concern, electronic types of funds may offer another basic option [3]. Here unfathomable sternness: Your standard government-backed cash, for example, Indian currency, should pass by its ridiculous name, fiat money, as progressive financial guidelines are near. Fiat is depicted as genuinely elegant as coins and banknotes that have gained some respect recently given the way society says so much.

4.1.3 Some Digital Currency History

The essential electronic currency was mostly Bitcoin. This is likely to be the cryptocurrency with which you are familiar [4]. Bitcoin was the result of the first Blockchain, which was created by Satoshi Nakamoto [5]. Satoshi passed on the

Bitcoin opportunity in 2008, portraying it as a "completely dispersed structure" of electronic cash.

Bitcoin was the centrally established cryptographic currency, but various attempts to introduce cash-related modernized rules occurred long before the definitive introduction of Bitcoin. Technically developed financial systems, such as Bitcoin, are generated by a so-called mining cycle.

Bitcoin remained the main type of modernized cash until 2011. By then, Bitcoin lovers had noticed shortcomings in this system. Thus, they decided to make altcoins, to improve the way Bitcoin operates in terms of speed, security, anonymity, and that's fair among the first altcoins was Litecoin. In any case, there are more than 1,600 mechanized financial directives open and the number will be expanded later [6].

4.1.4 Components of Blockchain

Blockchain may prove to be an amazing development, whose benefits can be quantified. However, if we sensibly understand three key Blockchain boundaries, consensus, gamification and openness, we can even more appropriately deal with what is essential for this advance in general and learn about their current and future applications [7]. Just over a decade ago, on September 18, 2008, the headline in the *Wall Street Journal* was as follows: "Obviously the most terrible crisis since the 1930s, with no end in sight." This was a reference to a financial crisis in the face of the subprime contract crisis, which led to the collapse of some of the major US and European firms and banks.

Announcement of the essential corporate identity from Bitcoin, another electronic cash structure that uses a common association to prevent double spending, is decentralized, meaning that it has no specialist or centralized force. A Blockchain is a distributed system that includes registrations or a database of transactions and has the ability to make exchanges at sensitive prices directly accesses any two social networks. The continuity of Blockchain has a unique ability to verify account ownership, validate ratings, and maintain transaction results without any need for a mediator or a middle source, such as a bank or a silver-based base [8]. The creator, or perhaps more accurately the manufacturers, of Bitcoin have tried to kill the conditions we have in the companies connected today to perform such tasks. Opportunities for joint ventures include public shops, central exchanges and banks. Instead we have limited control over these types of foundations and the global organization. The sustainability of these structures is based primarily on three things: internal control, law and external trust. Model authoritative models are Federal Reserve Board (FRB), Federal Deposit Insurance Corporation (FDIC), and the Securities and Exchange Commission (SEC) [9].

Bitcoin was a cryptocurrency that aimed to create a trading system that included transparent controls in its cycles. It is the practice of order, gambling and accountability that makes it possible. While you may not see all the details in the middle

listed after all, accompanying the descriptions should help you better understand the impact of usage support [10].

4.1.4.1 Consensus

We often supervise the negotiations. For example, we use BhimPay to get tea, a metro card to go by metro to go to work [11]. In these cases, the middle specialist to verify the ownership and balance of the record or assets and social issues required to comply with the terms set by the target company or organization, for example after online payment, the professional association knows that payment is considered, as indicated in my central bank register.

However, while it is a part of the surrounding Blockchain environment, the expert organization recognizes that we have the money to pay for it as enough people in the Blockchain agree that we have the money to pay for it. Getting a larger group of people to agree on ownership and the balance of assets is called understanding and placement is a key part of any Blockchain. Instead of making any merger to be the authority of my balance, Blockchain development incorporates that ability into individuals. To do this, copies of all value-based data are reproduced on each Blockchain hub in the assignment. With the calculation included in the Blockchain system, each intermediate point uses the same cycle to check account identity and record changes. As with the creation of an email record and a secret key, individuals can create Blockchain records or wallets. Transactions are viewed using the sender's record, such as sending or receiving email. By considering all messages or exchanges sent and received locally, we can determine the balance of any service. Like passwords, people have secret keys to their wallets, and only the owner of that key can control how their resources are used. Blockchain also uses cryptography to create closed exchanges. Each exchange with each square is subject to a single directional test known as a hash, which takes a set of pre-defined inputs and provides a separate line of novel length and location.

Below is an illustration of a 32-bit 64-character hash:

0000009a8a21adc53a473b165798ebd1d

If someone somehow managed to try to change the exchange, for example by converting it from "I got 5 BTC" to "I got 500 BTC", the hash result will change to the present time and will not coordinate any other person's hash for this exchange, which will subsequently invalidate it. Agreement is additionally necessary so that no one can use the same coin twice. This is known as double spending and taking care of double spending electronic money is one of the most outstanding achievements of Bitcoin. To validate an exchange without trusting each other, execution on the Blockchain is often called unreliable. Some Blockchain agreement conventions even contemplate verifying balances without information on the true balances themselves, which is called a proof of zero information. Finally, when enough hubs constituting 51% of the power of Blockchain processing confirm a trade square, the square is considered authoritative on the Blockchain.

Agreement between hubs is also needed in case someone needs to roll out improved guidelines for the Blockchain itself. If someone was able to control 51% of the processing power of a Blockchain, they could basically set the standards and give each other all of the pieces. From this composition, the Ethereum Blockchain has more than 16,000 hubs around the world, a figure which is increasing at around 10% each month. In addition to the fact that the size of the networks is struggling with gigantic acquisitions, it also makes the structure remarkably imperfect, open to deception. In the event that a few Blockchain nodes are cleared out of the blue, we currently have thousands more. However, consent is not sufficient. In addition, there must be sufficient motivating force for someone to invest energy and assets in building and maintaining the hub. For this reason, gamification is the next most important idea to drive innovation in the Blockchain.

4.1.4.2 Gamification

Preparing a Blockchain agreement is effective on the basis that, through gamification, people try to get compensation for doing work that helps keep the organization running and modifies overall network valuation [12].

The circle in which a hub does work, validates and adds exchanges to the Blockchain is called mining. Diggers claim fees for confirming exchanges and receive an even bigger reward for being the first to square the exceptional organization of exchanges and put that block in the organization called as the square price.

To pay prices, each Blockchain consists of their own crypto cash, for example, Bitcoin, Neo etc. Begin trading and largely offset the exchange fees, although a square price is given by the Blockchain itself by printing new tokens, this methodology may differ depending on the guidelines of the specific Blockchain.

To acquire a square prize some Blockchain requires that each hub create a huge irregular number, similar to a lottery that should fall inside a minuscule reach. Furthermore, that reach continues to get more modest and more modest until it sums to the total amount of coins printed. This requires a massive calculation, thereby driving the systems administration to become more grounded and keep up with the number of exchanges in the warranty. Your hub uses the latest innovation. Other blockbusters expect centers to play a vital role in the framework throughout a set timeframe to deal with a square. Saving more stakes and positions allows you to perform more confirmation manipulation. and acquire more expenses. Confirming share warrants works in the best interest of the organization, however, using significantly less processing energy.

The Bitcoin block reward (12.5 BTC) at the time of this composition is worth about $100,000 and the Ethereum reward (5 ETH) about $3000. Bitcoins with a limited amount stamped with the prize amount are continuously decreasing over the long term. Finally, the prize will fall to zero and at this point excavators will rely solely on exchange costs. In fact, all BTC has just been delivered, but Ethereum has no creation limit. There are currently around 97 million ETH at the point when one of these principles is refreshed, the chain will branch to another. The new standard of trading, dominated by new grounds, is considered another cash bitcoin gold (BTG) and bitcoin money (BCH), which is why these are all variants of the first bitcoin (BTC) [13]. One may be for faster processing, a second may be for more effective stockpiling of the exchange, and a third may be for a lower cost. All cash reserves are governed by clear and direct principles, and as a guide, in recent years, all proceedings on these guidelines require hub consent.

At this point, your mind may be off all of these guidelines, but in the end, run a series of business or social cycles with the rates, rewards, and benefits of a particular model. Imagine setting up an organization to do so. The principles will change without notice and the benefits will be eliminated. Concluding who can participate and who has the privilege to change management standards is the third element of the Blockchain. This degree of receptivity can have the greatest impact on our behavior.

4.1.4.3 Openness

Public support and reputation are particularly pervasive in the possibilities of the web. Linux Working Framework 67% of Universe web workers and more than 80% of Universe mobile phones are running themselves, relying on the open collaboration of many people.

4.1.4.4 Programming Engineer

The rally that oversaw Linux used a free open source authentication model. 250 is considered the world's largest single store of human information. With the idea of enabling decentralized associations such as open source programming, DAO crowdfunded $150 million in June 2016 [14]. Based on comparable Blockchain innovations such as the Bitcoin Blockchain, the DAO is in fact a regulator of sorts, whose rules and practices are carefully built on ideas of simplicity, theoretical basis, cryptography and science. publicity as opposed to a set of obscured cycles that can be affected by a limited aggregation of people.

Reasons can be taken in a publicly accessible space for evaluation so that governments, informal communities, property transactions and currency exchanges can be based on agreements which anyone can carry out and that will do it themselves on normal terms. Clear settlement, for example, selling 50 or more gadgets and getting 15% commission in any case, will get 10 billion VND commission.

Following the basic failure of the DAO, because of its inherent weaknesses, tweaks wete finally made to address the problem; recently, DAO has transformed into the ETH Blockchain network block with which we are now familiar. Although Bitcoin is primarily for installment purposes, Ethereum is intended to run decentralized projects or savvy contracts. Anyone can check out the code/reason behind a knowledge contract on the Ethereum Blockchain. Shrewd agreements can be used for a variety of functions: to track headlines for your property, to direct a bet or to create an understanding matrix of energy-haring zones. Like the site itself, public Blockchains for the most part have facilities that help to regulate or align important changes, but they mostly run autonomously by any individual or association.

Similarly, a privately owned business can have its own LAN or private entrance, and can have either private or participatory-based approaches to Blockchain creation. These are known as licensed records. Since large pieces in the private Blockchain are now trustworthy, they often do not take the same approach to preparing themselves as a public Blockchain to verify and secure exchanges, and this means that they can work very quickly. Similarly, in contrast to public Blockchains, independent and independent Blockchains do not require 51% approval of any advancement in their concept. Private Blockchains can be created. These show significant improvements in many common business areas, such as store networks, bookkeeping, and international financial transactions. In any case, while private and public restrictions may have the benefit of the exhibition over an open Blockchain, it can be argued that these benefits are undermined by the way a restricted public meeting can resolve decisions concerning their management. Disney Chain is a necessity for both public and private Blockchain management, creating the invisible creation we can hope to see from the Blockchain stages over the next decade which is completely independent, a variety of collective agreements, consolidation, and transparency [15].

We can expect to see an increase in empowered public and private administrations that are empowered and organized peacefully through management. For example, the use or loading of explicit functionality in Blockchains to perform administration, for example, identity verification, installment, resource exchange, exchange record keeping, and the authorization of robot contracts, Blockchain will also begin to play a role in ensuring that our data is used as guaranteed. When this establishment of shared services emerges as normal, I agree that the real opportunity for Blockchain is a place where it emphasizes its openness. Following the stock market crash in the US in 1929 and the fall of the 1930s, the administration President Franklin Delano Roosevelt deserved a certain credit for helping to stabilize the US. The main task was the production of new security organizations such as the 1934 Security Exchange Commission (SEC), which ensures increased business stability and a reduction in the level of risk that can be taken by organizations, such as focused trading, trading banks, brokers and advisors. The next task was the implementation of an app known as the New Covenant. The new deal brought about the formation of the Works Progress Administration (WPA) [16]. The WPA alone was answerable for making in excess of eight million positions. These projects did not just establish the country's infrastructure, such as the interstates, air terminals and transport connections, such as the expansion of their railroad frameworks, but also expanded scientific and cultural activities such as astronomical observatories, giving work to craftsmen, and sponsoring artistic events, such as symphony orchestras and celebrations. During a period of huge racial imbalance, one of the main considerations of the WPA's effectiveness was its comprehensive nature. The combination of consensus, gamification and openness creates opportunities and makes ideas of understanding, mixing management, and supporting the public with a sound natural environment New Deal sponsored by a government official. Now consider that worldwide it is supported by public works where anyone can eat as a detective, expert, or as a viewer of quality control. I am a Blockchain regulator and an open source public interest department, there is good reason to accept that the coming and future of online governance can use standards [17]. The same success that makes the financial department open to the international level.

Notwithstanding speaking to a computerized or actual resource, the blend of a Blockchain's agreement technique, gamification approach, and level of transparency can speak to one side to utilize an assistance, the option to perform work for that administration, the standing of a person or thing playing out that administration, or a mixture of these. Depicting these cash as resources, tasks, uses or prizes is a process called 'tokenization'. The boundaries between token alignment can be blurry and can use a large number of capacities (also known as half-and-half tokens), but for the most part we consider tokens to fall into five general classes. Some Blockchains simply create and verify exchanges. Despite being a computerized resource token, Bitcoin can likewise be viewed as a usage token. Some tokens are essentially related to real resources like Digix (DGD), which, like Bitcoin, are considered replaceable if there is no distinction between one token and another [18]. Like collectible baseball cards or crypto kitty, they can be irreplaceable. Working tokens like the Livepeer's LPT are earned by the hub when performing circulated video. The FileCoin Hub will procure work tokens when performing the deployed abilities, and the Executives and Jeweler Hub can direct the completion and installment of those performing micro-tasks such as photo alignment or marking.

The last type of token is known a stop sign or prize. A prize ticket refers to a school, rating or compensation for showing someone or something. The winner of the models rewards content providers with STEEM in terms of ideas and preferences for their work. Forecast rewards members with a reputation for excellence (REP) by performing specific expectations for sports, political events, or finances in the same way as evaluating event results. Livepeer uses and rewards the team to check the quality and performance of the hubs that provide broadcasting capabilities.

By combining all these ideas, we can simplify shared riding. Using resource tickets, we can empower members to sell value on their cars. Using work tickets, we can empower them to rent their cars to drivers. Cyclists can then compensate passengers for assistance tickets. Using profitable contracts, we can make an account passenger and cost passenger, reward senior drivers and loyal passengers with recognition tokens, ultimately calculate and possibly distribute profits or profits to all default quarterly price holders. Note that the SEC, from a management perspective, looks at tickets that fall into only two categories, help tickets and safety tickets. A ticket is considered useful when it is purchased to play a particular type of activity or management. The SEC ticket does not direct tickets. A ticket is considered collateral if it is purchased intentionally with the desire for a particular return method such as profit, sharing benefits, or an expected increase in value. Therefore, even tokens with all usage marks, can be ordered by the SEC as security.

Given current specialized and convenience challenges, Blockchain innovation will probably develop throughout the coming decade to turn into an indispensable piece of our specialized scene, not just helping in the productivity of assignments like confirmation of possession, installment, resource trade, exchange history support, and computerized implementation of agreements, yet in addition can possibly guarantee more noteworthy straightforwardness and improved administration over bigger concentrated associations like monetary foundations, trades, and online administrations. Furthermore, although not a solution for all advanced illnesses, Blockchain innovation presents opportunities for new and interesting capabilities for us to collaborate inside a safer, more secure and comprehensive computing world. From history, the possibility of inclusion can lead to sweeping constructive consequences for networks and nations. With a better understanding of how contract, wrongdoing and acceptability, influence Blockchain innovation, we can begin to anticipate, realize and participate in administrations. which opens entirely new financial open doors at a neighborhood and worldwide scale [19].

4.1.5 The Decentralization of Blockchain

In Blockchain, decentralization refers to a controlled and dynamic exchange of corporate components (individual, society, or assembled) to a conveyed network. Devolved institutions seek to reduce the amount of trust that members should give each other and prevent their ability to exercise authority or order over each other in morals that ruin the usefulness of the organization.

4.1.6 Why Devolution Matters

Devolution is definitely not another idea. When building an innovative agreement, three essential organizational models are often seen: grouped, decentralized, and decentralized. By decentralizing management and admitting assets in an application, more noticeable and pleasant support can be achieved. The lower the exchange throughput, however, the better the tradeoff deserves the improved level of reliability and governance they generate.

4.1.7 Advantages of Decentralization

■ **Gives a trustless surrounding:** In a decentralized Blockchain network, nobody needs to know or confide in any other person. Every part in the organization has a duplicate of precisely the same information as a disseminated record. On the off-chance that a part's record is adjusted or defiled in any capacity, it will be dismissed by most of the individuals in the organization.

■ **Improves information compromise:** Organizations frequently trade information with their accomplices. This information, thus, is regularly changed and put away in each gathering's information storehouses, possibly to reemerge when it should be passed downstream. Each time the information is changed, it opens doors for information misfortune or wrong information to enter the workstream. By having a decentralized information store, each element approaches a constant, shared perspective on the information.

■ **Diminishes purposes of shortcoming:** Decentralization can lessen purposes of shortcoming in frameworks where there might be an excess of dependence on explicit entertainers. These frail focuses could prompt foundational disappointments, including inability to give guaranteed administrations or wasteful assistance because of the fatigue of assets, intermittent blackouts, bottlenecks, absence of adequate motivations for good help, or debasement.

■ **Advances asset circulation:** Decentralization can likewise help streamline the conveyance of assets so that guaranteed administrations are given better execution and consistency, as along with a diminished probability of cataclysmic disappointment.

4.2 Working Principle of Blockchain

Decentralization should be used where it is most appropriate and it is not necessary that it should be 100% decentralized. The objective of any Blockchain arrangement is to convey what the clients of that arrangement need, and this could conceivably incorporate certain degrees of decentralization [20]. To comprehend decentralized organizations more readily, Table 4.1 shows how decentralized organizations contrast with the more normal unified and circulated networks. Each organization design has its pros and cons. For example, a decentralized Blockchain framework usually organizes run-time security, as opposed to a propagated framework. Along these lines, as the Blockchain network scales up or out, it turns out that the organization is safer, but execution is easy to return for all reasons. The part hub must approve all the information added to the record. Adding individuals to a decentralized organization is more secure, but not so fast. Who is building a Blockchain application using distributed?

Each Blockchain convention, dApp, DAO, or other Blockchain-related arrangement, receives a variable degree of decentralization. The selection level is usually based on the development of the arrangement, its motivational model and the time-proven unwavering quality of the consensus component, and the capabilities of the established group. To find some kind of harmony DAO has different segments at different stages of decentralization. Prophets (that is, external administrators who provide external data for clever consensus) are somewhat decentralized,

Table 4.1 Difference between Centralized, Decentralized and Distributed Organizations

	Centralized	*Distributed*	*Decentralized*
Resources in software and hardware	Kept up and constrained by single element in a unified area	Spread across different server farms and topographies; possessed by network supplier	Assets are claimed and shared by network individuals; hard to keep up since nobody possesses it
Components of solution	Kept up and constrained by single element in a unified area	Spread across different server farms and topographies; possessed by network supplier	Each member has exactly the same copy of the distributed ledger.
Data	Kept up and constrained by single element in a unified area	Usually owned and operated by the customer.	Added by group consensus.
Control in all	Kept up by single element in a unified area	Spread across different server farms and topographies; possessed by network supplier	No one owns the data but still everyone owns the data
Single point of failure in every organization	Yes	No	No
Tolerance in fault	Low	High	Highest
Security in all organizations	Kept up and constrained by single element in a unified area	Spread across different server farms and topographies; possessed by network supplier	Inversely proportional with network members
Performance shown in every organization	Kept up and constrained by single element in a unified area	It increases as network / hardware resources go up and down	Inversely proportional with network members
Examples	Enterprise resource planning	Cloud computing	Blockchain

knowledgeable consensus can be completely centralized, but the management cycle for changing boundaries is networked. It will be led and decentralized.

Larger decentralized Blockchain arrangements have been investigated and accepted by associations of various types, sizes and industries. Some prominent models incorporate applications that provide quick, unfamiliar or critical assistance to individuals who need it most, without bank intervention, government or outsider elements. Alternatively, there are applications that enable individuals to deal with their own developed characters and knowledge. Today, online media outlets, organizations, and various associations sell data without advantage. A decentralized methodology would help make it impartial for everyone [21].

For example, the legitimate model of Contura Energy, a leading UK-based coal provider, has relied on an obsolete letters of credit framework to handle its worldwide exchange installments. These letters of credit, issued by a representative bank for the benefit of their customers, complete as installment security for buyers. While this framework is reliable, it is also physically determined, slow and very wasteful. Contura Energy appreciates the significance and benefits of digitizing and mechanizing their credit measurement letters. The test they are, however, is the empowerment of trust and a shared check among merchants and buyers. This decentralized arrangement likewise extends its simplicity, giving all meetings a constant awareness of information and documents.

4.2.1 *Working of Blockchain*

The process of Blockchain development is still young and is likely to develop in future. Along these lines we must start to understand this innovation [22]. Blockchain is a mixture of three driving innovations. Shared records for

- Encryption key
- A processing Decentralized organization, including
- A method, exchange and record storage of organizations consisting of

4.2.1.1 *Encryption Keys*

There are two keys: the private key and the public key. These keys help to conduct a beneficial exchange between the two meetings. Every individual has these two keys that they use to create a protected advanced personality reference. This personality guarantee is a major part of Blockchain innovation. In the field of cryptocurrencies, this character is called a 'computer signature' and is used to approve and control exchanges [23].

Advanced markers are converged with the distributed organization; A large number of people become experts using computer signatures to reach agreement on the exchange, among various different issues. At the moment that they approve an agreement, it is secured by a digital check, which is effectively guaranteed. In short, Blockchain clients use cryptographic keys to execute various types of computer companies.

4.2.1.2 Transaction Process

One of the key highlights of Blockchain innovation is the way it validates and approves exchanges. For example, if two people want to have a private and public key exchange, the primary set of individuals will connect the exchange data with the public key of the next party. Notwithstanding leading monetary exchanges, the Blockchain can likewise hold conditional subtleties of properties, vehicles, and so on [24]. Here's a utilization case that outlines how Blockchain functions:

4.2.1.3 Hash Encryptions

Blockchain innovation mainly utilizes hash encryption to verify information according to SHA256 calculations to verify data. The sender's location (public key), the beneficiary's location, exchange and private key subtleties are: The encrypted data, the hash encryption, is sent around the world and added to the Blockchain after verification, and the SHA256 calculation rearranges the verification of the sender and receiver, making it difficult to hack the hash encryption [25].

4.2.2 Action Confirmation

In the Blockchain, each rectangle consists of four main headers: Past Hash: This hash address finds the past rectangle. Square's hash addresses: The hash address of the block: Everything mentioned above (before the hash, the subtle exchange and the temporary value) is sent via hashing calculations. This gives you a return containing a value of 256 digits and 64 characters long known as a special 'hash address'. As a result, it is hinted at as a square hash.

Different individuals around the world use computational calculations to classify incentives to meet predetermined conditions into the correct hash. The exchange will end when the predetermined conditions are met. More simply, Blockchain excavators strive to tackle the numerical mystery that is hinted at as evidence of work problems. Anyone who solves it wins the award first. The subtle rationale for current computerized/published records is called "mining." Although the term is related to Bitcoin, it is also used to refer to other Blockchain advances [26].

4.2.3 The Structure of Blockchain

To date Blockchains are considered the "fifth turn of events" of registration, the layer of trust is lacking for the Internet [27]. Blockchains can create confidence in modernized data. Exactly when the information has been made into a Blockchain database, it is difficult to do or change it. This possibility has never existed.

Blockchains are made up of three focus parts:

■ Square: The overview of transactions recorded over a given period of time. The size, duration and event set up for blocks Not to be confused with each Blockchain. Not all Blockchains are recording and guaranteeing the improvement of cash advance as item. However, all Blockchains record the advancement of their cryptocurrencies or tokens. The assignment of an engine to it (for example, that happens in financial transactions) is used to explain what the data suggest.

■ Chain: A hash that travels from one square to another and mathematically "moors" them together. This is one of the most inconvenient ideas to get a handle on the Blockchain. This is also a magic that allows the Blockchain to be glued and made mathematical. The hash of the trust Blockchain is generated using the data that was in the past squares. The hash is an interesting property of this data, confirming the square request and time. Hash was created over 30 years ago, despite the way the Blockchain is generally a new progression. This old advance is used to perform a single bearing operation that cannot be descrambled. Hash limits perform mathematical calculations that map data of any size to a fixed piece line. The piece string is typically 32 characters long and addresses the hashed data. Secure Hash Algorithm (SHA) is one of the cryptographic hash limits used on the Blockchain. SHA-256 is a mill count run that creates a nearly noteworthy fixed size 256-digit (32 bytes) hash. For practical purposes, consider a high-level exceptional sign of data used to verify a hash within the Blockchain as a hash.

■ Organization: The association consists of a "full center". Think of them as a PC running a secure map of alignment. Each central point contains an overall record of the huge number of transactions ever recorded in that Blockchain. Worked by anyone. Working at the full center is a daunting, exorbitant, and dull problem, so people don't do it in vain to their organization. The prize is usually token or cash advance, like Bitcoin [28].

4.2.4 Advantages of Structured Blockchain

Are you still convinced that advanced financial standards (or other types of decentralized money) are the predominant plans over traditional government-based money? There are various game plans that computerized currency formats may have alternatives to offer through their decentralized nature:

■ **Degradation reduction**: Immeasurable power comes with unusual obligations Giving lonely individuals and materials a huge pile of power increases their chances of beating their power. In the words of Sir Harold Acton, a senior British government official in the 19th century: "All power tends to corrupt; absolute power corrupts absolutely." Cryptocurrencies intend to determine the issue of world-class power by transferring power among various people or, much higher, among all people of society. That's the basic idea behind the development of Blockchain at any rate [29].

■ **Reproducing crazy money printing**: Public governments have one substantial financial institution, basically banks, and public banks can print money when they face a legitimate financial issue. This cycle is moreover called encouraging. Printing more money, an assembly may have the option to protect a commitment or reduce its cash. In any case, this strategy looks like putting a plaster on a broken leg. Not only is it rarely addressed, but the negative consequences can greatly outweigh the original problem. Countries such as Iran and Venezuela, for example, have abundant money. When they print more, its cash valuation drops significantly. Expanding skyrockets and people cannot afford to buy standard items and adventures. Their cash is not as important as the movement of the organization. Most cryptocurrency types of cash have a limited percentage of coins available. Whether coins are usable or a central substance, the association behind the Blockchain does not have a basic method for simply increasing or skillfully adding coins. If you trust the legislature, it's amazing, but remember that at any time your organization can essentially freeze your record, for example, in the United States, without a genuine will. If you own a bucket, kicking the bucket will give your organization an advantage in all its assets. Some governments can: It can even essentially invalidate guaranteed receipts, as India did in 2016. With advanced types of cash, you still don't have access to your resources.

■ **Completing the transaction:** With a regular currency, each time you make a trade, a professional such as your bank or high-level share organization is cut off. In a cash form, all the people you meet in the Blockchain are those experts; their compensation is arranged differently than the fiat money goes in and thus is not relevant to the assessment.

■ **Repayment of the Unpaid:** A large portion of the country's population does not have the means or permit reserved for the division of property such as banks. This problem is solved by spreading advanced exchanges everywhere so that anyone with a phone can start making parts. Otherwise, in fact, a larger number of people are closer to PDAs than banks. In all honesty, the most prominent population has cell phones rather than bathrooms, but this time Blockchain development will be unable to decide the final issue.

At the time of the release of Bitcoin, many disruptions to the entire business began to fade. These dreams may have received strength from the financial crash that followed the flood. The main thing to remember is that both Blockchain and development developments, the crypto in the coin market, are still in its infancy, and things are rapidly evolving.

4.2.5 Types of Blockchain

At present, there are four types of Blockchain networks: public Blockchain, private Blockchain, federated Blockchains, and cross Blockchains [30].

A. **Public Blockchain:** The public Blockchain is like becoming a validator (i., Participating in the implementation of an agreement protocol). Typically, such organizations provide financial incentives to individuals securing them and use some sort of Proof of Stake or Proof of Work calculation. Probably the largest public Blockchain, the best known are the bitcoin Blockchain and the Ethereum Blockchain.

B. **Private Blockchains:** This is more strictly known as a licensed private Blockchain. One cannot accompany it unless greeted by the organization directors. User access and validators are restricted. To recognize open Blockchains and other shared decentralized information base applications that are not open specially appointed process bunches, the phrasing Distributed Ledger (DLT) is ordinarily utilized for private Blockchains.

C. **Half-type Blockchains:** A Half-type Blockchain is a mix of integrated and decentralized functions. The specific activity of the chain may depend on which segment of centralization is utilized.

D. **Sideline Blockchain:** Items on the Mandatory Blockchain (the section that usually mentions computerized resources) can be linked with a sidechain. This allows the sidechain to operate autonomously of the essential Blockchain in any case (e.g. by utilizing alternative methods for record keeping, calculating alternative contracts, etc.) [31].

4.2.6 Security and Privacy Issues: Future Trends

Much equivalent to whatever else for the duration of regular day-to-day existence, advanced monetary standards go with their own things of peril. Whether or not you trade cryptos, put assets into them, or basically grasp them for the future, you ought to assess and fathom the risks ahead of time. Irrefutably the most-discussed computerized cash chances consolidate their shakiness and nonattendance of rule [32]. The levels of volatility became particularly high in 2017, when the expense of most critical computerized types of cash, including Bitcoin, increased by more than 1,000 percent, before falling equally dramatically. Rules are another critical topic in the business. Strangely, both non-attendance to the rules and prologue to rules can change into risk capacities for cryptographic cash examiners.

4.2.6.1 Learn to Do Transactions

Cryptocurrency makes transactions both simpler and faster. However, before abusing these options, you should take benefits of the convenience of cryptocurrency benefits, and find where you can get your hands on different advanced currencies. Cash and get acquainted with the crypto cash organization. These are parts of the nuts and bolts that consolidate computerized wallets and cash exchanges. Some crypto wallets containing the cryptocurrencies you have bought, are identical to the nest Applications have evolved like Apple Pay and PayPal. However, all things considered, interestingly associated with normal wallets and come with different game programs and security standards. You cannot participate in the cryptographic currency market without a crypto wallet.

Making care of your advanced currency forms on the exchange is considered a major threat if you consider that such various trades have been exposed towards deceptions in the past. trying to pull out with integrated joins. The third type of cryptocurrency is called a combination; this combines the advantages of the other two to make common, safer insights for customers.

4.2.6.2 Cryptocurrency Institutions

Becoming acquainted with a crypto organization can be a stepping stone to finding your way. A good website has a list of tourist attractions and care collections to make you feel better in the market and what people are talking about. There are a few different ways for you to install:

Crypto Specific Public Events: Advanced currencies have their own unique channels. in the Telegram program. To access them, you first need to download the Telegram Messenger program on your phone or PC; this is available on both the iOS and Android app stores.

Crypto on Reddit or Bitcoin Talk: Both Bitcoin Talk and Reddit have very stable crypto chatrooms. You can see a few focus without joining; however if you need to ask questions, you will need to sign in.

Trading the View Visiting Room: One of the best trading stages, TradingView provides social support for a wide range of representatives and currency experts to come together to share exams, questions and muses. If you are looking for a place that focuses more effort/trading to keep instead of less accumulated, you can join our theory assembly. Go ahead and bother people.

4.3 Make an Arrangement before You Jump In

There are more than 1,600 advanced types of cash available at the time they form, and this number continues to grow. You can choose advanced financial standards that depend on things like characterization, dominance, conviction framework, the organization behind the Blockchain, and its financial model.

As the crypto business is still relatively new, it's still extremely difficult to find the best crypto money and investment. That's the explanation you could benefit from by upgrading among different types and orders of cryptographic types of cash to manage your risk. Separating across whatever 15 cryptos, you can accumulate the odds of having champions in your portfolio. On the other hand, over-diversification can similarly become unsafe, so you need to take decided measures.

4.3.1 Challenges and Opportunity in Cyber Defense

As soon as you've restricted the advanced types of cash you like, you should then recognize the best an ideal occasion to get them. Shockingly, however, countless numbers of those people bungled the situation and bought when the expense had topped. Along these lines, they not only had the alternative to buy less bits of Bitcoin (just proposed), they also expected to sit on their setbacks and to keep things under control at the accompanying cost flood. Regardless, by analyzing the worth of the action and noting any authentic threat, you may have the alternative to stack the odds on the side of yourself and reap an enormous advantage at a later date.

4.4 Case Studies

Perhaps the clearest case for where the Blockchain could be profitable is origin and movement responsibility for it, and a land library is a particularly decent case. There have been a few pilot studies and confirmation of an idea, remembering Georgia, Sweden and Honduras, but none have yet become particularly large in scope. On the occasional occasion that the property exchange was processed on the Blockchain, it can record the entire property exchange history and increase the productivity of exchange preparation and battle pollution by circulating record keeping to all gatherings.

Leveraging a great agreement, resource trading can also follow explicit instructions encoded as a component of the exchange performed when the agreed model is met, and the productivity of the trading cycle. Let us further expand. As a public registration body, Blockchain acceptability is no obstacle. Members only need to know who will charge, sell, or split the land. In addition, an undeniable natural perspective helps to add simplicity as needed. The land vault Blockchain should start by tokenizing land resources. Each segment of land is legally portrayed as an equivalent computerized resource and placed on the Blockchain. It is tracked by ensuring that the current owners are responsible for the appropriate tokens assigned to them. This is very difficult because the existing framework is currently unpredictable and needs to be adaptable in future if the existing area certificate is an adjustment or part. Although Bitcoin works, it is an entirely online framework, and Blockchain applications in areas such as land libraries are now this now because all members agree to ownership and source records. It's more complicated because you have to take responsibility for the reality of the library and attach a record.

This is confusing. The register should definitely reflect the state of the real existence and resources of the Blockchain, even for parties who are not part of the Blockchain or do not remember it as genuine. When records indicate that these are retained, there must be a legitimate element to approve ownership. Expecting this difficulty to survive, then the vault Blockchain could record global deals (or other comparable exchanges), creating a more permanent and permanent record.

4.4.1 Digital Forms of Money

Having been a dispatched online currency, Bitcoin was converted into an electronic currency that can be distributed without the need for a national bank or other position to operate and maintain a record, and how real money is spent. The car that runs the bitcoin record is also different a large block, and some Blockchains run by a few hundred other businesses that can be compared with different principles. Bitcoin works by paying diggers – those who do the computer work of posting new exchanges – with newly printed bitcoins. The framework thus eliminates the hassle of exchange transfers and compensation for doing so to control the expansion.

Bitcoin appeals to clients for a number of reasons: The exchange costs paid by the lower payers; a significant increase since its creation; and the framework is much lower than traditional banking. Like a web-based currency, bitcoin also does not recognize the edges of the earth, which makes interregional migration similar to other installments.

4.5 Interbank Compromise

Blockchains are intended to be helpful in frameworks that require compromise between parties. Huge numbers of the significant portions in banking support the R3 consortium, which is investigating the use of a Blockchain-like spread record for interbank compromises and other financial applications.

A large amount of dollars has gone through each year, providing interbank records. On the off-chance that there is and could be a conveyed record arrangement that can handle the size of the interbank swaps, at that time this cost could be reduced dramatically. This type of use can be an independent record – where only accepted circles can view records or have an interest in creating new categories. This could reduce the important efforts that have been made in the letters issued to colleagues and considered a more productive financial framework in other recorded applications allocated to the financial space. However, we expect that this great difficulty can be overcome, this may be an important area for the use of the Blockchain. Some reconciliation of the production network for comparative reasons have been created and without the need to rely on the Consolidation of Concession to Agree on the Terms of Use. If it is approved, then a smart agreement will naturally fulfill its terms. This could mean submitting an installment following a specific letter, using a production product record or making a guess.

4.5.1 Keen Agreements

Keen agreements consider exchanges to be made consequently and without the need to depend on a focal gathering to arbitrate the activity of the agreement terms. Blockchain offers openings in this field, since shrewd agreement codes can be composed straightforwardly onto a square examinable at an early stage by the contracting parties, in much the same way as occurs with a conventional lawful agreement. In the event that it is consented to, at that point the shrewd agreement will naturally execute its own terms. This could mean delivering an installment following a specific trigger, running a product escrow record or making a speculation. One possible area of leeway of shrewd agreements over customary law is that they diminish counterparty hazard. With a customary lawful agreement, the courts go about as a fix to penetrates – if the agreement is broken, they can authorize the terms afterwards. Nonetheless, savvy agreements can be a precaution; they work on the expressed terms notwithstanding, which ties its gatherings. Additionally, savvy contracts are unambiguous – the agreement will do the unparalleled significance of its code.

There are a few difficulties to savvy contract selection. While the way toward executing a keen agreement may eliminate the requirement for a go-between, there may at present be a requirement for a confided-in expert (i.e., a software engineer) to make the brilliant agreement. In the event that institutional trust (and cost) moves from the legal counselors drawing up the agreement to the software engineers encoding it, there is no genuine preferred position to be picked up. Notwithstanding, we are presently on a reasonable route away from this reality. Courts would need to perceive that the activities of brilliant agreements are genuine approaches to move possession and incentive among parties, and that the conditions of savvy contracts are enforceable in the event that a penetrate by one way or another happens. Furthermore, an answer would need to be found to the inquiry: What change is accessible if the brilliant agreement is abused in a manner not expected by one of the gatherings? Could aim supersede the letter of the code?

This last issue is not hypothetical – when the DAO had quite a bit of its subsidizing commandeered through a proviso in an ineffectively composed brilliant agreement. This ultimately leads to a fork, with most members consenting to move back the deficiency of assets; however, some kept business as usual and turned into a different Blockchain, which presently exists under the name Ethereum Classic. This rollback was just conceivable in light of the fact that the greater part of the members consented to actualize it.

4.5.2 Store Network Recognizability

The current reserve chains are continuously capricious and range across edges, which implies monotonous, manual, inefficient and costly cycles for all get-togethers. Low perceptibility in a separated system can achieve prosperity issues, adulterated significantly. All the while, clients are mentioning more straightforwardness about the beginning stage and nature of the things that they buy. Blockchain advances could basically diminish taking care of time across every movement of this cycle. Each trade indicating an advancement of the product would be recorded, from unrefined materials to the finished article. Documentation would be made, revived, seen or affirmed by parties on the Blockchain, enabling detectable quality of the entire store organization.

A full survey trail would be made, which could be used to shield clients from counterfeit product. In addition to this, it gives associations extended trust in the authenticity and nature of items, influencing sourcing decisions. For example, portions could in like manner be begun perfectly between parties throughout the cycle, considering courses of action. As an increase, related sensors and clever devices could measure the condition of compartments and other information can be recorded to enlighten last settlements (e.g. if items have been hurt) [33].

4.6 Protection Preservation Policy

4.6.1 Privacy on Blockchain

Privacy Policy in Block Chain is designed to address managerial requirements of the authority in which Blockchain offers its Services and facility, including the General Data Protection Regulation ("GDPR"), as achieved by the European Commission.

Different Privacy Policy on Blockchain.

a. **Collection of Personal Data** - Information can be given by filling forms on website, email or through app. Various information is to be collected. These include

   Login Information: this includes type of browser and the version that is used, wallet identifier, last access of wallet and, finally IP, address that is used to access that wallet.

   Device Information: This collects Information about the device, Hardware model, OS and its version and software.

   Wallet Information: Wallet through our Services that will generate a public and private key pair and when we log-out from the Wallet it collects an encrypted file and if unencrypted key contains history along with the transaction.

   Transaction Information that collect and maintain information related to transaction, i.e. conversion of Bitcoin for Ether.

b. **Use of Personal Data** - Personal data is taken to understand how users uses the services and engages with the website, should manage and develop business and operations, and the prevention and investigation of dishonest or other criminal activities, addressing service request and resolving users questions and needs.

c. **Security of Your Personal Data** - Usually personal data comes via the Internet. Each member can protect their data using Blockchain security policies. In particular, server TLS (Transport Layer Security) protects the encryption of personal data and also prevents individuals from accessing such personal data that travels over the Internet.

4.6.2 Types of Blockchain in Privacy Systems

i. **Public Blockchain** – Also known as a permissionless Blockchain, in which anyone can join the network and also can read, write or participate within the Blockchain. This does not have a single entity that can control the network and also can be called as decentralized, but data are secure because no one can alter, delete or modify data once it has been validated on the Blockchain. Examples of such a system include Bitcoin and Ethereum.

ii. **Private Blockchain** – This is also known as a permissioned Blockchain. It restricts users to participation in the network. Entities who have knowledge about it can participate in the transaction. One example of such a system is the Hyperledger Fabric of the Linux Foundation.

iii. **Hybrid Blockchain** – This is a combination of public and private Blockchain solutions. We can see this as simultaneously providing both controlled access and freedom. It is not open to everyone, but still offers Blockchain features such as transparency, security, integrity, decentralization etc. Usually, it is entirely customizable in which members of a hybrid Blockchain can decide who can participate in the Blockchain or which transactions are to be made public [34].

4.7 Conclusion

In this chapter we read and gathered information about the security and assurance in cryptographic cash and Blockchain and, furthermore, read how it is not equivalent to other monetary sources. At first, we portray the stray pieces and working of cryptographic cash and Blockchain; a short time later, we talk about the security and insurance it offers. We also covered how encryption, lack of definition and various techniques has a tremendous effect in the turn of events and the advancement of Blockchain. With the creating interest of people in investigation and use of Blockchain, security issues have pulled in the concerns of people.

We assert that a beginning-to-end enthusiasm for the security and confirmation properties of Blockchain expects a fundamental occupation in improving the level of trust that Blockchain may give and in making mechanical enhancement for overpowering shield methods and countermeasures. We should calculate that growing lightweight cryptographic calculations comparatively as other traditional security and protection methodologies will be a key connecting with progression later on treatment of Blockchain and its applications. Blockchain is an emerging development, so ideas are still mixed with its ineffective limit. In a TechRepublic Research study, 70% of respondents said they did not use the Blockchain. However, 64%

of those said that they expect the Blockchain to affect their industry in one way or another, and the majority are anticipating a positive outcome.

Another Trend Insight report from the head company Gartner made a check:

■ By 2022, only 10% of users will achieve any unusual change using the Blockchain.
■ By 2022, at any one time a single Blockchain-based creative business will cost $10 billion.
■ By 2026, the Blockchain-enhanced business model will generate more than $360 billion; furthermore, by 2030, it will create more than $3.1 trillion.

Organizational insurance is perhaps one of the most promising areas for increased Blockchain development. Blockchain development can be used to prevent conversion, keep data secure and allow people to check the authenticity of the record.

■ Before we deal with each example in more detail, we should look at specific real factors and numbers that show how the Blockchain is rapidly transforming into a bit of our lives.
■ There are over 50 million crypto wallets used for portions far and wide.
■ The total market cap of all cryptographic types of cash is constantly changing and at the hour of making was over $360 billion.
■ 75% of Internet-of-Things (IoT) associations plan to start using Blockchain devices before the completion of 2020.

According to the financial processing company Accenture, money-related associations can save as much as $12 billion every year because of DLT courses of action. So Blockchain advancement will be unprecedented in the tech and IT region in the coming years, similar to what the web achieved for the world, beholding back to the 1990s and mid-2000s.

References

[1] Yaga, Dylan, Peter Mell, Nik Roby, and Karen Scarfone. "Blockchain technology overview." *arXiv preprint arXiv:1906.11078* 1(2), 121, (2019).
[2] Joshi, Archana Prashanth, Meng Han, and Yan Wang. "A survey on security and privacy issues of blockchain technology." *Mathematical foundations of computing* 1, no. 2 (2018): 121.
[3] Weiss, N. Eric, and Rena S. Miller. "The target and other financial data breaches: Frequently asked questions." In *Congressional Research Service, Prepared for Members and Committees of Congress February*, vol. 4, p. 2015. 2015. https://dennisnadeaucomplaint.com/wp-content/uploads/2015/06/Dennis-Nadeau-Complaint-The-Target-and-Other-Financial-Data-Breaches-Frequently-Asked-Questions-.pdf.
[4] Liu, Yukun, and Aleh Tsyvinski. *Risks and returns of cryptocurrency.* No. w24877. National Bureau of Economic Research, 2018.

[5] Tasatanattakool, Pinyaphat, and Chian Techapanupreeda. "7Blockchain: Challenges and applications." In *2018 International Conference on Information Networking (ICOIN)*, pp. 473–475. IEEE, 2018.

[6] Danial, Kiana. *Cryptocurrency Investing for Dummies.* John Wiley & Sons, 2019. https://books.google.co.in/books?hl=en&lr=&id=BsOKDwAAQBAJ&oi=fnd&pg=PT13&dq=Danial,+Kiana.+Cryptocurrency+Investing+for+Dummies.+John+Wiley+%26+Sons,+2019.&ots=PQqXLYEgcS&sig=CsXOtDCuTs2RFUu__VnbOu7vKu0&redir_esc=y#v=onepage&q=Danial%2C%20Kiana.%20Cryptocurrency%20Investing%20for%20Dummies.%20John%20Wiley%20%26%20Sons%2C%202019.&f=false.

[7] Tondello, Gustavo F., Rina R. Wehbe, Lisa Diamond, Marc Busch, Andrzej Marczewski, and Lennart E. Nacke. "The gamification user types hexad scale." In *Proceedings of the 2016 annual symposium on computer-human interaction in play*, pp. 229–243. 2016.

[8] Cai, Yuanfeng, and Dan Zhu. "Fraud detections for online businesses: a perspective from blockchain technology." *Financial Innovation* 2, no. 1 (2016): 1–10.

[9] Hagerman, Robert L., and Joanne P. Healy. "The impact of SEC-required disclosure and insider-trading regulations on the bid/ask spreads in the over-the-counter market." *Journal of Accounting and Public Policy* 11, no. 3 (1992): 233–243.

[10] Grant, Gerry, and Robert Hogan. "Bitcoin: Risks and controls." *Journal of Corporate Accounting & Finance* 26, no. 5 (2015): 29–35.

[11] Rastogi, Ayushi, and Madhavi Damle. "Trends in the growth pattern of digital payment modes in India after demonetization." *PalArch's Journal of Archaeology of Egypt/Egyptology* 17, no. 6 (2020): 4896–4927.

[12] Blohm, Ivo, and Jan Marco Leimeister. "Gamification." *Business & Information Systems Engineering* 5, no. 4 (2013): 275–278.

[13] Vujičić, Dejan, Dijana Jagodić, and Siniša Ranđić. "Blockchain technology, bitcoin, and Ethereum: A brief overview." In *2018 17th international symposium infoteh-jahorina (infoteh)*, pp. 1–6. IEEE, 2018.

[14] Santos, Francisco, and Vasileios Kostakis. "The DAO: a million dollar lesson in blockchain governance." In *School of Business and Governance, Ragnar Nurkse Department of Innovation and Governance* (2018).

[15] Teeluck, R., S. Durjan, and V. Bassoo. "Blockchain Technology and Emerging Communications Applications." In *Security and Privacy Applications for Smart City Development*, Tamane, S.C., Dey, N., and Hassanien, A-E. (eds.), pp. 207–256. Springer, Cham, 2021.

[16] Tews, Erik, and Martin Beck. "Practical attacks against WEP and WPA." In *Proceedings of the second ACM conference on Wireless network security*, pp. 79–86. 2009.

[17] Wang, Shuai, Wenwen Ding, Juanjuan Li, Yong Yuan, Liwei Ouyang, and Fei-Yue Wang. "Decentralized autonomous organizations: Concept, model, and applications." *IEEE Transactions on Computational Social Systems* 6, no. 5 (2019): 870–878.

[18] Vyzovitis, Dimitris, Yusef Napora, Dirk McCormick, David Dias, and Yiannis Psaras. "GossipSub: Attack-Resilient Message Propagation in the Filecoin and ETH2.0 Networks." *arXiv preprint arXiv:2007.02754* (2020).

[19] Holotescu, Carmen. "Understanding blockchain opportunities and challenges." In *Conference proceedings of» eLearning and Software for Education «(eLSE)*, vol. 4, no. 14, pp. 275–283. "Carol I" National Defence University Publishing House, 2018.

[20] Akram, Waseem. "Blockchain technology: Challenges and future prospects." *International Journal of Advanced Research in Computer Science* 8, no. 9 (2017): 642–644.

[21] Christodoulou, Panayiotis, Klitos Christodoulou, and Andreas Andreou. "A decentralized application for logistics: Using blockchain in real-world applications." *The Cyprus Review* 30, no. 2 (2018): 181–193.

[22] Shojaei, Alireza, Jun Wang, and Andriel Fenner. "Exploring the feasibility of blockchain technology as an infrastructure for improving built asset sustainability." *Built Environment Project and Asset Management* 10, no. 2 (2019): 184–199.

[23] Feng, Qi, Debiao He, Sherali Zeadally, Muhammad Khurram Khan, and Neeraj Kumar. "A survey on privacy protection in blockchain system." *Journal of Network and Computer Applications* 126 (2019): 45–58.

[24] Guerrero-Sanchez, Alma E., Edgar A. Rivas-Araiza, Jose Luis Gonzalez-Cordoba, Manuel Toledano-Ayala, and Andras Takacs. "Blockchain mechanism and symmetric encryption in a wireless sensor network." *Sensors* 20, no. 10 (2020): 2798.

[25] Seebacher, Stefan, and Ronny Schüritz. "Blockchain technology as an enabler of service systems: A structured literature review." In *International Conference on Exploring Services Science*, pp. 12–23. Springer, Cham, 2017.

[26] Gorkhali, Anjee, Ling Li, and Asim Shrestha. "Blockchain: a literature review." *Journal of Management Analytics* 7, no. 3 (2020): 321–343.

[27] Qi, Zhuyun, Yan Zhang, Yi Wang, Jinfan Wang, and Yu Wu. "A cascade structure for blockchain." In *2018 1st IEEE International Conference on Hot Information-Centric Networking (HotICN)*, pp. 252–253. IEEE, 2018.

[28] Lin, Iuon-Chang, and Tzu-Chun Liao. "A survey of blockchain security issues and challenges." *IJ Network Security* 19, no. 5 (2017): 653–659.

[29] Chen, Weili, Zibin Zheng, Mingjie Ma, Pinjia He, Yuren Zhou, and Jing Bian. "Hierarchical bucket tree: an efficient account structure for blockchain-based system." *International Journal of Embedded Systems* 12, no. 4 (2020): 554–566.

[30] Andreev, R. A., P. A. Andreeva, L. N. Krotov, and E. L. Krotova. "Review of blockchain technology: Types of blockchain and their application." *Intellekt. Sist. Proizv.* 16, no. 1 (2018): 11–14.

[31] Liu, Manlu, Kean Wu, and Jennifer Jie Xu. "How will blockchain technology impact auditing and accounting: Permissionless versus permissioned blockchain." *Current Issues in Auditing* 13, no. 2 (2019): A19–A29.

[32] Joshi, Archana Prashanth, Meng Han, and Yan Wang. "A survey on security and privacy issues of blockchain technology." *Mathematical Foundations of Computing* 1, no. 2 (2018): 121.

[33] Aitzhan, Nurzhan Zhumabekuly, and Davor Svetinovic. "Security and privacy in decentralized energy trading through multi-signatures, blockchain and anonymous messaging streams." *IEEE Transactions on Dependable and Secure Computing* 15, no. 5 (2016): 840–852.

[34] Feng, Qi, Debiao He, Sherali Zeadally, Muhammad Khurram Khan, and Neeraj Kumar. "A survey on privacy protection in blockchain system." *Journal of Network and Computer Applications* 126 (2019): 45–58.

Chapter 5

Robust Digital Medical Image Watermarking and Encryption Algorithms Using Blockchain over DWT Edge Coefficient

Paresh Rawat
S.N. Technology, India

Piyush Kumar Shukla
University Institute of Technology Rajiv Gandhi Prodyogiki Vishwavidyalaya, India

Contents

DOI: 10.1201/9781003129486-5

5.1 Introduction

The watermarking algorithms designed specific for medical images are used for data security and protecting it from any kind of temper due to attacks [1–7]. Therefore, it is necessary to design a robust watermarking method. An embedded watermark must be perceptually invisible, must have only minor changes in medical image brightness values and must not be visible to the human eye. Therefore, invisible watermarking [1] is designed to minimize the error between cover image and watermarked image. Blockchain [2] has emerged as a modern security trend to improve the robustness of encryption standards. Blockchain-based security methods are using the genesis blocks for embedding, meaning that they are supposed to be more robust and secure. This chapter takes the advantage of Blockchain and the transformations-based watermarking methods for improving the medical image authentication and security.

The basic process of the Blockchain-based watermarking is presented in Figure 5.1 as a block diagram. The proposed embedding method is a three-stage process. It can be observed from Figure 5.1 that the SHA256 [3, 4] based Blockchain method is first used to generate the encrypted image data. These data are transmitted between the transmitters and the receiver. At the receiver, the decryption is done to recover the image back. This process is the simplexes implementation of the Blockchain-based security in watermarking. Here the genesis blocks or encrypt data are used as the watermark.

In the basic method presented in this chapter no additional image is used as a watermark. The level of security is greater as every block is unique.

5.1.1 Secure Hash Algorithm (SHA) for Blockchain

Blockchain is a technology for securing the large database records. The method uses the secure hash algorithm (SHA256) to protect records from fraudulent activity, tampering, and copyrighting using the chain participants. The algorithm used is a crypto hash algorithm-2 (called SHA-2), along with a Genesis blocks-based Blockchain. Blockchain technology was initially adopted as the background to cash

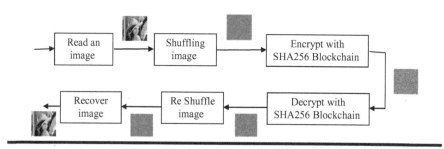

Figure 5.1   Basic Block diagram of the Blockchain based Watermarking

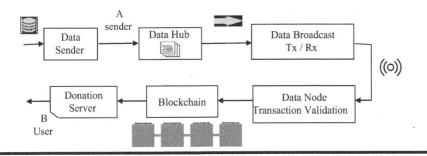

Figure 5.2   Process of Bitcoin based Blockchain process

transactions using the Bitcoin cryptocurrency [8]. Bitcoin is an advanced service capability for financial cash transactions and its characteristic features involve accurate tracing, and transaction record management, from anywhere [9]. Blockchain is a decentralized system which initially offers a digital technology for information and records management for a distributed database (Figure 5.2).

In recent years, Blockchain technology has been used to improve integrity, initially for handling money transactions. This chapter uses the integrity of Blockchain to improve the security in the watermarking method. Prince waqas Khan et al. [1] have discussed about a safe picture encryption algorithm for an IoT-situated network figuring framework dependent on a Blockchain has demonstrated support in terms of securely downloading information from gadgets. They completed a few tests to check that their proposed calculation is secure. There are still, nonetheless, a few impediments in the utilization of this innovation, including restricted figuring assets and the speed of exchanges. Numerous IIOT gadgets such as sensors have inadequate memory; therefore, it makes it difficult to handle network assets, and keeps them as alive nodes in the Blockchain. Web administrations can resolve this issue; however, this issue should actually be attended to. Later on, image security over the cloud subsequent to downloading can likewise be thought of as the serious challenge.

Mohammad Ali Bani Younes et al. [2] presents a square-based change calculation in light of the mix of picture change and a well-known encryption and unscrambling calculation called Blowfish. The first picture was separated into blocks, which were revised into a changed picture utilizing a change calculation introduced here; later, the changed picture was scrambled utilizing the Blowfish calculation. The outcomes appeared that the connection between picture components was essentially diminished through the use of the proposed method. The outcomes moreover show that expanding the quantity of squares by utilizing more modest block sizes brought about a lower relationship and higher entropy. Lukman et al. [3] have used the ShA256-based crypto hash algorithm for the encryption of the oil and gas industry for managing the decentralized data. Sheping Zhai et al. [4] have addressed different applications of the crypto hash SHA256 method using the Blockchain applications.

K. Sivaranjani et al. [5] proposed a half-and-half encryption method for the shading picture based on the arbitrary change, pivot activity, figure block fastening (CBC) strategy. At that point, scrambling is implemented in the try color RGB planes in fixed direction viz. diagonal, horizontal or vertical, askew. This strategy totally destroys the diagrams of the scrambled pictures, obscures the dispersion qualities of RGB-level grids, and adequately ensures against the unscrambling under various attacks. In the proposed framework, improved security is achieved without the utilization of change area. The testing and examination of a piece of the picture can done utilizing different boundaries to guarantee the security and adequacy of this proposed approach.

J. Mahalaxmi et al. had presented an inventive security-for-the-administration application for encrypting the images. The encryption is implemented in the clears to achieve high security for image transmission over cloud networks. The proposed strategy utilizes the improved code block-binding encryption mode that upgrades the calculation to scramble the RGB pictures of different volumes. Key age is created as intricate with numerical model that defeats the dilemma key issue exists in prior strategies, which additionally overhauls nature of encryption. Their results over standard images and their examination demonstrates the robustness of this strategy. Execution of the proposed technique is investigated with some security investigation like entropy measure, factual measure.

S. Pramothini et al. [9] presents a cross-breed security plot that utilizes steganography joined with Blockchain innovation to improve the security of picture posts makes data authentication over for web-based media application. A single block of a Blockchain [9] contains a body and header. Blockchain encryption uses public key cryptography for image transaction validation. In the embedding process the Blockchain body portion is the generated hash values of cover image having its fingerprint hidden a stago in it by steganography.

SHA ALGORITHM

The SHA256 algorithm is a two pass *process*

1. Initially the input message vector S is padded with 512 bits block lengths.
2. In the second pass processed the each block of 512 bits independently and represented as

$$S = \left[S^{(1)}, S^{(2)}, \ldots\ldots\ldots S^{(M)} \right] \qquad 5.1$$

Method randomly begins with the first hash value as $H^{(0)}$.then sequentially calculated the hash for message blocks as

$$H^k = H^{k-1} + C^f_{S^{(k)}} * H^{k-1} \qquad 5.2$$

Where, $C_{S^{(k)}}^{f}$ is the compression function for the SHA256 algorithm, and $S^{(k)}$ is the kth message Block where

$$k = 1, 2 \cdots\cdots\cdots, M \qquad\qquad 5.3$$

Here vector H^k the hash of the kth message. In this chapter the SHA256 algorithm is used for generation of the Blockchain based encryption for medical image watermarking.

5.2 Medical Image Watermarking

Medical image watermarking is a procedure for embedding watermark data within digital medical images. In other words, watermarking is a method of hiding logo or text images within the cover medical images. An efficient watermark must satisfy the following major requirements [2]:

1. The watermark for most of the applications must be invisible and must not affect the host or protected images' perceptual quality.
2. Watermark must be easily reconstructed and must also be reliable.
3. An embedded watermark must be robust against the various types of fragile or semi-fragile attacks.
4. Watermark must be statistically irremovable after it is embedded within the image.
5. It must be capable enough for providing the highest degree of image security.
6. The capacity and information within the watermark must be capable enough of holding the valuable information.

5.3 Previous Related Works

There are many types of watermarking methods available in the literature. In this chapter, our major concern is on the transform domain-based methods and on the methods using a digital signature. The transform domain-based medical image watermarking methods can be classified, as shown in Figure 5.3. Invisible watermarking is commonly implemented in the transform domain based methods.

Transform-based methods are widely opted for in medical image watermarking, including the following transforms: Discrete Wavelet Transform (DWT) [11, 12], Discrete Cosine Transform (DCT) [13, 14], Singular Value Decomposition (SVD) and various hybrid combinations of these transformations [1, 6, 7].

Watermarking for medical images is designed to authenticate the medical data and prevent the unauthorized copying of patient images. In recent decades, a number of watermarking techniques were proposed to improve the robustness of medical image

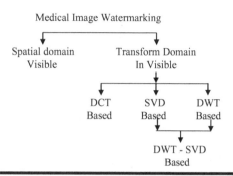

Figure 5.3   Classification of watermarking methods using transform domains

watermarking. Wavelet transform [1, 11, 12] is the most commonly used for implementing the digital image watermarking, and has been used for many years. Tao and Eskicioglu [10] have designed a watermarking method using the wavelet transform technique. Tao and Eskicioglu have embedded a watermark logo using four wavelet sub-bands, but they have used a varying scaling factor for each sub-band based on the features present. But the method was unsuitable for medical image authenticating since using the all sub bands may have the higher probability of the information changes.

A. DCT-based Watermarking

Kasmani et al. [6] have designed a hybrid combination of the DWT and DCT for embedding the watermarking as the binary image. Kasmani proposed to use three levels of DWT decomposition and then watermark is embedded is DCT domain. But method seems to be computationally complex.

Saeed et al. [7] proposed watermarking in the Joint DWT-DCT Transformation domain. The binary watermark logo is first scrambled using Arnold cat map and then embedded within the 3-level DWT coefficients of a input image. Next, PN-sequences of watermark bits are hidden in the wavelet coefficients in the computed DCT transform in the middle frequencies coefficients. The method was bit complex and needs larger processing time.

B. Wavelet-based Watermarking

Xia, et al. [13] has designed a early transform domain watermarking method using multi-resolution characteristic of the Discrete Wavelet Transform (DWT). The Gaussian noise is modeled as watermark and embedded to high-frequency sub bands of the images.

C. SVD-based Watermarking

Deepa Mathew K, [15] has proposed a robust method of watermarking using the D and V components of the SVD coefficients. But the method was rather simple and requires more robustness.

D. Hybrid Watermarking Methods

Akshya Kumar Gupta et al [16] have proposed the design of a watermarking method using the hybrid combination of the DWT- and SVD-based domains. The watermark is embedded using the singular values in high-frequency sub bands. The digital signature is also used for the embedding, which adds to the robustness.

Nilesh et al. [17] have used the hybrid combination of DWT-DCT-SVD for embedding the watermark logo for the medical images. Their method uses the single key-based signature generation mechanism and embeds the watermark in LL and HH coefficients after four-level DWT. Their method seems to be efficient against various attacks and is capable of retrieve the watermark efficiently.

5.4 Basic Transformations Used for Watermarking

Usually, wavelet transform is widely used for watermarking in the past. Singular value Decompositions (SVD) is also merged with the DWT to improve the robustness as in [1, 7].

A. Discrete Wavelet Transform (DWT)

This is a widely used transform for watermarking the medical imaging algorithms. Because DWT wavelets actually sub-divide the image into its multiple approximation sub-bands, thus are widely used for watermarking applications for medical images. The DWT-based wavelets efficiently isolates and thus manipulates the high-frequency HH and low-frequency LL sub-bands so that watermarks can be embedded in the sub-band making them less sensitive to human vision and capable of improving the invisibility. The multi-resolution property of the wavelet adds robustness to the system. Multiple wavelets are obtained from a basic prototype mother wavelet $\psi(t)$ using the scaling and shifting functions.

$$\psi_{a,b}(t) = \frac{1}{\sqrt{a}} \psi\left(\frac{t-b}{a}\right) \qquad 5.4$$

Where, a is the scaling parameter of the scaling function and b is the shifting parameter of the shifting function for the generation of the different wavelet filter coefficients. The direct transformation approaches are usually adopted [11]. Let I_0 is the gray scale image decomposed by wavelet decomposition. Then the first-level decomposition can be represented as:

$$I_0 = I_{LL1} + I_{LH1} + I_{HL1} + I_{HH1} \qquad 5.5$$

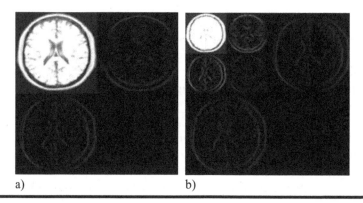

a)   b)

Figure 5.4   Example of the DWT decomposition of the CT image 1 a) for 1st level, b) for 2nd Level decomposition

Where I_{LL1} represents the low-frequency sub-band parts and I_{LH1}. I_{HL1}, I_{HH1} respectively represents high-frequency bands with edges. Figure 5.4 shows the example of a two-dimensional, two-level discrete wavelet decomposition for CT image.

It can be observed from the high-frequency sub-band of Figure 5.4(b) that it has very few features. Therefore, they provide more invisibility if used for watermarking.

B. Singular value Decompositions (SVD)

SVD is an eigenvector decomposition method which is frequently used for watermarking. The SVD decomposition is based on finding the eigenvalues and the eigenvectors of input square matrix as β using the $\beta\beta^T$ and $\beta^T\beta$.

$$[SVD = \underset{MxM}{\text{eigen}}\left(\beta\beta^T \ \& \ \beta^T\beta\right) \qquad 5.6$$

The eigenvectors calculated for the $\beta^T\beta$ represents the columns of V. The eigenvectors corresponding to $\beta\beta^T$ terminate to the columns vector U.

Finally, the most important values in S in *vector* are real singular values and are square roots of eigenvalues from $\beta\beta^T$ or $\beta^T\beta$. These singular values are used for the watermarking rules for robustness.

5.5 Validation of Basic Blockchain-Based Watermarking

A sequential process of the basic Blockchain-based encryption implemented in this section is given in Algorithm 5.1. The process of the decryption is just the inverse

ALGORITHM 5.1   BLOCKCHAIN WATERMARKING

1. Read the input image $\rightarrow$ X_ $\rightarrow$ rgb2gray $\rightarrow X$
2. Declare Genesis Blocks $\rightarrow Gb_{BxB}$ for B = 32
3. Initialize SHA256header
4. Shuffle the Image $\leftarrow y$ *while M blocks*
5. a1 = X(:) $\rightarrow x$ = 512 $\times$ 512 $\rightarrow Gb \otimes x$
6. Encrypt y using SHA256 algorithm
7. Decrypt $y \rightarrow$ z $\rightarrow$ re shuffle $\rightarrow Z$

of the encryption process. method is based on the bit vise XOR of the genesis jesh block and the shuffled data block.

This section presets the basic validation of the results of Basic Blockchain-based watermarking and image encryption explained earlier. Figure 5.5 presets the sequential validated results for Lena image of 512 $\times$ 512 and the 256 $\times$ 256 sizes. Results of the process mentioned in Figure 5.1 are validated in Figure 5.5. The actual performance can be evaluated from the sequential histogram comparison for 128 $\times$ 128 Blockchain watermarking of Lena image presented in Figure 5.6. In order to compare the performance of these histograms stage wise or different image sizes the entropy of the different stage of encryption process is compared in Table 5.1 for 128 and 512 image sizes. It can be seen from Table 5.1 that the Lena image is successfully decrypted with very little change in entropy of images. For 128 size the percentage change is 3% and for 512 image size 2.7% approx. Thus, the method is an efficient one.

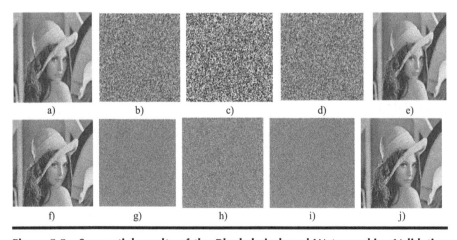

Figure 5.5   Sequential results of the Blockchain-based Watermarking Validation of results for Lena images for two different image sizes as a-e) for 512 × 512, f-j) for 256 × 256 image suz

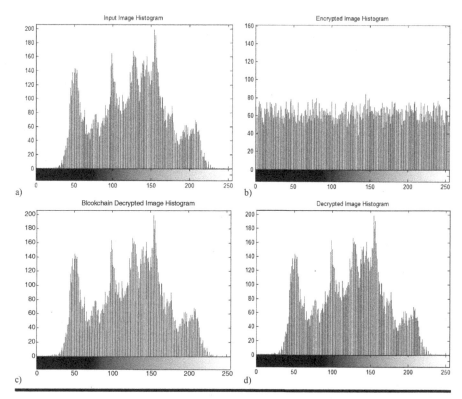

Figure 5.6 Sequential histograms for 128×128 Blockchain watermarking of Lena image a) input histogram, b) Encrypted Histogram c) Blockchain decrypt histogram d) Decrypted Histogram

Table 5.1 Comparison of the Entropy of Different Stages for Different Image Sizes and Methods

Images Sizes2	Original image	Shifted image	Encrypted image	Block chain Decrypted	Decrypted Image
128 × 128 without DWT	7.4101	7.4101	7.9880	7.4124	7.4124
512 × 512 without DWT	7.4450	7.4450	7.9994	7.4454	7.4454

5.6 Proposed DWT-SVD-Based Blockchain Encrypted Watermarking

Many wavelet-based watermark embedding methods have been designed in the past, but today they can easily be decoded by hackers. The existing watermarking methods have focused solely on the perceptual quality of watermarked image. But there has been little exploration of the process of generation and the memory storage of the watermark images. Thus, this section of the chapter has designed a new methodology for generating and decoding the digital watermark. This has involved the design of a robust algorithm as a combination of the DWT-SVD watermarking and Blockchain-based hash functions. This Blockchain in watermarking algorithm is used to safely store the watermark information. The discrete wavelets transform (DWT)-based watermarking method was also evaluated in this chapter. An encryption method unsighted hash-256 function is used to generate hash value based on the local image features. The watermark rule must be simple, but also robust. This chapter aims to design a watermarking method using DWT and edge detection coefficient values and the robust block chain technique. The edge detection using wavelet adds the invisibility to watermark. The chapters have illustrated the basic medical image-authenticating methods using the different combinations of the DWT- and SVD-based embedding rules for a fixed block of chain. A generated Blockchain is shuffled and encrypted using the SHA-256 algorithm. Proposed method adopts the energy-efficient wavelet coefficient for minimizing the spatial localities for better invisibility.

5.6.1 DWT-SVD Watermark Embedding

The process of embedding is sequentially presented for proposed watermark embedding method. The proposed method first takes the cover image (512 × 512) and a watermark logo (256 × 256). Takes wavelet decompositions of cover image and then the SVD of LL component are replaced by the SVD of the watermark component. A watermark rule is used to embed the logo image to cover image. Sequential procedure for embedding the watermark and decoding is presented as follows;

1. Read the input color or gray medical images as cover image.
2. Convert RGB to gray components stores it in to separate variables.
3. Read the watermark logo image to be embedded in the cover image.
4. Applying the DWT decomposition of cover image up to $\log_2(M)$ where M is the ratio of size of cover and logo images.
5. Calculate the SVD decomposition of the LL component of cover image and replace it with the SVD of logo image for embedding.

6. Take the inverse SVD and then inverse DWT decomposition to reconstruct the watermarked medical image
7. Generate the shuffle image the SHA256 encryption using Genesis block of 32 lengths as Blockchain. Generate the encrypted image.

The process of watermark extraction is simply the reverse of the extraction process.

5.7 Results

Some of the results are presented in this section for Lena and the medical CT, MRI images. The input images are shown in Figure 5.7. Here the Lena image is just used for validation purposes. The method is robust and good enough to improve the efficiency of the watermarking technique. The method also provides opportunity to transmit the encrypted data easily.

The sequential results of the proposed DWT-SVD-Blockchain method are shown in the Figure 5.8.

The comparison of the crypto weights in terms of histograms are presented in the Figure 5.9.

It can be observed from Figures 5.8 and 5.9 that the proposed method efficiently recovers the image and the watermark. The efficiency of the proposed method is also presented in Table 5.2, where the entropy is compared for basic Blockchain and the DWT-SVD-BC method.

The watermarking results for the medical images are shown in Figure 5.10.

The watermarking and extraction results for MRI and CT scan images are shown in Figures 5.11 and 5.12, respectively. The watermark extraction efficiency can be clearly seen from the figures. It is clear that the method is robust as it is a hybrid combination of DWT-SVD watermarking and Blockchain-based encryption,

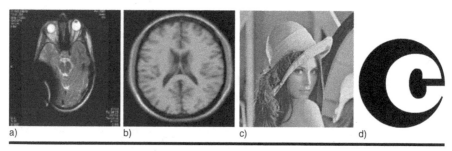

Figure 5.7 Input image database and the watermark used for study. a) MRI b) Ct-Scan_1 c) Lena d) Watermark

Figure 5.8 Sequential results of the DWT-SVD-Blockchain algorithm for the LENA image

although there is a grate scope of improvement in the retrieval quality of images and watermark extraction.

5.8 Conclusions

This chapter outlines a new methodology for generating and decoding the digital watermark. A robust algorithm as a combination of the watermarking and Blockchain-based hash functions is designed. The Blockchain in the watermarking algorithm is used for safely storing the watermark information. A discrete wavelet transform (DWT)-based watermarking method is evaluated in this chapter.

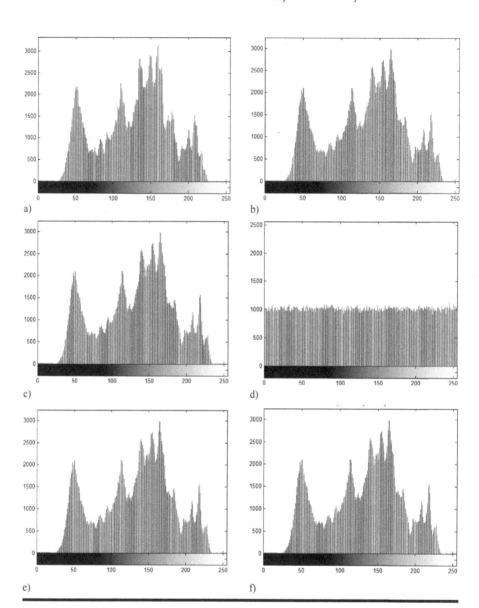

Figure 5.9 Sequential crypto weights histogram for proposed DWT-SVD-Blockchain method. a) Original image Histogram b) Watermarked image histogram c) Shuffled histogram, d) SHA encrypted histogram, e) Blockchain decrypted histogram, f) Recovered image histogram

Table 5.2 Comparison of Entropy of Different Stages for Lena Image and Proposed Methods

Images Sizes2	Original image	Watermarked image	Block chain Decrypted
512 × 512 without DWT	7.4450	7.9994	7.4454
512 × 512 DWT-SVD-BC	7.4450	7.4745	7.4747

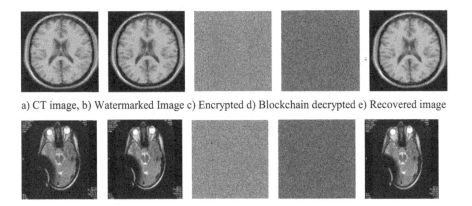

a) CT image, b) Watermarked Image c) Encrypted d) Blockchain decrypted e) Recovered image

f) MRI image, g) Watermarked Image h) Encrypted i) Blockchain decrypted j) Recovered image

Figure 5.10 Results of the medical image watermarking using the DWT-SVD-BC method. a) CT image b) Watermarked Image c) Encrypted d) Blockchain decrypted e) Recovered image f) MRI image, g) Watermarked Image h) Encrypted i) Blockchain decrypted j) Recovered image

An encryption method unsighted hash-256 function is used to generate a hash value based on the local image features. In the first section, a basic Blockchain-based image encryption method and its results are validated. Then, in the second part of chapter the DWT-SVD-based watermarking is combined with Blockchain encryption in order to improve the robustness.

It is to be observed that Lena image is decrypted with very less change of entropy of image without uses of DWT. For 128 size the percentage change is 3% and for 512 image size 2.7% approx. Thus, the method is an efficient one. However, there is a great scope for improvement in the recovered image quality for extracted watermark. Overall, chapter presents considerable insight into the application of Blockchain for medical image watermarking.

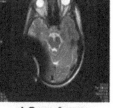
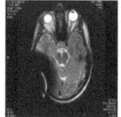

a) Cover image   b) Watermarked image

c) Watermark logo   d) Extracted watermark

Figure 5.11   Results of watermarking and extraction using DWT-SVD-BC for MRI image

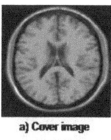
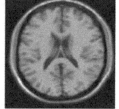

a) Cover image   b) Watermarked image

c) Watermark logo   d) Extracted watermark

Figure 5.12   Results of watermarking and extraction using DWT-SVD-BC for CT scan image

References

[1] Prince Waqas Khan, Yungcheol Byun "A blockchain-based secure image encryption scheme for the industrial internet of things", *MDPI Journal of Entropy 2020* Vol. 22, 175December2019.

[2] Mohammad Ali Bani Younes, Aman Jantanon "Image encryption using block-based transformation algorithm", *MDPI Journal of Entropy* Vol. 22(2), 175, 2020.

[3] Lukman Adewale Ajao, James Agajo, Emmanuel Adewale Adedokun, Loveth Karngong, "Crypto hash algorithm-based blockchain technology for managing decentralized ledger database in oil and gas industry", *MDPI Multidisciplinary Scientific Journal* Vol. 2, 300–325, 2019.

[4] Sheping Zhai, Yuanyuan Yang, Jing Li, Cheng Qiu, Jiangming Zhao "Research on the application of cryptography on the blockchain", *Journal of Physics Conference Series* Vol. 1168, p.0320772019\.

[5] K. Sivaranjani, P. Bright Prabahar, "A Hybrid Image Encryption Algorithm for secure communication"; in *NCICCT' 14 Conference Proceeding, International Journal of Engineering Research & Technology IJERT*, 2014.

[6] S.A. Kasmani, A. Naghsh-Nilchi *A New Robust Digital Image Watermarking Technique Based on Joint DWT-DCT Transformation, Third International Conference on Convergence and Hybrid Information Technology* 99. 539–544, 2008.

[7] Saeed K. Amirgholipour, Ahmad R. Naghsh-Nilchi, "Robust digital image watermarking based on joint DWT-DCT", *International Journal of Digital Content Technology and its Applications* Vol. 3(2), pp. 42–54, June 2009.

[8] R. Diego, S. Giovanni "Beyond Bitcoin: A critical look at block chain based systems", *Cryptography* Vol. 1(2), p. 15, 2017.

[9] S. Pramothini, Y.V.V.S. Sai Pavan, N. Harini "Securing images with fingerprint data using steganography and blockchain", *International Journal of Recent Technology and Engineering (IJRTE)* ISSN: 2277-3878, Vol. 7(4), pp. 82–85, December 2018.

[10] P. Tao, Ahmet M. Eskicioglu, "A robust multiple watermarking scheme in the discrete wavelet transform domain", in *Symposium on Internet Multimedia Management Systems V*, Philadelphia, PA2004.

[11] Salima Lalani, D.D. Doye "A novel DWT-SVD canny-based watermarking using a modified torus technique", *Journal of Information Processing Systems* Vol.12(4), pp. 681–687, December 2016.

[12] B.M. Lavanya "Blockchain technology beyond bitcoin: An overview", *International Journal of Computer science and Mobile Computing* Vol. 6, 76–80, Appl. 2018.

[13] Xia Xiang-Gen, C.G. Boncelet, G.R. Arce, "A multiresolution watermark for digital images", in the *Proceedings of IEEE International Conference on Image Processing*, Vol. 1, pp 549–551, October 1997.

[14] Vikas Tyagi "Data hiding in image using least significant bit with cryptography", *International Journal of Advanced Research in Computer Science and Software Engineering*, Vol. 2(4), 120–123, April 2012.

[15] K. Deepa Mathew, "svd based image watermarking scheme", *IJCA Special Issue on Evolutionary Computation for Optimization Techniques*, 2010.

[16] Akshya Kumar Gupta, Mehul S. Rawal, "A robust and secure watermarking scheme based on singular values replacement", *SadhanaIndian Academy of Sciences* Vol. 37(Part 4), 425–440, August 2012.

[17] Nilesh Rathi, Ganga Holi, "Securing medical images by watermarking using DWT-DCT-SVD", *International Journal of Computer Trends and Technology (IJCTT)* Vol. 10, 1–9, 2014.

[18] Vandana S. Inamdar, Priti P. Rege, "Dual watermarking technique with multiple biometric watermarks", *Sadhana* Vol. 39(Part 1), 3–26, February 2014. Indian Academy of Sciences

[19] Ranjan Kumar Arya, Ravi Saharan, "A novel digital watermarking algorithm using dual keys with RMI", *International Journal of Computer Science & Communication Networks* Vol. 4(3), 119–124, 2016.

[20] Smita Agrawal, Manoj Kumar, "Reversible data hiding for medical images using integer-to-integer wavelet transform", in *IEEE Students' Conference on Electrical, Electronics and Computer Science, (SCEECS)*, 2016.

[21] Nai-Kuei Chen, Chung-Yen Su, Che-Yang Shih, Yu-Tang Chen "Reversible watermarking for medical images using histogram shifting with location map reduction", in *IEEE International Conference on Industrial Technology (ICIT)*, 2016.

[22] Narong Mettripun, "Robust medical image watermarking based on DWT for patient identification", in *IEEE 13th International Conference on Electrical Engineering/Electronics, Computer, Telecommunications and Information Technology (ECTI-CON)*, July 2016.

[23] Ramanand Singh, Piyush Shukla, Paresh Rawat, Prashant Kumar Shukla "Invisible Medical Image Watermarking using Edge Detection And Discrete Wavelet Transform Coefficients", *International Journal of Innovative Technology and Exploring Engineering (IJITEE)*, Vol. 9(1), 2019.

Chapter 6

Enhanced Privacy and Security of Voters' Identity in an Interplanetary File System-Based E-Voting Process

Narendra Kumar Dewangan and Preeti Chandrakar
National Institute of Technology Raipur, India

Contents

DOI: 10.1201/9781003129486-6

113

6.1 Introduction

The traditional voting system has many flaws, including the leakage of the vote, revealing the voter's identity, biasing, fraudulent ballots, and many other things. In the electronic voting system, some problems are supposed to be paperless. Using the Internet of Things (IoT) devices and smartphones in the voting system, election and voting can be made straightforward and transparent. However, the data storage is still in the centralized store, which means that they remain at risk of a hacker's attack. Simultaneously, the transmission of the data from IoT devices to remote storage is another problem. In a traditional e-voting system, the voter's identity can be revealed and the device id provides evidence of voting. In an IoT-based voting system, if the device is cloned or the there is a "man-in-the-middle" attack, then the voting process is compromised and this leads to a failure of the system. Furthermore, a Distributed Denial of Services (DDoS) attack is possible in a traditional e-voting system. As the result of a DDoS attack, the voter cannot vote on time and the session is expired before voting. Accordingly, this is a violation of the right to vote. Managing user identity in a transaction in the Blockchain is an essential factor for the preservation of privacy. For example, to vote in a country the age and qualification are critical criteria. These may be done through the unique identification number of the voter's identity card. A voter's identity depends upon various factors, including the voter's address and the place in which the election is to take place.

In a decentralized and non-electronic system, paper-based identity management is processed. This is both vulnerable and alterable and can lead to identity fraud and impersonation. The same problem occurs with the e-voting system with IoT and cloud servers, where the devices are vulnerable and there is a high risk of identity fraud on such devices. Blockchain offers the promise of a trusted, privacy-preserving, transparent and decentralized data storage scheme. It uses the distributed ledger to store data in the immutable format and links between blocks using a hash. Cryptographic tools are used in Blockchain to secure the transmitted data between the nodes in a peer-to-peer manner. The digital signature and the one-way hash function measure both the authentication and the integrity of data. In a decentralized storage system, we can store our data in different systems and recall them when we want. In the Blockchain, elliptic curve cryptography is used for the digital signature and encryption of data. SHA-256 is used as a cryptographic hash function. According to Asamoah et al. [1], privacy preservation is imperative on a Blockchain platform since all of the data stored on a Blockchain is public and everyone can see it. It means that the credentials and data about the transactions made by participants on a Blockchain are publicly available.

The interplanetary file system (IPFS) is a decentralized file storage platform to store a Merkle-directed acyclic graph (DAG). In this, mostly large files can be stored in splitter hash formed in the different connected nodes. The root hash generated in Merkel DAG can retrieve these files. In some cases, files are not allowed to share with some nodes that do not provide consent for sharing. Without verifying the identity of nodes in the network, IPFS does not enable the sharing of files, especially in this case, when a node requires the sharing of chunks of a file [2]. The best e-voting model conceals the identity of the user mysterious and unidentifiable once the process is done. Smooth e-voting protects democracy. One reason behind the use of the Blockchain e-voting process is the transparency of records and the anonymity of participants [3]. Transaction malleability is identified as a threat for Blockchain-based applications as it leads to a double-spending attack [4]. We use elliptic curve cryptography and the ECDSA signature scheme as a cryptographic tool for the proposed system. The user interface and the IPFS is implemented in PHP-based Blockchain.

6.1.1 Motivations and Goals

The two critical challenges in e-voting are preserving the voter's identity and applying a GDPR audit to the system. In our attempt to address these issues, we list the following contributions made in this chapter:

i. The proposal of an e-voting system based on Blockchain and IPFS.
ii. The generation of the identity of voters, officers, and candidates and the protection of their identity.
iii. The proposed system follows GDPR audit, security analysis, comparison with previously developed systems and novel models.
iv. The proposed procedure of the storage and verification of tokens during various stages of polling.

6.1.2 Chapter Organization

Section 6.2 offers a literature review. Section 6.3 outlines the proposed system, along with the theoretical analysis. Section 6.4 is system implementation and experimental analysis of the proposed system. Section 6.5 discusses the results of the experiments and compares them with the previously developed systems. Section 6.6 is security and privacy analysis. Finally, conclusions are drawn in Section 6.7.

6.2 Literature Review

There are many models on the Blockchain-based e-voting system that have already been developed and still have some issues; here, we summarize the latest of them in a brief literature review. Babu & Dhore [5] used multilevel authentication to ensure the establishment of correct voter identity using Blockchain. In another contribution, Bellini et al. [6] described the privacy and security of voters in the Blockchain e-voting system, and they used agent-based modeling to implement Blockchain e-voting in ethereum. Braghin et al. [7] developed a model for e-voting based on ethereum. This was a system based on the same principles as Bitcoin and calculated hash working of proof-of-work. Khan et al. [8] proposed an e-voting model based on multi-chain Blockchain. They assigned tokens to the voters and candidates for identity purposes. Their proposed system is based on the Bitcoin generation method; at the time of casting a vote and also when it is being counted, a wallet is required. Verwer et al. [9] described a Blockchain-based e-voting model with key generation-based voter registration and auditing in the personal data. They used a Quick Response (QR) code for the private key of the voter. Their model used private key as voter's id, so if it is being stolen, then fraud voting is possible.

Awalu et al. [10] proposed a system dedicated to the stand-alone mobile interface for the voter's use. This involved the proposed auditability and security during the voting process and after the voting process tally of votes. Blockchain implemented in multi-chain Blockchain and used a proof-of-stake (PoS) consensus algorithm, including nonce and zero transaction fees. Watanavisit & Vorakulpipat [11] proposed an entire process of the e-voting system in the distributed ledger. In their system, no Blockchain is implemented and cryptographic keys are not used for identity and security. Politou et al. [12] proposed a model for the erasure of IPFS files from a node that does not want to store that file content or hash in their system. They used proof-of-ownership in their model. They used probabilistic polynomial time (PPT) for erasure time and consent management to protect data from erasure from all nodes. Mukne et al. [13] proposed a system for land record management in the IPFS and Blockchain. They manage land records in Hyperledger fabric. Their system has a lack of data privacy and identity security.

Kumar & Tripathi [14] proposed an IPFS-based student data-sharing system based on student data, yet this system is incompatible with maintaining the privacy and identity of students as they're sharing directly personally identifiable information of students in IPFS. Karapapas et al. [15] explained a ransomware attack performed in ethereum and IPFS Blockchain with key generation for the attacks, which releases the victim. They use proof-of-concept consensus with costing gas as per transactions. They use the Rinkeby test network for ethereum implementation. Pham et al. [16] proposed a Blockchain-based model for the storage of files using IPFS. Many certification authorities are used to store files in IPFS and users are connected through one ethereum Blockchain in their system. Their proposed system worked in high latency. Krejci et al. [17] proposed Blockchain and IPFS based e-voting system used multi-chain to deploy the Blockchain. Token use for the address of voters and candidates. Naz et al. [18] proposed a key selection-based voter registration with auditing, sorting is proposed. Private keys are in the form of a QR code.

Mamun et al. [19] presented a dedicated stand-alone mobile interface for the voter's uses. They proposed auditability and security during the voting process, and after the voting process a tally is made. They implemented Blockchain in multi-chain with PoS consensus algorithm with zero transaction fees. Li et al. [20] proposed a system based on the ethereum and bitcoin systems for e-voting. It takes a massive amount of gas burning, costing 57.15 euros for contract deployment and vote casting costs 18.60 euros. Makhdoom et al. [21] proposed an ethereum-based Blockchain for e-voting with the matching of identity in the time of voting. However, under this system a person can change their identity at any time. Kassem et al. [22] proposed a group signature-based Blockchain to sign a single transaction with multiple groups. They use multi-signatures with assets. Patole et al. [23] proposed a Blockchain system with privacy preservation to share data of assets and this was implemented using Hyperledger. Their system controls various Blockchain services using a single Blockchain.

In spite of the above e-voting systems which have been proposed previously, there are currently many gaps in the research Many e-voting systems are implemented using the ethereum Blockchain, a cost transaction in gas; in the real world of e-voting, this costs a tremendous amount of money. Some of them do not comply with the GDPR and find themselves unable to protect the identity of voters. Some used weak cryptographic methods and signatures. These research gaps are vital to the proposed enhanced identity management for the voters in the e-voting system using Blockchain.

6.3 A Proposed E-voting System in Blockchain

We divided our proposed system into four parts. These parts are:

i. Voter identity generation, registration and privacy preservation before voting.

  ii. Pre-voting process, candidate registration, authority verification and set up for voting.

  iii. Voting process, security and privacy management during the voting process.

  iv. Post-voting process, counting, result declaration and identity protection of voters.

For an explanation of the theoretical part of the proposed system, we are using some notations. A list of all notations in this chapter is given in Table 6.1. In Figure 6.1, the overall proposed system architecture is shown

6.3.1 Voter Identity Generation, Registration and Privacy Preservation before Voting

In this section, voter identity generation using the Elliptic Curve Digital Signature Algorithm (ECDSA), registration of identity with the authority and privacy preservation during this process are mentioned. In this process, registration is done in IPFS and it is available publicly.

  i. **Voter Identity Generation:** In this section, we generated the voter identity using a unique identification number (**UIN**) and the ECDSA. UIN is a 256-bit random generated number, which works as the input private key for the ECDSA and generates public key via this private key. Identity generation is shown in Figure 6.2.

Table 6.1 List of Notations Used in This Chapter

S.N.	Notation	Description
1	$hash(.)$	Hash function
2	$E(.)$	Encryption function
3	V_{pubk}	Voter public key
4	V_{privk}	Voter private key
5	R_{pubk}	Registrar public key
6	R_{privk}	Registrar private key
7	$EdDSA(.)$	Edward curve digital signature
8	$Hash_{IPFS}(.)$	Generated IPFS hash
9	$KeyPair(x_{pubk}, x_{privk})$	Elliptic curve key pair generator for x

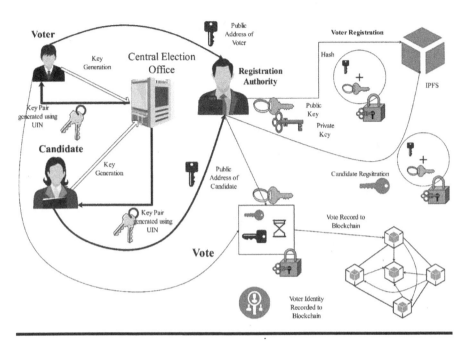

Figure 6.1   Overall proposed system architecture

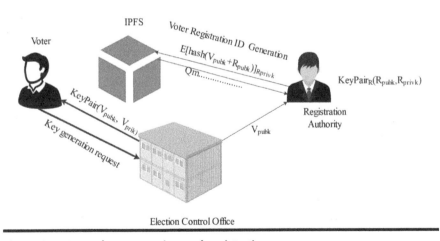

Figure 6.2   Voter key generation and registration process

ii. **Voter Registration:** A voter has to register their identification within the election authority. Thus, at the time of voting, the authority can verify the identity of the voter. For registration purposes, the voter public key is used as the primary field and the voter is verified with the local authority for authentic identity. Then, the authority-generated key within the token and ECDSA nodal to register the voter on the list authority-generated address is ORed with the private key of the voter and result hashed with a SHA256 hashing algorithm. This record is stored in the IPFS with the election commission.

iii. **Privacy Preservation before Voting:** Before the voting process, if anyone wants to know about an individual voter on the list, then they must have the voter's private key and the authority address to generate ORed result and then convert it to the 256-bit hash. Let anyone have both addresses and generate the hash. After all these processes, they cannot identify the person because no personally identifiable information is stored in the IPFS. So the adversary cannot verify the person whether or not the voter is the same person. This voting system also supports remote voting using IPFS and IPFS erasure processes.

6.3.2 Pre-voting Process, Candidate Registration, Authority Verification and Setup

The pre-voting process included preparing the list of eligible candidates and publication of the list of the candidates and the voters. The functions within this part of the system are as follows:

i. **Candidate Registration:** Candidates generate their public address using the Edward Curve Digital Signature Algorithm (**EdDSA**) with a random number. This public key is hashed with the registration authority's public address. The result of this operation generates the candidate's registration number for the election. The registration is stored with the IPFS in encrypted form with the private key of the registration authority.

ii. **Authority Verification and Setup:** At the final stage of registration for voting and fixing the candidature of candidates. The election authority had to verify this with the registration authority's public key and the candidate's public key hashed and match the stored IPFS file. If this match is successful, then candidature is verified.

ALGORITHM 6.1   E-VOTING PROCESS WITH IPFS

Terms: V = Voter, R = Registration Authority, hash(.) = SHA256, E(.) = Encryption Function, $KeyPair_{(Xpubk, Xprivk)}$ = Key Pair for x,
x_{pubk} = Public Key of x, , x_{privk} = Private Key of x, T = Timestamp
$Hash_{IPFS}(x)$ = IPFS hash of x
Pre-voting Process:-
1: $V \rightarrow R)$
2: $V \leftarrow R(KeyPair_{(Vpubk,Vprivk)}) \leftarrow Random(UIN)$ // Key pair Generation for Voter
3: $V_{regid} \leftarrow E(hash(V_{pubk} + R_{pubk}))$
4: $Hash_{IPFS}(E(hash(V_{pubk} + R_{pubk}))) \rightarrow StoredIPFS$

```
5:  C → R)
6:  C ← R(KeyPair_(Cpubk, Cprivk)) ← Random(CIN) + UIN  // Key
    pair Generation for Candidate
7:  C_regid ← E(hash(C_pubk + R_pubk))
8:  Hash_IPFS (E(hash(C_pubk + R_pubk)))→StoredIPFS
Voting Process:-
1:  Verify(V_regid) → True, then
2:  VoteProcess:
    EC ← EdDSA(Transaction(C_regid, V_regid + T_v,
    TransactionHash))_R
    (Vote as transaction)
    EC ← Approved (EdDSA(Transaction(C_regid, V_regid + T_v,
    TransactionHash))_R)
    Block = Block + 1 (Vote recorded to the Blockchain)
3:  Verify(V_regid) → False, then voter failed on
verification
Post-voting Process:
1:  VoteCount := Count(C_regid) ← Number of vote per candidate
2:  Result: = Highest number of vote
(Voter id generated at last vote submission table is V_regid
    + T)
```

6.3.3 Voting Process – Security and Privacy Management during Voting Process

There are two types of e-voting which can be carried out. First, the polling centers specially created and second from the devices for secured voting from remote locations. These two scenarios are:

1. When voters vote in the polling center, the registration authority must verify the voter's identity stored in the IPFS. The registration authority performs a hash operation with the voter's private key and matches with the IPFS stored hash. After the verification of voter's identity generated hash used for making transaction while voting. Polling is a transaction making by the hash generated in IPFS and approved by the signature of authority. The transaction structure is shown in Figure 6.3.

2. When a voter is in a remote station and wants to participate in the polling process, they must share the keys securely with the verification authority. The transaction structure is the same as in the first case. Each transaction in the Blockchain is counted as a vote. After ten transactions polling authority approved the transaction, these transactions are added to the block, and these blocks are added into the Blockchain. The voter verification and the voting process are shown in Figure 6.4.

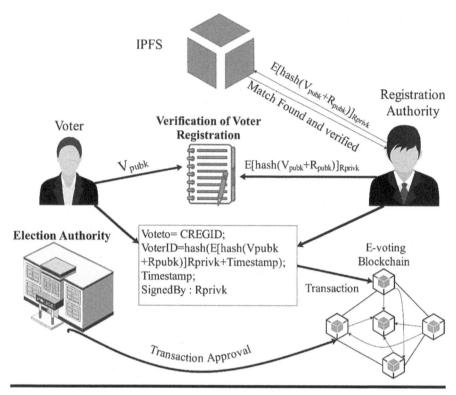

Figure 6.3   Transaction structure from voter for voting process

Voteto= CREGID;
VoterID=hash(E[hash(Vpubk+Rpubk)]Rprivk+Timestamp);
Timestamp;
SignedBy : Rprivk
Transaction To- Election Authority
Transaction Hash=(CREGID+Timestamp+VoterID+Rprivk)

Figure 6.4   Voter verification and voting process

6.3.4 Post-voting Process – Counting, Result Declaration and Identity

After polling, it is necessary to count the votes and to announce the result. The counting process in the total vote according to each candidate is calculated. The result is declared based on that. Voter's and registration authority's identity protection is done in Blockchain by generating ORed hash for vote transaction and registration number of the candidate.

6.4 System Implementation and Experimental Analysis

This section implemented the proposed system in Hypertext Preprocessor (PHP)-based Blockchain and IPFS. We were storing shared values in the MySQL database and immutable format database. The system remarks are shown in Table 6.2.

6.4.1 Key Generation

To generate a public address and private key for the voter, we used a 256-bit random number generator. This 256-bit number was known as UIN and used with ECDSA. This registration is stored in IPFS. An example of key generation for the voter is as follows:

UIN: 626988886
Hash of UIN: 374d3d0716d5a45fdd79209d4f0496a0e1f6e9b8a0462a93a a75498270b87ee8
Public Key:510e17df8e6611b37fd7ad367e3ecdc8c88f70391fccf28a2b96ab53 aef66106
Private Key: 374d3d0716d5a45fdd79209d4f0496a0e1f6e9b8a0462a93a a75498270b87ee8

Table 6.2 System Remarks

S.N.	Hardware/Software	Details
1	System configuration	AMD Athlon Processor, 12 GB RAM, 500 GB HDD
2	Operating system	Ubuntu 20.10
3	IPFS	Go Language
4	Front end	PHP, JavaScript
5	Back end	MySQL
6	Cryptographic tools	SHA-256, EdDSA (ed25519)

6.4.2 Candidate Registration

To register a candidate for the election an EdDSA-based 256-bit private and public key is generated. The candidate's public key is hashed with the EdDSA-based generated public key of the registration authority. This registration is then stored in IPFS. An example of candidate registration might be as follows:

Candidate_Identity (PublicKey): 374d3d0716d5a45fdd79209d4f0496a0e-1f6e9b8a0462a93aa75498270b87ee8

- Block Address: 34
- Polling Area: ABC
- Assembly Code:34
- Party: ABC
- Registrar Public Key:374d3d0716d5a45fdd79209d4f0496a0e1f6e9b8a0462a93aa75498270b899e8
- Registrar Private Key:510e17df8e6611b37fd7ad367e3ecdc8c88f70391fccf28a2b96ab53aef66106

6.4.3 Polling Process

At the polling center, a voter is verified by providing a private key in the portal and the verification officer ORed the private key with the registering officer's public key. The rest of the process is as follows: convert the result into the 256-bit hash to generate voter registration ID; match this ID with the voter ID stored in the IPFS; if a match is found, then the voter is able to cast their vote at the polling center.

During the polling window, voters have to press the symbol of the candidate or picture of the candidate, converted into the hash in transactions. This transaction is a Blockchain transaction and after every ten transactions a block is created by the polling authority. The transaction hash indicates that the voter has cast a vote. A voter can see the caste vote at the Blockchain window. This block is stored in a distributed system and all participated nodes in the polling process.

6.4.4 Counting and Results

During the polling process, the voter's vote is a transaction and is stored in all polling nodes. The hash generated by the election symbol is the same for all transactions. Therefore, for the election result, we have to count the number of the same hash generated for the candidate.

6.5 Analysis of Security and Privacy

6.5.1 Security Analysis

The election Blockchain has been implemented in the private network with interplanetary storage. A voter can cast their vote either in a polling center or through remote devices. For both processes it is necessary to ensure security in an open channel for the transaction of data. The following attacks on the system are possible and their prevention methods are as follows:

i. **Fake voter:** If a voter's private key is revealed and the attacker knows the public key of the registration authority, he can generate the registration identity of the voter. At the polling center, the registration ID matching process is done via IPFS; after the match, the poll button is enabled. In this method, there are the highest chances of the failure of voter registration ID and fake voting. For the remote voting method, the device and biometric identity generates the registration identity of the voter and sends that to the registration authority. When voters apply for the verification of a registered id at the polling process, a secure connection is established between the voter and the registration authority devices. After the matching of voter identity by the registration authority, the voter is enabled for voting. In this case, the authentication and non-repudiation of the registration authority's signature guarantee that a fake voter cannot vote.

ii. **Duplicate Voting:** If a voter wants to vote twice and tries to generate a double key to register identity, then he/she is required to register with the public key of the registrar and the required private key of the registration authority for signing the voter registration. Therefore, the attacker fails at the registration process and not able to vote again. In the remote voting registration process, the voter verification also falls at the time of voting and the attacker cannot vote twice.

iii. **Man-in-the-middle Attack:** In this attack, the adversary can listen to the voter's vote and disclose it. Let adversary A be the attacker in-network and sniff out the vote cast by voter Vn at timestamp Tm for candidate Ca. In this scenario, every value is composed of a hash and form of 256-bit hash. Thus, the voter's identity is not revealed and the candidate id is not revealed due to the combination of the registrar and candidate registration as a generation of the candidate's identity for reregistration.

iv. **Authentication:** For the authentication of voters and candidates, the registration authority and polling officers are responsible. In IPFS, the registration of polling officer, registrar, voter and candidates are already saved. At the time of verification, these details are matched from the record. If verification is successful, then the information signature is verified after the confirmation of the signature voter allowed to vote.

v. **Integrity:** In the voting process, the nodes are the polling centers, the verification officers and the election commission. So the transaction included the voter's temporary id generated for voting, vote and candidate's identity generated for the poll. The SHA256 hashes the transaction, and at the approver point this transaction hash is part of the Markle tree. In the final stage, the block contains this tree. At each point of approval, the hash is generated and the integrity is verified.

vi. **DDoS Attack:** Suppose that adversary A wants to attack in voting and wishes to interrupt the remote vote network using the DDoS attack. In order to do this, the adversary flooded the authority nodes with the meaningless request. At this point, the Blockchain network closes the authority system as this is a distributed and decentralized The SHA256 hashes the transaction, and at the approver, point this transaction hash is part of the Markle tree network. Then the authority moved to the new system with the same identity. In this way, DDoS attacks and is prevented by the authority system. For the voting node, if the DDoS attack is performed in the insecure online network, then the only ten identified votes are mined at once and after the one-time system is restarted automatically if DDoS halting is detected.

6.5.2 Privacy Maintenance and GDPR Compliance

In this proposed system, the goal is to maintain the voter's identity from the registration to the counting process. The following point is proof of privacy maintenance during the process and compliance with GDPR.

I. **Identity generation of voter and voting process:** A key generation UIN is used as the necessary information, a randomly generated integer with 256 bits. This UIN is hashed with SHA256 and used EdDSA to create key pairs for the voter. Therefore, if an adversary has the UIN, they can generate the key pair for the voter registration. In the registration process, the private key of the registrar is in concatenation with the public key of the voter. This process generates the voter's registration identity, which is stored in the IPFS. If an adversary knows this information, he can try to create the registration identity of voters, but no personal information is available at any point in any registration stage. So the adversary is unable to identify the voter.

II. **After the voting process:** The transaction is in the form of a vote initiated by the voter to the election authority. In this transaction, the hashing and signature verification of voter registration is done by the registration authority. In the voting process's transparency mode, the voter identity generated in the final transaction of the vote is in the format of the concatenation of the previous transaction hash, registration authority private key and voter registration identity. Therefore, the adversary cannot combine any of them at any time. Every transaction hashes the timestamp and this timestamp is unique, meaning that this transaction or any data is not generated again. In this way, the adversary is unable to identify the voter.

6.6 Comparisons and Results

To prove the strength of our proposed system, we compared it with previously developed systems. Table 6.3 shows the advantages of our proposed system over the previously developed systems. In the resulting point of view, we are discussing the following points as the strength of our proposed system:

i. **Storage:** from the storage point of view, the proposed system storage used the public IPFS for the key storage requires 74 bytes for the voter data and 74 bytes for the candidate data in single voter and single candidate cases. After the polling process, the vote transaction needs 78 bytes of storage. Previously developed system storage and proposed system storage comparisons are illustrated in Figure 6.5. The total IPFS storage required for a single instance is 228 bytes.

ii. **Cost:** The proposed system is implemented using the customized PHP-based Blockchain with public IPFS storage. A one-time installation cost is required for this Blockchain. No transaction cost is needed for the polling process or the counting process, as previously developed systems in the ethereum required the burning of ether and gas to complete the process. Proof-of-Work (**PoW**)-based systems require high computation power. In our proposed system, however, this type of cost is not required. Cost comparisons with the previously developed system are shown in Figure 6.6. For setting a system cost in terms of the amount needed to run the script the figures are as follows: for the key generation of voter 405.13 kb; for the key generation of the candidate 403.7 kb; for voter registration 406.84kb; for candidate registration 408.84kb; and to vote 406.13kb. Thus, the required total cost of script setup is 2030.64kb.

iii. **Privacy and Security:** In Section 6.5, security and privacy analysis are done. Our proposed system is secure against various attacks and maintains the privacy of voter identity, when compared with the previously developed systems.

iv. **Time for transactions:** The time required for the key generation per voter is 0.09245s. The time needed for the registration of a voter is 0.14422s. The time required for voting is 0.42541s. The time required by the key generation per candidate is 0.36245s. The time needed for the registration of a candidate is 0.20509s. The time required for voting is 0.42541s. The time needed for counting and result declaration is 0.37573s. This means that the total time needed for a single voter through the complete process is 1.60535s. The time

Table 6.3 Comparison between the Previously Developed Systems and the Proposed System

Property	Braghin et al. [7]	Khan et al. [8]	Verwer et al. [9]	Awalu et al. [10]	Proposed system
Data Encryption	Yes	No	No	No	Yes
Public/Private	Private	Public	Private	Private	Private
Platform	Ethereum	Ethereum	Consortium	Multichain	PHP based customized
Consensus algorithm	Proof-of-work	Proof-of-work	Proof-of-work	Proof-of-work	Proof-of-work
Security Analysis	No	No	No	No	Yes
Privacy Protection	No	No	No	No	Yes
Remote Voting	Yes	Yes	Yes	Yes	Yes
IPFS-based	No	No	No	No	Yes

Note: Yes= feature supported, No= feature not supported by system

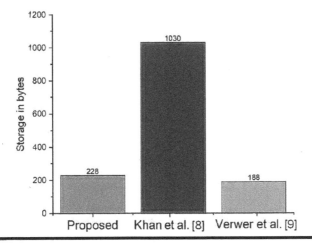

Figure 6.5 Single voter data storage in different systems

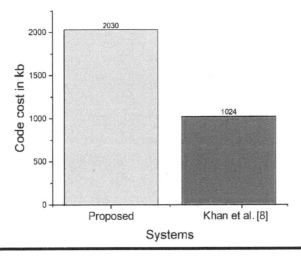

Figure 6.6 Code implementation cost in kb in different systems

required for the whole process in previously developed systems is compared in Figure 6.7.

v. **Hash and Encryption bits required:** in key generation, SHA256 and EdDSA are used to generate the 512 bits required. For registration, 830 bits are needed. For the polling process and signature verification, 256 bits of the hash are required. The proposed system hash functions required in its implementation are shown in Figure 6.8. For a single voter and candidate total, nine hash and four encryptions are needed for the entire process.

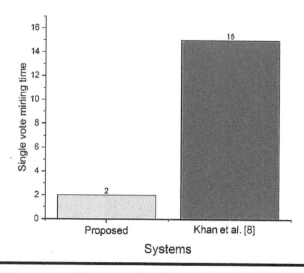

Figure 6.7 Time required for system implementation in different systems

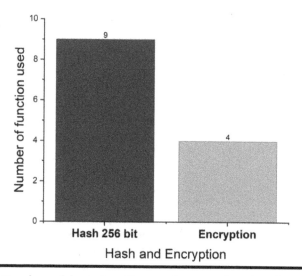

Figure 6.8 Number of hash functions and encryption functions used in the proposed system

6.7 Conclusion and Future Work

In this chapter, we have proposed a Blockchain-based secure, voter privacy-preserving e-voting system. We design transaction and block validation protocols to share votes between the voter and the election authority. This proposed system is protected from intruder and identity theft-type attacks. The comparison section shows that our proposed system is superior to any previously developed systems in terms of security and privacy concerns. Overall, our work provides various benefits to the Blockchain-based election and voter identity security, which are superior to the earlier developed systems. In future research, we will be applying this model to higher education and skilled employment management services. Furthermore, we can undertake more analysis on the security of Blockchain nodes in different attack scenarios with distinct node malfunctions.

References

[1] Asamoah, K.O., Xia, H., Amofa, S., Amankona, O.I., Luo, K., Xia, Q., Gao, J., Du, X. and Guizani, M., 2020. Zero-chain: A blockchain-based identity for digital city operating system. *IEEE Internet of Things Journal*, 7(10), pp. 10336–10346.

[2] Khan, K.M., Arshad, J. and Khan, M.M., 2020. Simulation of transaction malleability attack for blockchain-based e-voting. *Computers & Electrical Engineering*, 83, p. 106583.

[3] Steichen, M., Fiz, B., Norvill, R., Shbair, W. and State, R., 2018, July. Blockchain-based, decentralized access control for IPFS. In *2018 IEEE International Conference on Internet of Things (iThings) and IEEE Green Computing and Communications (GreenCom) and IEEE Cyber, Physical and Social Computing (CPSCom) and IEEE Smart Data (SmartData)* (pp. 1499–1506).

[4] Reddy, M.N.K. and Reddy, L.M.M., 2020, June. An integrated and robust e-voting application using private blockchain. In *2020 4th International Conference on Trends in Electronics and Informatics (ICOEI)* (48184) (pp. 842–846). IEEE.

[5] Babu, A. and Dhore, V.D., 2020. Electronic polling agent using blockchain: A new approach. In *IC-BCT 2019* (pp. 69–77). Springer, Singapore.

[6] Bellini, E., Ceravolo, P. and Damiani, E., 2019, July. Blockchain-based e-Vote-as-a-Service. In *2019 IEEE 12th International Conference on Cloud Computing (CLOUD)* (pp. 484–486). IEEE.

[7] Braghin, C., Cimato, S., Cominesi, S.R., Damiani, E. and Mauri, L., 2019, June. Towards Blockchain-Based E-Voting Systems. In *International Conference on Business Information Systems* (pp. 274–286). Springer, Cham.

[8] Khan, K.M., Arshad, J. and Khan, M.M., 2020. Investigating performance constraints for blockchain based secure e-voting system. *Future Generation Computer Systems*, 105, pp. 13–26.

[9] Verwer, M.B., Dionysiou, I. and Gjermundrød, H., 2019, December. Trusted E-Voting (TeV) a Secure, Anonymous and Verifiable Blockchain-Based e-Voting Framework. In *International Conference on e-Democracy* (pp. 129–143). Springer, Cham.

[10] Awalu, I.L., Kook, P.H. and Lim, J.S., 2019, July. Development of a Distributed Blockchain eVoting System. In *Proceedings of the 2019 10th International Conference on E-business, Management and Economics* (pp. 207–216).

[11] Watanavisit, S.T. and Vorakulpipat, C., 2020, February. Learning Citizenship in Practice with School Vote System: A Participatory Innovation of Blockchain e-Voting System for Schools in Thailand. In *Proceedings of the 2020 9th International Conference on Educational and Information Technology* (pp. 254–258).

[12] Politou, E., Alepis, E., Patsakis, C., Casino, F. and Alazab, M., 2020. Delegated content erasure in IPFS. *Future Generation Computer Systems*, 112, pp. 956–964.

[13] Mukne, H., Pai, P., Raut, S. and Ambawade, D., 2019, July. Land Record Management using Hyperledger Fabric and IPFS. In *2019 10th International Conference on Computing, Communication and Networking Technologies (ICCCNT)* (pp. 1–8). IEEE.

[14] Kumar, R. and Tripathi, R., 2020. Blockchain-based framework for data storage in peer-to-peer scheme using interplanetary file system. In Krishnan, S., Balas, V.E., Julie, E.G., Robinson, Y.H., Balaji, S., and Kumar, R. (eds.) *Handbook of Research on Blockchain Technology* (pp. 35–59). Academic Press.

[15] Karapapas, C., Pittaras, I., Fotiou, N. and Polyzos, G.C., 2020, May. Ransomware as a Service using Smart Contracts and IPFS. In *2020 IEEE International Conference on Blockchain and Cryptocurrency (ICBC)* (pp. 1–5). IEEE.

[16] Pham, V.D., Tran, C.T., Nguyen, T., Nguyen, T.T., Do, B.L., Dao, T.C. and Nguyen, B.M., 2020, October. B-Box-A Decentralized Storage System Using IPFS, Attributed-based Encryption, and Blockchain. In *2020 RIVF International Conference on Computing and Communication Technologies (RIVF)* (pp. 1–6). IEEE.

[17] Krejci, S., Sigwart, M. and Schulte, S., 2020, September. Blockchain-and IPFS-based data distribution for the Internet of Things. In *European Conference on Service-Oriented and Cloud Computing* (pp. 177–191). Springer, Cham.

[18] Naz, M., Al-Zahrani, F.A., Khalid, R., Javaid, N., Qamar, A.M., Afzal, M.K. and Shafiq, M., 2019. A secure data sharing platform using blockchain and interplanetary file system. *Sustainability*, 11(24), p. 7054.

[19] Al Mamun, M.A., Alam, S.M., Hossain, M.S. and Samiruzzaman, M., 2020, March. A Novel Approach to Blockchain-Based Digital Identity System. In *Future of Information and Communication Conference* (pp. 93–112). Springer, Cham.

[20] Li, C., Wang, L.E., Xu, Q., Li, D., Liu, P. and Li, X., 2020, June. Groupchain: A Blockchain Model with Privacy-preservation and Supervision. In *Proceedings of the 2020 4th International Conference on High Performance Compilation, Computing and Communications* (pp. 42–49).

[21] Makhdoom, I., Zhou, I., Abolhasan, M., Lipman, J. and Ni, W., 2020. PrivySharing: A blockchain-based framework for privacy-preserving and secure data sharing in smart cities. *Computers & Security*, 88, p. 101653.

[22] Alsayed Kassem, J., Sayeed, S., Marco-Gisbert, H., Pervez, Z. and Dahal, K., 2019. DNS-IdM: A blockchain identity management system to secure personal data sharing in a network. *Applied Sciences*, 9(15), p. 2953.

[23] Patole, D., Borse, Y., Jain, J. and Maher, S., 2020. Personal Identity on Blockchain. In Sharma H., Govindan K., Poonia R., Kumar S., El-Medany W. (eds) *Advances in Computing and Intelligent Systems* (pp. 439–446). Springer, Singapore.

Chapter 7

Blockchain-Enabled Secure Internet of Vehicles: A Solution Taxonomy, Architecture, and Future Directions

Mohd Zuhair, Pronaya Bhattacharya, Ashwin Verma, and Umesh Bodkhe
Nirma University, India

Contents

DOI: 10.1201/9781003129486-7

7.1 Introduction

The recent advances and development of the automobile industry with the integration of the Internet of Things (IoT) has created an enhanced driving experience. The vehicles and the surrounding support system are equipped with numerous sensors that generate heterogenous data through advanced on-board devices [1]. The vehicles share, collect, and perform computations on the generated data to create an intelligent transportation system. According to the requirements and expectations of users, technology in today's scenario must be scalable, flexible, and convenient; it also requires continuous updates. As far as the transport system is concerned, the researchers integrate various technologies, such as IoT, vehicular ad hoc networks (VANET), cloud computing, IoV, and Artificial Intelligence (AI) to design an intelligent transportation system.

Bearing in mind the increased population, the number of vehicles, and their users, IoV has become one of the most profitable ecosystem in today's world. The vehicles are equipped with smart devices, such as sensors and data communication modules, which are being used to broadcast information such as speed, road conditions, etc. to other vehicles and roadside units (RSU). The three main components of communication in IoV are inter-vehicle, intra-vehicle, and vehicle mobile Internet [2]. Communication in IoV includes different types of vehicles, ongoing passengers, bicycle riders, and pedestrians. The communication of IoV can be categorized into five distinct types: i) Vehicle-to-Vehicle (V2V); ii) Vehicle-to-Personal devices (V2P); iii) Vehicle-to-Roadside Units (V2R); iv) Vehicle-to-Sensors (V2S); v) Vehicle-to-Infrastructure of cellular networks (V2IC).

The devices share multivariate data, such as audio, video, sensor readings, and text messages. The sharing of data in the IoV creates the issues of data privacy such as data tampering, identity counterfeiting, and sensitive information disclosure. For example, Sybil attacks for counterfeiting the identity, it fakes the identity of the vehicle to control other vehicles through the counterfeit node. Through counterfeit nodes, it sends false information to the connected server in order to misrepresent the traffic conditions, which might result in in either a traffic jam or accidents. Therefore, given such dangers it is crucial to secure the vehicle's privacy (identity, location, history of the driver, etc.) and the authentication of the message. The challenges, such as privacy-preserving [3], broad-cast collision-avoidance, and resource scheduling [4], adversely affect the circulation of the vehicle data. Thus, the issues of privacy protection in IoV may lead to low adoption of the proposed technology.

Blockchain is an emerging trend in the computing system, which designed to secure the shared information among different entities in a network. Recently, the integration of Blockchain technology with IoV has attracted increasing attention on the part of both researchers and developers because of the decentralization, anonymity, and trust characteristics of the Blockchain [5]. A secure trusted, and decentralized intelligent transport ecosystem is established by the Blockchain to solve vehicle data-sharing problems. Some of the largest global automobile companies, such as Volkswagen and Ford, have integrated Blockchain to secure communication between vehicles, and they have even filed the patent for this technology [6]. Research in this field is now moving towards designing the proof of driving and the privacy prevention mechanism using Blockchain to support safe and secure data transmission and communication between vehicles [7], and secure and authorized unmanned aerial vehicular communication for military, healthcare and other services [8].

There are a few pertinent issues which should be borne in mind when implementing Blockchain in IoV. For example, the existing Blockchain systems have a tendency to be either too weak or too strong. The Zerocoin and Monero Blockchain systems [9, 10], for instance, protect user privacy by implementing ring signature or zero-knowledge proof [11]. In the case of IoV, vehicles' privacy should be made conditional. If zero-knowledge proof or ring signature is used, then revealing the true identity of a vehicle will become a challenging task [12]. The developed cities will have a large-sized IoV deployment; given the large number of vehicles in the city, this will generate huge volumes and varieties of data over a short period of time. Therefore, there would be a need for a Blockchain network that can store this huge volume of data efficiently and quickly [13].

7.1.1 Architecture, Characteristics, and Application of IoV

The architecture of IoV endorses the existing vehicular ad hoc networks (VANETs) with new advancements. The comparison between VANET and IoV is presented in Table 7.1. Kaiwartya *et al.* [14] have proposed the five-layer architecture as presented in Table 7.2. The five layers are perception, coordination, artificial intelligence (AI), application, and business layers [14]. Each of the layers has its own particular functionality.

IoV has similar characteristics to IoT, but IoV is much more complex and dynamic in nature as the vehicles are mobile and move quickly in and out of the system. This makes the IoV system highly mobile, involving a short duration of connection within a specific network. The vehicles may have different drivers, which will impact the communication between the vehicles and the driver. The V2S will depend on the driver and different drivers will also impact the V2S communication. The vehicle is moving that will frequently change the V2R as well as V2I communications. Thus, IoV will change much more frequently than the IoT due to changes in drivers, vehicles, sensors, and roads.

The size of the network of vehicles is dynamic and depends on the population density of the city. The number of vehicles is increasing on a daily basis and the movement of vehicles depends on various factors, such as office timings, vacations,

Table 7.1 Comparison of VANET and IoV

Features	VANET	IoV
Goal	To improve traffic safety, avoid causalities, and upgrade the traffic effectiveness (Time, cost, and environment) but lack in entertainment features for passengers.	To enhance traffic safety, efficiency, and commercial infotainment.
Communication	Two kinds of communications i) V2I; ii) (V2V)	Five types of communication i) V2V; ii) V2R; iii) V2I; iv) V2S; v) V2P.
Compatibility	Compatibility issues with personal devices (smartphones, laptops, etc.)	Personal devices are compatible with IoV
Range	The range is local and suitable for limited scale	Global scope and sustainable
Processing	Limited computing power	Involves big data and using advanced computing techniques (Fog computing, Edge computing, etc.)
Network	Uses singleton network architecture	Uses heterogeneous networks (WAVE, Wi-Fi, 4G/LTE, satellite networks)
Data size	limited data as decision making is done based on the local information	Big data as a huge amount of data is generated in real-time
Cloud Computing	Not Supported in VANET	Cloud computing is used for storage, processing, and data analysis

etc. Therefore, the network that handles the IoV must be scalable and have the ability to adapt according to the demand.

The applications of IoV can be divided into four broad categories: i) Safety applications; ii) Comfort and entertainment; iii) Efficiency and management of traffic; and iv) Healthcare applications [15]. The safety aspect is to reduce and avoid road accidents. The intention is to provide proactive messages about traffic and road conditions to the driver. Entertainment applications in the IoV are designed to increase

Table 7.2 Architecture of IoV

Layers	Visualization	Function
Business	Graphics, flowchart, diagram, table	Investment and business model design; resource utilization and pricing for application; and budgeting and data aggregation
Application	Intelligent applications for vehicles dynamics	intelligent service user; discovery and integration of services; usage of data and corresponding statistics
AI	Cloud computing, expert systems, data analytics	Storage, processing, and analysis of data; decision making based on analysis; service management
Coordination	Diversified networks like WIFI, LTE	Unified transformation; interoperability provisions; secure exchange of information
Perception	The sensor of vehicles, RSU, personal devices (PD)	Data collection: vehicle, traffic, PD; digitization and communication; energy optimization

travellers' comfort. Gaming, searching the nearest restaurants, drama and movie theatre, coffee bar, parking slot, video streaming, car-pooling, etc. are all different examples of entertainment [16].

The efficiency and management of traffic in IoV are designed to avoid accidents and to prevent congestion by optimizing the flow of the traffic. The vehicles' drivers are informed in advance about traffic situations that allow them to divert their routes if required, thereby reducing travel time [17]. The healthcare applications are done through wireless body sensors networks to provide better communication between patients and healthcare professionals. Personal health information, such as blood pressure, body temperature, etc., is gathered and transmitted through body sensors. The outside environment conditions are transmitted by the ambient sensors to the health center's [18].

7.1.2 Platform for IoV

The traditional vehicle has basic controllers such as microcontrollers (MCU) and digital signal processing (DSP) to process the data generated from various components of the vehicle. Functions such as air conditioning, the operation of the tail light, driver assistance functions, and so on are operated through these controllers [19]. In contrast to that, in the IoV network, the processor has to compute millions of lines of code to execute the intelligent algorithms. Therefore, it requires a powerful computation platform, which has appropriate hardware and software capabilities.

The graphics processing unit (GPU) and field-programmable gate arrays (FPGA) have a wider application in the field automobile industry in the future. The GPU has the capability of image processing using parallel computing [20]. This makes GPU ideal for complex systems in self-driving like obstacle detection and collision avoidance. The FPGA is capable of parallel computing with optimized energy usage.

The software module is another crucial component for the IoV platform. The software for the automotive industry has its own customized requirements. The European automotive industry has developed a real-time operating system OSEK/VDX for automotive applications [21]. Japan has established an Automotive Software Platform and Architecture (JASPAR) in 2004 with the collaboration of automobile companies such as Honda, Nissan, and Toyota. The OSEK/VDX and JASPAR have the drawback of not incorporating the demand of re-usability for the current automotive industry. The AUTO-motive Open System Architecture (AUTOSAR) standard was developed to separate the software applications from the associated hardware. It has reduced the development cost, but needs further improvement to support AI applications [22]. The AUTOSAR, in collaboration with its global partners, is developing an adaptive platform to provide the programming interface that supports Ethernet-based architectures.

The existing nature of the software industry has concerns for the security and updating their products and services [23]. The same can be experienced while using Android smartphones. The new versions and updates are available for the phone as well as the applications installed on the phone. Similarly, in the case of IoV it is necessary to install new versions and updates of the software that are already being installed in the vehicle. Security during the updates is very important and has become an interesting research topic for researchers [24].

The network of IoV has to observe the vehicles as well as the surroundings. The situation beyond the range of the normal vision will also be required in the IoV to optimize the path for the vehicle; therefore, the vehicles are required to install the advanced sensors. These sensors shall detect and classify the objects in both normal and adverse weather and lighting conditions. The inputs from the sensors must be reliable to ensure the safe functionality of the vehicle.

The combination or fusion of the multiple sensors is used to ensure the reliability and robustness of the information of the surroundings [25]. The commonly used sensors for IoV are Light Detection and Ranging (LiDAR), visual sensors, and Radar. LiDAR enables the vehicles to observe the outside world. This will provide a 360-degree view of the world through different laser channels. The multimedia wave Radar was deployed in high-end vehicles. This radar can penetrate non-transparent material such as snow, dust, and fog. The monocular visual and stereo vision systems are the two important intelligent visual sensors deployed in automated vehicles. At present, they are being used for the detection of a target, fatigue detection, etc. [26]. AI techniques such as deep learning are used with the inputs of the visual sensors to produce accurate results [27]. The drawback of visual sensors is its sensitivity to external conditions like light and weather. Therefore, rather than relying on one type of sensor data at the moment, the fusion of different sensor data makes it possible to fuse different information from the different sensors to ensure reliability.

7.2 The Security Aspect of IoV

The benefits of IoV are evident, but they come with the challenges and issues concerned with security, authentication, and privacy within the network. Security is one of the major issues in IoV as the hacker or intruder may gain access to and control of the vehicle with an ulterior motive [28], and may then induce traffic accidents. Attackers can intercept, modify, reproduce, and stall the messages disseminated in the IoV network [29]. In the case of the messages being altered and then disseminated then the vehicles may be diverted towards dense traffic and issues of road accidents, parking problems, etc. might be the outcome. Therefore, to make the IoV affective, to be used in a practical scenario, the security challenges and issues must be addressed first.

The primary security requirement for the IoV is to identify the security goals of the IoV network. These security goals are confidentiality, authentication, data integrity, nonrepudiation, access control, privacy, etc. Confidentiality ensures that privacy and secrecy shall be provided for the communication of sensitive data [30]. The authentication ensures that the sender of messages is authentic. Data integrity ensures that the generated data shall not be altered by any means. The non-repudiation mechanism prevents the denying of sender/receiver about the transmitted messages [31]. The access control measure will assign different privileges to the participating vehicles/nodes in the network. This will ensure that each node shall perform its assigned functions based on the entitled services. The privacy ensures that the driving traces, history, and the drivers' information shall not be revealed to an unauthorized person.

The security challenges for IoV can be categorized into the following aspects: error tolerance, key management for encryption and decryption of messages, scalability, stability, security, the privacy of the network, and the mobility of the vehicle. The error tolerance in the IoV network is high when compared to the IoT network. The problem of network quality and low bandwidth can be a deterrent to real-time communication. A slight delay in communication and a minor mistake can lead to fatal accidents [32]. Key management is vital in encrypting and decrypting sensitive communications due to a large number of nodes; it creates a huge overhead in the IoV network [33]. The IoV requires a large amount of data storage and high-performance computers for analysis. Therefore, cloud services are used for data management and computing. Data transmission between the user and the cloud platform has potential hazards. Therefore, in order to preserve privacy, efficient encryption techniques are required for data transmission and data storage [34].

7.3 Taxonomy of IoV Attacks

IoV is vulnerable to numerous types of attacks and threats. The threats to the security of IOV must be proactively resolved in order for it to be deployed successfully. However, the prediction of every possible threat to the network is not feasible in a practical scenario; therefore, reactive approaches shall be effective. Figure 7.1 presents a taxonomy that focuses on two major attack scenarios: i) Authentication-based, and ii) Accountability-based attacks. The details of these are presented below:

7.3.1 Authentication

■ *Wormhole Attack*: A wormhole attack is a well-known issue in wireless networking. It is generally performed by two or more attackers/nodes who place themselves at strategic positions in the network. They utilize their strategic location and advertise among other nodes that they have the shortest path for transmitting the information. Through this, the attacker creates a direct link between each other and the attacker at one end receives the packet and transmit/tunnel the same to the other side of the network. The attack can be performed without compromising any of the hosts/nodes by the attacker.

■ *Sybil Attack*: The Sybil attack is one of the most dangerous attacks on IoV. A Sybil attack *occurs* when a node behaves as if it were legitimate, but creates multiple false identities by changing the MAC/IP addresses or any other identifying information. This creates confusion for the centralized authority in terms of identifying the legitimate nodes. Therefore, the vehicles/nodes are unable to distinguish whether or not the information is coming from a single or a multiple vehicle/node. The Sybil attack is classified as both the most

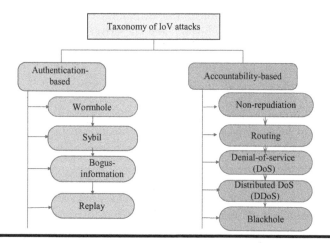

Figure 7.1   Taxonomy of selected attacks in IoV ecosystem [35]

dangerous as well as the most difficult to detect. The attacker can use this to divert the traffic by creating a large number of identities at a particular location, which give the impression that there is huge traffic in a particular portion of the road.

■ *Bogus Information Attack*: In bogus information attacks, the vehicle could generate and send false information to the network. The attacker intends to manipulate other vehicles in the network with *malicious* intent. A vehicle in IoV can generate false information about an accident on the road and send that false information to other vehicles in the network to divert the route. Through this, the attacker can also create the congestion by diverting several vehicles on a particular road. This attack is computationally inexpensive and very commonly used due to its huge impact on the IoV. If an attacker can convince only a single vehicle, then that vehicle would unknowingly become an attacker and start propagating the falsified information to the other vehicles in the network.

■ *Replay Attacks*: The replay attacks are related to blackhole attacks (discussed below) and are a variation on man-in-the-middle attacks. The attackers continually resend the valid frames to disrupt the real-time functioning of IoV. In this, the attacker can gather and store the *information*; at some later point, can send the same into the network, even though that information is invalid. In IoV, the attacker can save the information regarding the previous traffic congestion, accidents, etc., and then he can send the same to the network later.

7.3.2 Attacks on Accountability

■ *Non-repudiation attack*: In this, the vehicle can deny the reception or transmission of messages. This causes the sender to retransmit the message, thereby consuming extra resources of the network and causing a delay in the IoV network.

■ *Denial of Service attacks (DoS)*: Denial-of-service (DoS) attacks come in many forms, all of which prevent the normal functioning *of* the system. The attacks are attempted by the non-legitimate users to exhaust the resources, flooding the host/server in the network by sending a large number of bogus packets/messages to overload it. Thus, these resources will be unable to service the legitimate user's requests. In IoV, an attacker can attempt to shut down the network established by RSUs; this will close the communication between vehicles and RSUs. Among the well-known DoS attacks are JellyFish, flooding, and intelligent cheater attacks [36, 37]. The DoS attacks can be attempted by anybody having a little knowledge of networking. The attack may block communications and vehicles will stop receiving real traffic events. The impact and the probability of the attack are very high; therefore, it must be detected as quickly as possible and the response must be activated in a timely manner.

■ *Distributed Denial-of-service attacks (DDoS)*: In DoS attacks, the attacker uses a single IP address to generate the attack, and therefore it places a considerable burden on the resources of the attacker. In DDoS, the attacker uses multiple IP addresses of compromised systems to attack the targeted *system*. The flooding of bogus packets/messages to the target system will force the target system to deny the service to legitimate users. Like DoS, DDoS attacks can be executed on both RSUs and other vehicles in a network. The DDoS attacks are even tougher to tackle and mitigate, as the messages are coming from different IP addresses.

■ *Blackhole attack*: Blackhole attacks are very common in communication systems. In this, the attacker exploits routing protocols by sending a piece of fake routing information in the network, claiming that it has an optimum route for the destination (vehicle/RSU). The broadcast of false routing information in the network makes the RSU/vehicles send the messages/packets through the attacker's node. The attacker has control of the node and generally discards the incoming messages thus it creates a hole from where no packets/messages can circulate within the network. The attack can have very serious implications on the performance of the IoV network. The consequences of the attack are life-critical as the packet/message loss may lead to severe accidents.

7.4 Blockchain-Based Secured IoV Ecosystem

Blockchain has attracted the interest of many researchers in areas where security is a big concern. It is a chain of immutable blocks that keep all the transactional details of any participating members in the network. Each block in the Blockchain is partitioned into header and body. The header contains information about itself and other blocks and these are linked together, similar to a linked list. The first block is called the genesis block. It maintains the ownership of every transaction and it does not point to any previous block. Each transaction on a Blockchain will require a key pair (public-private) for the validation of data. Each block of Blockchain uses a private key for validating the transactions [38].

The application of Blockchain is enormous and researchers have implemented it in almost every field where security is a concern. Similarly in IoV, researchers have proposed the Blockchain models to trace, control, and ownership of the messages/content that is being shared in the IoV network.

Blockchain technology is an important component in managing the information generated from IoV. The communication in the IoV (V2I, V2V, V2R, etc.) can be made secure through the use of the Blockchain platform. The transaction in IoV can be an observation or any activity of the vehicle, such as traffic, weather information, etc. The platform stores every transaction generated by vehicle and RSU in the blocks of a Blockchain network.

The Blockchain allows the decentralized, anonymous, secure, and traceable content in the distributed network, as presented in Table 7.3. The implementation of Blockchain technology for IoV can be summarized as follows:

1. *Big Data Storage and Data Management*: The IoV will generate data from the sensors from inside as well as outside the vehicle, including driving patterns, traffic data, human–computer interfaces, and RSU. The data will also include

Table 7.3 Integration of Blockchain and IoV

Feature of Blockchain	Description	Impact on IoV
Immutability	Each node in the IoV shall have a digital copy of the transaction	Fault-tolerant, transparent, non-corruptible, and organized
Decentralized	No central governing body	Third-party is not required, user control reduced chances of a breakdown
Consensus	The participating nodes have the authority for approval of the transaction	Enhances reliability, transparent and fast transactions
Security	Ensures security and privacy through cryptographic hash functions	Creation of privacy preserved transportation system
Transparency	The transactions are stored in each node and open for scrutiny	Build trust among nodes
Time-stamped records	Each block is time-stamped before being added to the Blockchain network	Ordering of each event in the intelligent transportation system
Traceability	Identification of each recorded data	The timestamped data record ensures identify the chronology order of events
Non-Repudiation	The integrity and proof of origin for data	Once the transactions are recorded successfully then the IoV network cannot deny it
Pseudo Identity	The user name, keys, and digital signatures are used for the identification of the user	The vehicles and RSU's can be identified with their public key and username

e-commerce transactions, vehicle insurance, refuelling, etc. The vehicles, as well as the road network, is increasing and the data generated by them will have high volume. This means that the concept of centralized and distributed storage of Blockchain can be utilized. The Blockchain is adopted to resolve the concerns of security privacy concerns, as well as to build trust among the edge nodes [39]. The immutability feature of Blockchain is applied in order to secure the data communication among the vehicles [40].

2. *Resource Sharing*: In IoV, there are opportunities that the vehicles can share the resources among themselves. This will enable the vehicles to share the spare computational resources with nearby entities. The benefits of this are obvious, but there are also implementation issues. The two major issues are: (i) building trust among the parties; and (ii) providing economic benefits to encourage participation in resource sharing. The Blockchain supports the decentralized platform and the nodes can share their resources. The Blockchain will ensure trust-building and will take care of the security and privacy concerns [41, 42]. In this chapter, a reputation-based consensus mechanism is presented to establish trust among parties and to decrease the dependency on the computationally costly mining process. The incentive schemes for resource sharing are designed that provide a 30% better costing than the unified pricing scheme.

3. *Vehicle Management*: The management of vehicles, RSU, parking lots, and other resources is a complicated task. The most well-known issues for vehicle management are vehicle platooning and smart parking. The problem with the increasing number of vehicles is parking management as well as the maintenance of the privacy and security of the user using a central management system. The Blockchain is implemented to address these issues of data leakage [43]. The researchers have developed a Blockchain integrated platform to search the available parking spots to do the bookings [44]. The platooning is done usually for long-distance transportation of cargo through heavy vehicles with the concept of reducing the air friction, thus improving the fuel efficiency. The researchers have proposed a platform for Blockchain-enabled IoV platform to create the group of anonymous vehicles that can be referred to as platoon [45]. The vehicles do not have to pay to be part of the platoon and it uses matching of the path to select the matching vehicles for the platoon

   a. *Decentralization and Redundancy*: The properties of Blockchain include decentralized environments, immutability, security, and extremely fault tolerance among a group of nodes in the IoV network. A distributed cloud data center can be created on different designated nodes within a specific area.

   b. *User Privacy*: In Blockchain technology, every user manages his keys and every data block node stores encrypted user data. Therefore, the issue of privacy can be resolved in IoV by implementing Blockchain technology.

   c. *Traffic Control and Management*: The technologies developed in the current decade have made traffic management and control easier than before. Now the vehicles and RSU generate traffic data, incidents of accidents and congestion, maintenance work on-road, and other relevant information that makes it easier to manage the traffic. This information can be utilized to design the smart transportation system, mitigation of traffic congestion, etc. The benefits come with the issues of security of the data storage and the vehicles as well as RSU will be vulnerable to attacks. This will affect the availability, accessibility, integrity, and privacy of data. The Blockchain platform can be one of the solutions for this problem as it supports decentralized management, availability, automaticity, and immutability [46].

7.5 Attack Countermeasures

The section depicts the parametric classification of the various security attacks in IoV ecosystems. Table 7.4 present the possible attack vectors based on the related parameter and present the possible countermeasures.

1. *Authentication-based attacks*: In the case of authentication attacks, an adversary gets access to the identity information of IoV nodes, and can further join the network and perform masquerade. For the same, Blockchain is a potential solution as transactions store the hashes of previous blocks, and any attempt of forging the transactions results in block invalidation [47]. For signing, Blockchain employs the elliptic-curve digital signature algorithm, and thus adversary node requires to solve the discrete log problem in short time duration to forge an attack. This requires access to high computational power, and storage, which is infeasible in approach.

2. *Attacks on availability*: In such attacks, the role of the adversary is to get access to open sensor ports and send resource reservation requests at servers, and RSUs. In case of access, the malicious intruder forms a bot-swarm on the server, forcing it to reserve resources for each malicious request. With a high influx of incoming requests, the server cannot grant access to authorized users. Moreover, an adversary tries to hinder the communications, by mixing it with noise signals, and passively by eavesdropping on an open communication link. In such cases, the source and destination have to process the information confidentially, and elliptic curve cryptography allows them to exchange keys securely based on agreed group.

3. *Attacks on confidentiality*: In such cases, the adversary can detect the sent messages on the channel with the granting of shared secret keys of the communicating entities during the exchange process. Thus, an adversary can withhold the message, until the message purpose is withheld [48]. To counter such attacks, Blockchain and proper signing schemes are required at communicating entities to record the transacting blocks through shared consensus.

4. *Attacks on integrity*: Integrity-based attacks involve the fabrication of sent data, through manipulating the hash codes. An adversary can launch blackhole

Table 7.4 Attack Vectors and Their Possible Security Countermeasures

Security aspects	Type of Attacks	Countermeasures
Attacks on Authentication	Replay, Sybil	Hash chains Elliptic Curve Cryptosystem (ECC)
	Message Falsification	Blockchain, ECC, Bilinear pairing Hash functions, Chinese Remainder Theorem
	Replay	Bilinear pairing
	Linkage	Discrete logarithm problem, ECC
	Flow of bogus information	Discrete logarithm problem, ECC
Attacks on Availability	DoS	PKI, Blockchain, Symmetric encryption
	DDoS	
	Channel hindrance	
Attacks on Confidentiality	Eavesdropping	Blockchain, Encryption
	Message holding	
	Message deletion	
Attacks on Integrity	Data Falsification and Manipulation Attack	IDS, Packet message entropy
	Malware	
	Blackhole	

attacks that drain network power. The other IoV nodes are made to believe that the malicious node has an optimum path to the destination at a lower cost. For the same, effective and secured routing policies needs to be built that selects the optimum path based on trust. Also, packets can be encrypted and then sent on the channel, but it increases the overhead of each node.

7.6 A Case Study on BC-Based Certificate Generation Scheme in IoV

Any transaction can be added to a block after the verification of each member of the Blockchain network, as presented in Figure 7.2. The proposed framework protects the privacy of the user by integrating the signature-less public key mechanism.

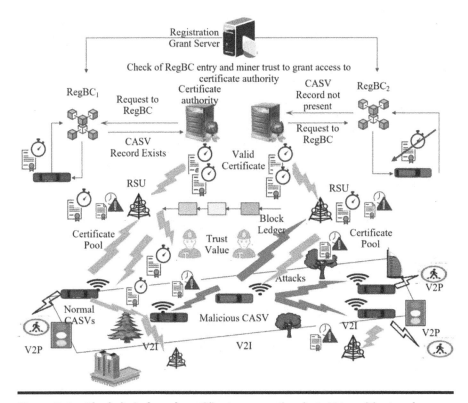

Figure 7.2 Blockchain based certificate generation in IoV to mitigate adversary attacks [49]

Any node (vehicle, RSU, etc.) can enter into the IoV network. The public–private key for the nodes is being initialized and submitted to a certificate authority for the verification process [50]. The credentials of the nodes are verified; if it is valid, then it will generate the certificate for the vehicle otherwise it rejects the certificate. The certificate will contain the key, as well as a timestamp for the expiration of the certificate.

Suppose two vehicles, *V1* and *V2*, are there in the network and *V1* wants to communicate with *V2*, then *V1* sends the validated certificate to *V2* for validation. *V2* will check the certification validity, expiration, and key. Additionally, *V2* will check the existence of *V1* at a certification authority. If the key, timestamp, and certification are valid then only *V1* and *V2* can start the communication. Following the validation of *V1*, *V2* will check the trust value of *V1* with the RSUs. The RSU will check the id of *V2* and validate it, if the id of *V2* is validated then RSU will check the trust value from the server and send the same to *V2*.

Once the identities are validated, *V1* and *V2* can exchange the communication between one another. Whenever *V1* sends a message *M1* to *V2*, the credibility of *M1* is being evaluated by the *V2* to determine the trustworthiness of *M1*. The trust of every event/message is being calculated and stored in the trust set. If *M1* has a probability greater than the threshold then *M1* will be accepted; otherwise this is given as a false report. The *V2* will generate a positive rating for the accepted *M1* and a negative rating for the false report. The message ratings will define the trustworthiness of the vehicle/node.

In case if *V1* and *V2* have not done any communication before the update of the Blockchain network then the trust value of *V1* will be unchanged. In case if there is successful communication between *V1* and *V2* then the RSU has to fetch the updated trust ratings of *V1*. Thereafter, the RSU will calculate and update the trust ratings of *V1*. The trust value offset of every vehicle is being calculated in the network.

Each RSU will register the timestamp and evaluate the hash function. In such a case, the hash function evaluated by the RSU is lower than the threshold function the RSU will cross-verify the trust offset and maximum summation of absolute value. In the event that the absolute value is less than the maximum sum for an RSU then it is elected as minor. After the election of the miner that RSU will publish itself in the network.

7.7 Research Challenges and Directions for Future Research in IoV

The Blockchain has a number of implementation issues. The research challenges of Blockchain-enabled IoV that need attention at this time are as follows:

1. *Throughput of System*: The consensus algorithm of Blockchain requires huge resources and computing power for updating and synchronizing the data copies communicated among vehicles in the network. The existing technologies in the vehicle have limited capabilities for processing and computing thus reduces the throughput and increases the latency of the system [51]. Therefore, the consensus algorithm shall be designed according to the demand of latency and throughput.

2. *Cyber-attacks*: Though Blockchain technology assures safe and secure infrastructure for IoV, there are still loopholes for cyber-attacks. These attacks can occur due to the permissionless nature of Blockchain. The permissioned Blockchain is not viable for the IoV networks due to distinct participating vehicles from different locations. The problem of the permissionless Blockchain network is that any malicious vehicle can compute and solve the proof-of-work (PoW) problem and become a part of a Blockchain network.

3. *The Issue of Scalability*: The Blockchain network maintains the backup of all the transactions to ensure data transparency and availability. To maintain the backup at each block is unrealistic in IoV as it has huge memory requirements for data storage. Therefore, the Blockchain will become complex, with a

degradation of network performance through increasing the number of vehicles in the network.

4. *Authentication*: The most suitable type of Blockchain in IoV is public Blockchain. In this system, the vehicles can perform PoW to join the network. In the public Blockchain, the probability of adding a malicious vehicle is high. Therefore, appropriate authentication for adding the nodes is a challenge.

5. *Trust on IoV*: The requirement for establishing the trust between the participating nodes or members of a Blockchain network is very important. The vehicles are operating on a public network that is prone to malfunction. This creates a challenge to establish trust among the vehicles, as well as RSU.

6. *Wireless Connectivity*: The IoV is dependent on the internet and theres are connectivity issues in developing countries such as India. In order to implement the Blockchain-enabled IoV network connectivity has to be enhanced, and error rates in wireless communication infrastructures have to be minimized. For high-performance computing in wireless networks, optical core networks are considered a viable choice [52].

7.8 Conclusion

In modern sustainable transport ecosystems, IoV plays a prominent role in terms of effectively sharing data through open channels. For this reason, IoV networks are susceptible to informed attack vectors by an adversary, and thus require trust, privacy, and confidentiality in data sharing among nodes. Due to the immutable and chronological nature of Blockchain, it can drive secure and trusted IoV-enabled ecosystems. The proposed survey highlights the integration of Blockchain in IoV to leverage the trust and privacy of shared data among different vehicles. A solution taxonomy of IoV attacks is proposed, and Blockchain-assisted solutions are discussed. A case study of the Blockchain-based certificate generations scheme for IoV is discussed. Finally, research challenges of incorporation of Blockchain in IoV and future research directions are proposed. Thus, the proposed survey presents a holistic overview of attacks in IoV and driving Blockchain as the solution. The key direction would help automotive stakeholders, research scholars, and industry to deploy Blockchain-based smart IoV solutions. In future, we would like to investigate the effect of 5G network orchestration in IoV through the introduction of secured Blockchain-assisted solutions to enhance the bandwidth, reduce latency, and increase the service availability of possible integration in IoV ecosystems.

References

[1] A. Ladha, P. Bhattacharya, N. Chaubey, and U. Bodkhe, "Iigpts: IoT-based framework for intelligent green public transportation system," in *Proceedings of First International Conference on Computing, Communications, and Cyber-Security (IC4S 2019)*, (P. K.

Singh, W. Pawlowski, N. Kumar, S. Tanwar, J. J. P. C. Rodrigues, and O. M.S, eds.), vol. 121, pp. 183–195, Springer International Publishing, 2020.

[2] J. Liu, J. Li, L. Zhang, F. Dai, Y. Zhang, X. Meng, and J. Shen, "Secure intelligent traffic light control using fog computing," *Future Generation Computer Systems*, vol. 78, pp. 817–824, 2018.

[3] J. Lim, H. Yu, K. Kim, M. Kim, and S.-B. Lee, "Preserving location privacy of connected vehicles with highly accurate location updates," *IEEE Communications Letters*, vol. 21, no. 3, pp. 540–543, 2016.

[4] C.-Y. Wei, A. C.-S. Huang, C.-Y. Chen, and J.-Y. Chen, "Qos-aware hybrid scheduling for geographical zone-based resource allocation in cellular vehicle-to-vehicle communications," *IEEE Communications Letters*, vol. 22, no. 3, pp. 610–613, 2017.

[5] A. Shukla, P. Bhattacharya, S. Tanwar, N. Kumar, and M. Guizani, "Dwara: A deep learning-based dynamic toll pricing scheme for intelligent transportation systems," *IEEE Transactions on Vehicular Technology*, vol. 69, no. 11, pp. 12510–12520, 2020.

[6] J. Kang, Z. Xiong, D. Niyato, D. Ye, D. I. Kim, and J. Zhao, "Toward secure blockchain enabled internet of vehicles: Optimizing consensus management using reputation and contract theory," *IEEE Transactions on Vehicular Technology*, vol. 68, no. 3, pp. 2906–2920, 2019.

[7] M. Singh, and S. Kim, "Blockchain based intelligent vehicle data sharing framework," *arXiv preprint arXiv:1708.09721*, 2017. https://arxiv.org/abs/1708.09721

[8] S. B. Patel, H. A. Kheruwala, M. Alazab, N. Patel, R. Damani, P. Bhattacharya, S. Tanwar, and N. Kumar, "Biouav: Blockchain-envisioned framework for digital identification to secure access in next-generation UAVs," in *Proceedings of the 2nd ACM MobiCom Workshop on Drone Assisted Wireless Communications for 5G and Beyond, DroneCom '20*, (New York, NY, USA), pp. 43–48, Association for Computing Machinery, 2020.

[9] E. B. Sasson, A. Chiesa, C. Garman, M. Green, I. Miers, E. Tromer, and M. Virza, "Zerocash: Decentralized anonymous payments from bitcoin," in *2014 IEEE Symposium on Security and Privacy*, pp. 459–474, IEEE, 2014.

[10] S. Noether, "Ring signature confidential transactions for Monero," *IACR Cryptol. ePrint Arch.*, vol. 2015, p. 1098, 2015.

[11] L. Li, J. Liu, L. Cheng, S. Qiu, W. Wang, X. Zhang, and Z. Zhang, "Creditcoin: A privacy-preserving blockchain-based incentive announcement network for communications of smart vehicles," *IEEE Transactions on Intelligent Transportation Systems*, vol. 19, no. 7, pp. 2204–2220, 2018.

[12] P. Bhattacharya, S. Tanwar, U. Bodke, S. Tyagi, and N. Kumar, "Bindaas: Blockchain based deep-learning as-a-service in healthcare 4.0 applications," *IEEE Transactions on Network Science and Engineering*, vol. 8, no. 2, pp. 1242–1255, April–June 2021, DOI: 10.1109/TNSE.2019.2961932.

[13] U. Bodkhe, S. Tanwar, P. Bhattacharya, and N. Kumar, "Blockchain for precision irrigation: Opportunities and challenges," *Transactions on Emerging Telecommunications Technologies*, p. e4059, 2020, DOI: 10.1002/ett.4059

[14] O. Kaiwartya, A. H. Abdullah, Y. Cao, A. Altameem, M. Prasad, C.-T. Lin, and X. Liu, "Internet of vehicles: Motivation, layered architecture, network model, challenges, and future aspects," *IEEE Access*, vol. 4, pp. 5356–5373, 2016.

[15] L. C. Hua, M. H. Anisi, L. Yee, and M. Alam, "Social networking-based cooperation mechanisms in vehicular ad-hoc network—a survey," *Vehicular Communications*, vol. 10, pp. 57–73, 2017.

[16] Y. Toor, P. Muhlethaler, A. Laouiti, and A. De La Fortelle, "Vehicle ad hoc networks: applications and related technical issues," *IEEE communications surveys & tutorials*, vol. 10, no. 3, pp. 74–88, 2008.

[17] R. G. Engoulou, M. Bellaïche, S. Pierre, and A. Quintero, "Vanet security surveys," *Computer Communications*, vol. 44, pp. 1–13, 2014.

[18] R. Gupta, A. Shukla, P. Mehta, P. Bhattacharya, S. Tanwar, S. Tyagi, and N. Kumar, "Vahak: A blockchain-based outdoor delivery scheme using uav for healthcare 4.0 services," in *IEEE INFOCOM 2020 – IEEE Conference on Computer Communications Workshops (INFOCOM WKSHPS)*, pp. 255–260, 2020.

[19] J. Xu, and F. Zhong, "Automotive air conditioning control system based on stcl2c5a60s2 singlechip," *Auto Electric Parts*, pp. 14–16, 2014.

[20] E. Lindholm, J. Nickolls, S. Oberman, and J. Montrym, "Nvidia tesla: A unified graphics and computing architecture," *IEEE micro*, vol. 28, no. 2, pp. 39–55, 2008.

[21] B. Liu, and Y. Sun, "Osek/vdx: An open-architectured platform of vehicle electronics system," *Acta Armamentarll the Volume of Tank, Armored Vehicle Engine*, vol. 2, pp. 61–64, 2002.

[22] C. Guettier, B. Bradai, F. Hochart, P. Resende, J. Yelloz, and A. Garnault, "Standardization of generic architecture for autonomous driving: A reality check," in Langheim J. (eds) *Energy Consumption and Autonomous Driving*, Springer, Cham, pp 57–68, 2016.

[23] S. Fürst, and M. Bechter, "Autosar for connected and autonomous vehicles: The autosar adaptive platform," in *2016 46th Annual IEEE/IFIP International Conference on Dependable Systems and Networks Workshop (DSN-W)*, pp. 215–217, IEEE, 2016.

[24] F. Sagstetter, M. Lukasiewycz, S. Steinhorst, M. Wolf, A. Bouard, W. R. Harris, S. Jha, T. Peyrin, A. Poschmann, and S. Chakraborty, "Security challenges in automotive hardware/software architecture design," in *2013 Design, Automation & Test in Europe Conference & Exhibition (DATE)*, pp. 458–463, IEEE, 2013.

[25] M. Dibaei, X. Zheng, K. Jiang, S. Maric, R. Abbas, S. Liu, Y. Zhang, Y. Deng, S. Wen, J. Zhang, et al., "An overview of attacks and defences on intelligent connected vehicles," *arXiv preprint arXiv:1907.07455*, 2019. https://arxiv.org/abs/1907.07455.

[26] Y. Dong, Z. Hu, K. Uchimura, and N. Murayama, "Driver inattention monitoring system for intelligent vehicles: A review," *IEEE transactions on intelligent transportation systems*, vol. 12, no. 2, pp. 596–614, 2010.

[27] R. Singh, A. Singh, and P. Bhattacharya, "A machine learning approach for anomaly detection to secure smart grid systems," in Ashwani Kumar and Seelam Sai Satyanarayana Reddy (eds.) *Advancements in Security and Privacy Initiatives for Multimedia Images*, IGI Global, pp. 199–213, 2020.

[28] I. Ali, A. Hassan, and F. Li, "Authentication and privacy schemes for vehicular ad hoc networks (vanets): A survey," *Vehicular Communications*, vol. 16, pp. 45–61, 2019.

[29] P. Bhattacharya, P. Mehta, S. Tanwar, M. S. Obaidat, and K. F. Hsiao, "Heal: A blockchain-envisioned signcryption scheme for healthcare iot ecosystems," in *2020 International Conference on Communications, Computing, Cybersecurity, and Informatics (CCCI)*, pp. 1–6, 2020.

[30] S. M. Ghaffarian, and H. R. Shahriari, "Software vulnerability analysis and discovery using machine-learning and data-mining techniques: A survey," *ACM Computing Surveys (CSUR)*, vol. 50, no. 4, pp. 1–36, 2017.

[31] F. Wang, Y. Xu, H. Zhang, Y. Zhang, and L. Zhu, "2flip: A two-factor lightweight privacy preserving authentication scheme for vanet," *IEEE Transactions on Vehicular Technology*, vol. 65, no. 2, pp. 896–911, 2015.

[32] S.-W. Kim, B. Qin, Z. J. Chong, X. Shen, W. Liu, M. H. Ang, E. Frazzoli, and D. Rus, "Multivehicle cooperative driving using cooperative perception: Design and experimental validation," *IEEE Transactions on Intelligent Transportation Systems*, vol. 16, no. 2, pp. 663–680, 2014.

[33] W. Xi, C. Qian, J. Han, K. Zhao, S. Zhong, X.-Y. Li, and J. Zhao, "Instant and robust authentication and key agreement among mobile devices," in *Proceedings of the 2016 ACM SIGSAC Conference on Computer and Communications Security*, pp. 616–627, 2016.

[34] C. Castelluccia, and P. Mutaf, "Shake them up! a movement-based pairing protocol for cpu-constrained devices," in *Proceedings of the 3rd International Conference on Mobile Systems, Applications, and Services*, pp. 51–64, 2005.

[35] P. Bagga, A. K. Das, M. Wazid, J. J. P. C. Rodrigues, and Y. Park, "Authentication protocols in internet of vehicles: Taxonomy, analysis, and challenges," *IEEE Access*, vol. 8, pp. 54314–54344, 2020.

[36] I. Aad, J.-P. Hubaux, and E. W. Knightly, "Denial of service resilience in ad hoc networks," in *Proceedings of the 10th Annual International Conference on Mobile Computing and Networking*, pp. 202–215, 2004.

[37] A.-S. K. Pathan, *Security of self-organizing networks: MANET, WSN, WMN, VANET*. CRC press, 2016.

[38] A. Srivastava, P. Bhattacharya, A. Singh, A. Mathur, O. Prakash, and R. Pradhan, "A distributed credit transfer educational framework based on blockchain," in *2018 Second International Conference on Advances in Computing, Control and Communication Technology (IAC3T)*, pp. 54–59, 2018.

[39] J. Kang, R. Yu, X. Huang, M. Wu, S. Maharjan, S. Xie, and Y. Zhang, "Blockchain for secure and efficient data sharing in vehicular edge computing and networks," *IEEE Internet of Things Journal*, vol. 6, no. 3, pp. 4660–4670, 2018.

[40] Y. Chen, X. Hao, W. Ren, and Y. Ren, "Traceable and authenticated key negotiations via blockchain for vehicular communications," *Mobile Information Systems*, vol. 2019, Article ID 5627497, 2019.

[41] H. Chai, S. Leng, K. Zhang, and S. Mao, "Proof-of-reputation based-consortium blockchain for trust resource sharing in internet of vehicles," *IEEE Access*, vol. 7, pp. 175744–175757, 2019.

[42] P. N. Sureshbhai, P. Bhattacharya, and S. Tanwar, "Karuna: A blockchain-based sentiment analysis framework for fraud cryptocurrency schemes," in *2020 IEEE International Conference on Communications Workshops (ICC Workshops)*, pp. 1–6, 2020.

[43] S. B. Patel, P. Bhattacharya, S. Tanwar, and N. Kumar, "Kirti: A blockchain-based credit recommender system for financial institutions," *IEEE Transactions on Network Science and Engineering*, pp. 1–1, 2020 aop, DOI: 10.1109/TNSE.2020.3005678.

[44] W. Al Amiri, M. Baza, K. Banawan, M. Mahmoud, W. Alasmary, and K. Akkaya, "Privacy-preserving smart parking system using blockchain and private information retrieval," in *2019 International Conference on Smart Applications, Communications and Networking (SmartNets)*, pp. 1–6, IEEE, 2019.

[45] C. Chen, T. Xiao, T. Qiu, N. Lv, and Q. Pei, "Smart-contract-based economical platooning in blockchain-enabled urban internet of vehicles," *IEEE Transactions on Industrial Informatics*, vol. 16, no. 6, pp. 4122–4133, 2019.

[46] L. Cheng, J. Liu, G. Xu, Z. Zhang, H. Wang, H.-N. Dai, Y. Wu, and W. Wang, "Sctsc: A semicentralized traffic signal control mode with attribute-based blockchain in iovs," *IEEE Transactions on Computational Social Systems*, vol. 6, no. 6, pp. 1373–1385, 2019.

[47] U. Bodkhe, P. Bhattacharya, S. Tanwar, S. Tyagi, N. Kumar, and M. S. Obaidat, "Blohost: Blockchain enabled smart tourism and hospitality management," in *2019 International Conference on Computer, Information and Telecommunication Systems (CITS), Shanghai, China*, pp. 1–5, IEEE, 2019.

[48] P. Bhattacharya, S. Tanwar, R. Shah, and A. Ladha, "Mobile edge computing-enabled blockchain framework—A survey," in *Proceedings of ICRIC 2019* (P. K. Singh, A. K. Kar, Y. Singh, M. H. Kolekar, and S. Tanwar, eds.), (Cham), pp. 797–809, Springer International Publishing, 2020.

[49] U. Bodkhe, D. Mehta, S. Tanwar, P. Bhattacharya, P. K. Singh, and W. Hong, "A survey on decentralized consensus mechanisms for cyber physical systems," *IEEE Access*, vol. 8, pp. 54371–54401, 2020.

[50] N. Kabra, P. Bhattacharya, S. Tanwar, and S. Tyagi, "Mudrachain: Blockchain-based framework for automated cheque clearance in financial institutions," *Future Generation Computer Systems*, vol. 102, pp. 574–587, 2020.

[51] Verma A., P. Bhattacharya, U. Bodkhe, A. Ladha, and S. Tanwar (2021) DAMS: Dynamic association for view materialization based on rule mining scheme. In: Singh P.K., Singh Y., Kolekar M.H., Kar A.K., Chhabra J.K., Sen A. (eds) *Recent Innovations in Computing. ICRIC 2020. Lecture Notes in Electrical Engineering*, vol 701. Springer, Singapore. DOI: 10.1007/978-981-15-8297-4_43.

[52] Singh, A, Tiwari, A. K. and Bhattacharya, P. "Bit Error Rate Analysis of Hybrid Buffer-Based Switch for Optical Data Centers," *Journal of Optical Communications*, 2019. DOI: 10.1515/joc-2019-0008.

Chapter 8

Blockchain-Based Federated Cloud Environment: Issues and Challenges

Ashwin Verma, Pronaya Bhattacharya, Umesh Bodkhe, and Mohd Zuhair
Nirma University, India

Ram Kishan Dewangan
Thapar Institute of Engineering and Technology, India

Contents

DOI: 10.1201/9781003129486-8

8.1 Introduction

The recent never-ending growth of Big Data, Internet of Things (IoT), Fog computing, and Cloud computing are driving a rapid increase in demands for novel technologies and solutions to handle decentralized systems that are distributed across the network [1]. The deployment of trusted, secure, and verifiable services is much in demand, as the volume of user's data connected over the network increased greatly along with vulnerable devices through which it is connected. Unfortunately, on a large scale user's data breaches are intractable firm rapidly, exposing vast volumes of private information, and thus trust becomes the main issue among the stakeholders. As a prime weakness in multitudinous computing architectures and centralization creates an unbalanced relationship between Cloud User (CU) and Cloud Service Provider (CSP), which makes difficult for CU's to handle information by creating a single point of failure for the exploiters.

A Blockchain (BC) is a decentralized transaction database that is distributed in nature and duplicated across the network of computing systems [2, 3]. Each block of the BC consists of several transactions, which are added to every stakeholder's ledger whenever a new transaction is recorded or happens in the BC network. BC has a distributed ledger, which records a cryptographic hash that is immutable in nature. BC is an alternative to building a trustworthy network due to its characteristics of tamper resistance in data and data traceability. Because of this attribute, it is commonly believed that BC is applicable in every field where trust and the tamperproof system is required, from financial services (Bitcoin, Ethereum, etc.) to application-oriented system [4–7]. In BC-enabled systems, the SC is a significant driving force which can control system processes automatically [8]. The trustful system is created by BC and is tied with different operations and processes with the help of SC. Introducing BC-enabled solutions is a strategic plan to solve different issues in cloud data centers. Based on our findings, many studies in this field are seeking solutions to empower the current system with the help of BC technology. The restructuring of cloud-based systems and data centers through BC is reliable and trustworthy in intercrossed-networking environments [9, 10]. As is generally acknowledged, few significant advantages of BC enabled technologies to include transparent governance [11], education [12], healthcare supply management through unmanned aerial vehicles [13], tamper resistance protection [14–16], novel business models [17, 18] and decentralization-powered security [19–22]. Furthermore, despite the prospect for BC to revolutionize decentralized architectures which are distributed in nature, create problematic outcomes in practice that require resolution [23–25], any system vulnerabilities in the implementation or elementary process will create open doors and loopholes for malicious subversion in the entire system or to the users. From this point of view, it is imperative that a comprehensive evaluation be carried out thoroughly to understand the technological implications.

In this survey, we have assessed the adequacy of emerging and current BC-enabled technology. We have explored the relevant techniques, underlying concepts, and critical features. In particular, we have investigated BC technology from the perspective of emerging applications, such as healthcare, Big Data, IoT, Cloud, and Fog computing as an important paradigm to serve full integrated computing services and the use of BC. In FCE, multiple cloud service providers (CSP) come together to offer their services to cloud users (CU). CU consumes offered services and pays only to the limited use of that services or through subscription charges involved with that service. The centralized information related to the multiple CSP needs to be stored on a centralized server which is prone to vulnerable attacks not only to the user's data, but also related to the important service information; thus, the security and access control is an important aspect of the federated centralized environment along with the data storage, where the user needs tamperproof data along with storage optimization, and resource allocation and resource identification is an important aspect of service provisioning, the offloading of resources and its proper management, resource exchange and making them available for exchange or on the contract is currently the optimal utilization of resources.

Thus, to handle the aforementioned issue in FCE, where CU and CSP offer and consume services in a decentralized system, trust framework is required between the different stakeholders of the system. Hence BC is an apparent revolution that can provide anonymous trust among all the stakeholders on the agreed set of truths. A BC forms and creates a decentralized trustworthy information-sharing ledger that addresses the above-mentioned issues. Figure 8.1(a) shows the total size of the public cloud computing market (in millions of USD) in the industry from 2010 to 2020, and, in future, it is expected to grow exponentially due to the reliable availability and high response from the infrastructure. In Figure 8.1(b), the average usage of one organization in each quarter of the year is depicted from the year 2016 to 2020, where each quarter value shows the usage of consumer and enterprise from the organization, the fourth quarter of 2020 shows 1,564 different cloud services consumed by the enterprise. Figure 8.1(c) shows the different areas where BC provide solutions in FCE.

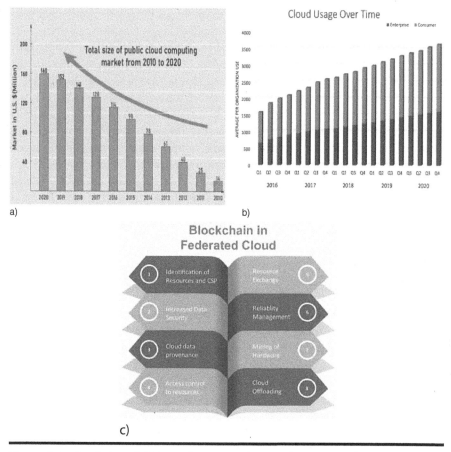

Figure 8.1 Statistics of CSPs and CUs service involvement and BC adoption in FCE (a) Cloud computing usage from last 10 years, (b) Average number of cloud service in use as per organization type, and (c) Adaption of BC in FCE

8.1.1 Contribution

- The role of BC in FCE, along with a detailed study, is presented.
- Comparative analysis of several approaches to FCE with several parameters is discussed in detail.
- Finally, an open issue and research opportunity along with future directions for further research in BC enabled FCE.

8.1.2 Chapter Layout

This chapter is organized as follows: background knowledge and the important necessity of BC in FCE is presented in Section 8.2. In Section 8.3 we have highlighted the solution taxonomy of BC in FCE. Section 8.4 presents the open issues and research opportunities, along with the future directions. Finally, Section 8.5 presents some conclusions.

8.1.3 Scope of the Survey

The comprehensive and intricate study is carried out as follows, Firstly, the digital repositories of the library are searched extensively, using different keywords to locate specific contributions related to the survey over the past five years (Year:2016 to Year:2020). The keyword is searched for both in isolation and in conjunction with other words with the help of operators like AND OR, e.g. "*Blockchain AND cloud computing*", "*Blockchain AND multi-cloud environment*", "*Blockchain AND service provisioning*", "*Blockchain AND cloud security*" and "*Blockchain AND cloud resource management*". A total of 73 papers have been found, of which 48 research articles are considered for the detailed survey for research work towards the novelty of BC in FCE.

The main reason for conducting this survey is to analyze the current BC study that can be used to power up the cloud-based applications and novel mechanisms that uses a cloud-based approach to improve the system. Each technological dimension, such as performance (throughput), compatibility (network, database), computation energy cost, privacy, and security, addresses the key aspects of the BC framework.

To date many surveys has been conducted that have explored various aspects in FCE; however, as per our literature survey, many of these works have focused primarily virtual machine (VM) attacks, attacks in a tenant network, resource exchange, storage optimization, cloud offloading, resource allocation, data duplication, and resource identification. Motivated by the aforementioned facts, we have analyzed the different research articles and provided novel insights into the field of FCE. First, this survey provides a thorough analysis, concentrating on the re-engineering of FCE from the implementation point of view of BC. In this work, comparisons are made in the same technical dimension, which offers explicit research and practical guidance for practitioners and scholars. Second, this survey gives useful insights on the recommended system for identifying suitable CSP from a pool of providers; this work relies on a variety of technical aspects that assist with academic/industrial engagement and is also essential for the implementation of cloud systems or cloud-based BC systems.

8.2 Background

In the current epoch, computing is not limited simply to a desktop PC; rather, it is becoming a global architecture that consists of a customized set of services that are delivered in just the same way as conventional utilities, such as electricity distribution, telephone connection, water & gas distribution and which is charged according to the user's consumption. In the current era users access the services via an application programming interface (API) based on their requirements irrespective of the services hosted and being delivered. In the cloud computing capabilities of the business, applications are made available to use in a sophisticated manner over the internet. In market-oriented cloud computing, multiple cloud providers come together to a common platform to provide services to CU, the environment is referred to as FCE. Traditionally, each CSP offers its services from their portal service or API provided to CU, and CU's task is to search each portal and identify the best services. In market-oriented FCE, the biggest challenges along with data storage and bandwidth are standardization to offered services and its centralization to a distributed server, a legal framework that should be implemented for FCE. Apart from this, CSP needs to create trust among its CUs by providing a guarantee through service-level agreement (SLA) resource identification, it should be verified against the service-level objectives (SLO) defined in the SLA, CSP identification during resource exchange between multiple CSP is another challenge in FCE to create a trustworthy framework.

BC is a distributed system for recording information in a linked data structure in a way that makes it impossible to alter the system. If any block in the chain is altered, that changes the hash of the block, which eventually changes the previous hash value for the successor block. It is therefore impossible to alter any block in the chain and hence to maintain the trust and security in the system. It is a ledger of transactions that is duplicated and distributed across all the nodes in the network. Figure 8.2 represents the internal structure of a block. Each block in the BC consists of version information, a hash of the previous block, Merkle root (data structure), difficulty target, timestamp, and nonce.

These connected block-like structures are stored across the network on all the nodes, which means that adding a new transaction in a block requires an agreement between the users. They use a consensus algorithm to verify the block before adding it into the chain, which makes the system trustworthy without requiring trust in any other user of the system [36]. Blockchain at least contains these two things. Firstly, the hash of the previous block links the current block hash, and secondly, the stored information can be any generic transactions that depends on the application which is using it. In the case of Bitcoin [37], for example, the data segment stores transactions. BC may be divided into three categories [38], based on write permissions on blocks. (i) Public BC: This system has an open network and permissionless nature due to which anyone (participants) can view, read and write data in the BC which will be accessible to all the nodes and no specific participants have special control over the data in the BC, i.e. any participants can add the block. (ii) Private BC: This is governed by a single entity (e.g. administrator) and only the administrator can add the block other participants need permission to read, write or audit the block. (iii) Consortium BC: This system is governed by a predefined set of multiple participants

Table 8.1 Comparative Analysis between the Existing State of the Art and the Proposed Survey along with Its Pros and Cons

Author	Year	1	2	3	4	5	6	Pros	Cons
Uriarte et al. [26]	2018	Y	Y	N	Y	Y	Y	BC-enabled decentralized cloud solutions were compared along with its analysis	Lack of validation for computational results
Zhang et al. [27]	2018	Y	Y	N	N	Y	Y	Cloud I model was proposed and taxonomy of security attacks was discussed	The detection of users cloud security state was not shown in an effective way
Sukhodolskiy et al. [28]	2018	Y	Y	N	N	N	Y	Proposed privacy-enabled set of cryptographic protocols	Resource Provisioning was not highlighted by the authors
Gao et al. [29]	2018	Y	N	N	Y	Y	Y	Vulnerabilities for various major cyber attacks are discussed in detail	Barriers encountered in Cloud computing due to usage of BC technology was not focussed
Jiao et al. [30]	2019	Y	Y	Y	Y	Y	Y	Trust and computational efficiency	Communication constraint in the ecosystem was not taken into account during simulation
Xie et al. [31]	2019	Y	Y	N	N	Y	Y	Pros of decentralize BC-based CloudEX platform was discussed in the paper	Unfairness in the transactions
Baniata et al. [32]	2020	Y	Y	N	Y	N	Y	Deployment and integration of FC and BC	Implementation or Simulation of BC-enabled Fog model was not proposed even at a small scale

(Continued)

Table 8.1 (Continued) Comparative Analysis between the Existing State of the Art and the Proposed Survey along with Its Pros and Cons

Author	Year	1	2	3	4	5	6	Pros	Cons
Sohrabi et al. [33]	2020	Y	Y	N	Y	Y	Y	Shamir secret key based BACC model was proposed in the paper	SLA validation is not discussed
Kumari et al. [34]	2020	Y	Y	N	N	Y	Y	Integration of Blockchain and AI techniques for energy management in the cloud	Lack of actual simulation of ECM system
Bodkhe et al. [35]	2020	Y	N	N	N	Y	Y	In-depth survey for Industry 4.0 applications	SLA validation, Network latency were not explored
Our Proposed Survey	2021	Y	Y	Y	Y	Y	Y	Technological aspects namely security, service, and performance of FCE covers all the aspects of a multi-cloud architecture	-

1.Trust, 2.Chronology, 3.SLA Validation, 4.Resource Provisioning, 5.Data provenance, 6.Data Privacy Y-Yes, N-No

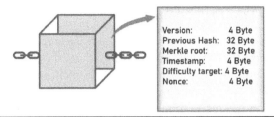

Version: 4 Byte
Previous Hash: 32 Byte
Merkle root: 32 Byte
Timestamp: 4 Byte
Difficulty target: 4 Byte
Nonce: 4 Byte

Figure 8.2   The internal structure of a block

and these can only add the block in the system and it is not a public platform. Public BC is permissionless while private and consortium BC is permissioned. Generally, we use Hyperledger Fabric which is permissioned BC [39].

8.3 BC in a Multi-Cloud Environment: A Solution Taxonomy

In recent years, BC has emerged as trusted distributed technology based on a secure list of the transaction record. It allows other stakeholders to transact with untrusted parties over the network [40]. Efforts have been made to analyze the potentials of BC in FCE.

In this section, we are going to present the solution taxonomy for BC in a multi-cloud environment. Figure 8.3 presents the BC-based taxonomy for federated cloud environments.

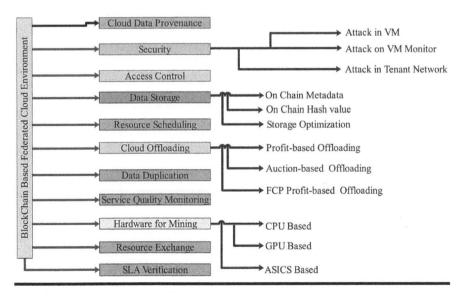

Figure 8.3   Taxonomy of Multi-Cloud Environment

8.3.1 Cloud Data Provenance

Cloud computing-based IoT networks are focused largely on hard real-time systems where time is an important parameter, such as industrial power, smart grids, security, and digital automated surveillance systems. In such networks, the number of IoT devices gather data from multiple remote environments and depend on storage, review, and decision-making to multiple intermediate agents through wireless connections to the cloud. To guarantee correct and timely decisions, such systems need highly trustworthy data [41]. In most cases, however, the Internet of Thing (IoT) data become uncertain during transfer to the cloud server. This becomes a crucial security issue to ensure the origin of data in a heterogeneous multi-layered environment.

To address the same, Ali et al. [42] proposed a stable cloud-centric data provenance system for leveraging the irreversible and deterministic BC intelligent contracts for the conventional cloud-centric IoT network. The proposed framework stores the cryptographic hash key of each device on the BC network, whereas the actual data is stored off-chain. Cloud making it highly available and scalable for dense IoT devices, to guarantee the origin of data stored on the cloud multiple SC are deployed on the BC. The proposed framework consists of three main components: cloud storage, BC network, and IoT devices as its gateway nodes [43]. The IoT devices sense the data and send it to gateway nodes that act as an intermediate between the cloud and the BC network. The cloud provides the analysis of data, decision-making, and storage services, while the BC network is used to have only metadata of the devices like device identity and periodic traffic profile. Each IoT device registers itself using a domain name system (DNS) and is mapped as a unique ID, i.e. public/private key. After receiving the data from IoT devices, the gateway verifies the authenticity and integrity of the data with the digital signature of the device. The gateway aggregates the data and sends it to the BC network in the form of a transaction. The provenance of data is ensured by executing the SC.

8.3.2 Security

With the extensive use of applications based on cloud computing, security is the most important part of it. CU needs a secure environment where it can transfer its sensitive information on external servers which is controlled by CSP. Because of rapidly increasing CU and CSP in FCE, there is an increase in the vulnerability and attack vectors. Many surveys have been provided based on intrusion detection systems for detecting intrusions. Zhang et al. [44] summarized the various attack and their taxonomy, and the illustration is depicted in Figure 8.4.

8.3.2.1 Attacks in Virtual Machines

Cross VM side-channel attack where the attacker bypasses the logical isolation by accessing the other VM from the same memory in which he is working with current

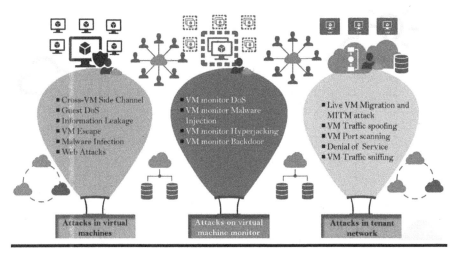

Figure 8.4 Cloud computing Attack taxonomy [44]

VM, Guest Denial of Service (DoS) due to improper configuration of the hypervisor, a single VM consumes almost all the resources which cause DoS to other VM application executing on the same machine, Information leakage by accessing the hardware like random access memory or cache data read, Accessing other VM's memory, use of malware to corrupt the guest OS and with the help of side scripting and cookie manipulation.

8.3.2.2 Attacks on Virtual Machine Monitor

Attackers can exploit the code of a virtual machine (VM) monitor and, with the help of DoS, can create resource starvation like CPU, RAM and inject rootkit applications so that the entire control of the server is hijacked. By exploiting backdoors attackers can manipulate the kernel data in the guest operating system by overwriting the code of the hypervisor.

8.3.2.3 Attacks in Tenant Network

When VM is migrating from one machine to another, an attacker can modify the data of communication with the CSP on behalf of legitimate CU. An attack traffic is generated with the help of IP spoofing in which several attacks are generated on behalf of legitimate CU. Port scanning also provides information of working ports through which attackers can initiate other attacks, flood the VM with spoofed packet so that it would not be able to provide services running on, will create DoS attack in the system, Traffic sniping is a common attack where VMs are connected with the virtual switch.

8.3.3 SLA Verification

As the CSP is responsible for managing the security and physical infrastructure when a local computing resource moves to a commercial cloud, then CU loses full control of the physical servers, and it becomes CSP's responsibility to manage and monitor resource allocation, performance, security, etc. which create a trust issue between CU and CSP. CSP fulfill the trust issue with SLA, which builds trust between CSP and CU, and SLA defines the rights and obligations of all the stakeholders involved, along with the targeted QoS. On violation of service-level objectives (SLO) defined in SLA, its CU responsibility to identify the violation and check the penalty accordingly. At CSP side, CSP check and apply the penalty only when it finds the violation. So, in order to remove the dependency from both sides and simultaneously automate the task, third-party verification from both sides is required.

Wonjiga et al. [45] proposed a BC-based SLA verification approach for the cloud. CU can perform verification at any time, the verification process where CU and CSP both participate to make verification data secure. A BC is used to remove the third party, the distributed ledger store a part of the evidence for checking the correctness of the outsourced data. It consists of two phases; in the first phase, CU sends the data and its hash to CSP, and the hash is used to check the correctness of the file uploaded on the cloud; after uploading the data, both CU and CSP update the hash on the ledger. In the verification phase, in order to check the integrity of the stored data, CU requests the current state of the stored data on the cloud by requesting the current hash of the data, and CU can verify the current hash with the stored hash. If the hash is mismatched, CU can claim the violation using the proof stored on the distributed ledger.

8.3.4 Access Control

In recent years, there has been an increase in services that store and synch users' data remotely on the cloud. Many users store their important confidential data in this way; the main problem arises when these data transferred to the external environment and apart from the owner, anyone else gets access to this information. There are several ways to solve the problem of remote data stored securely; one effective way is to encrypt the data before sending it to the cloud from the user's end. However, this imposes some hurdles in terms of using and accessing the data collectively. Among the tools which encrypt the file before sending it to the cloud services are "BoxCrypt", "CryptDB" [46], "ARX" [47] and "BigchainDB" [48], which ensure integrity and non-repudiation.

Sukhodolskiy et al. [28] proposed a BC-based access control method for storing data on an untrusted cloud by implementing Ethereum-based SCs. The data will be stored on the cloud while the information which identifies the data/file will be stored on the BC. The public cloud information is stored as it is, while the restricted information that requires authorized accessed needs to be encrypted before it transfers to the external cloud. The user will create a SC for each file which stores the information about the access policy, owner, identification of the cloud, changes that occur with the file, and a hash of the stored information, i.e. using the BC system will maintain the log of all meaningful security events, access requests, and revocation request. Ethereum-based SC is executed and only ciphertext if hash data is transferred to the BC ledger.

8.3.5 Cloud Resource Scheduling

Due to the recent developments in network speed, the ability to store and retrieve information is increased, and to deal with a huge amount of data all of the information is stored on the cloud to make it easy to retrieve at any point in time. Cloud environments provide infrastructure and application as service to users, these applications have complex scheduling on VMs, with different configuration and deployment conditions [49]. Therefore, there is a need to optimize scheduling criteria to ensure the recoverability and security of cloud data [50].

Zhu et al. [27] proposed a BC-based distributed approach for job scheduling in the cloud environment, which stores scheduling information in the cloud cluster. The authors have used a decentralized and distributed solution that combines the BC in combination with a conventional approach to solve the problem of task scheduling and maintain the integrity and security of cloud information. The system consists of four components: BC network, cloud database, control system, and cloud cluster. First, register each entity inside the cloud cluster. Then log files are collected, which is generated by task scheduling in the cluster, the metadata related to this is transferred to the control system, the hash of it is forwarded to the BC, and raw data are stored on the cloud database. Once the data are collected and uploaded on the BC network, the events are captured as a transaction that provides authentication, auditing, and tracking information. Then the transaction is confirmed by hashing, and the block is verified and added as a part of a tamper-proof ledger.

8.3.6 Cloud Storage Reliability

Most of the organizations rely on cloud computing infrastructure for their data storage, communication, and computational requirements because cloud services provide their benefits by replacing the cost of IT infrastructure. However, this model also produces some serious issues as users are privacy-conscious and put only less sensitive data on the cloud, thereby limiting the full potential of the paradigm. Organizations are not ready to move their sensitive data onto the servers they do not control, and there are also some legal implications of the application and data held on third-party servers geographically with different norms of data protection legislation. How to resolve the issues when some unexpected situation occur, which makes data inaccessible. So both CU and CSP face the challenge of accountability.

G D'Angelo et al. [51] proposed a system that records the flight data. The idea is to accomplish all the stored data on the cloud in the BC network. The events are recorded on the BC, which are VM initialization, the timestamp of accessed resources, deletion, modification, and file upload. All these events need to be notified either by the CU or by the CSP; these events help to identify the cause of SLA violation. To understand these better let's consider the data archive and backup of Amazon Glacier. These services allow you to: (i) store a data block k; (ii) read back data block k; and (iii) delete data block k. Now let's assume CSP cannot deliver the requested block k to the CU or the provided block k is different than expected. In such cases, series of inspections on BC can reveal whether CSP lost k, or CU updated k, or CU has deleted or never uploaded k on the cloud server.

8.3.7 Service Quality Monitoring

The current demand of cloud usage has forced the CSP to maintain a massive pool of computing resources in the infrastructure in order to avoid SLA violation. To alleviate the issue of underutilized and overprovisioned resources, CSPs come together to scale and share their resources in FCE so as to maximize their profit and provide better Quality of Service (QoS) [52]. Due to some unbending issues, including FCE stability, long-time commitments from CSP's to CU's, a fair revenue-sharing model, and the presence of untrusted unknown stakeholders, a cloudchain was proposed [53]. A cloudchain allows CSP to outsource their resources and maintain a history of values changed during the exchange. BC-based model removes the barriers of traditional cloud computing and offers a fully transparent and distributed administration by maintaining the agreement between CU and CSP over the services. For a BC-based FCE, it is crucial to avoid blind trust in SLA and at the same time to maintain QoS without any problem. Due to the unaccessed outside data, BC is unable to handle the misbehaviors of CSPs in the system.

Taghavi et al. [54] introduced a Oracle-based verifier agent that monitors the QoS and the same is reported to the SC deployed on the BC network. Oracle is a trusted third party that communicates outside of the BC network. The interaction between CSP and CU while providing services or a request from another CSP comprises of autonomous system through SC. The CU seeks high-quality monitored services at nearly no cost and CSP aims to achieve balanced services with less conserved capacity. A SC which is deployed is executed, which provides a proof that whatever data is retrieved is tamperproof. The service quality is monitored with the help of five multi-agent models, i.e. Request Agent, CSP Agent, Verifier Agent, and two SC agents, one is the Registry Profile Contract Agent and the other is the Registry Verifier agent. The Registry Profile Contract agent triggers the SC when a new transaction takes place, and a BC node is updated based on the data received from SC. The Registry Verifier agent checks and detects any unusual activity by the request agent.

8.3.8 Resource Sharing in FCE

Generally, CU purchase a cloud service from a single CSP as each CSP maintains their marketplace and, due to the absence of a competitive environment, CU struggles to choose the appropriate cost-effective services. That becomes the reason for higher pricing, and a single CSP cannot maintain different types of competitive structure. Cloud exchange is the potential solution for a single CSP, which adopts the conventional model in which it is fully controlled by an organization; due to centralization, it suffers from a single point of failure and tempering of transaction. While CU looking for suitable services, dishonest CSP may display harassment advertisement and, in the case of a transaction dispute between CU and CSP, the final judgment can be unfair or biased towards a certain CSP.

Xie et al. [31] presented an overview of BC-based cloud exchange. The problems and challenges are depicted in Figure 8.5. Few BC-based markets named as 'Nasdaq linq' which is a private security-based cloud market for buying and selling securities with less risk exposure and settlement time, which eventually lowers the administrative burden. The counterparty digital currency market on Bitcoin, which is safer and lower in transaction fees, is a digital decentralized currency exchange where a user creates its own asset and trades without middlemen. Bitshare digital asset market, with lower transaction fees and more reliable than others, an organization can issue their stock in bitshare network. In Enerchain, an energy product market which is

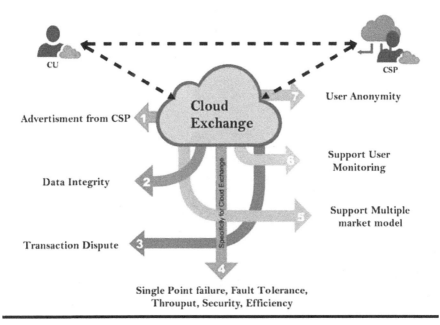

Figure 8.5   Problems and Challenges in Cloud Exchange [31]

safer and more reliable, a user can trade power and gas without third party interaction. Still, cloud exchange suffers security and privacy, vulnerable repudiation, and transaction disputes.

8.4 Open Issues and Challenges

Although BC has provided the solution to various issues in FCE as a result of its unique features such as trust, immutability, transparency, and disintermediation, there are still issues and challenges which cannot be addressed with the help of BC, due to its existing limitations. Figure 8.6 depicts the issues and challenges of BC-based FCE environments.

Standardization of SLA in FCE: In multi-cloud environment number of CSPs come together to provide services in a federated environment, traditionally each CSP has their own API and advertising offerings, but a federated environment requires all offerings in standard format, so that all the service offerings can be easy to analyze for consideration from CU.

Suitable CSP identification in FCE: In a competitive cloud environment when multiple CSP come together to utilize the resources and offer their services from a common API, where CU needs to exhaustively search for the best possible

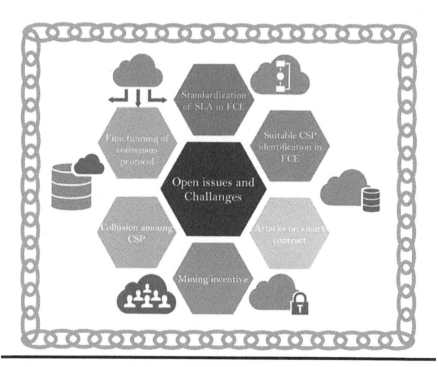

Figure 8.6 Issues and Challenges in FCE

economical CSP. So, there is a need for an automated program that takes the CU's request and searches for a suitable CSP. After identifying CSP, the system executes the SC between CU and CSP.

Attacks on SC: SC is a program that executes automatically, i.e. without the involvement of a third party, and resides within a decentralized BC network. They are capable of executing commands on their own on some specific incident triggered in the system. Once it is deployed, it cannot be changed, which does not allows it to update through any security patch found against any vulnerability. The most common attack on SCs are parity wallet hack and decentralized autonomous organization attack, so it's very crucial to deploy a strong security strategy in it. The following seven attack techniques severely impact the SC.

- Re-entrancy
- SC overflow and underflow
- Short address attack
- Default visibility
- Transaction ordering dependence
- Timestamp dependence
- Code injection attack

Mining incentive: The miner is flooded with a large number of transactions at any given time, the number of transactions in a block is determined by block length and size of the block. When the sender includes the amount of information in the message, it will be difficult for the miner to pick the block. Moreover, if we use a proof-of-stack (PoS) consensus algorithm to verify the block, multiple miners come together and create a federation in the mining community due to higher stack count they easily got a chance to participate in mining and create a monopoly which restricts this system to provide fair mining chances to all the miners [41]. Likewise, in PoW the miners with better infrastructure, provide a difficult target value faster when compared with miners with moderate infrastructure, which is not fair in a decentralized system.

Collusion among CSP: In a multi-cloud environment when two or more CSP form their federation and offer services, then they can manipulate the services with higher price and low QoS. BC has no control over this type of monopoly by CSP.

Fine-tuning of the consensus protocol: In the present day, BC has become common to use along with cryptocurrency and smart contracts in different applications and BC applies a consensus protocol to verify the block in the network; in a distributed network there is no perfect consensus protocol. As attackers need only 50% of the computational power to generate a private chain to replace the original one to have a double-spend attack and a proof-of-work protocol consumes substantial computational power, which is not good for low-powered devices in the federated environment [55]. Fault tolerance, low power consumption, and scalability are among the issues of consensus protocol used in the FCE. Moreover, consensus schemes might require effective rule mining schemes for low-powered computations, which requires tight optimization constraints [56]. Thus, the fine-tuning of pre-defined consensus schemes is a practiced art.

8.5 Conclusion

This chapter presents a systematic survey of the technological aspects for the re-engineering of cloud computing using BC technologies. BC, due to its chronological and auditable nature, has matured to provide smart solutions to FCE. The proposed survey includes three technological aspects; namely, the security, service, and performance of FCE. We have focused on state-of-the-art schemes of BC-based FCE to provide solutions for cloud re-engineering, cloud data provenance, BC-based cloud offloading, cloud exchange in market-oriented BC-based network, different security attack on FCE, BC-based SLA verification, access control to data centers, BC-based resource scheduling, BC-based storage reliability on cloud and resource sharing. A detailed taxonomy and challenges of BC deployments are discussed. The proposed survey would serve as a guideline for research scholars, industry practitioners, and FCE stakeholders to provide secure cloud-based solutions with BC. In future, we would like to explore recommender models to cloud users in terms of services offered through FCE.

References

[1] A. Ladha, P. Bhattacharya, N. Chaubey, and U. Bodkhe, "Iigpts: IoT-based framework for intelligent green public transportation system," in *Proceedings of First International Conference on Computing, Communications, and Cyber-Security (IC4S 2019)*, (P. K. Singh, W. Paw lowski, N. Kumar,, S. Tanwar, J. J. P. C. Rodrigues, and O. M.S, eds.), vol. 121, pp. 183–195, Springer International Publishing, 2020.

[2] U. Bodkhe, and S. Tanwar, "Secure data dissemination techniques for iot applications: Research challenges and opportunities," *Software Practice and Experience*, pp. 1–23, 2020, doi: 10.1002/spe.2811.

[3] P. N. Sureshbhai, P. Bhattacharya, and S. Tanwar, "Karuna: A blockchain-based sentiment analysis framework for fraud cryptocurrency schemes," in *2020 IEEE International Conference on Communications Workshops (ICC Workshops)*, pp. 1–6, 2020.

[4] L. Da Xu, and W. Viriyasitavat, "Application of blockchain in collaborative internet-of-things services," *IEEE Transactions on Computational Social Systems*, vol. 6, no. 6, pp. 1295–1305, 2019.

[5] T. Aste, P. Tasca, and T. Di Matteo, "Blockchain technologies: The foreseeable impact on society and industry," *computer*, vol. 50, no. 9, pp. 18–28, 2017.

[6] P. Bhattacharya, S. Tanwar, U. Bodke, S. Tyagi, and N. Kumar, "Bindaas: Blockchain-based deep-learning as-a-service in healthcare 4.0 applications," *IEEE Transactions on Network Science and Engineering*, pp. 1–1, 2019, doi: 10.1109/TNSE.2019.2961932.

[7] U. Bodkhe, P. Bhattacharya, S. Tanwar, S. Tyagi, N. Kumar, and M. S. Obaidat, "Blohost: Blockchain enabled smart tourism and hospitality management," in *2019 International Conference on Computer, Information and Telecommunication Systems (CITS)*, pp. 1–5, Aug 2019.

[8] A. Dorri, M. Steger, S. S. Kanhere, and R. Jurdak, "Blockchain: A distributed solution to automotive security and privacy," *IEEE Communications Magazine*, vol. 55, no. 12, pp. 119–125, 2017.

[9] H. Zhou, X. Ouyang, Z. Ren, J. Su, C. de Laat, and Z. Zhao, "A blockchain based witness model for trustworthy cloud service level agreement enforcement," in *IEEE INFOCOM 2019-IEEE Conference on Computer Communications*, pp. 1567–1575, IEEE, 2019.

[10] K. Gai, K.-K. R. Choo, and L. Zhu, "Blockchain-enabled reengineering of cloud data-centers," *IEEE Cloud Computing*, vol. 5, no. 6, pp. 21–25, 2018.

[11] F. S. Hardwick, R. N. Akram, and K. Markantonakis, "Fair and transparent blockchain based tendering framework-a step towards open governance," in *2018 17th IEEE International Conference On Trust, Security And Privacy In Computing And Communications/12th IEEE International Conference On Big Data Science And Engineering (TrustCom/BigDataSE)*, pp. 1342–1347, IEEE, 2018.

[12] A. Srivastava, P. Bhattacharya, A. Singh, A. Mathur, O. Prakash, and R. Pradhan, "A distributed credit transfer educational framework based on blockchain," in *2018 Second International Conference on Advances in Computing, Control and Communication Technology (IAC3T)*, pp. 54–59, 2018.

[13] R. Gupta, A. Shukla, P. Mehta, P. Bhattacharya, S. Tanwar, S. Tyagi, and N. Kumar, "Vahak: A blockchain-based outdoor delivery scheme using uav for healthcare 4.0 services," in *IEEE INFOCOM 2020 – IEEE Conference on Computer Communications Workshops (INFOCOM WKSHPS)*, pp. 255–260, 2020.

[14] B. Chen, Z. Tan, and W. Fang, "Blockchain-based implementation for financial product management," in *2018 28th International Telecommunication Networks and Applications Conference (ITNAC)*, pp. 1–3, IEEE, 2018.

[15] A. Hari, and T. Lakshman, "The internet blockchain: A distributed, tamper-resistant transaction framework for the internet," in *Proceedings of the 15th ACM Workshop on Hot Topics in Networks*, pp. 204–210, 2016.

[16] S. B. Patel, H. A. Kheruwala, M. Alazab, N. Patel, R. Damani, P. Bhattacharya, S. Tanwar, and N. Kumar, "Biouav: Blockchain-envisioned framework for digital identification to secure access in next-generation uavs," in *Proceedings of the 2nd ACM MobiCom Workshop on Drone Assisted Wireless Communications for 5G and Beyond, DroneCom '20*, (New York, NY, USA), pp. 43–48, Association for Computing Machinery, 2020.

[17] K. Biswas, and V. Muthukkumarasamy, "Securing smart cities using blockchain technology," in *2016 IEEE 18th international conference on high performance computing and communications; IEEE 14th international conference on smart city; IEEE 2nd international conference on data science and systems (HPCC/SmartCity/DSS)*, pp. 1392–1393, IEEE, 2016.

[18] R. Cole, M. Stevenson, and J. Aitken, "Blockchain technology: Implications for operations and supply chain management," *Supply Chain Management: An International Journal*, vol. 24, no. 4, pp. 469–483, 2019.

[19] N. Fabiano, "Internet of things and blockchain: Legal issues and privacy. the challenge for a privacy standard," in *2017 IEEE International Conference on Internet of Things*

(*iThings*) *and IEEE Green Computing and Communications (GreenCom) and IEEE Cyber, Physical and Social Computing (CPSCom) and IEEE Smart Data (SmartData)*, pp. 727–734, IEEE, 2017.

[20] W. Meng, E. W. Tischhauser, Q. Wang, Y. Wang, and J. Han, "When intrusion detection meets blockchain technology: A review," *IEEE Access*, vol. 6, pp. 10179–10188, 2018.

[21] U. Bodkhe, S. Tanwar, P. Bhattacharya, and N. Kumar, "Blockchain for precision irrigation: Opportunities and challenges," *Transactions on Emerging Telecommunications Technologies*, p. e4059, 2020, doi: 10.1002/ett.4059.

[22] U. Bodkhe, and S. Tanwar, "A taxonomy of secure data dissemination techniques for iot environment," *IET Software*, pp. 1–12, July 2020.

[23] R. Matzutt, J. Hiller, M. Henze, J. H. Ziegeldorf, D. Müllmann, O. Hohlfeld, and K. Wehrle, "A quantitative analysis of the impact of arbitrary blockchain content on bitcoin," in *International Conference on Financial Cryptography and Data Security*, pp. 420–438, Springer, 2018.

[24] H. S. Yin, and R. Vatrapu, "A first estimation of the proportion of cybercriminal entities in the bitcoin ecosystem using supervised machine learning," in *2017 IEEE International Conference on Big Data (Big Data)*, pp. 3690–3699, IEEE, 2017.

[25] Z. Zheng, S. Xie, H.-N. Dai, X. Chen, and H. Wang, "Blockchain challenges and opportunities: A survey," *International Journal of Web and Grid Services*, vol. 14, no. 4, pp. 352–375, 2018.

[26] R. B. Uriarte, and R. De Nicola, "Blockchain-based decentralized cloud/fog solutions: Challenges, opportunities, and standards," *IEEE Communications Standards Magazine*, vol. 2, no. 3, pp. 22–28, 2018.

[27] H. Zhu, Y. Wang, X. Hei, W. Ji, and L. Zhang, "A blockchain-based decentralized cloud resource scheduling architecture," in *2018 International Conference on Networking and Network Applications (NaNA)*, pp. 324–329, IEEE, 2018.

[28] I. Sukhodolskiy, and S. Zapechnikov, "A blockchain-based access control system for cloud storage," in *2018 IEEE Conference of Russian Young Researchers in Electrical and Electronic Engineering (EIConRus)*, pp. 1575–1578, IEEE, 2018.

[29] W. Gao, W. G. Hatcher, and W. Yu, "A survey of blockchain: Techniques, applications, and challenges," in *2018 27th international conference on computer communication and networks (ICCCN)*, pp. 1–11, IEEE, 2018.

[30] Y. Jiao, P. Wang, D. Niyato, and K. Suankaewmanee, "Auction mechanisms in cloud/fog computing resource allocation for public blockchain networks," *IEEE Transactions on Parallel and Distributed Systems*, vol. 30, no. 9, pp. 1975–1989, 2019.

[31] S. Xie, Z. Zheng, W. Chen, J. Wu, H.-N. Dai, and M. Imran, "Blockchain for cloud exchange: A survey," *Computers & Electrical Engineering*, vol. 81, p. 106526, 2020.

[32] H. Baniata, and A. Kertesz, "A survey on blockchain-fog integration approaches," *IEEE Access*, vol. 8, pp. 102657–102668, 2020.

[33] N. Sohrabi, X. Yi, Z. Tari, and I. Khalil, "Bacc: Blockchain-based access control for cloud data," in *Proceedings of the Australasian Computer Science Week Multiconference*, pp. 1–10, 2020.

[34] A. Kumari, R. Gupta, S. Tanwar, and N. Kumar, "Blockchain and AI amalgamation for energy cloud management: Challenges, solutions, and future directions," *Journal of Parallel and Distributed Computing*, vol. 143, pp. 148–166, 2020.

[35] U. Bodkhe, S. Tanwar, K. Parekh, P. Khanpara, S. Tyagi, N. Kumar, and M. Alazab, "Blockchain for industry 4.0: A comprehensive review," *IEEE Access*, vol. 8, pp. 79764–79800, 2020, doi: 1109/ACCESS.2020.2988579.

[36] U. Bodkhe, D. Mehta, S. Tanwar, P. Bhattacharya, P. K. Singh, and W. Hong, "A survey on decentralized consensus mechanisms for cyber physical systems," *IEEE Access*, vol. 8, pp. 54371–54401, 2020.

[37] S. Nakamoto, and A. Bitcoin, "A peer-to-peer electronic cash system," *Bitcoin*, vol. 4, 2008, URL: https://bitcoin.org/bitcoin.pdf

[38] D. Guegan, "Public blockchain versus private blokhain," 2017, https://halshs. archives-ouvertes.fr/halshs-01524440/, last accessed 23-07-2021.

[39] E. Androulaki, A. Barger, V. Bortnikov, C. Cachin, K. Christidis, A. De Caro, D. Enyeart, C. Ferris, G. Laventman, Y. Manevich, et al., "Hyperledger fabric: A distributed operating system for permissioned blockchains," in *Proceedings of the thirteenth EuroSys conference*, pp. 1–15, 2018.

[40] J. Mendling, I. Weber, W. V. D. Aalst, J. V. Brocke, C. Cabanillas, F. Daniel, S. Debois, C. D. Ciccio, M. Dumas, S. Dustdar, et al., "Blockchains for business process management challenges and opportunities," *ACM Transactions on Management Information Systems (TMIS)*, vol. 9, no. 1, pp. 1–16, 2018.

[41] P. Bhattacharya, P. Mehta, S. Tanwar, M. S. Obaidat, and K. F. Hsiao, "Heal: A blockchain-envisioned signcryption scheme for healthcare iot ecosystems," in *2020 International Conference on Communications, Computing, Cybersecurity, and Informatics (CCCI)*, pp. 1–6, 2020.

[42] S. Ali, G. Wang, M. Z. A. Bhuiyan, and H. Jiang, "Secure data provenance in cloud-centric internet of things via blockchain smart contracts," in *2018 IEEE SmartWorld, Ubiquitous Intelligence & Computing, Advanced & Trusted Computing, Scalable Computing & Communications, Cloud & Big Data Computing, Internet of People and Smart City Innovation (SmartWorld/SCALCOM/UIC/ATC/CBDCom/IOP/SCI)*, pp. 991–998, IEEE, 2018.

[43] A. Shukla, P. Bhattacharya, S. Tanwar, N. Kumar, and M. Guizani, "Dwara: A deep learning-based dynamic toll pricing scheme for intelligent transportation systems," *IEEE Transactions on Vehicular Technology*, vol. 69, no. 11, pp. 12510–12520, 2020.

[44] J. Zhang, L. Zheng, L. Gong, and Z. Gu, "A survey on security of cloud environment: Threats, solutions, and innovation," in *2018 IEEE Third International Conference on Data Science in Cyberspace (DSC)*, pp. 910–916, IEEE, 2018.

[45] A. T. Wonjiga, S. Peisert, L. Rilling, and C. Morin, "Blockchain as a trusted component in cloud sla verification," in *Proceedings of the 12th IEEE/ACM International Conference on Utility and Cloud Computing Companion*, pp. 93–100, 2019.

[46] R. A. Popa, C. M. Redfield, N. Zeldovich, and H. Balakrishnan, "Cryptdb: Protecting confidentiality with encrypted query processing," in *Proceedings of the Twenty-Third ACM Symposium on Operating Systems Principles*, pp. 85–100, 2011.

[47] R. Poddar, T. Boelter, and R. A. Popa, "Arx: A strongly encrypted database system.," *IACR Cryptol. ePrint Arch.*, vol. 2016, p. 591, 2016.

[48] T. McConaghy, R. Marques, A. Müller, D. De Jonghe, T. McConaghy, G. McMullen, R. Henderson, S. Bellemare, and A. Granzotto, "Bigchaindb: A scalable blockchain database," *white paper, BigChainDB*, 2016, https://git.berlin/bigchaindb/site/raw/ commit/b2d98401b65175f0fe0c169932ddca0b98a456a6/_src/whitepaper/big-chaindb-whitepaper.pdf.

[49] R. K. Ko, and M. A. Will, "Progger: An efficient, tamper-evident kernel-space logger for cloud data provenance tracking," in *2014 IEEE 7th International Conference on Cloud Computing*, pp. 881–889, IEEE, 2014.

[50] U. Bodkhe, S. Tanwar, P. Shah, J. Chaklasiya, and M. Vora, "Markov model for password attack prevention," in *Proceedings of First International Conference on Computing,*

Communications, and Cyber-Security (IC4S 2019), (P. K. Singh, W. Pawl owski, N. Kumar,, S. Tanwar, J. J. P. C. Rodrigues, and O. M.S, eds.), vol. 121, pp. 831–843, Springer International Publishing, 2020.

[51] G. D'Angelo, S. Ferretti, and M. Marzolla, "A blockchain-based flight data recorder for cloud accountability," in *Proceedings of the 1st Workshop on Cryptocurrencies and Blockchains for Distributed Systems*, pp. 93–98, 2018.

[52] M. M. Hassan, A. Alelaiwi, and A. Alamri, "A dynamic and efficient coalition formation game in cloud federation for multimedia applications," in *Proceedings of the International Conference on Grid Computing and Applications*, p. 71, 2015.

[53] M. Taghavi, J. Bentahar, H. Otrok, and K. Bakhtiyari, "Cloudchain: A blockchain-based coopetition differential game model for cloud computing," in *International Conference on Service-Oriented Computing*, pp. 146–161, Springer, 2018.

[54] M. Taghavi, J. Bentahar, H. Otrok, and K. Bakhtiyari, "A blockchain-based model for cloud service quality monitoring," *IEEE Transactions on Services Computing*, vol. 13, no. 2, pp. 276–288, 2019.

[55] P. Bhattacharya, S. Tanwar, R. Shah, and A. Ladha, "Mobile edge computing-enabled blockchain framework—A survey," in *Proceedings of ICRIC 2019* (P. K. Singh, A. K. Kar, Y. Singh, M. H. Kolekar, and S. Tanwar, eds.), (Cham), pp. 797–809, Springer International Publishing, 2020.

[56] A. Verma, P. Bhattacharya, U. Bodkhe, A. Ladha, and S. Tanwar, "Dams: Dynamic association for view materialization based on rule mining scheme," in *The International Conference on Recent Innovations in Computing*, pp. 529–544, Springer, 2020

Chapter 9

Blockchain-Based Secured Data Management in Confidential Cyber Defence Applications

S. Satheesh Kumar
KPR Institute of Engineering and Technology, India

S. Gokul Kumar
Ros Tech (A&D), India

S. Chandraprabha
KPR Institute of Engineering and Technology, India

B. Maruthi Shankar
Sri Krishna College of Engineering and Technology, India

S. A. Siva Kumar
Ashoka Women's Engineering College, India

Contents

DOI: 10.1201/9781003129486-9

9.1 Introduction

Blockchain Technology does not solve complex issues. Rather, it makes the complexities more organized in order to improve real-time efficiency in the current defence system. The complexities cluttered in the current system in terms of managing data and the protection of critical data are the major challenges that industry aims to resolve.

Government's involvement could create central repositories or enterprise systems for sharing information internally and across private agencies. Under any circumstances, these data must not be accessible by any third parties or private sectors indiscriminately. Thus, Blockchain provides an environment in which the data can be shared easily across individuals and organizations systematically and each person can take ownership of their data and control the flow of information.

Emerging Blockchain technology can support this situation so that each defence sector can upload the information, the records of every transactions, information, test result in a dedicated ledger within the encrypted database of Blockchain. Either individuals or the sector can access the information through the internet. Every user is given the authorization of read or alter the information with their individual private-key cryptography. In this situation, certain specified information can be exposed to designated agencies meeting the predefined conditions [1].

9.2 System Overview

Implementation on a Control Unit (CU) level is essential for the defence industry to store the testing data according to the industrial standards because CUs are unchallengeable for consumers and can only be changed by the producer. On-Board Diagnostic II (OBDII) socket is implemented to accumulation and transfer testing variables, although it is not considered to be adequate as they are likely to influence and hacking of data from the dongles. Hence, retrieving data is recommended directly from the Control Unit.

As an additional security protocol, the Enigma Coding Method is initiated to control private sectors to view or analyse the portal. The secret code will be randomly generated and will be shared in an encrypted manner to the users who want to enter the portal instantly.

The Ethereum calligraphy is Turing full, which allows the executing some encoding judgment on Blockchain and the implementation of smart contracts. Thus, the execution and monitoring of test data and storing process once the ownership is changed becomes crucial. So, the Ethereum system uses a consensus mechanism called "Mining codes" ensuring the high time and consumption of resources through Proof of Work (PoW).

Novel Blockchain-based prototype architectures include all interactions and concerned parties for smart contracts. The primary party is the operating party, who initialized the accounts, i.e., the testing unit has a private key. The light client had the deposit of the private key, which is obtainable for the testing unit holder who can pass information/specimen results to the database of the Blockchain network. In this chapter, a variety of security upgrading and modern cryptography provenance using Blockchain is addressed. This provides us greater assurance and information security in defence applications. The architecture of Blockchain is shown in Figure 9.1.

9.3 Blockchain in Defence Sectors

Defence and military sectors across the world are confronted by a wide range of cybersecurity threats. Hackers continue to steal information and sell or pass to this to other private and negative groups, which will end up damaging public life. The problems faced by military and defence organizations are the same as those faced by most other groups: Tracking of transactions; A ack of integrity in the ERP Systems; Poor quality; and Lack of automation. These are also among problems faced by defence and military sectors in India, which may lead information leakage.

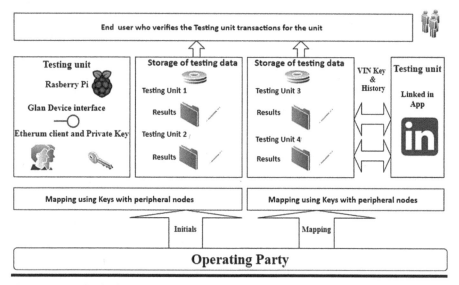

Figure 9.1 Block chain architecture

9.3.1 Objectives/Framework

This chapter addresses one of the solutions that Blockchain can be used to reorganize the data essential to store tested data in the system. With regard to the Blockchain-level security for the military schemes, serious data could confirm that all received data are precise, and the data could continue as protected as possible from external intimidations.

9.3.2 Motivation for the Work

In the field of defence, Blockchain is mentioned as an emerging technology, which provides efficient output and solution when executed in recent years. Involving multiple parties, Blockchain provides the solution mentioned below:

- **Content:** Alteration of the data is not possible without the concerned knowledge. This also concludes all data transactions can be tracked and monitored end to end.
- **Transparency:** Blockchain technologies helps to integrated Product Lifecycle Management (PLM) and Enterprise Resources Planning (ERP) systems end to end, which ensures all the parties concerned can remain on the same page and transactions cannot be lost in the systems.

- **Validation:** Business rules automation and validating the data will reduce the cost, increase efficiency, diminish exceptions and improve reconciliation.
- **Quality improvement:** 100% quality achievement and trust across the team.
- **Accurate reporting:** Through the decentralized nature of block technology, it is possible to streamline the business, and to achieve both reporting regularization and operational consistency.
- **Data security:** With no single point of failure, encryption for record-level data security, and greater network resiliency are possible. Automation of access rights is possible.
- **A step towards digitalization:** In the defence field, Blockchain can be used to achieve end-to-end digitalization and countries all over the world can invest in this technology.

9.3.3 Existing Proof-of-Concept

- **Design and implementation of a wireless OBD II fleet management system [8]:** In this article terms the effort that has been complete in the plan and progress of a wireless OBD II fleet organisation system. The scheme goals to amount the speed, distance and fuel ingesting of vehicles for tracing and investigation resolutions.
- **Trusted systems of records based on Blockchain technology—a prototype for mileage storing in the automotive industry [9]:** A scheme model to decrease mileage deception on car markets. The method validates possibility of important process of proceedings for (vehicle) information like mileage information expending a disseminated database founded on the open Ethereum network and smart bonds
- **PUFchain [10]:** Article states the historic block chain that can instantaneously lever equipment that is good at information safekeeping, which is significant for the evolving **Internet-of-Everything (IoE).** Article states an exclusive idea of block chain which assimilates physical safety primitives named **Physical Unclonable features (PUFs)** that can resolve scalability, delay, and energy obligation tasks and is named as PUF chain.

9.4 Requirements of a Trusted Defence System

Once any block has been introduced to the Blockchain, modification is impossible. If modification of data does take place, then the block becomes invalid. Thus, blocks should be added correctly the first time they are generated. The testing of Blockchains has processes which are both critical and complex. The transaction involves the following processes: validating, decryption, encryption, transmission etc. The general layout of Blockchain technology is shown in Figure 9.2. In order to ensure the smooth running of processes, testing need to be done end to end. This property of the process allows the whole technology to block the hacking.

9.5 Type of Testing Needed for Blockchain

■ **Functional Testing**
Testing of each function is needed to ensure the component in the system is working correctly. If there are any problems in the function, then the whole transaction in the block chain becomes invalid.

■ **Integration Testing**
Several systems and environments can be spanned in the whole cycle of Blockchain. So as to ensure consistent performance, it is necessary to ensure

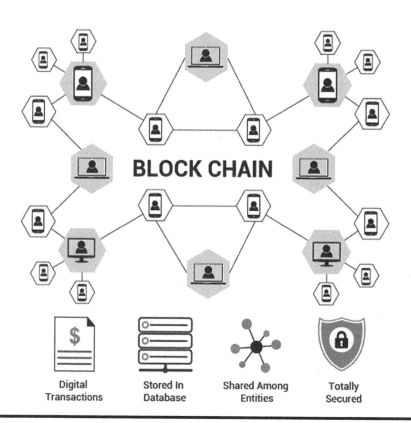

Figure 9.2   Layout of Block chain Technology

the working of interfaces and the integration of different parts of the system. Integration testing is very important.

■ **Security Testing**

Security testing for Blockchain applications is the most important of all the testing parameters. Security testing ensures that the authorization systems are robust and adequate protection is implemented and free from malicious attacks. Integrity, authentication, confidentiality, and non-repudiation are also checked during security testing.

■ **Performance Testing**

Finally, the performance of any system needs to be ensured if the application is to be successful. The system must be quick enough to cope if the number of transaction increases and users become robust. Bottlenecks must be addressed and solutions must be developed to overcome them. If there is any change in the applications, the Blockchain technology will adapt such that the performance is not affected. This trust in the system will support the defence sectors in preventing changes in the data and any hacking of the system [7].

9.6 Preliminary Assessment of Blockchain

Blockchain technology is based on two strategies. The first one is a **transparent-privacy access prevention**, which permits the open accounting of transactions and privacy and also eliminates double entries. This privacy access prevention can be controlled by an organized way of providing permission to the user and equal rights for the transactions and contributions [6].

The second strategy is a **conflict between security and latency.** The immunity of the accounted transaction is hold by the "Norm logic", which is solved in every block added to the chain. This Norm logic helps in any kind of change or manipulation. This logic increases the travel time and cost, which reduces the process speed when a new block is added. This can be avoided by giving permission for everyone in the group to write a block ensuring the set of nodes are limited.

The block of total transactions can be modified to the statements of ledgers once the network node reaches the end of the validation. This proposes the creatio of a new algorithmic logic to understand the addition of new transactions. The verification of the transactions is confirmed by the nodes which eliminates the double spending and confirms data have not been hacked [3].

9.7 Data Manipulations in Defence Industries

Currently, there is no proper solution to prevent the data hacking and testing reliable system. We recommend a process using Blockchain technology to solve this problem of information storage in defence systems. To test a product, not all of the facilities are available in a single sector. The product has to travel to different government labs, testing environments, and private sector labs, where testing is carried out.

During this time, data are not stored in a trusted environment and access can be done by any means. Thus, this technology eliminates the third party by facilitating the timestamped and immutable distributed system of records. The documentations are kept as secret by the sectors and this can be manipulated when transferred from one system to another through dongles or service devices. It is hard to disclose the data hacking scam. It is necessary to address this problem and store the data in a scattered record.

9.8 Requirements of a Reliable Defence Data-Storing Arrangement

Technically, the solution can be limited, result to verify or check multiple party access data storage system in the defence sector. Thus, a trustworthy solution is proposed to overcome this problem of variable or data leakage in this sector. So, a decentralized application using Internet of Things and software/hardware setup to a third party which is independent in order to ensure the security of any data that are generated, which does not void the stored data setup output [4].

In the prototype setup as shown in Figure 9.3, the data storage and reading can be given as T1 and T2 and the interface can be T3. The request to change can be T4. Manual intervention is to be minimized and the complete automation process will be made to check and verify the data with complete security enforcement. This can be regarded as T5. The frequency of data change needs to be monitored, which is T6. The project name of test data can be stored with **Unique number (UNR)**. Every testing result should be stored in the Control Unit-Gland device database and any user who accesses the data must register the login with authorization [3].

As a test case, we are going to test a mechanical actuator system and the testing data are stored in the Blockchain environment in order to share data in the defence sector. Generally, the testing facility is unavailable in a single facility, meaning that the unit needs to travel to different labs in the sector and that testing needs to be completed.

A mechanical system to be used in the defence field has to undergo the following tests:

- Environmental Stress Screening Test
- Burn-In Test
- Random Vibration Test
- Thermal Cycle test
- Random Vibration Test

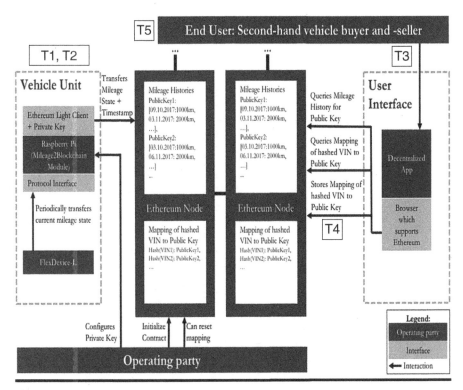

Figure 9.3 Prototype setup

- Fabrication Heat Treatment Test
- Component Inspection Test
- Subassembly Inspection Test
- Main Assembly Inspection Test
- Testing Equipment
- Physical Appearance Test
- Insulation Resistance Test
- Load Test
- Electrical and Mechanical Travel Tests

All the tested data results can be stored in the hardware and secured using Blockchain.

9.9 Proposed Architecture and Its Implementation

This section explains the solution and methodology of working, as well as the test setup. The result of each test data needs to be transmitted and stored in Blockchain. The generated data are interlinked with Gland device which works with the testing device, say an actuator, and then transmits the data into the block chain and stores it. The setup is also attached to a Raspberry Pi computer, which is a gateway from the testing device to the Blockchain module. Every piece of output data is transmitted and stored in the Blockchain module. To store the time and level of complexity of data, we need a web-based application, which is accessed from any browser module.

This prototype consists of all parties who are responsible for the transactions. Accounts initialization is carried out by the first party, through the private key of each testing unit. While the key is stored in the Raspberry Pi, the key will be available with the tester. The first party initializes and can verify the testing data [2, 3].

Figure 9.4 demonstrates the hardware arrangement of the closed network. The Gland device G and M uses buses to simulate to the CU. The Gland device tracks the testing data from the testing data hardware setup, as shown in Figure 9.5, and sends it to the next module.

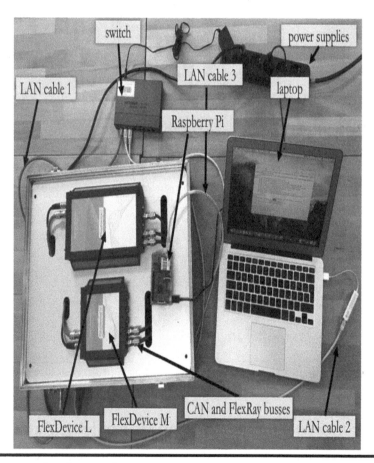

Figure 9.4   Closed network

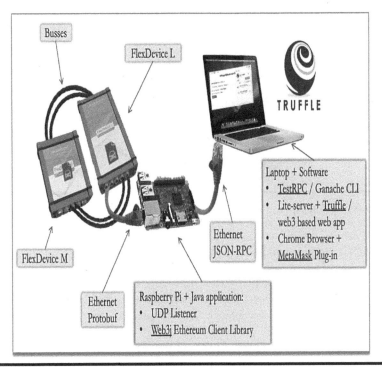

Figure 9.5   Testing data Hardware setup

9.10 Design Changes

The data created in the Gland device simulate the testing data result and send it to the Blockchain module using the LAN cables. The module consists of a test node, which monitors the transaction; through the private key, the data are becoming scrambled and transmitted. The first login is assigned to the tester and the second login is given to those parties who want to access the testing data. There will be a timestamp for every data modification. The Blockchain client ensures data storage once the one variety of testing is done. Then, using the Gland device, the authorised person can log in through the developed web application and check the data results.

The data creation, tracking and storing can be monitored using this entire module. The data can be serialized using the buffer protocol of Google and transmitted as packed data using the transmission protocol [2].

A separate server is allocated to store and monitor the static files, to serve the front end. The public key is mapped through the source code, including the time and testing result storage.

Test Setup II

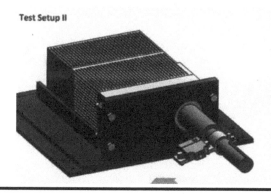

Figure 9.6   Test setup

9.11 Acceptance Procedure

The tester performs the acceptance test procedure of the unit and the full actuator system shall meet the relevant requirements on the order stated and compliance with the conditions of the acceptance. The recorded results ensure that the procedure is met.

Different tests, such as the Electrical Connector Verification, Quiescent Current, and Bond Resistance Test of the Product, is carried out according to the procedure using the test setup (as shown in Figure 9.6) and data are created and transferred to Blockchain modules. Like-wise, the data are created, stored, tracked and transmitted through the modules.

9.12 Promoting Enigma Coding

At this point we introduce the Enigma web-based application. The user, who wants to analyse the data, must have the password and a code data. Once the password is triggered, the Enigma will produce the scramble code, with the other half being found on the Code sheet. These two halves are then typed together to open the login.

9.13 Methods based Evaluation and Discussion

This type of methodology can help the user in military and defence sectors to work on the confidential data without there being any danger of hacking.

Meeting method 1: No limitation in storing data in the modules
Meeting method 2: No limitation in copying the test result data

Meeting method 3: Perfection in user interface coordination
Meeting method 4: High security in database, no one can hack
Meeting method 5: Cost-efficient and user satisfaction

9.14 Needs based Evaluation and Discussion

Need No. 1: There is no restriction to verifying testing data storage and verification of histories
Need No. 2: No restriction in editing and entering the data
Need No. 3: Extended decentralized application for high interface usability
Need No. 4: The data are more reliable and manipulation-free
Need No. 5: Completely automated process for every transaction
Need No. 6: Completely cost efficient

9.15 Challenges and Limitations

■ **Limited scalability in application**
If the units are testing more for any project, then the data storage will increase. This will reduce the system speed, making it a burden for the software and hardware setup. Thus, the system may slow down. Upgrading may be required if the storage capacity needs to be increased.

■ **Transaction cost**
For maintaining the setup, the cost is needed. Accordingly, over a specific period of time, if the number of users increases, so will the cost per transaction.

9.16 Conclusion

The prototype stores the testing data and the resulting values are protected and its cost is very low patronised way on scattered database established on Blockchain expertise. The storage procedure is totally involuntary, and it requires no human intervention. When established, the system ensures that there is no need for any reliable other party because of the arrangement of the data on the private Ethereum network and the execution of keen agreements.

Testing information is available and apparent to any who recognises the **testing identification number (TIN),** when the TIN is enumerated on the Blockchain by a user. The information would be regained by ingoing the TIN in instinctive web application so the consumers will not want familiarity of basic Blockchain technology. Hence, there is no need for dominant expert requests to be reliable in order to authorize the database.

9.17 Future Work

Information in the Blockchain is absolute, being stored in a scattered database that sorts it forcefully and protected in contradiction of influence or possible hackers in contrast to an essential database. In demand to fulfil with information security and assurance anonymity of the users, the planning of a TIN to a distance information record on the Blockchain will be capable of being updated. The testing of the statement between the reader and the emulator verified that the structure could edge with an objection testing unit and retrieve sensor measurements.

Different technologies are integrated in this device to reduce the cost of designing various pieces of equipment with dissimilar abilities. In future developments of the function we can introduce GPS tracking of data, and WIFI implementation to monitor data in movable systems.

The limitations of the Ethereum network need to be solved through a scaled application. The PoW consensus mechanism needs sufficient power to compute, which leads to scalability and latency limitations. The testing data can cover 1000 transactions per module unit; if this increases, then the process cost will increase. It remains a challenge when the data fluctuate.

Going forward, the Blockchain might overcome the limitation by providing higher fabric limits in the network of trusted nodes and a centralized system of users. This will contradict the requirement of potential buyers in the market. The planned alteration of Ethereum from a PoW to a PoS accord device is predictable in order to report restrictions.

The ability to decentralize is a core feature of Blockchain technology, regardless of how it is used. This function eliminates the single point of vulnerability that could be exploited. As a result, infiltrating networks or locations where access control, data storage, and network traffic are no longer in a single location becomes nearly impossible. As a result, in the near future Blockchain could be one of the most effective cyberthreat prevention techniques. Nonetheless, Blockchain, like any other disruptive technology, faces numerous startup obstacles as it goes through the painful process of growth.

References

[1] Yan Z, Zhang P, Vasilakos AV. A survey on trust management for Internet of Things. *J Netw Comput Appl.* 2014; 42:120–134

[2] Rimba P, Tran AB, Weber I, Staples M, Ponomarev A, Xu X. Quantifying the cost of distrust: comparing blockchain and cloud services for business process execution. *Inf Syst Front.* 2018; 22:489–507

[3] Salimitari M, Chatterjee M. A Survey on Consensus Protocols in Blockchain for IoT Networks.

[4] Katarina Preikschat, Moritz Böhmecke-Schwafert, Jan-Paul Buchwald, Carolin Stickel. Trusted systems of records based on Blockchain technology—A prototype for mileage storing in the automotive industry. *Concurrency and Computation: Practice and Experience* 2021; 33:e5630

[5] CoinDesk. $6.3 Billion: 2018 ICO Funding Has Passed 2017's Total. 2018. https://www.coindesk.com/6-3-billion-2018-ico-funding-alreadyoutpaced-2017/. Accessed October 02, 2019. 14.

[6] Wright A, De Filippi P. Decentralized blockchain technology and the rise of lex cryptographia. *SSRN Electron J.* 2015. 15:2580664.

[7] Nakamoto S. Bitcoin: a peer-to-peer electronic cash system. 2008

[8] Malekian, Reza, Ntefeng Ruth Moloisane, Lakshmi Nair, Bodhaswar T. Maharaj, and Uche AK Chude-Okonkwo. "Design and implementation of a wireless OBD II fleet management system." *IEEE Sensors Journal 17*, no. 4 (2016): 1154–1164.

[9] Preikschat, Katarina, Moritz Böhmecke-Schwafert, Jan-Paul Buchwald, and Carolin Stickel. "Trusted systems of records based on Blockchain technology-a prototype for mileage storing in the automotive industry." *Concurrency and Computation: Practice and Experience* 33, no. 1 (2021): e5630, pp. 1–18.

[10] Mohanty, S. P., V. P. Yanambaka, E. Kougianos, and D. Puthal. "PUFchain: Hardware-assisted blockchain for sustainable simultaneous device and data security in the Internet of Everything (IoE), Sept 2019." (2019), pp. 8–10.

Chapter 10

Blockchain Technology for Privacy and Security Issues and Challenges in IOT-Based Systems

C. J. Raman
St. Joseph's College of Engineering, India

S. Usha Kiruthika
Vellore Institute of Technology, India

L. Javid Ali
St. Joseph's Institute of Technology, India

S. Kanaga Suba Raja
Easwari Engineering College, India

Contents

DOI: 10.1201/9781003129486-10

10.1 Privacy and Security Issues in IoT Systems

Owing to the rapid growth of the Internet of Things (IoT), a number of day-to-day real-time applications are highly influenced by IoT applications. These make human life more sophisticated by making their presence felt in almost everything, ranging from customary equipment to normal household objects. The IoT is of great potential. There are various challenges in terms of making IoT much more user-friendly. Scalable applications in IoT demand a large number of devices that are practically hard to be met due to constraints on time, memory, processing power and energy consumption. Take, for instance, an IoT application that deals with recording the variations in temperature for the entire country. It is more easily said than implemented. Such an application may require hundreds of thousands of devices, churning out huge quantities of data. There are usually inherent variations found in operational characteristics of hardware IoT devices, such as varying sampling rates and variations in error rates. In addition, the sensors and actuators deployed in the IoT environment for monitoring events and data collection/transmission operations are intrinsically complex. Such components of varying complexity are deployed in the IoT environment, leading to the formation of heterogeneous IoT network, where the IoT data may vary. The huge quantity of aggregated IoT data need to be subjected to compression and fusion techniques for smoother transmission and the minimizing of communication costs.

Awareness related to standardized data processing for future IoT is highly recommended. The most disturbing feature in the IoT data transmission is the fact that the integrity of data transmitted or received in an IoT environment is less trustworthy. IoT data is constantly under a variety of threats, from hackers, malicious software, virus etc. The entire IoT environment is highly vulnerable, giving rise to information insecurity. IoT had gained a concrete foothold in several day-to-day applications, which includes smart grid, smart transportation, smart security and smart homes. Varying sizes of applications, like access cards and bus cards, can be developed using IoT technology. Even though the IoT technology influences human life by providing various conveniences, its insecure operating environment cannot ensure personal privacy, leading to the exploitation of personal information by the adversaries. Hence the security aspect of IoT needs further in-depth analysis and cannot be set aside. The exploitation of IoT signals will have a direct impact on the information exchanged between the devices. The IoT growth simultaneously triggers uneasiness pertaining to data exploitation by adversaries. Thus, these security concerns in IoT need to be addressed adequately in order to reap its entire benefits.

10.2 Security Architecture of IoT

The security issues prevailing in various types of networks such as mobile networks and the Internet also exist in IoT technology. The more prominent security concerns in IoT include (but are not limited to) privacy, access control, data storage and network management [1, 2]. Application-level challenges arise through data and privacy protection [3]. The IoT, like RFID (Radio Frequency Identification) technology, relies on password encryption techniques for maintaining the integrity and confidentiality of the transmitted information [4–8]. Other techniques also persist in maintaining the secrecy like random hash lock protocol, hash chain protocol, managing and generating keys from transmission channels, encrypted identifiers etc. The trustworthiness of an ongoing communication can be ascertained by employing identity authentication and access control techniques to alleviate disguised attacks and uphold the integrity of the information exchanged [9–13]. Two security issues had been identified in the IoT data transmission, of which one is inherent in IoT technology itself and the other one pops up due to the technology that had been applied for constructing and implementing the network functions [10]. IoT includes multiple heterogeneous networks that are integrated together giving rise to compatibility issues raising, security concerns.

The constantly changing trust relationship amongst nodes in such networks can be normalized by applying key management and choosing appropriate routing protocols [14–16]. Security of the transported information in IoT could be threatened by a number of different attacks, such as DoS/DDoS (Distributed Denial of Service), masquerading, man-in-the-middle attacks, application risk attack due to IPv6 (Internet Protocol version 6), conflicts arising due to WLAN (Wireless Local Area Network) applications, and so on. The core network of IoT could be easily affected by congestion since the volume of data transported is massive. Capacity and connectivity issues, including address space, reference network redundancy and security standards, should be given much greater importance in IoT. Application security issues that emerge in IoT include information access and user validation, data confidentiality, middleware security etc. IoT comprises of a layered architecture that includes three layers, namely the perception layer, the transportation layer and the application layer. A detailed study of the IoT security issues could be carried out by dividing the perception layer into perception nodes and perception network, the transportation layer into access network, core network and LAN and, finally, partitioning the application layer into application support layer and IoT applications. Every layer is bound with a certain responsibility that it is expected to provide. The security architecture of IoT is depicted in Figure 10.1.

All the layers of IoT need to be secured from unpredictable events. Apart from its layers, IoT should confirm the security of the entire system cutting beyond its own layers. At the perception layer, the types of security afforded includes RFID security, WSN (Wireless Sensor Network) security, RSN (Robust Secure Network) security and other similar types of security. The transport layer's access sub-layer takes control of ad hoc security, GPRS (General Packet Radio Service) security, 3G

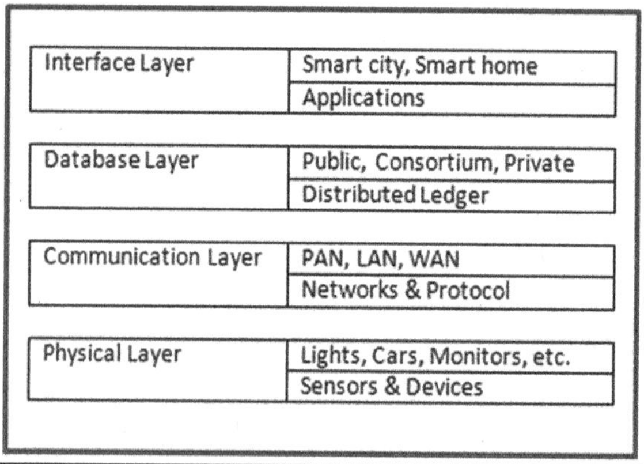

Interface Layer	Smart city, Smart home
	Applications
Database Layer	Public, Consortium, Private
	Distributed Ledger
Communication Layer	PAN, LAN, WAN
	Networks & Protocol
Physical Layer	Lights, Cars, Monitors, etc.
	Sensors & Devices

Figure 10.1 Security architecture of IoT

security and WiFi (Wireless Fidelity) security. As part of core network sub-layer, Internet security and 3G security are taken care of. The LAN sub-layer takes care of the security pertaining to local area networks. The application layer consists of an Application support layer and IoT applications take care of security pertaining to middleware technology safety, cloud computing platform safety etc. Industries have varying application security requirements that are catered for by IoT applications security sub-layer. Therefore, affording security under the IoT environment needs to be a large multi-layered security that should include, apart from the security of each layer, also the cross-layer integration of varying network security issues.

10.3 Security Issues Analysis of IoT

To date, a standardized architecture for IoT has not yet been established. In 2002, the ITU-T (International Telecommunication Union Telecommunication Standardization Sector) had proposed that the IoT should comprise of three layers: namely, the perception layer, the transportation layer, and the application layer.

10.3.1 Perception Layer

The scope of the perception layer includes the collection of information, object insight and object control. The perception layer is sub-divided into two divisions; namely, the perception node, that could be sensors, controllers etc., and the perception network, which oversees the relationship with the transportation network. Data are collected and aggregated at the perception node, which is sent to the gateway or passed as control information by the perception network. Technologies managed by the perception layer include RFID, WSNs, RSN, GPS (Global Positioning System) and so on.

The following sub-section analyzes these technologies for identifying the security issues managed by the perception layer [6].

10.3.1.1 Security Issues of RFID Technology and Solutions

The RFID technology is a contactless technology for identification that can detect the target tag signal automatically and convert it into relevant data without any manual intervention [17]. The RFID can be deployed in tough environments. In spite of its wider applications there are several issues that are shown below:

10.3.1.1.1 Uniform Coding

RFID technology does not have any standard encoding technique defined to the present day. There is at present a standard defined and supported by Japan, which is known as Universal Identification, and one defined and supported by European countries, which is known as the Electronic Product Code (EPC). Due to the non-availability of a standardized encoding technique, obtaining tag information may be hampered or it may result in errors while reading is in progress.

10.3.1.1.2 Conflict Collision

When various RFID tags convey their information to the readers simultaneously, data interference occurs at the reader resulting in failure during data read operation. The anti-collision technique can be applied to apprehend multiple tags to transmit their information to the reader simultaneously. Collisions can be categorized into two types, namely collisions due to tags and collisions due to reader. When multiple tags transmit their information to the reader simultaneously, the reader may be unable to extract the data properly, leading to a collision of tags. The scope of RFID sensor needs to be of broader range, where the cooperative work of multiple sensors is equally important. But such collaboration may result in the overlapping of read information. This results in redundant information being read and increases the network load. This type of collision is known as a reader's collision.

10.3.1.1.3 RFID Privacy Protection

The tags employed in RFID are highly economical, which can also contribute to low storage space consumption. The computational complexity involved in RFID is simple, due to which it could afford only simple solutions for preserving the privacy. Data privacy and location privacy are the type of privacies that are preserved through RFID.

Data Privacy

The security and privacy preservation techniques in RFID can be broadly classified into two types: physical-based techniques and password-based techniques. In the physical-based schemes, a variety of techniques are employed, including block tags, signal interference, deactivation of kill command, clip tags, pseudonym tags, antenna energy analysis, Faraday nets etc. The techniques included under the password-based scheme are hash lock technique, random hash lock technique, hash chain mechanism, anonymous ID creation technique, and re-encryption technique. In addition to these schemes, industries for their part employ different types of privacy protection techniques based on their type of IoT infrastructure. For instance, the national research agency in France employs the T2TIT framework that utilizes the Host Identity Protocol (HIP) as a solution for overcoming data privacy issues. Considering the type of security techniques and the level of computational complexity applied in RFID, it makes sense to have less sensitive information in the tag and move out highly sensitive information to the next higher-level service.

Location privacy

Even though the critical information is not stored at the tag level, the tag id is still in the reach of hackers. Through acquiring the tag id, the hackers could easily track the location of the tag. For instance, if a vehicle is fitted with a navigation and tracking system such as the Global Navigation Satellite System, then the system could easily read the tag id through which it could track the location of the tag based upon its operational features like range and capability.

10.3.1.1.4 Trust Management

The privacy of any participating node in IoT should be ensured. Hence the trust management features should be incorporated into the RFID system. Trust needs to be ensured between the readers and the tags and also between the readers and the adjacent base stations. The digital signature scheme can be employed to establish trust between parties. It could be applied for authenticating the data exchanges that are taking place between various communicating entities applications. The digital signature can be generated using cryptographic algorithms and security protocols. These algorithms and security protocols consume considerable storage space as well as computing resources that are already scarce in RFID. Therefore, the authentication algorithm used in RFID should take into consideration the tag's storage and processing power, apart from the usual storage and privacy constraints. Currently, the research is focused on the complexity level of the security in proportion to prevailing resource constraint issues.

There are four technologies that could be applied as a solution for security concerns in RFID: trust management, conflict collision, uniform encoding and privacy protection. By encoding the tag data uniformly, the information exchanges can be maximized. By employing an efficient technology for resolving collisions, the accuracy of information read by RFID readers can be increased through a reduction in data interference. The application of lightweight data privacy protection techniques results in the securing of both data and location privacies. By incorporating efficient trust management algorithms, the trust between readers, tags and the base stations can be enhanced.

10.3.1.2 Security Issues and Technical Solutions in WSNs

The wireless sensor networks have the capability to self-organize. They possess a lively network topology and a broadly scattered multi-hop transmission characteristic. The sensors present in WSN have inherent limitations in the form of limited storage, less computing power, and limited sensing capability, and thereby they are more vulnerable to a variety of attacks. The perception later has a goal of forming a fully aware environment. Due to the limitations within sensors, the complexity of the network structure increases by the presence of several sensor nodes. The perception layer concentrates more on data and the aggregation of the same. While considering the WSNs, analysis of data collected is the most researched topic. Data collection in WSNs may give rise to a variety of attacks, such as eavesdropping, malicious routing, modifying the integrity of the transmitted message and other similar issues that pose a serious threat to the entire IoT environment. Security issues related to data that should be focused upon include data confidentiality, data legitimacy, data reliability and data timeliness. Solutions for these data breaches could be obtained through designing efficient cryptographic algorithms, key management techniques, and implementing both secure routing and node trust establishment techniques.

10.3.1.3 The Problems of Heterogeneous Integration

The integration of RFID and WSNs leads to a RFID sensor network, which is extensively applied in the IoT environment. The assimilation between RFID and WSN can be carried out in four different ways, namely by integrating the tag with sensor node, integrating the tag with wireless sensor node, integrating the RFID reader with both the wireless sensor and node and wireless sensor device and, finally, combining the RFID and sensor node. Since IoT is a type of heterogeneous network, the RFID Sensor Network can provide a solution to the issues arising from heterogeneity. IoT aggregates a huge quantity of data from a variety of sources. Such varying sources contribute data in varying formats. Effective analysis of the collected data needs to be done by applying data unification techniques. Failing to adhere to this may result in a loss of data, destruction of data or data becoming compromised. The adversaries could resort to activities like node monitoring and capturing, stealing data, thereby rendering the privacy protection measures inefficient. When data from multiple sources gets integrated, a number of security issues pop out. The most critical of such issues arising out of data integration arise from the heterogeneous data. WSNs and RFID employ various procedures to collect data, thereby giving rise to compatibility disputes related to data format, communication protocols. In order to combat these issues there is a need for both data encoding standard and data exchange protocol. To enforce a system-level collaboration between the RFID and WSNs, they should be compatible at the software level. This needs to be introduced, in spite of differences found in storage formats, data access formats and the employment of different security control measures resulting from RFID and WSN technology. Due to such differences, both RFID and WSN process data differently while carrying out activities such as filtering, aggregation and data processing. Hence the research should be focused upon these variations mentioned (data access format, data storage format, data processing procedures and security control mechanisms).

10.3.2 Transportation Layer

The transportation layer of the IoT has been given the responsibility of providing access to the perception layer in a ubiquitous mode, storage and transmission of the information generated by the perception layer and other related tasks. The transport layer can be categorized in to three sub-layers, based on the function it delivers. The three sub-layers are access network, core network and local area network. The transportation layer is an amalgamated mixture of several heterogeneous networks.

10.3.2.1 Security Issues Related to the Functional Architecture of the Transportation Layer

10.3.2.1.1 Access Network

A ubiquitous access infrastructure is created by the access network to the perception layer. Security issues pop up when the perception layer accesses the core network. The access network could be of any type, such as wireless network, ad hoc network and so on. Taking into consideration the structural differences in the network, the wireless network can be further sub-divided into the center network and the non-center network. Communication in the center network between the mobile nodes is routed through the base stations, as found in the common cellular networks and wireless local area networks. In the non-center network, communication between the mobile nodes need not be routed through the base station.

Analysing Security Issues in WiFi

WiFi is abbreviated as Wireless Fidelity and it has been defined under the IEEE 802.11 wireless LAN standard. It is the most widely used wireless standard, in which the wireless terminals are connected to each other in wireless mode. In the IoT, WiFi-based applications include accessing the Internet through WiFi, accessing the email server, downloading online contents, watching online videos etc. Security is a major issue in the WiFi access mode. The user, surfing through the Internet, may be encountering various phishing websites [88, 89], leading to the compromise of user's account and password details. The security vulnerability in WiFi could be categorized into two forms—creating a network trap for users in the network and exploiting the trap to launch network attacks. The security concerns in WiFi include access attacks, phishing attacks, DoS/DDoS attacks and so on.

Analyzing Security Concerns in Ad Hoc Networks

Ad hoc networks are infrastructure-less networks that are created readily to perform a specific task The nodes in the network still communicate in the wireless mode, making use of the distributed network management policies. They are self-creative, self-organizing types of networks. In the IoT, the ad hoc network falls under the non-center category. The heterogeneity present between the nodes of perception layer is eliminated in the network through the network's routing protocol. The nodes in the network can adapt to any type of changes encountered during the network run time changes in network. The nodes adapt dynamically without creating any issues during the perception layer network communication that takes place in the core network. Security concerns in an ad hoc network pop up from radio channels and network type. A wireless channel is always susceptible to eavesdropping and interference. Since the ad hoc network falls under the non-center category, it is highly vulnerable to attacks like cheating, vulnerable posing and other similar type of attacks. In the IoT environment, the following are the security concerns related to ad hoc networks:

Illegal Node Access Security Issues: Nodes that are engaged in communication can establish the identity of each other before they begin any exchanges. Failing which the attacker may impersonate or capture any node leading to revealing of critical information present in nodes. This security breach could be addressed through proper authorization and authentication. Security certificates of each node establish their identity to each other. Authorization decides the access right of each node upon any system resources.

Data Security Issues: The communication taking place in wireless ad hoc network is unidirectional, where the sensors transmit their data to the base station or any designated sink node. There are more chances of data being revealed to unauthorized users present in the network. The network routing information may also be tampered and the location of communicating users can be identified. Such breaches could be overcome by implementing appropriate authentication and key management techniques in the network.

Analyzing Security Issues in 3G Network: The various security concerns that pop out when the 3G networks are deployed as access network are revealing of user details, data inaccuracy, unethical attacks and other similar type of attacks. These security issues could be addressed through by employing measures to protect the confidentiality of user information, efficient key management techniques, authentication techniques and cryptographic encryptions. But in reality all these techniques are still evolving. During the transmission of data several violations like data revelation, violation of access rights and unethical attacks could occur. Apart from the above mentioned issues there are some other common attacks that occur in 3G networks namely DoS/DDoS attacks, identity theft attacks and phishing attacks.

10.3.2.1.2 Core Network

Data transmission in the IoT takes place through the core network, which is primarily the Internet. The Internet is susceptible to a number of attacks. The wireless environment comprises of several sensor nodes that need to have an IP address to communicate their information. Since the number of IPv4 addresses are in scarce, the demand could not be met. This could be addressed by turning to IPv6 addresses. The power consumed by the sensor nodes using IPv6 addresses could be managed by utilizing the 6Lowpan technology.

10.3.2.1.3 Security Analysis in Local Area Network

The local area network in the IoT ought to be designed in such a way that it should be robust enough to thwart unauthorized data access, attacks on the server, etc. The local area network management security principles need to be strengthened [6]. Access to the network resources should be provided only to legitimate users, which will go a long way to protecting the network's security. Other security steps, such as identifying any malicious code in any system, flushing off unwanted system services that are installed without necessary permission, the regular updating of operating system patch files, and using a strong password for resource access, could be implemented to protect the LAN.

10.3.3 Application Layer

10.3.3.1 Analyzing Security Issues in the Application Support Layer

The application support layer is placed above the transportation layer. This layer renders all kinds of support to realize business applications, computational amenities, and the allocation of resources to applications in an optimal way, projecting, selecting, and data processing. It is capable enough to differentiate between legal data, spam data and malicious types of data and accordingly decides either to allow or to discard the same in a timely manner. Its organization varies according to the various services it provides. The security scope of this layer includes middleware support, cloud computing support, machine-to-machine communication support, service support and other similar types of platforms [6]. Core technologies are used for developing middleware in the IoT. The communication component includes the middleware servers that enable the deployment of software on different operating systems. The volume of information generated in the IoT is humongous and vibrant in nature. Therefore, the middleware deployed in IoT should be capable enough to handle such huge data and should have self-provision for linear expansion of its storage. Functions such as controlling ambient temperature, maintaining ambient state that are encapsulated in the deployed middleware of IoT are usually complex. In these cases the middleware should be handling simultaneous correlated data requests coming from several devices from different locations. These requests resemble a context, lasting for a limited duration. Several contexts carry out several functions, thereby catering to the varying needs of the users. Incoming requests are serviced based on their arrival time. Still, there are a lot of real-time applications that needs to be given priority. Therefore, the system should differentiate such emergency services and service them immediately.

In the IoT, machine-to-machine communication models have become increasingly prominent. Even such models are not devoid of security risks. In these models, data in the form of signals are transferred through physical cables or through air. Three types of security issues are identified at the machine-to-machine model of the application layer. Applications that involve back-end terminals and middleware should be highly secured since they are responsible for collecting and analyzing the data such that there is an increase in the level of business processing intelligence.

The source code of such applications needs to be equally secured. Other security concerns that are identified at this level include access control, privacy protection, authorization of users, preservation of data integrity, real-time servicing etc. Among the major security risks identified in the cloud computing platform are: risk in prioritizing various processes; risk from management agencies; risk at data location; risk in isolating data; risk in data recovery; risk in providing investigation support; and risk pertaining to long term development.

10.3.3.1.1 Security Threats Identified from IDC Survey

The aspect of security is of high concern in the cloud environment. All respondents of the cloud environment have intrinsic technical security issues. The data stored in the cloud are encrypted before being stored. In addition, the backup of user data remains in the cloud for a particular period of time. Therefore, some sorts of immediate security measures are imminent before storing the data in the cloud platform. Many leading enterprises in the world take risks by choosing cloud storage to retain their enterprise-level data. Regardless of whether any security breaches through hackers occur or not protection needs to be given. Due to the prevailing insecurity pertaining to data storage in the cloud, enterprises, including medical, and financial, are generally recommended to abstain from cloud storage.

10.3.3.1.2 Issue of Service Interruption and Attacks

In the cloud, based on its history service interruptions are unavoidable. Common services that are interrupted include data backup, shutting down of machines and data centers going to offline mode. However, such untoward happenings can be predicted. Furthermore, the possibility of DDoS attacks also cannot be avoided in the cloud. In the cloud, DDoS would disrupt the legitimate users from availing the cloud services, manipulating certain cloud services to consume enormous system resources like memory, CPU time, network bandwidth etc. All of these result in slowing down the performance efficiency of the cloud service providers' server.

10.3.3.2 IoT Applications Security Analysis

There are integrated as well as application-specific businesses that are provided with required service at the application layer of the IoT environment. Security issues that pop up at this layer like the protection of privacy have less chance of getting realized at the transportation or perception layers. At the application layer, in certain contexts, they pose serious threat to users as well as data. Location privacy discusses the past or current position of the user and query privacy involves information pertaining to the query posed and the resolution for the same. Take, for instance, when a query for identifying restaurants or amusement parks is posted by a user, it could be exploited by any adversary and the user's location, salary, lifestyle, social behavior and other private information could be tracked easily. Presently, privacy protection techniques include camouflaging user location, creating an anonymous space, space encryption and so on.

10.3.4 Security of IoT as a Whole

As the IoT is growing in popularity, the security issues pointed above need to be addressed appropriately. Solutions prescribed under each layer/sub-layer, though effective, cannot be integrated together and provided as a single solution. IoT has gained a foothold in almost all domain-based applications, including smart transportation, smart home solutions, intelligent urban management, smart medical applications and the intelligent grid. The security requirements of all these applications vary. Consider, for instance, the smart transportation and smart medical applications where the security related to data privacy is of the utmost importance. In the case of intelligent urban management and the intelligent grid, however, the authenticity of data processed is of utmost concern. Hence different weightings need to be given for each type of application. From the above discussion, it is clear that a single technology in a single layer is not sufficient to provide the needed security. Take, for instance, an IoT system where the application layer is weak and insecure., the system as a whole is vulnerable to an intelligent hacker. Hence, in such circumstances, cooperation between layers is of primary importance. The design of future policies should be centered around this cross-layer inter-operations.

10.4 Security Issues Comparison between IoT and a Traditional Network

From the above discussions it is evident that the security requirements and solutions provided for each shortcoming do not fall into the similar category in the case of the IoT domain and the network security domain. IoT comprises of RFID nodes and wireless sensor nodes which are resource-starved. Internet, on the other hand, consists of computers, servers, and mobiles, which are equipped with sufficient resources. It is therefore possible to use complex lightweight, hybrid algorithms to afford maximum security by expending minimum resources like the memory, storage and processing power. In IoT, lightweight algorithms are utilized to seek a balance between security and power consumption. IoT applications are integrated into our day-to-day life where they collect our everyday details, making our life easier. These IoT applications can even go to the extent of controlling our living environment. If such applications are not controlled properly, we are in the risk of losing our private information. Hence comprehensive solutions are needed to safeguard the IoT environment.

The security and privacy concerns of IoT can be addressed through excluding the centralized maintenance of data by incorporating Blockchain technology, which is based on novel distributed ledger-based technology[4]. This technology permits the sensed information to run across the distributed ledger for every transaction made with proper verification.

10.5 Blockchain Concepts

At present, the idea of Blockchain is gaining a lot of attention. The blocks present in the chain provide data veracity among the contributors with the help of a working proof, which guarantees necessary trust among the participants in a distributed environment.

Each block is formed by a node, which contains a header, along with data and metadata. A cryptographically linked list of these blocks creates the Blockchain. The Blockchain is a distributed ledger involving a distributed agreement, which maintains a list of records which can grow. The records present are all prevented from amendment and meddling. Since the data present in the blocks of the chain are all protected from tampering and modification, the Blockchain is considered as an appropriate technology to provide a tamper resilient distributed ledger of data.

10.5.1 The Structure of Blockchain

Blockchain is characterized by a list of blocks with transactions in a particular order. Figure 10.2 represents the structure of the Blockchain mechanism. The two important data structures used in the Blockchain architecture are pointers and linked lists.

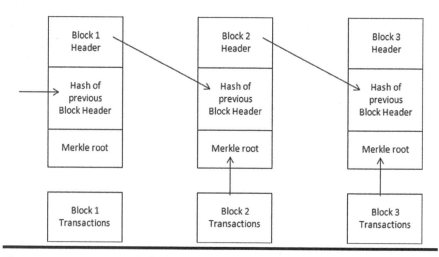

Figure 10.2   Structure of Blockchain

While pointers hold the information about the next block, linked lists represent a sequence of blocks.

A block header is used to recognize a specific block, which is hashed repetitively to produce proof of work for mining rewards. The previous block is linked to a particular block with the help of its preceding block's header hash value. A Merkle root is the hash of all the transactions that are represented by a block in the network.

10.5.2 The Working of Blockchain

Basically, the Blockchain offers global availability, integrity, candidness and the capability to hoard and handover data in a safer way. The data can be of any type, including documents, monetary transactions, signatures or contracts. Blockchain is capable of supporting a broader category of tasks without the need for any intercessor. Blockchain allows entities to generate a communal record of asset tenure. It belongs to an open distributed environment, where the practices are all subjected to investigation and expansion. Essentially, it is a distributed ledger whose replicas are found on all the machines present in the network. The presence of the replicas, which are scattered throughout the network, eradicates the chances of overall data sleaze.

The Blockchain maintains the whole registered transactions history on a system. Each system present in the network maintains its own residential copy of the database and the presence of the consensus algorithms make the copies synchronized irrespective of their whereabouts. Precisely, a Blockchain is made up of blocks which maintain transactional data. Every block in the Blockchain includes the hash of the preceding block.

Nodes present in the network are unidentified entities. They may be either processes or users. Nodes on their presumed part can start and endorse a transaction apart from authenticating themselves. They also perform mining to maintain consensus among other nodes in order to maintain data integrity. Whenever a node initiates a transaction which is to be transferred to other nodes, it utilizes its private key to sign the transaction, which authenticates itself as the factual owner of the transaction. A peer-to-peer network and consensus algorithms are essential for Blockchain to offer replication across the nodes.

The distributed ledger is maintained by the peers present in the network. The peer-to-peer network functionality ensures that there is no centralized control in the network, apart from allowing the participating nodes to connect to other nodes present in the network to exchange the transactional data. The peers present in the network can be categorized into two types; namely, committing peers and endorsing peers. While the endorsing peers accomplish and permit the transactions based on the endorsement policies, the committing peers receive the endorsed transactions, verify them and then update the ledger. The committing nodes can also play the role of the Orderer node, which receive endorsed transactions, order them and forward them to other committing peers.

Nodes also play the role of miners, producing fresh blocks with appropriate information. They can also add new transactions and authenticate themselves. Nodes are otherwise known as block signers and their responsibility is to authenticate and sign the transactions digitally. The major factor to be considered in a Blockchain network is to find out the nodes which are competent enough to affix as the subsequent block to the chain. The consensus algorithms help in making such decisions. In order to strongly recognize the source node and the sink node, all the communications made in the network are secured cryptographically. If a miner desires to add data, then the consensus algorithm is applied to determine where it has to be bagged in the network. The blocks present in the network are categorized as child blocks and parent blocks. The child blocks contain the collections of transactions, their timestamps and the corresponding link to the parent block, which forms the chain of blocks.

The consensus algorithms employed in the network constitutes of three major phases. In the first phase, an endorsement of the transaction is made; in the second phase, the transactions endorsed are all written into the ledger in a sequential manner; finally, in the third phase the received transactions are validated and committed to the ledger. The nodes present in the network make use of peer-to-peer messages to identify other peers, inquiring, invoking and installing transactions, ensuring the synchronization of the nodes and authorizing the transactions.

A transaction made is apprehended by a host node, which is then distributed to the network. The transaction is then validated using some standards and algorithms. Scripts are normally used to validate the digital signature of the host node embedded in the transactions against its public key. If all the conditions mentioned on the scripts are satisfied, the transaction is said to be host verified, following which the documentation of the transaction is pooled with others to generate a fresh chunk of data for the ledger.

The freshly generated block is then supplemented to the prevailing Blockchain in such a way that it marks the transaction as both stable and unchangeable. Blockchain is a communal database; the records it contains are explicitly open and directly confirmable. Since there is no centralized control of the information, it is not possible for a hacker to control, operate, tamper or delete the information.

When a miner node is connected to the peer-to-peer network it has to perform some tasks which are listed below. Synchronizing with the network (i.e.) download the relevant Blockchain by demanding the past chronological chunks from others, authenticating the transaction (i.e.) by verifying and validating the digital signature of the transactions and their output, validating the block (i.e.) validating using a set of recognised rules, creating new blocks (i.e.) proposing a fresh chunk by merging the authenticated transactions obtained from others, perform proof of work (i.e.) discovering a legal chunk by resolving a puzzle, fetching the reward (i.e.) after solving the proof of work the node announces the outcome to others to authorize and admit the block. If the block is recognized by other nodes, the miner node is satisfied.

Hashing plays a major role in Blockchain. A hash algorithm is a mathematical algorithm which produces a value centered on a data object by mapping the data object to a fixed size hash. Essentially, the hash function is a one-way function that it is not possible to invert. In a hash tree also known as the Merkle tree, the nodes at the lowest level represent the hash value of the data block and those in between nodes represent the hash of the label of its child nodes. In the Blockchain, every transaction that encompasses a block is hashed to produce a hash value. Hashes are joined to form the Merkle tree. The output produced by the hashing process is supplemented to the header of a block, together with the hash of the preceding block's header and a timestamp. The fresh header is then given as the input to the cryptographic procedure to generate a nonce which is then supplemented to the Blockchain.

10.5.3 Types of Blockchain

There are four main categories of Blockchain: public Blockchain, private Blockchain, consortium Blockchain and hybrid Blockchain. Regardless of the variations, the nodes present in the Blockchain are operating on a peer-to-peer network system. Nodes present in the network maintain a replica of the shared ledger, which is updated periodically. Nodes are capable of initiating, approving and receiving the transactions, in addition to creating blocks.

10.5.3.1 Public Blockchain

Public Blockchain is a non-restraining distributed ledger system without any authorization. Anybody with Internet access can turn into this platform and become an integral part of the network. A node which joins this Blockchain is approved to obtain the present and historical records, validate the transactions or do the proof-of-work and to perform mining.

Example: Ethereum

10.5.3.2 Private Blockchain

Private Blockchain is a restraining or permission-oriented Blockchain functioning only in a secured network. They are utilized within a group, where there is a very limited number of participants. The level of safety, approvals, authorizations and convenience is determined by the controlling group.

Example: Corda

10.5.3.3 Consortium Blockchain

This is a semi-distributed kind, where two or more organizations manage the Blockchain network. This differentiates it from the private Blockchain, which is controlled by a solitary group. This type of Blockchain can be useful to exchange information between organizations and to perform mining.

Example: Energy Web Foundation

10.5.3.4 Hybrid Blockchain

This combines the features of both private and public Blockchains. In this network, permission to access the data stored in the Blockchain is restricted by the user. Only a designated portion of data from the Blockchain can be permitted to go public while the remaining portion is kept private. This system of Blockchain is malleable for the users to connect to a private Blockchain with multiple public Blockchain. An agreement in a private network of a hybrid Blockchain is usually confirmed within it, but manipulators can also announce it in the public Blockchain to get confirmation.

Example: Dragonchain

10.5.4 Blockchain Solution to IoT

The security and privacy concerns of IoT can be addressed by excluding the centralized maintenance of data by incorporating Blockchain technology, which is based on novel distributed ledger-based technology [18–20]. The technology permits the sensed information to run across the distributed ledger for every transaction made with proper verification. Blockchain guarantees the necessary data integrity to the IoT systems. Even though it guarantees data integrity, its prevailing features, such as peer-to-peer network contribution, functionalities offered by endorsing peer and committing peers, the use of consensus algorithms, proof of work and other related things, may introduce additional intricacy if the peer-to-peer network infrastructure is recognised across the IoT environment. Because of these additional intricacies, it is unviable to use a complete Blockchain safeguarded network in the IoT environment.

Blockchain technology provides appropriate solutions to the issues faced by IoT systems. In the emerging situations of IoT systems, there is demand for an escalation in the amount of devices interacting in the network. Whenever there is an upsurge in the amount of interacting devices, it may cause additional problems in the IoT environment since the sensed information is upheld in a centralized server. Whenever advanced technologies are integrated with IoT to portray it as a large-scale system, the centralized approach will not be effective. The demand of the large-scale IoT system in processing the data will not be catered by the prevailing internet infrastructure. To cater the same, it is desirable to have peer-to-peer networking, dispersed file allocation and independent device coordination. The Blockchain mechanism can perform these necessary functionalities and hence, if incorporated within the IoT environment, can help the IoT systems to track a large collection of interconnected devices.

Blockchain enables the devices existing in the IoT environment to process the transactions among them with coordination. It will also improve the privacy and dependability of the system and also accelerate the messaging process between the peers with the aid of the distributed ledger. When Blockchain is incorporated into the IoT environment, the data flow of the environment varies considerably from the original. The flow of data will be from sensors to user, which will be as follows: From the sensor, data are transmitted to the network; from where it is transmitted to the router; and from the router it is transmitted to the Internet. From the Internet, data flow is directed towards the distributed Blockchain and from there to the analytics and then to the user. Since the distributed ledger is tamper-proof, this will not allow meddling and erroneous data authentication. Blockchain also eradicates the single thread communication in IoT and makes the data flow more secure and dependable.

Blockchain offers four different characteristics to protect the integrity of the data. They are as follows:

10.5.4.1 Encryption and Validation

After a transaction is started by a node, the data block corresponding to the transaction is validated by means of the consensus algorithms. Unless any approved modifications are made to the data, it is confirmed permanently. By employing cryptographic protocols, the data are then encrypted to assure data security.

10.5.4.2 Decentralized Database

Since the Blockchain technology is decentralized in nature, there is no single node which holds the entire data altogether and the possibility of breaking into the system by the hackers is made tougher. The replica of the complete database is made available in every single node present in the network and so a fault in a single node will not present any issues to the complete network. It is also not essential to have a third-party verification for a transaction since all nodes having access to the authenticated encoded data.

10.5.4.3 Private and Public Blockchain

While the permission less nature of the public Blockchain has attracted a lot of people, the security offered by it is based on the authentication and encryption made initially. It offers privacy. The private Blockchain is permission-based, where the nodes need to identify themselves explicitly to access the network which incorporates an additional level of security into the network.

10.5.4.4 Immutable and Virtually Tamper-proof Network

The blocks present in the Blockchain are tamper-proof in nature and the data present in the blocks are protected by means of encryption. The entire system is designed in such a way that even if a few nodes are compromised by the hackers, the system will not fail. Blockchain is a distributed ledger; for every change made to a record entered earlier in the ledger, changes are recorded together with the new timestamp.

To tamper or to modify the data present in a block it becomes mandatory to modify all the blocks preceding it, which is not an easy task.

10.5.5 IoT Framework with Blockchain

Figure 10.3 shows the IoT framework with Blockchain. It consists of four layers; namely, the physical layer, the communication layer, the database layer and the interface layer.

10.5.5.1 Physical Layer

This contains all smart devices that are equipped with sensors and actuators. These devices gather the data and transfer it to the layers, which lie above. In the normal scenario, it is not mandatory to have a single standard for the devices to share the information in order to provide the necessary cross-functionality. However, when Blockchain is incorporated into the IoT environment it becomes mandatory to procure all the sensor devices from the same manufacturer functioning on the same network.

10.5.5.2 Communication Layer

Smart devices present in the IoT environment employ various communication mechanisms to exchange information. The security and privacy of the communicated

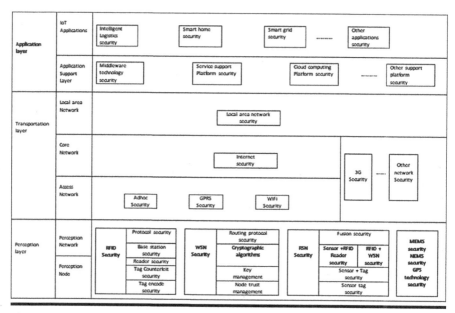

Figure 10.3 IoT framework with Blockchain

data within the system are seen as particularly vital. This issue is addressed by incorporating Blockchain into the system.

10.5.5.3 Database Layer

Blockchain is a distributed database, which holds an unchallengeable and an unceasingly rising number of transactions. Another major advantage of the Blockchain is the public confirmation and reviewing mechanism.

10.5.5.4 Interface Layer

It consists of applications that interconnect with each other to make a beneficial decision cooperatively. Typical IoT applications include smart cities and smart homes.

Advantages of having Blockchain technology for large-scale IoT systems include

- Eradication of a centralized controlling authority
- Distributed file sharing
- Reliability
- Robustness
- Trustless peer-to-peer messaging
- Maintaining the history of the transactions

10.5.6 Difficulties in Incorporating Blockchain with IoT

When Blockchain technology is incorporated with the IoT environment, it addresses the issues of privacy and dependability of IoT. However, incorporating it into the IoT environment is not an easy task to do. There are a lot of difficulties in integrating Blockchain with IoT. Restricted ledger storage capacity, the absence of appropriate code and standards, and the differences in the processing capability and scalability are among those highlighted.

10.6 Conclusion

Technological development in the field of wireless sensor networks enables the sensors and actuators to associate to endpoints via the Internet gateways, thereby forming a unified network. Devices present in such networks share the information and, based on the information exchanged, the systems in the endpoint may initiate suitable actions. The majority of these IoT devices are vulnerable to attacks. They can be easily negotiated and slashed. A technique based on the dissemination and replication of the digital record of the exchanged information known as Blockchain addresses this issue. The devices present in the network form the nodes. Every active node present in the network upholds a copy of the Blockchain. All the active nodes of the network share the saved ledger, which is computationally very much impossible to tamper. By incorporating the framework offered by Blockchain into the IoT-based systems, the security and privacy issues are all addressed with ease.

References

[1] Jing Qi, Athanasios V. Vasilakos, Jiafu Wan, Jingwei Lu, & Dechao Qiu (2014), "Security of the Internet of Things: Perspectives and challenges", *Wireless Networks*, 20(8), 2481–2501.

[2] C. Tsai, C. Lai, & V. Vasilakos (2014). "Future internet of things: Open issues and challenges", *ACM/Springer Wireless Networks*, doi: 10.1007/s11276-014-0731-0.

[3] J. Wan, H. Yan, H. Suo, & F. Li (2011), "Advances in cyberphysical systems research", *KSII Transactions on Internet and Information Systems*, 5(11), 1891–1908.

[4] G. Yang, J. Xu, W. Chen, Z. H. Qi, & H. Y. Wang (2010), "Security characteristic and technology in the internet of things", *Journal of Nanjing University of Posts and Telecommunications (Natural science)*, 4, 20–29.

[5] H. Liu, M. Bolic, A. Nayak, & I. Stojmenovic (2008), "Taxonomy and challenges of the integration of RFID and wireless sensor networks", *IEEE Network*, 22(6), 26–35.

[6] Manoj Kumar Nallapaneni, & Pradeep Kumar Mallick (2018), "Blockchain technology for security issues and challenges in IoT", *Procedia Computer Science*, 132 (2018), 1815–1823

[7] Jayavardhana Gubbi, Rajkumar Buyya, Slaven Marusic, & Marimuthu Palaniswami (2013), "Internet of Things (IoT): A vision, architectural elements, and future directions", *Future Generation Computer System*, 29(7), 1645–1660, doi: 10.1016/j.future.2013.01.010.

[8] Manoj Kumar Nallapaneni, & Archana Dash (2017), "The Internet of Things: An opportunity for transportation and logistics." *Proceedings of the International Conference on Inventive Computing and Informatics (ICICI 2017)*, pp. 194–197, Coimbatore, Tamil Nadu, India.

[9] Daniel Minoli, & Benedict Occhiogrosso (2018), "Blockchain mechanisms for IoT security", *Internet of Things*, 1–2 (2018), 1–13

[10] M. Pilkington (2016), Blockchain technology: principles and applications, in: F.X. Olleros, M. Zhegu (Eds.), *Research Handbook on Digital Transformations*, Edward Elgar Publishing, Northampton, MA, pp. 225–253.

[11] M. Samaniego, & R. Deters (2016), "Blockchain as a service for IoT", *Proceedings of the 2016 IEEE International Conference on Internet of Things (iThings) and IEEE Green Computing and Communications (GreenCom) and IEEE Cyber, Physical and Social Computing (CPSCom) and IEEE Smart Data (SmartData)*, Chengdu, China, Dec. 2016.

[12] Y. Zhang, & J. Wen (2017), "The IoT electric business model: Using blockchain technology for the Internet of Things", *Peer-to-Peer Networking and Applications*, 10 (4), 983–994.

[13] S. Huckle, R. Bhattacharya, M. White, & N. Beloff (2016), "Internet of Things, blockchain and shared economy applications", *Procedia Computer Science*, 98, 461–466, ISSN 1877-0509.

[14] S. Huh, S. Cho, & S. Kim (2017), "Managing IoT devices using blockchain platform", *Proceedings of the 2017 Nineteenth International Conference on Advanced Communication Technology (ICACT)*, Bongpyeong, South Korea, Feb. 2017.

[15] M. Samaniego, & R. Deters (2016), "Using blockchain to push software-defined IoT components onto edge hosts", *Proceedings of the International Conference on Big Data and Advanced Wireless Technologies BDAW '16*, Blagoevgrad, Bulgaria, Article No. 58, November 2016.

[16] I. Bashir (2017), *Mastering Blockchain*, Packt Publishing, Birmingham, UK, ISBN 978-1-78712-544-5.

[17] International Telecommunication Union (2005), "Internet reports 2005: The internet of things", Geneva: ITU.

[18] Ben Dickson (2016), "Decentralizing IoT networks through blockchain", https://techcrunch.com/2016/06/28/decentralizing-iot-networksthrough-blockchain/

[19] Ahmed Banafa (2017), "IoT and blockchain convergence: Benefits and challenges", https://iot.ieee.org/newsletter/january-2017/iot-andblockchain-convergence-benefits-and-challenges.html

[20] M. Conoscenti, A. Vetrò, & J. C. De Martin (2016), "Blockchain for the Internet of Things: A systematic literature review." *IEEE/ACS 13th International Conference of Computer Systems and Applications (AICCSA)*, Agadir, pp. 1–6. doi: 10.1109/AICCSA.2016.7945805

Chapter 11

A Secure Online Voting System Using Blockchain

Mehak Wadhwani
Monash University Melbourne, Australia

Nisha Mansoori
EZDI Solutions and Healthcare, India

Shivangi Tanwar
John Deere Technology Centre, India

Aanchal Handa
HSBC Technology, India

Bhavesh N. Gohil
Sardar Vallabhbhai National Institute of Technology, India

Contents

DOI: 10.1201/9781003129486-11

11.1 Objective

The main objective is to achieve a decentralized, immutable and secure **e-voting** (electronic voting) system to promote a higher level of participation. This advancement will facilitate voting in a more flexible and efficient manner. As a preliminary, it is important to recognize the shortcomings of current voting practices and how Blockchain can help overcome them through its inherent properties. The implementation procedure of the proposed e-voting system will be explained thoroughly and presented to help readers interpret the content appropriately. Further, there will be a briefing on digital identity management in Blockchain and its utilization as a tool to eliminate sharing and storing of personal credentials.

The expected audiences of this chapter are Blockchain enthusiasts and individuals aiming to develop an online Blockchain-based voting system. The application presented in this chapter is primarily created for elections held in educational institutes. However, this case study is also explored in corporate and government elections. According to this system, students in educational institutes would no longer be reliant on the institute staff to provide them with a location, time and the access rights for casting votes. An immutable and decentralized model of elections will greatly enhance the verifiability and security of votes being recorded.

Another intent is to learn how digital identity management in Blockchain can be used as a tool to eradicate the need of sharing and storing personal credentials and aid voting. This advancement in e-voting is aimed at all voters around the world and governments which can implement or adopt the same.

11.2 Introduction

A fundamental pillar in any democratic system is the elections; a process that enables citizens to express their opinions through the use of votes. The election process should be reliable and transparent, thereby confirming the participants of its reliability and trustworthiness. This is primarily due to the great role they play in today's society. As a consequence, the approach to voting has been an ever-evolving domain with the main motive of making the system transparent, secure, and verifiable. Since its impact is so vast, many efforts have been made to increase the overall efficiency and resilience of a voting system. The creation of e-voting or electronic voting certainly made its mark. Since the first use of punched-card ballots in the 1960s, voting systems have displayed remarkable progress through the adoption of internet technologies [1]. There are some guidelines which must be adhered to as they specify the benchmark parameters for widespread acceptance. These consist of anonymity of the voter, non-repudiation among others and integrity of the vote.

Some countries have taken serious measures to improve their voting systems by incorporating decentralized peer-to-peer networks via the use of Blockchain technology. This is accompanied by a public ledger. The first country to use Blockchain technology to verify votes was Sierra Leone. This was carried out during their nationwide presidential elections in March 2018. The key attribute of Blockchain technology is the inability to delete or change information residing in preexisting blocks. The backbone of Blockchain technology is the distributed network built up of a large number of interconnected nodes. Every node in the distributed system has its own copy of the distributed ledger holding the full history of all the transactions the network has processed. In this kind of network, no single entity or individual has the authority to control the flow. If the majority of the nodes approve, the transaction is accepted. The anonymity of the user is maintained in this network through cryptographic measures. An overly simplified statement that allows one to understand Blockchain technology suggests that it is an extremely viable basis for electronic voting. In addition, it has the potential to make e-voting more credible and acceptable.

This chapter evaluates the use of Blockchain as a service to implement an electronic voting (e-voting) system for annual elections during an academic year in educational institutes. This chapter makes the following original contributions:

1. Review on existing Blockchain frameworks suited for constructing Blockchain-based e-voting system.
2. Proposes a Blockchain-based e-voting system for education institutional level elections by utilizing private Blockchain to enable liquid democracy.

11.3 Theoretical Background

11.3.1 Hyperledger

Hyperledger is an umbrella project created with the aim of promoting an open-source collaborative effort to allow the use of Blockchain technology in various business verticals. Several leaders of finance, banking, supply chain, and technology have come together in collaboration to support the development of Blockchain-based distributed ledgers. This technology does not support Bitcoin. Its main focus is on the generation of new transactional applications that establish transparency, accountability, and trust [2]. This must happen alongside increasing the efficiency of business processes and strategies.

1. **Hyperledger Fabric:** Hyperledger Fabric is an enterprise-grade permissioned distributed ledger framework for developing solutions and applications. Its versatile and modular design is utilized by a broad spectrum of industries. Hyperledger Fabric uses the concept of consensus to optimize performance without hindering privacy constraints. [3]. Within private industrial networks, the verifiable identity of a participant is a primary requirement. All network participants are expected to have known identities in the case where permissible membership exists. This is the case with Hyperledger Fabric.

   Hyperledger Fabric has a modular layout, which is segregated into three different stages. The first stage consists of smart contracts which comprise the distributed logic processing. It then transitions to the next stage, where transaction ordering takes place. The third and final stage is the validation and committing of the transactions into the Blockchain. There are multiple benefits of the segregation, such as improving the network scalability, and decreasing the number of trust levels and verification which keeps the network running without hindrance and yields a better overall performance [4].

   ■ **Hyperledger Fabric CA**

   The **Hyperledger Fabric CA** is a Certificate Authority (CA) for Hyperledger Fabric. Features like assurance of enrollment certificates (ECerts), registration of identities, certificate revocation and renewal are available through the Hyperledger Fabric CA [5].

   There are two ways of interacting with the Fabric CA server which include interacting through the Fabric CA client and via the Fabric **SDK**s (Software Development Kits). The entire communication process is conducted with the help of **REST** (Representational State Transfer) **API**s (Application Programming Interface). Applications interact with the network with the help of APIs and then run smart contracts. These smart contracts or chain codes are hosted by the network and have unique names and versions associated with them. APIs are accessible with an SDK. A pictorial representation of the Hyperledger Fabric CA structure can be observed in Figure 11.1.

2. **Architecture:** Hyperledger Fabric has its own set of components which function in harmony with one another. Each component is integral to the working of the system and has its own role to play. Every component runs as a separate docker container and is engineered to work side by side with other containers. The docker containers can communicate with each other despite running on different physical machines on the network [6]. These components are:

   ■ **Certificate Authority**: The access control logic, user permissions and identity management of members in the Hyperledger Blockchain network are all responsibilities of the certificate authority.

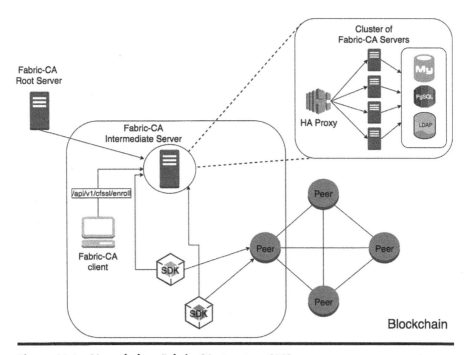

Figure 11.1   Hyperledger Fabric CA structure [22]

- **Orderer:** Its main function is to keep every component and member functioning in a synchronized manner. The orderer informs all the peers present in the system about the newly committed transactions. Increasing the number of orderers in the system reduces the number of faults that the system may face.
- **Peers:** Every peer in the network contains its own copy of the world state and only peers have the permission to commit transactions in the network. The information is also transferred to CouchDB which operates as the database [7]. Systems can have multiple peers and anchor peers. Anchor peers are pivotal for communication with other organizations in the network [8].

A sample network of two machines is shown in Figure 11.2, depicting a single machine acting as the orderer, certificate authority along with single or multiple peers. Other machines in the network act only as peers. This is the architecture for a single organization. Hyperledger Fabric also provides the functionality to deploy multi-organization networks, where each organization has a separate anchor peer. Some organizations also have multiple anchor peers in order to avoid a single point of failure.

3. **Smart Contract:** A computer program stored on the Blockchain network itself is referred to as a Smart contract. Its fundamental function is to execute the terms defined and laid out in the program. When invoked by an external

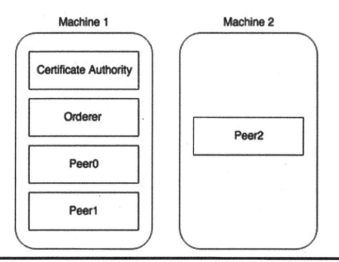

Figure 11.2   Multi-peer Network Architecture [28]

event, or if some preset condition has been fulfilled, only then does the smart contract begin executing [9]. Contract-oriented high-level languages, such as **LLL** (LISP Like Language), Serpent or Solidity, are used in **EVMs** (Ethereum Virtual Machines) and programming languages such as Javascript, Go and Java are used in Hyperledger Fabric.

4. **Consensus in Hyperledger:** Hyperledger makes use of the permissioned voting-based consensus from a pool of other consensuses, named the lottery-based consensus [10]. The working assumption for Hyperledger engineers is that business Blockchain networks work in a climate of incomplete trust. To summarize, voting-based algorithms are more favorable since they offer a low latency strategy. When a major proportion of the nodes validate a block to enter the chain, consensus prevails and finality occurs. Hence, the block is added to the Blockchain. However, there exists a significant trade-off. The voting-based algorithm requires nodes to transfer information to all the other nodes existing in the network. As a result, when more nodes are present in the network, a longer time is required to reach a consensus. Thus, there is a major trade-off between time and scalability.

Consensus in Hyperledger occurs in three phases, namely endorsement, ordering and validation. Observe the process of consensus in Figure 11.3. Endorsement is driven by policy, as shown in steps 1 and 2. Endorsing peers in the network send appropriate messages back to the client to endorse the transaction. Subsequently, transaction ordering is performed by the Ordering Service in step 3 and finally validation takes place in step 4. Upon validation, the transaction is committed to the Blockchain network by the committing peer.

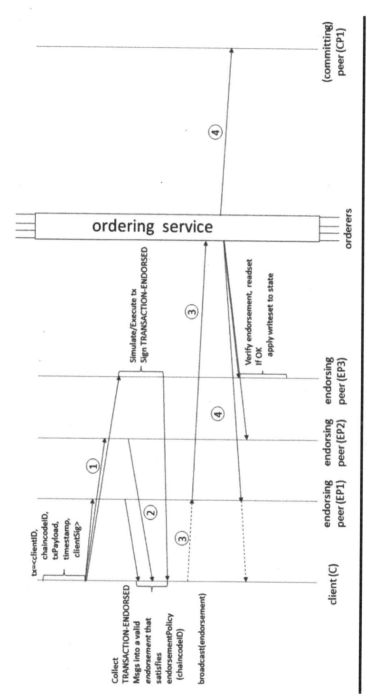

Figure 11.3 Sequence Diagram of Consensus in Hyperledger Fabric [5]

11.3.2 Hyperledger Composer

Hyperledger Composer comprises a set of tools that help in the creation of the Blockchain network. It is implemented by various business owners and developers for Blockchain-based applications and smart contracts. The primary aim behind this is to help solve business problems and to promote operational efficiency. It has an inbuilt functionality which provides the user with a Digital Subscriber Line (DSL) to state transactions, assets and participants in the network.

- ◾ **.BNA Files:** When trying to build a business network, access controls are of the utmost importance. They are enforced as per the access control rules specified in the Business Network definition [11]. Before the business network definition can be deployed, it must be compressed and packed into a (Business Network Archive) (**.bna**) file [12]. It can be observed in the work-flow (Figure 11.4) that the generated .bna file is an integral part in the functioning of a Hyperledger Composer application. The contents of a .bna file are model file, script file, access control file and a query file. Figure 11.5 shows these components, along with their descriptions. These four files are packaged to create the Business Network Archive.

11.3.3 Electronic Voting System

In the early 1980s, the idea of electronic voting was brought to light by David Shaum [13]. The system made use of public-key cryptography, which helped cast votes while keeping voter identities hidden. The Blind Signature Theorem was used in order to ensure that there were no links between voter and ballots.

For the past several years, many governments have shown a strong interest in e-voting systems. This interest, however, has often been followed by security issues which start becoming prominent upon usage. Quite a few approaches have been suggested that contribute to a more transparent voting system, but they are both expensive and infeasible to be implemented on a large scale. As a population becomes

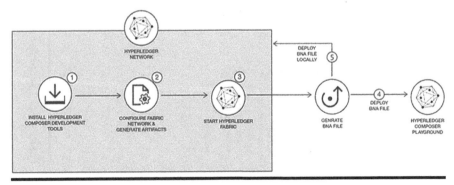

Figure 11.4 Hyperledger Composer Application Workflow [23]

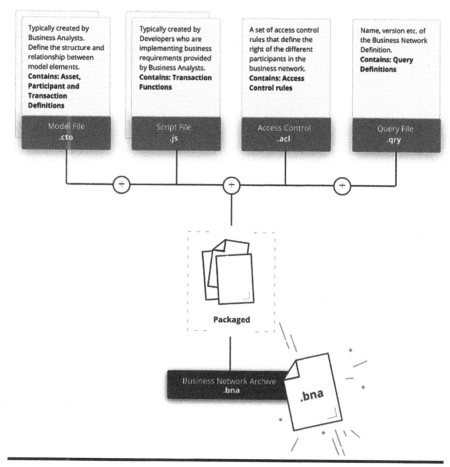

Figure 11.5 Components of .bna files [12]

more technically advanced, electronic and remote voting becomes an incentive for greater participation in democracy.

The replacement of traditional schemes of voting, the electronic voting system, must be made while keeping a few points into consideration. These include the fraud detection and allowing the voting process to be verifiable and traceable. In this section, we are going to discuss the desired criteria for an electronic voting system and how beneficial Blockchain technology is in this vertical. Blockchain can prove to be a transparent and cost-effective method to verify transactions taking place in large-scale voting systems and this is another reason why the use of Blockchain is being promoted.

1. **Key Features of an E-voting System** [14]

Altogether, for an e-voting ballot system to be regarded as secure, certain for-mally expressed properties must hold true.

a. Fairness

No early results should be obtainable before the completion of casting a ballot procedure; this ensures that no voter will be influenced by the votes cast by another individual.

b. Eligibility

This property expresses that only eligible voters should be permitted to cast their votes, and that they can do so only once. Verification is the principle of this property, as voters need to prove their identity before being considered as eligible or otherwise.

c. Privacy

This property expresses that privacy of the voters should be maintained. Voters need to register for voting using their personal details; as a result, security should also be a major concern.

d. Verifiable

This property guarantees that all voters included can check whether or not their votes have been counted. Normally, two types of verifiability are defined: individual and all-inclusive verifiability. Individual verifiability enables an individual voter to check that his vote has been counted [15]. All-inclusive verifiability facilitates that anybody can check that the election result declared is indeed the one distributed [16].

e. Coercion-Resistant

A coercer is a person who tries to make the voter cast a vote of his preference and communicates with the voter before and after the election. Coercion resistance refers to the property of voting systems that allows a voter to be unable to prove to a coercer in what manner they cast the vote. This allows for votes to not be bought or blackmailed in order to rig the outcome for an election.

To understand if a voter casts a vote under coercion, a system should ideally be able to detect it. Yet coercion resistance will not be effectively sought after since it was regarded unrealistic to be accomplished simply with mechanical methods in a remote e-vote ballot convention.

2. **Problems with the Proprietary Voting System**

The existing e-voting system encounters significant design flaws. This is due to its proprietary feature that there is a single supply that concurrently controls the code base, database, system outputs and also supplies the monitoring software. The architecture, in other worlds, is centralized. The lack of an open-source, independently verifiable output makes it difficult for such centralized systems to accumulate trust from the voters and election organizers. Without easy and free access to effective and secure electronic voting technology, political participation is scarce and limited to on-site elections, given the high setup cost of election preparation, supervision, and post-election operations [17]. This design flaw is therefore limiting electronic voting applications at a time when literacy and use of technology is increasing. This should, in fact, foster their widespread adoption of Blockchain in the voting industry.

3. **How can Blockchain Overcome it?**

   If Blockchain is utilized within the online voting system, it is possible to implement better electronic management. This will be used to check whether or not voters cast their votes and also the counting of votes, thereby making the voting system more efficient.

   The advantages of the Blockchain-based online voting system are as follows:

   a. Time and cost reduction

   The Blockchain-based online voting system can reduce time and cost compared to conventional voting. According to the existing voting method, it takes some time before the ballot counter counts all the votes. If the voting is done on the Blockchain server, however, it will be possible to see the voting result immediately after voting. So it is not necessary to wait for the voting result to come in after a certain time. Also, due to the simplified voting process, voting costs can also be expected to be reduced. The Blockchain-based online voting system can reduce the cost of voting and ballot counting compared to that of the conventional voting methods, and, in contrast to the existing online voting system, the Blockchain-based online voting system can also reduce the cost of implementing the central server and the security system.

   b. Increased participation of voters

   The Blockchain-based online voting system can increase citizens' participation in voting. Everyone finds it difficult to participate in the current direct voting, but if the Blockchain is used for voting, it will be possible to overcome physical limitations and more people can participate in the policy-making process. Also, as the online ballot paper provides a link to the information on each candidate, they could get information more easily and faster than in the conventional voting.

   c. Security and reliability

   Regarding the online voting system, there are concerns about the secrecy of voting, the personal information security issue and the abuse and fabrication of the right to vote. However, the decentralized information-sharing system of the Blockchain can secure integrity and security on its own [18]. In the conventional online voting system, as the central server and the central database manage and process voting values, there is a high risk of fabricating voting results.

   In the Blockchain-based online voting system, not all voting values are stored in the central server and the central database, but they are disclosed to everyone participating in the voting on the Peer to Peer (**P2P**) distributed network. So voting can be done transparently. Also, in the Blockchain-based online voting system, voting values are connected using the keys and hash functions of other voting values. So, it is impossible to arbitrarily modify or omit them. Since one-way calculation is easy, but inverse calculation is very difficult, the input value cannot be inferred or calculated, no matter which method is used. As a result, it is difficult to forge or alter them and voting can be conducted transparently.

4. **Digital Identity Management**

One of the main problems faced during elections is that of authentication. Authentication is the process of determining whether someone is in fact who they are declaring themselves to be. This is a key component in any trustworthy online system, which handles sensitive transactions. It seems very straightforward, yet the entire authentication process lacks opacity. The problem lies in how transparent and visible it is to the users. This correlates directly to their perception of trust. Without this key attribute, an online voting system fails its purpose. A good authentication process should be able to verify the users' credentials without compensating on the users' privacy [19]. Identity management (ID management) is the organizational process for identifying, authenticating and authorizing individuals or groups of people to have access to applications, systems or networks by associating user rights and restrictions with established identities. The managed identities can also refer to software processes that need access to organizational systems. An encryption scheme proposed by MIT researchers Silvio Micali, Shafi Goldwasser, and Charles Racko in the 1980s is a good fit for having a digital identity management framework [20]. Here one party (ie. the Prover) can prove to another party that a specific statement is true. This party is referred to as the verifier and this process is done without disclosing any additional information. It is commonly referred to as the Zero Knowledge Proof method [24].

11.4 Secure Online Voting Using Blockchain

11.4.1 Existing Voting System

The existing voting system in educational institutes comprises the central server called the admin, which regulates the entire voting process. All students are eligible to vote using their enrollment numbers as usernames for the system that enables them to cast votes. Additionally, a list of passwords is prepared and distributed to the faculties. This process which requires distribution of password along with the username can be easily exploited by an adversary.

Drawbacks to the Existing System

■ The administration holds the entire record, i.e. all the votes cast. Hence, if the system breaks down, then it has detrimental effects on the entire voting procedure.

■ The system fails to handle a large number of entries simultaneously. There have been many instances where the votes went to waste because the system was unable to record them appropriately.

■ The password for casting a vote is randomly generated by some algorithm. However, the password is not confidential. In fact, a list of all student IDs and passwords is circulated among the people, who are assigned duties during the voting process. As a result, an anonymous person can cast votes using someone else's credentials.

■ This voting system requires all of the institute's students to be present on the institute campus to cast their votes. Many day scholars do not feel the need to come to the institute just to cast their votes. As a result, a major portion of the day scholars' are wasted.

■ The atmosphere during the day of voting is quite tense, with different candidates trying their best to gather more votes. Many students prefer to not vote in order to avoid such extreme conditions.

■ Since, there is no alternate copy of the data recorded, no one will be aware of any changes made even if some data is maliciously altered.

11.4.2 Proposed System

The flowchart in Figure 11.6 depicts the flow in perspective of the user. A user will enter their respective email ID and roll number. An **OTP** (One-time password) will be sent to them. If the OTP is correctly inputted, they will be asked to fill in their personal information. If the OTP the user has entered is incorrect or if they have filled their personal information wrong, the system will automatically not allow them to pass to the next stage. The user will be again asked to enter their email ID and roll number. If both the entered OTP is correct and the personal information entered is valid (i.e. it will be verified using Institute data), a login password will be sent to the user's registered mail ID. After which, the user will be added as a voter. Now the user can cast the vote. Once they select their candidates and click the submit button, the system will log them out. If the vote is successfully submitted, it is added as a transaction in a block which is further added onto the Blockchain network. However, if the attempt is unsuccessful, the user can enter their roll number and login password to login onto the system again. Once that is verified, they will be able to select candidates and cast the vote again.

One of the main objectives of building an online voting system using Blockchain is decentralization. In other words, being able to run the application on multiple peers gives rise to various perks. During the process, the voter is first verified before registering to vote. After the vote has been casted the data is transferred to the Orderer (it can be solo or a cluster) which compiles the transaction and the world state variable, forming the block to be appended to the chain. The peers used in this application are the committing peers, which do not endorse the transaction but commit the block to the chain. So after the Orderer creates a block that is

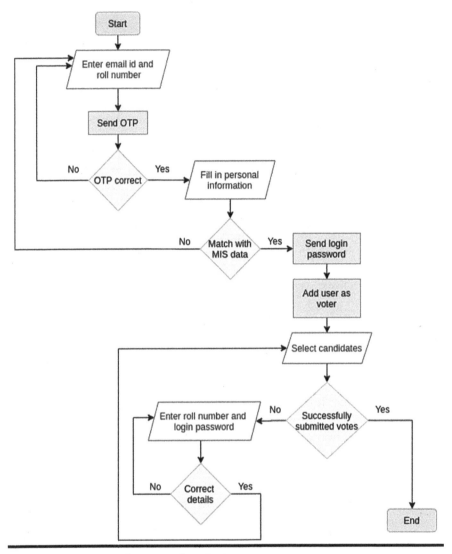

Figure 11.6 Proposed System Flowchart

transmitted to the committing peers for adding blocks of transactions to the shared ledger and updating the state variables.

1. **Why are we opting Hyperledger over Ethereum?**
   The innovation of fabrics introduced a whole new take on the Blockchain architecture. It was directed at improving its confidentiality, resilience, scalability and reliability. Designed as a modular and extensible general-purpose permissioned Blockchain.

Fabric is the first Blockchain system to support the execution of distributed applications written in standard programming languages, in a way that allows them to be executed consistently across many nodes, giving the impression of execution on a single globally distributed Blockchain computer.

Fabric happened to be the first distributed operating system in the permissioned Blockchain network. The architecture of the Hyperledger Fabric follows the "execute–order–validate" format. This is the path traditionally followed in any distributed execution of code that users do not trust, in an unsafe environment. The transactional flow is segregated into three phases, which can run on different entities within the system [21]:

a. Endorsement—endorsing a transaction, checking its accuracy and validating it (corresponding to the execution of transaction).

b. Ordering—ordering through a consensus protocol, regardless of any transaction semantics

c. Validation—transaction validation takes place that is targeted to applications. This boasts the trust assumptions and wipes out any race condition states occurring due to concurrency.

11.4.3 Modular Design

The entire system is to be divided into four sub-modules. These modules are responsible for carrying out particular tasks of the system. The following functionalities are carried out by the sub-modules.

1. **Verification Module:** The first phase of the online voting system is the verification process. This module verifies the details filed during the process of registration with the details of the student in Institute data. The verification process verifies the OTP sent to the registered email id along with other details (such as details present in the institute).

   Authentication is the process that occurs when an entity proves an identity. We have implemented a multi-step authentication. The roll number of the student is checked against the Institute database. OTP is sent to their registered email ID to confirm that the student has provided the correct details. Voter-related information will be sent to their registered email id. Personal details are cross-checked from the Institute database (dummy database in the application demonstration). If someone performs identity spoofing, then they are bound to fail at any one of the three steps.

2. **On-boarding Module:** The second module in the online voting process is on-boarding. This means that after the students' details have been completely verified using the Institute data, now they need to be linked to the application in order to vote (or perform the transaction). This is done by sending a secret key to the registered email id of the student, which is used to login into the system. The secret key is an 8-digit random key created using a powerful

cryptography library which provides various sets of functions to generate unpredictable data, and hence is very effective in order to create secret keys. It is important to create a login page instead of just redirecting the voters to the page for casting votes directly. By having a login page, the students will be obligated to login in again in case of power outage or system failures and then cast the vote. During the on-boarding process, the voters are created as participants in the Blockchain with their user id, name and enrollment number. Hence, on successful login the voters can perform the voting (transaction).

3. **Casting the Votes:** On-boarded students can cast their votes during the election period. After successful verification and linking them as participants in the Blockchain the voters can cast their votes. The administrative nodes, including peers, add the votes onto the Blockchain, hence making their votes secure and immutable. Their votes are sent as a transaction for a block to be added in a Blockchain. Single transaction refers to a single vote which includes the student's admission number and the time at which the vote is submitted, i.e timestamp. Time can be set to regulate the number of transactions in a block. The block entry is sent as input to the hashing algorithm so that the corresponding hash can be sent to the next block.

4. **Declaration of Results:** The admins will be able to receive the count of votes after the ending of voting procedure.

11.5 Implementation Methodology

We have followed a similar systematic approach to building and developing the back end of the Blockchain voting model. Throughout this chapter, code snippets and screenshots of the working model are presented.

11.5.1 Peer Network

We have built a network comprising two peers, which includes an admin node and a peer node. The admin node also serves as the Orderer, Certificate Authority and a Peer itself. Below there are some screenshots of the working model. One can also see code snippets depicting the above-mentioned theory.

YAML is a human-readable data-serialization language. It is commonly used for configuration files and in applications where data are being stored or transmitted. With docker-composer, YAML is used to configure the application's services. As can be seen in lines [11] and 29 in Figure 11.7, a multi-container docker configuration is created wherein Fabric CA, Orderer, Peer and CouchDB services are isolated from each other.

Along with creating the configuration, this file also provides the location of the CA. The CA filename is updated every time the server is generated, and the filename

Figure 11.7   Docker-compose.yml File Screenshot

needs to be updated in the docker-compose.yml file, according to the filename in the respective directory [22]. The location of the CA directory is provided in Figure 11.8. Additionally, for the peers to be able to connect to the network, their **IP** (Internet Protocol) address needs to be written under the extra hosts section of the code above (172.21.1.211 is the IP of the second peer, peer1.org1.example.com).

Start.sh script first removes the previous instances of all the peers and orderer and then creates new docker containers. There is one container for each image. All the services are listening at different ports and will later help in providing authentication, database, transaction ordering facility and to establish communication with the client. The unique docker container IDs and status of the same can be seen in Figure 11.9. This output is observed on the console when the start.sh script is executed.

Moving on to the configuration of the second peer, peer1.org1.example.com. This peer (peer1.org1.example.com) is using port 8051 to communicate with the server residing (peer0.org1.example.com) at port 7051. See Figure 11.10. Extra hosts are the server machine, which also serves as the orderer and certificate authority providing authentication details to all the peers wanting to connect to the network. The IP address 172.16.2.237 is of the server machine. Like the server machine, the contents of docker can be seen in Figure 11.11.

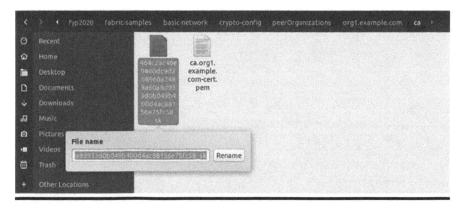

Figure 11.8   CA File For Peer Authentication

```
docker-compose -f docker-compose.yml up -d ca.example.com orderer.example.com peer0.org1.example.com couchdb
Creating couchdb ...
Creating peer0.org1.example.com ...
Creating ca.example.com ...
Creating couchdb ...
Creating peer0.org1.example.com ...
docker ps -a
CONTAINER ID    IMAGE              COMMAND              CREATED          STATUS                   PORTS
                                   NAMES
3207d95c04f2    hyperledger/fabric-peer   "peer node start"    5 seconds ago    Up Less than a second    0.0.0.0:7051->7
051/tcp, 0.0.0.0:7053->7053/tcp    peer0.org1.example.com
140b1fa5a9d2    hyperledger/fabric-couchdb   "tini -- /docker-ent."   15 seconds ago   Up 5 seconds         4369/tcp, 5984/
tcp, 9100/tcp, 0.0.0.0:8050->8050/tcp   couchdb
249ee20af34f    hyperledger/fabric-ca    "sh -c 'fabric-ca-se."   15 seconds ago   Up 6 seconds         0.0.0.0:7054->7
054/tcp                              ca.example.com
e3dcd817074b    hyperledger/fabric-orderer   "orderer"            15 seconds ago   Up 6 seconds         0.0.0.0:7050->7
050/tcp                              orderer.example.com
```

Figure 11.9   Server Started

```
40         8051:7051
41         8053:7053
42
43       - /var/run/:/host/var/run/
44       - ./crypto-config/peerOrganizations/org1.example.com/peers/peer1.org1.example.com/msp:/etc/hyperledger/msp/peer
45       - ./crypto-config/peerOrganizations/org1.example.com/users:/etc/hyperledger/msp/users
46       - ./config:/etc/hyperledger/configtx
47
48     - "orderer.example.com:172.16.2.237"
49     - "peer0.org1.example.com:172.16.2.237"
50     - "ca.example.com:172.16.2.237"
51
52       - couchdb1
53       #   - orderer.example.com
54       #   - peer0.org1.example.com
55
56     - basic
57
58                    : couchdb1
```

Figure 11.10   Docker-compose.yml file for peer1

```
shivangi@shivangitanwar-laptop:~/fyp2020/fabric-samples/basic-network$ docker ps -a
CONTAINER ID    IMAGE              COMMAND              CREATED          STATUS          PORTS
                NAMES
91072c5fe069    hyperledger/fabric-peer   "peer node start"    6 minutes ago    Up 6 minutes    0.0.0.0:8051->7051/tcp, 0.0.
0.0:8053->7053/tcp    peer1.org1.example.com
d4cd3c1ef342    hyperledger/fabric-couchdb   "tini -- /docker-ent."   6 minutes ago    Up 6 minutes    4369/tcp, 9100/tcp, 0.0.0.0:
6984->5984/tcp    couchdb1
shivangi@shivangitanwar-laptop:~/fyp2020/fabric-samples/basic-network$
```

Figure 11.11   Docker containers status in peer1

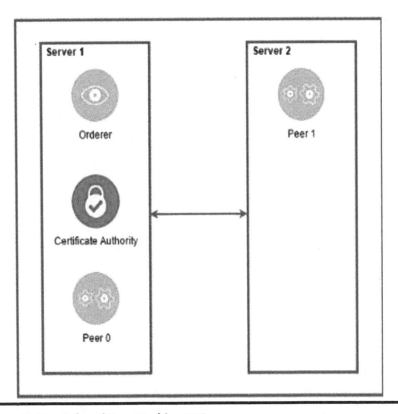

Figure 11.12   Roles of Peer Machine [29]

There are two peers present in the current network. The first peer (peer0) also acts as the certificate authority and orderer whereas the second peer, peer1, acts as a regular peer who takes part in endorsing an incoming transaction. Figure 11.12 is used to depict the same.

Hyperledger Fabric supports two types of peer databases: LevelDB is the default state database embedded in the peer node and stores chaincode data as simple key-value pairs; and CouchDB is an optional alternate state database that supports rich queries when chaincode data values are modeled as **JSON** (JavaScript Object Notation). CouchDB is a JSON document data store rather than a pure key-value store, thereby enabling indexing of the contents of the documents in the database. Therefore, CouchDB is also in one of the docker containers to maintain the world state database. One of the advantages of our network connection is that the peers and server stay active until there is a stable internet connection and the machines are turned on.

11.5.2 Blockchain

The file shown in Figure 11.13 defines the structure of the voting business network. The model.cto file has two participants, one asset and one transaction definition. Voter and Candidate participants contain parameters for relevant information, which will be used for verification of voter's identity and for the submission of votes. Since an asset is anything of value, the Vote asset here is a registry of all the votes that have been cast by a Voter with voteID (as denoted by String voteID parameter) to a list of candidates of different posts. Lastly, VoteLog is the immutable record of vote transactions which contains the parameters as Vote asset, along with timestamp and transactionID.

The Logic.js file, shown in Figure 11.14 contains the transaction logic these functions are called transaction processor functions. It defines what actions are to be performed before the vote can be submitted in the ledger. The above code snippet implements the functioning of adding the vote as an asset before it is submitted as a transaction. Updates to vote assets can be used by voters or participants in the business network to check whom they have voted for without the need to extensively search in the whole transaction log. Transaction processor functions use async functions for promises to be resolved before committing the transaction.

```
namespace org.example.empty
asset Vote identified by voteID {
    o String voteID
    --> Candidate[] candidate
}
participant Voter identified by voteID {
    o String voteID
    o String password
    o String rollNumber
    o String fullName
}
participant Candidate identified by candidateId {
    o String candidateId
    o String post
    o String firstName
    o String lastName
}
transaction VoteLog {
    o String voteID
    --> Candidate[] candidate
}
```

Figure 11.13   Model.cto File

```
/**
 * @param {org.example.empty.VoteLog} tx
 * @transaction
 */
async function logAdd(tx) {
    let assetRegistry = await getAssetRegistry('org.example.empty.Vote');
    var factory = getFactory()
    var asset = factory.newResource('org.example.empty', 'Vote', tx.voteID)
    asset.candidate = tx.candidate
    await assetRegistry.add(asset);
}
```

Figure 11.14   Logic.js File

```
/**
 * Access control rules for vote-network
 */
rule Default {
    description: "Allow all participants access to all resources"
    participant: "ANY"
    operation: ALL
    resource: "org.example.empty.*"
    action: ALLOW
}

rule SystemACL {
    description:  "System ACL to permit all access"
    participant: "ANY"
    operation: ALL
    resource: "org.hyperledger.composer.system.**"
    action: ALLOW
}
```

Figure 11.15   Permissions.acl File

As suggested by the second line in the code snippet in Figure 11.15, these are the access control rules for the vote network. These rules define what role is played by each identity in the network on different resources. The Default rule states that any participant is allowed to access any operations on all resources. Resources here mean participants (candidate and voter), assets (vote), and transaction (VoteLog). Hyperledger Composer system namespace, in rule SystemACL, is the base definition of all business network class definitions. All asset, participant, and transaction definitions extend those defined here. SystemACL is permitting all access.

After setting the foundation of our business network, the next essential task is the generation of cards. In our vote network, there are two cards, PeerAdmin@hlfv1 and admin@vote-network (see Figure 11.16). The PeerAdmin is used to administer the local Hyperledger Fabric and it's a special role reserved for deploying business networks as well as creating, issuing, and revoking identity cards for business networks. So, with the help of PeerAdmin card, admin@vote-network is generated. Using this card, the running business network will be updated and querying the various registries (participant, identity, and so forth) [23].

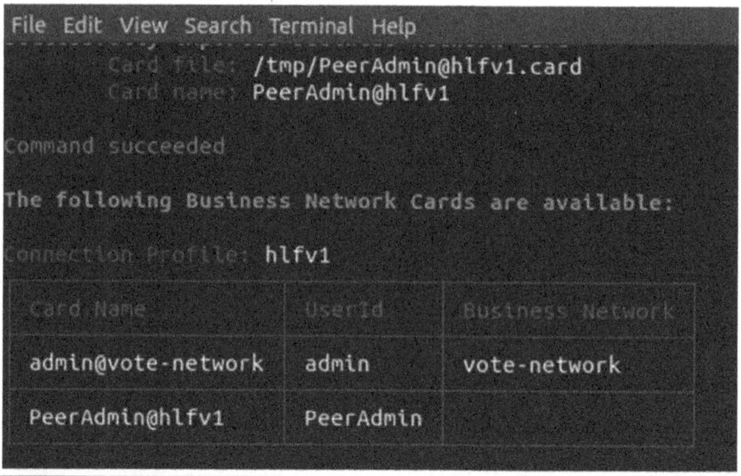

Figure 11.16   Cards Used In The System

11.5.3 REST Server API

Once the business network is deployed locally, there must be an interface which can help a secondary user use all the operations related to a participant, an asset or a transaction. Composer REST server api serves this purpose by bridging the gap between a client application and Blockchain. The default port number used by composer rest server is 3000 and it runs on localhost. Any request made to the business is done via REST server by calling the api and different functions in a jquery script over at the client web application. The general operations are get, post, delete, etc. These are also visible in Figure 11.17, where Candidate participant operations are listed in the REST server explorer.

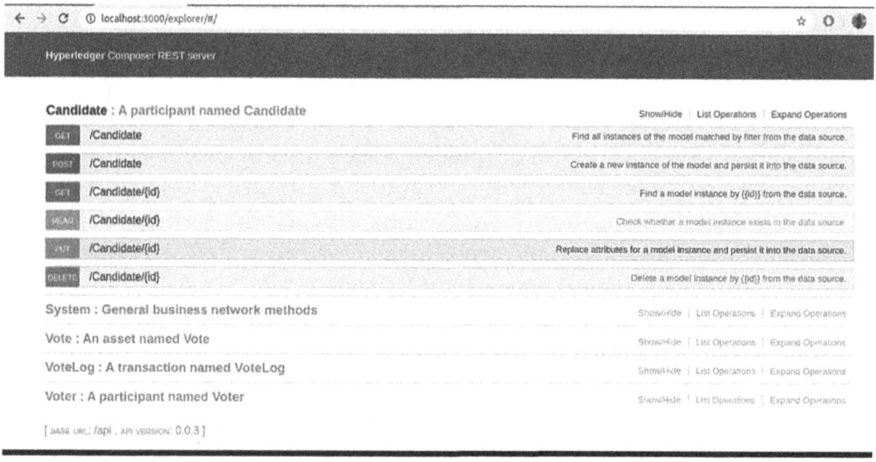

Figure 11.17   Composer REST Server Explorer

11.5.4 Client-side Application

As depicted in the proposed flow, the first step is for the voter to enter their roll number and email id, so that an email can be sent to them with OTP. Once the OTP is verified, the student is redirected to the personal details verification page. The student's mother's name, father's name and date of birth are requested. Details such as mother's name and father's name are not even known to the closest of friends. Ideally, these details will be checked with the actual Institute database. However, we have used dummy data provided by fellow batchmates to aid the demonstration of the verification process.

After the details entered by the voter are successfully verified against the Institute data, the student's roll number and a few other parameters are added in the Voter participant, wherein a voteID is also generated by compiling personal details and generating a **SHA**-256 (Secure Hash Algorithm) hash. A unique password is also generated and mailed to the student. The student is then redirected to the voting page (see Figure 11.18). In the voting page, names of all the candidates will be displayed according to the posts they will be contesting for and each student will have to vote for every post and only then will the votes be added to the transaction. In the event of a bad internet connection where the student may be unable to vote, they must use the login details sent to them to login and cast their votes.

Once the users have submitted their votes for every post using their voteID, the candidate roll numbers will be sent in a candidate array. The sample transaction can be seen in Figure 11.19, where the array is followed by transactionID and timestamp.

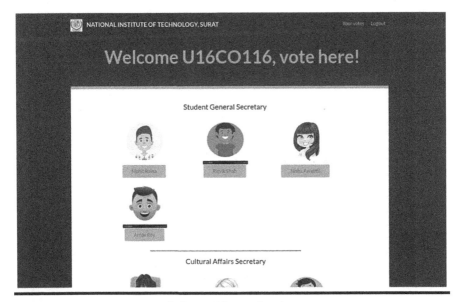

Figure 11.18   Voting Page of Client-side Application

```
{
  "$class": "org.example.empty.VoteLog",
  "voteID": "0001",
  "candidate": [
    "resource:org.example.empty.Candidate#1906",
    "resource:org.example.empty.Candidate#3891",
    "resource:org.example.empty.Candidate#5686",
    "resource:org.example.empty.Candidate#7832"
  ],
  "transactionId": "e68884d8-fb04-4c31-af75-cbe367c3cd16",
  "timestamp": "2020-06-02T05:06:33.198Z"
}
```

Figure 11.19   Transaction data

After the voting is completed, all the admins and peers will have to bring down the composer rest server. Once this is done, after a pre-decided time interval, a button to view the results will become active and the admin will be able to view the results. The results for each post will be visible in graph format as shown in Figure 11.20.

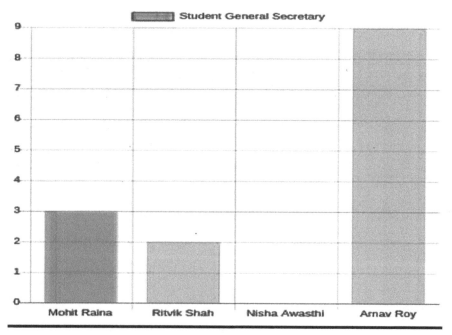

Figure 11.20   Results Representation

11.6 Results and Analysis

The key areas where we focused on result and its analysis are as follows:

DECENTRALIZATION The proposed system provides a decentralized online voting application which is not monitored by a singular authority. All the votes will be submitted to different peers, all of which will be connected to the rest server. If anyone with malicious intent will try to alter the votes, they will have to do the same for all the peers in the network as each peer will contain a local copy of the ledger. Therefore, the server to which all requests are made is reliable and trustworthy. The more the number of peers, the better the decentralization. However, this would also require more storage in each peer machine.

IMMUTABILITY Immutability is defined as the ability of distributed ledger to remain unchanged. Firstly, this voting network allows votes to be cast only once per voteID. If a transaction is submitted with a previously used voteID through hacking the client application, then it is denied by the system. Hence, once submitted, nobody's votes can be changed. For an outsider to orchestrate a false vote, the attacker first needs to have a valid login. Once they are part of the network, they would need to have the hash of the previous block, only then can they attempt to submit or alter a vote. Moreover, since the network is distributed to multiple peers, if a change is successful given the condition above is satisfied, then the change must be transmitted to all the peers and the blocks following it.

PRIVACY (OF VOTES) Votes are submitted using unique voteIDs which are generated using a cryptographic hashing algorithm. Hence, when the votes are added to vote asset and transaction log, even the peers will not be able to understand as to which students has cast a particular vote.

AUTHENTICATION This online voting application has the primary goal of allowing students to vote regardless of their location. Therefore, it is increasingly important that the correct authentication schemes are applied. In this two step verification, email ids of students are verified through OTP verification and then their details are checked against Institute data. In the current system, all authentication-related information is stored in a database with the admin. In this case, however, only the login password is stored in the Blockchain, which is also encrypted. So unless someone knows the components of their password, they cannot login into any student account to vote.

ILLEGAL CHECKING OF VOTES Another problem significant to the current voting system is the admin's ability to check vote count amidst the voting process. This leads to practices where students are told by other students to vote for person A who is x votes behind person B. To overcome this problem, the button used to count the votes is only active after the composer rest server is brought down for a certain amount of time. This preserves the fundamental attribute of any voting process.

Apart from the analysis on how well it overcomes some of the existing problems faced by an education institute voting system, the implementation of Blockchain technology brings with it some new challenges and drawbacks.

Drawbacks
Server crash
In the event of the administration system crashing, i.e. shutting down, the whole peer network will come down and will not function as admin is the also the Orderer and CA server. However, if any of the peers stop working, it will not affect the functioning. In any case, the world state database will still have the most recent transactions stored.

Fixing faults
In the event of any faults occurring, it will be difficult for anyone other than a person having Blockchain knowledge to fix a problem.

11.7 Conclusion and Future Work

The idea of adapting and reshaping an education institute's voting system to make the public election process cheaper, easier and quicker is quite a gripping one. The addition and implementation of Blockchain technology opens the door for a more direct style of democratic system. It allows voters to know the value of their vote, make sure their voice is heard and that their vote is not going to be tampered with. In this system, we have implemented a unique, Hyperledger Blockchain system that utilizes chain code to enable efficient and secure mechanisms to cast a vote. We have outlined the proposed flow of the system, the systems architecture, the design, and working implementation of said system.

By comparison to the previous system, this new voting method overcomes a lot of the disadvantages faced by education institute students during the election period. On a demo-run election, the results, the working and flow of the entire system yielded good results. The Primary aim of bringing more transparency to the system and expanding voter participation is achieved via our application [24].

It would be extremely helpful for us to see how our application stands up once students use it to cast the votes and whether or not any bugs, flaws, or problems arise once many users enter the system and cast their votes. Given more time and resources, we would want to use an authentication platform instead of OTP/Institute details for verifying a student's identity. Platforms such as Google OAuth should integrate well with our system.

The present application does not use any third party for authorization; instead, it creates passwords for the authenticated voters. However, this process of giving access to the students can be improvised using the OAuth framework [25]. It enables a third-party application (client) to obtain access with specific permissions to a protected resource, with the consent of the resource owner. Access to the resource is achieved through access tokens. **JWT** (JSON Web Tokens) is an open standard that defines a compact format to transmit claims between parties as a JSON object.

An extension to the current implementation can be binding identities with participants. Identities are provided in the form of cards, which are generated and issued by the network admin when a participant is added to the network. These cards are stored in the local wallets of network admin and composer performs participant to identity mapping. So, whenever a participant wants to access resources, their identity card is used.

Usually, participants with identities are implemented when participants are recurring users of the business and want to exchange or own certain assets. That being said, they do provide a more controlled access to operations as permissions defining access can be altered for each type of participant. In the proposed voting application, voter participant is used to merely store student information for use during login activity and providing voteID. However, identities can be used for a more defined access control.

References

[1] J. Gobel, H. Keeler, A. Krzesinski, and P. Taylor, "Bitcoin Blockchain dynamics: The selfish-mine strategy in the presence of propagation delay," *Performance Evaluation*, vol. 104, pp. 23–41, 2016.

[2] "Electronic voting system using Blockchain," *International Research Journal of Engineering and Technology*, vol. 7, no. 7, p. 332, 2020.

[3] J. Frankenfield, "Hyperledger Fabric", Investopedia-Blog, 2020.

[4] E. Androulaki, A. Barger, V. Bortnikov, C. Cachin, K. Christidis, A. De Caro, and S. Muralidharan, (2018, April). "Hyperledger fabric: a distributed operating system for permissioned Blockchains". *Proceedings of the Thirteenth EuroSys Conference*, pp. 1–15.

[5] "Architecture Origins," *hyperledger*. Available: https://hyperledger-fabric.readthedocs. io/en/release-1.4/arch-deep-dive.html.

[6] Y. Emre, A. Kaan Koc, U. Can Cabuk, and G. Dalk. "Towards secure e-voting using ethereum Blockchain." *2018 6th International Symposium on Digital Forensic and Security (ISDFS)*, pp. 1–7. IEEE, 2018.

[7] H. Rifa, and B. Rahardjo. "Blockchain based e-voting recording system design." *2017 11th International Conference on Telecommunication Systems Services and Applications (TSSA)*, pp. 1–6. IEEE, 2017.

[8] Hjalmarsson Fririk, K. Hreiarsson Gunnlaugur, Hamdaqa Mohammad, and Hjalmtysson G Sli. "Blockchain-based e-voting system." *2018 IEEE 11th International Conference on Cloud Computing (CLOUD)*, pp. 983–986. IEEE, 2018.

[9] K. Kashif Mehboob, J. Arshad, and M. Mubashir Khan. "Secure digital voting system based on Blockchain technology," *International Journal of Electronic Government Research (IJEGR)*, vol. 14, no. 1, pp. 53–62, 2018.

[10] W. Jan Hendrik. "The Blockchain: A gentle four page introduction," *arXiv preprint arXiv:1612.06244*, 2016.

[11] EkS S. Mukhekar, "Deploy Business Network Archive (.bna) les to your IBM Blockchain," *BlogSaays*, 13-Sep-2017. Available: https://www.blogsaays.com/deploy-business-network-archive-to-ibm-blockchain/.

[12] "Deploying business networks | Hyperledger Composer," Hyperledger.github.io, 2017.

[13] K. Fung, "Network Security Technologies", Boca Raton, FL: Auerbach Publications, 2005, p. 14.

[14] H. Freya Sheer, A. Gioulis, R. Naeem Akram, and K. Markantonakis. "E-voting with Blockchain: An e-voting protocol with decentralisation and voter privacy." *2018 IEEE International Conference on Internet of Things (iThings) and IEEE Green Computing and Communications (GreenCom) and IEEE Cyber, Physical and Social Computing (CPSCom) and IEEE Smart Data (SmartData)*, pp. 1561–1567. IEEE, 2018.

[15] A. Ahmed Ben. "A conceptual secure Blockchain-based electronic voting system," *International Journal of Network Security Its Applications*, vol. 9, no. 3, p. 5, 2017.

[16] A. Jadhav, "What is Ethereum Blockchain and How it Works and What it can be Used for?", Linkedin, 2018.

[17] Barnes Andrew, Christopher Brake, and Thomas Perry. "Digital Voting with the Use of Blockchain Technology", Team Plymouth Pioneers-Plymouth University, pp. 3–10, 2016.

[18] S. Karim, U. Ruhi, and R. Lakhani. "Conceptualizing Blockchains: Characteristics applications," *arXiv preprint arXiv*, 1806, 03693, 2018.

[19] R. Zhang, R. Xue, and L. Liu, "Security and privacy on Blockchain," *ACM Computing Surveys*, vol. 52, no. 3, pp. 1–34, 2019.

[20] S.B. Mills, "Blockchain design principles," *Medium*, 22-Mar-2017. Available: https://medium.com/design-ibm/blockchain-design-principles-599c5c067b6e.

[21] S. Kumar, "The Ultimate Guide to Consensus in Hyperledger Fabric | Skcript", Skcript—Blog, 2018.

[22] "Fabric CA user's guide," *hyperledger*, 2017. Available: https://hyperledger-fabric-ca.readthedocs.io/en/release-1.4/users-guide.html.

[23] B. Ekici, "Blockchain-based vote application on hyperledger composer," *Medium*, Available: https://medium.com/coinmonks/blockchain-based-vote-application-on-hyperledger-composer-e08b1527031e.

[24] F. Francesco, M. Ilaria Lunesu, F. Eros Pani, and A. Pinna. "Crypto-voting, a Blockchain based e-Voting System." In *KMIS*, pp. 221–225. 2018.

[25] V. Siris, D. Dimopoulos, N. Fotiou, S. Voulgaris, and G. Polyzos, "OAuth 2.0 meets Blockchain for authorization in constrained IoT environments," *IEEE 5th World Forum on Internet of Things (WF-IoT)*, vol. 152, pp. 364–367, 2019.

[26] S. Panja, and B. Kumar Roy, "A secure end-to-end verifiable e-voting system using zero knowledge based Blockchain," *IACR Cryptol. ePrint Arch.*, pp. 466–473, 2018.

[27] J. Lopes, J. Pereira, and J. Varajao, "Blockchain Based E-voting System: A Proposal", *Twenty-fifth Americas Conference on Information Systems, Cancun, 2019*, 2019.

[28] V. Raj, "Setting up a Blockchain Business Network With Hyperledger Fabric & Composer Running in Multiple Physical Machine," *Skcript*, 2-Jan-2018. Available: https://www.skcript.com/svr/setting-up-a-blockchain-business-network-with-hyperledger-fabric-and-composer-running-in-multiple-physical-machine/.

[29] D. Bascans, "Setup Hyperledger Fabric in multiple physical machines," *Medium*, 18-Sep-2018. Available: https://medium.com/1950labs/setup-hyperledger-fabric-in-multiple-physical-machines-d8f3710ed9b4.

Chapter 12

Secure Electronic Health Records (EHR) Management Using Blockchain

Atharva Kalsekar, Avinash Jaiswal, Rogin Koshy,
Sameer Mandloi, and Bhavesh N. Gohil
Sardar Vallabhbhai National Institute of Technology, India

Contents

DOI: 10.1201/9781003129486-12

12.1 Objective of the Chapter

This chapter primarily aims to develop a Blockchain system that implements and maintains Electronic Health Records (EHR) among various participating medical organizations and patients. This system would provide smooth interoperability and transfer of patient health records among the peer medical institutions whenever a patient might want to change his/her ongoing consultancy from one medical practitioner to another. "The secondary objective of the chapter would be to provide the implementation details and subtle instructions required to setup the system". This system would be made interactable with participants of the network through a web application.

12.2 Introduction

Developing countries are carrying the burden of the most deadly chronic diseases, including cancer, HIV/AIDs and diabetes. These countries are under pressure to provide superior healthcare services amid a shortage of qualified healthcare professionals. As a key component of medical informatics, the EHR symbolizes potential solutions for enhanced healthcare. The EHR is a digital version of a patient's paper records. The EHR structures hold vital and highly confidential private details for healthcare diagnosis and treatment, often spread and exchanged among peers such as healthcare professionals, insurance agencies, hospitals, academics, patient families, among others.

In the healthcare context, EHR systems requires to work jointly within and across organizational boundaries in order to advance the effective delivery of health-care for individuals and societies and also enable cost savings and efficiencies. In addition, the lack of integration makes it difficult to maintain the privacy and security of a patient's confidential information. Security of the EHR is a matter of concern, especially where patient data are transmitted over a network. Recently, Blockchain technology has been advocated as a promising solution to solving EHR interoperability and security issues in developing countries.

Blockchain is a decentralized [1], trustless protocol that combines transparency, immutability, and consensus properties to enable secure [2], pseudo-anonymous transactions stored in a digital ledger. Systems built on the Blockchain technology achieve secure distribution of entities amongst untrusted nodes. In the healthcare industry, the Blockchain technology has the potential to address the interoperabil-ity and security challenges currently present in EHR systems [3]. The technology has the ability to provide technical architecture that enables individuals, healthcare providers, disparate entities and researchers to securely share electronic patient's data across multiple platforms.

In this chapter, we propose a Blockchain system for implementing and main-taining the EHRs.

12.2.1 Application

i. This system provides transparency between patients and doctors and makes the patient in charge of his own data. The age-old problem of patients being restricted to a single doctor is solved and gives him the freedom to change doctors without the hassle of maintaining a record of all the previous visits.

ii. The doctors get a summary of the patient and don't have to manually go through the entire patient history.

iii. Since the whole record is maintained on the Blockchain, it is tamper-proof and trustworthy.

12.2.2 Motivation

The healthcare industry is known to have fallen behind other sectors in the usage and deployment of emerging digital technology, such as the finance sector. Manual processes account for a significant part of the processes. These systems are suffering from a lack of data ownership, poor data quality, poor data security and backup pro-cedures and therefore rarely used for decision-making. This also presents difficulties when documenting what is currently occurring in healthcare to improve epidemic monitoring, preparation, clinician and strategic decision-making. The lack of data integration makes it difficult to offer 360° of patient health history, and to share information between different entities [4–6]. Interoperability in data health is an issue which remains open until now. The main question is how to give open access to sensitive data (health data), preserve privacy, anonymity and avoid misuse of data.

These existing scenarios motivate us to design a system that can make these health data transactions smooth, secure and invulnerable to tampering and interoperable among organizations having least trust among them; however, they share some common assets like patients.

12.2.3 Contribution

The chapter aims to develop a Blockchain system for the ecosystem of doctors and patients to maintain the EHRs and manage their update and retrieval. The entire system is ensured by reliability of the Blockchain consensus protocol. The EHRs will be readily available for easy access for patients and doctors, so that they can refer these on demand. Our project lays a foundation for further research for leveraging this to a greater level. The implementation has done on IBM's Hyperledger Fabric with working transactions.

12.2.4 Organization of the Chapter

Section 12.2 presents a brief introduction of the chapter, its application in the real world, the motivation behind choosing this topic, its objectives and our contribution towards this topic.

Section 12.3 presents the background study which gives the overview of the technology we are using namely Blockchain and EHRs and gives an overview about some of its concepts relevant to our chapter.

Section 12.4 presents the implementation details and the tech stacks which we are utilizing to implement the project.

Section 12.5 & 12.6 present our conclusions drawn to possible future works that can be built upon the proposed system.

12.3 Background Study

Here we present the overview of technologies involved and some concepts that are essential for getting a good idea about their utilization in this chapter. This section has been divided in the following Subsections 12.3.1 Presents introduction to the EHRs and their essential requirements. Subsection 12.3.2 explains the Blockchains in a bird's-eye view and also important components of it, which are necessary to understand their role in this project.

12.3.1 Electronic Health Records (EHR)

An Electronic Health Record (EHR) is an electronic version of a patient's medical history. This is maintained by the provider over time, and may include all of the key administrative clinical data relevant to that persons care under a particular provider, including demographics, progress notes, problems, medications, vital signs, past medical history, immunizations, laboratory data and radiology reports. The EHR automates knowledge exposure and has the ability to streamline workflow for the clinician. The EHR also has the ability to directly or indirectly support other care-related activities through various interfaces, including support for evidence-based decision-making, quality management, and reporting of outcomes. EHRs are the further part in continued healthcare progress, which can strengthen the relationship between patients and clinicians [7]. The data, as well as its timeliness and availability, will allow providers to make better choices and give better care. For example, the EHR can upgrade patient care by:

i. Reducing the occurrence of medical mistakes and keeping patient reports more precise and transparent.
ii. Making the health information accessible, reducing test duplication, reducing treatment delays and informing patients to make better decisions.
iii. Reducing medical error by making medical records more accurate and concise.

12.3.2 Blockchain

Blockchains systems are tamper-proof, seldom cryptographic ledgers deployed in a de-centralized way (i.e., without a central repository) and typically without any central authority (i.e. a bank, corporation, or government). On an intuitive level, they enable a group of users to record transactions in a shared ledger within that group, such that under normal circumstances of operation of the Blockchain network no transaction can be modified or changed once published to the system. A typical Blockchain can be thought of as shown in **Figure 12.1**.

The technology of Blockchain lays the foundation of modern world cryptocurrencies, such terminology being employed because of the heavy usage of cryptographic functions. For cryptocurrency-based Blockchain networks that use mining, users can solve puzzles using cryptographic hash functions in the enticement of getting fixed amount of the cryptocurrency reward. However, Blockchain technology is more broadly applicable beyond mere cryptocurrencies. In this work, we focus on the healthcare use case, since this field has received much attention by various researchers around the globe today.

12.3.2.1 Blockchain Categorization

Generally based on the permission model, the Blockchain networking systems are categorized, which determines who can look after, cater and modify them (e.g., publish blocks). If anyone can publish a new block, it is permissionless. While in permissioned block chains only specific authorized users can publish blocks. In simple terms, a permissioned Blockchain network is like a corporate intranet that is, in some manner, controlled, while a permissionless Blockchain network is open to all like the public Internet, where anyone can participate.

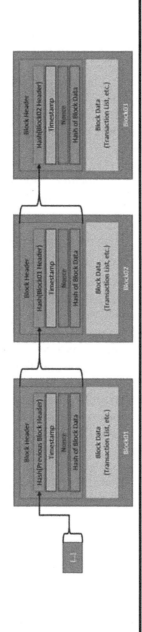

Figure 12.1   A typical Blockchain [8]

12.3.2.2 Permission-less

1. Being open to all, permissionless networks of Blockchain allow any user to publish blocks on to it, without any authorization requirement.
2. These are generally open source software, which can be simply acquired by downloading.
3. As anyone is allowed to publish blocks on such a network, it also enables them to read the ledger as well as issue any transactions on it.
4. As these permissionless networks of Blockchains are open to all, malicious activities may pose a threat to such systems.

12.3.2.3 Permissioned

1. Unlike permission-less Blockchains, permissioned Blockchain networks, as the name suggests, are those where users who publish blocks to the network must be authorized.
2. It is possible to control read access and who can issue transactions over the network because some authorized group of users are maintaining the Blockchain.
3. Open source as well as closed source software can be used to maintain these permissioned Blockchains.
4. These networks employ consensus models for maintenance. The group of users maintaining the Blockchain have a level of trust with each other, which is a result of the confirmation of user's identity required to participate as a member of the network. In case of any misbehaviour or malicious activity, that users' authority can be revoked.

Due to the above-mentioned features we have decided to use a permissioned network of peers in this project.

12.3.3 Cardiology

Cardiology is the study and treatment of disorders of the heart and the blood vessels. A person with heart disease or cardiovascular disease may be referred to a cardiologist. In this project, we have laid our focus on cardiologists in particular and mentioned the various factors required for a doctor to provide a basic diagnosis. Since we only have one field on which we are focusing and all the doctors are in the same field, all the doctors can view the records added by all other doctors. However, the future scope of this project will aim to include doctors from different fields. The doctors in one field can only access the records of specialists within the same specialty. We have used various fields in particular to cardiology for this project. This can be varied according to the field to which the doctor tends. The doctor takes inputs like RBC (Red Blood Count), WBC (White Blood Count), heart beat count etc. for the diagnosis. This is explained further in the coming sections (see **Table 12.1**).

12.3.4 The Medical Council of India

The Medical Council of India is a statutory body for establishing uniform and high standards of medical education in India until the formation of the National Medical Commission on 14 October 2019. Here we can use the Medical Council of India as the certification authority which can be used to verify the doctors. Every doctor has a Doctor Registration number by which he/she can be identified. The authenticity of the doctor can be identified using this number, following which the doctor can be uploaded. This can be developed in future work. However, the doctor ID can be corresponded to the Doctor Registration number, thereby validating the doctor.

12.4 Secure EHR Using Blockchain

We aim to build a system that brings health organizations that have weak trust among them to participate in a peer-to-peer Blockchain network to maintain the data of their patients and share their reports [7]. The Blockchain network will consist of doctors or health organizations as peers. This system will be available to them as a web app. The web app will have different variants for doctors and patients. The doctors can update as well as read the data, whereas the patients can only read it. The interactions with the system involved are: onboarding process of a medical practitioner; uploading the new transaction of a patient by the doctor; and retrieval of medical reports of the patient's record. These are described below in the respective order.

12.4.1 Entities

The architecture consists of certain terms that needs to be introduced before we move on to the exact implementation details. These are:

> *Certification Authority*: The certification authority is responsible for handling all of the logic of access control, issuing the users' identities and permission in the Blockchain network of Hyperledger.
>
> *Orderer*: The orderer is used to keep the whole network in a synchronized state. Whenever a new transaction is to be made, the orderer is the one who informs all peers of the transaction. A network can have multiple orderers; it's also advised to keep fewer faults.
>
> *Peers*: Only peers in the business network are allowed to commit transactions. In addition, each peer has its own copy of the entire world state. It is linked to instances of CouchDB, which serves as the database.
>
> *Block contents*:
> i. *@PatientID*—The id of the patient being queried.
> ii. *@ehrID*—The unique ID generated for the patient's diagnosis EHR.

iii. *@doctorID*—The id of the doctor currently accessing the her.

iv. *@lastModifiedTime*—The time of the current transaction.

v. *@doctorName*—The name of the doctor currently accessing the her.

12.4.1.1 EHR Structure

Table 12.1 EHR Structure

EHR	Sub-Fields: Data Type
Symptoms	Fainting: Boolean Yes/No Heartbeat: int Chest Tightness: Boolean Yes/No Chest Pain: Boolean Yes/No Swelling: Checkbox ■ legs ■ feet ■ ankles ■ abdomen Weight: Float
Any Other Problem	Text Area
Patient Feedback	Text Area
Blood Test	WBC: int RBC: int Total Cholesterol: float LDL: float HDL: float Triglycerides: int
util	Next Appointment date: date Fees: int Payment: string
Prescribed Medicines	List[obj]=>obj: { medicine: string, dosage: string}

Where,

LDL – Low Density Lipoprotein.

HDL – High Density Lipoprotein.

WBC – White Blood Count.

RBC – Red Blood Count.

12.4.2 Architecture

Figure 12.2 describes the following architectural setup of our system. Following are the interactions among them:

1. The patient or the doctor devices interact with the frontend servers for authentication purposes and logging into the system.
2. The frontend server interacts with the backend for retrieving patient's details or updating them and conveying transaction alerts to the user.
3. The backend server is responsible for managing the EHRs, validating the update and fetch request and generating verification codes.
4. The Blockchain server hosts the Blockchain and the peer network.

12.4.3 Working Methodology of the System

The system consists of doctors and patients as its peers. The doctor is more privileged than a patient. Both of the peers interact with the ledger through an interactive web application. The web application has different interfaces for doctor and patients. The following subsections explain in a step-by-step manner all the possible interactions with the ledger.

12.4.3.1 Onboarding

The onboarding process will be quite different in the case of both of the participants. The doctor onboarding can be initiated and completed by the doctor him-/herself but for the patient on boarding, the patient has to visit a doctor at least once in the beginning.

The Doctor onboarding process is as follows:

1. The Doctor opens the application and fills his details like his name, contact and medical credentials, i.e. the registration number provided by Medical Council of India (MCI), which serves the purpose of authentication and also the doctor as to provide a unique username. Then an onboarding request is sent to the certification authority.
2. On receiving an onboarding, request the central authority verifies the doctor's credentials and sends appropriate message back to the doctor depending on the status of the onboarding request process.
3. The doctor notes this down and this completes the onboarding process as shown in **Figure 12.3**

The Patient onboarding process is as follows:

1. The patient visits a doctor who is already registered on the system.

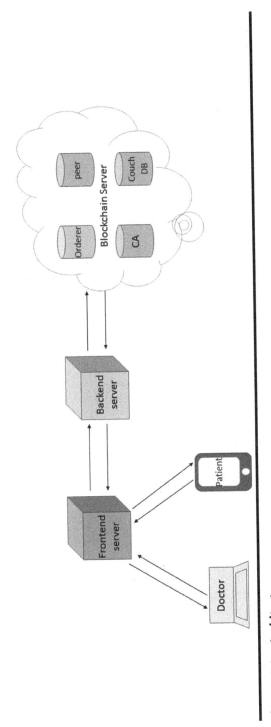

Figure 12.2 Architecture

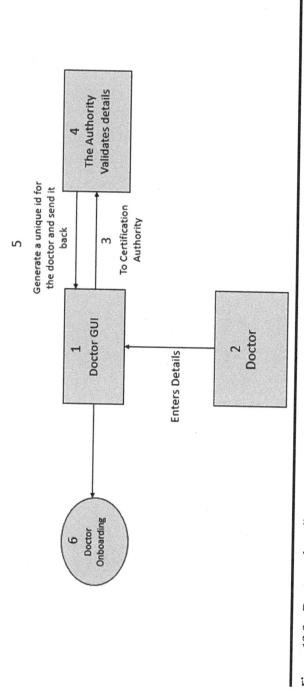

Figure 12.3 Doctor onboarding process

2. The doctor then feeds in the patient's email ID and username which henceforth will serve as the patient's ID, the uniqueness can be ensured by the doctor using the prompts in the UI (User Interface).
3. This successfully onboards the patient.

12.4.3.2 Uploading the Data

Updating or creation of a new record can only be carried out by a doctor, which can be visualized from **Figure 12.4**.

1. Doctor logs into his homepage.
2. Doctor has to choose between new patient and old patient to proceed to its diagnosis.
3. Then, depending on the selected patient type, an OTP (One Time Password) or a verification code is sent to the onboarded patients registered email address. *NOTE:* If the patient is not onboarded, then an appropriate message is displayed to the doctor.
4. The patient then tells this OTP to the doctor. This authentication process shows that the patient and the concerned doctor are in contact, which ensures that the doctor is authorized now to update the data of the patient.
5. The doctor then is presented with the diagnosis form and, after filling it up appropriately, the record can be submitted.
6. If the record is submitted successfully, then message is prompted to the doctor accordingly.

Here various cases are involved like: Case 1: Patient visits doctor.

Case 1.1

Patient visiting doctor for the very first time.

If the patient is visiting the doctor for the very first time, the patient has to be onboarded first. For the onboarding, the details of the patient, such as a unique username, First Name, Last Name and the Email Id of the patient needs to be added. For further access to the patient's profile, the patient needs to enter the OTP sent to his/her email id, after which a password can be set for future login. This is shown in **Figure 12.5**.

Case 1.2

Patient has already visited the doctor.

In this case there are two possibilities which are: (i) the patient was assigned to the current doctor itself; or (ii) the patient was previously under any other doctor. In both of these cases, the patient has to provide the consent (in the form of OTP) for the doctor to add any diagnosis or even view the history of the patient.

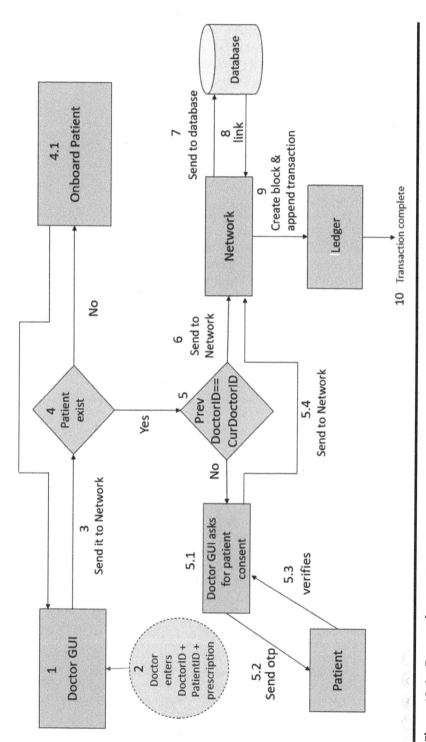

Figure 12.4   Data update process

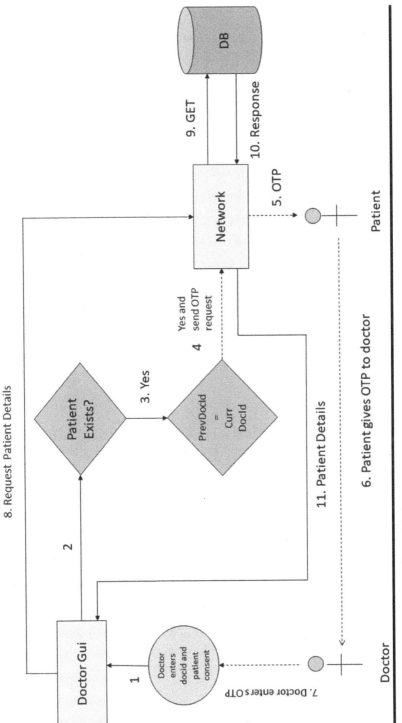

Figure 12.5   Patient Interaction with doctor

Case 2

An onboarded patient to a new doctor with whom he has no history but was getting treatment from another doctor previously.

In this case,

(1) The doctor asks for the patient's consent and then the doctor is asked by the web application to enter the verification code, which would be sent to the concerned patient.

(2) The patient tells the verification code to the doctor.

(3) Then steps (4) to (7) are followed.

(4) The doctor uploads his DoctorID, the PatientID and medical prescriptions to the web application, which then verifies some rules and send it to the peer network.

(5) The system then stores the medical prescription data to a secure database, which generates a link that maps to the location of this data and sends it back to the system.

(6) The system generates a block and BlockID for the same.

(7) This block as a transaction is then appended to the existing ledger. This completes the data updating process.

12.4.3.3 Data Retrieval

The patient can read the data at any time just by clicking a button in the patient's GUI (Graphical User Interface), but if a doctor wants to read a patient's data then again the verification code process is followed as described above.

12.4.4 Configuration

The User Interface is the part of the application that any user will directly interact with. It handles some of the essential application features, such as the hashing of the password and authorization while sharing the authentication mechanism partly with the backend. The backend is the realm that the user will never actually see. It contains a set of hosted Application Programming Interfaces (APIs) that processes data on request and return responses appropriately. The backend of this application consists of a node server that hosts logic related to data preprocessing and is the site of origination of requests to the Blockchain server.

The Blockchain server is an imaginary entity that, in reality, contains four different docker containers hosted at four different ports. These containers are responsible for maintaining the state of our Hyperledger Fabric. Things such as issuing a certificate to an entity, maintaining the order of execution of the transaction and operating through the ledger are all handled in these docker containers.

Let us now look at both of these servers in more detail and learn how to set up the development environment and necessary system configuration.

12.4.4.1 The Primary Nodejs Server

The node server is the site that hosts API for our application. Along with the express framework to handle the routing and handling the HTTP (Hypertext Transfer Protocol) server operations, we have used some other npm packages that handle the heavy lifting of activities like session management or mailing services. The list of packages that we use in the application are:

1. Fabric-contract-API—This is a package provided by the Hyperledger node SDK (Software Development Kit), which is used for communication with the Blockchain server.
2. Fabric-shim—The fabric shim is an abstraction that adds new Javascript-related functionality to the methods provided by the fabric-contract-API. It is a useful library provided along with the SDK that will help to interface the code in Nodejs easily.
3. Express—This is a framework for Nodejs built to handle the route and server management. It abstracts many of the Nodejs server-related methods and can help you spin up a server using just 10 lines of code. Routing is also made easy using express as readily available endpoints and their handlers can be encapsulated in a single block of code, which otherwise could create havoc in heavy projects.
4. Body-Parser—This package is used to handle the post requests coming to the server. It helps in creating a JSON object of the body that is received in the API request. This is useful to work with data when the fields are deeply located using multi-level keying.
5. Cors—This is a package that attaches necessary cors headers to all the outgoing responses so that they are not blocked by the browser under the cors policy. It is a very useful utility when it comes to making good APIs.
6. Morgan—This is used for logging all the HTTP requests to the terminal. The logs include the type of request, their origin, the route requested and other request-related fields. It helps in debugging your backend, when the number of API requests exceeds more than a normal threshold.
7. Fs—Fs is a Nodejs module that is used for all the file system-related operations. It can help you read or write a file synchronously as well as asynchronously depending on the use case.
8. Uuid—This package is being used to generate random ids for the EHRs in our system. We are using a random number generation techniques that are provided by version 4 of this package.
9. Nodemailer—As the name suggests, nodemailer is being used to send emails from our node server for the patient OTPs.

10. Mongoose—It is an ORM over the popular NoSQL database, MongoDB. It returns promisified responses that can be used effectively in building scalable nodeJS applications.
11. JsonWebToken—This package is being used for the generation of the random JWT token that will be used for session management with the frontend of angular.

Our primary backend server consists of two very important files, i.e the app.js and the network.js. The app.js is the seat of all the router endpoints. We listen for all the requests primarily in the app.js. The network.js is used for communicating with the Blockchain server. It contains methods abstracted from the fabric-contract-API which are then used for manipulating or querying the Blockchain as per the use case.

12.4.4.2 The app.js

The app.js contains nearly 1k lines of code and presents a total of 19 different API endpoints for handling the requests from the frontend server. It is also the seat of database communication and the JSON (JavaScript Object Notation) webtoken creation. Depending on the use case we have API endpoints hosted that can be used to manipulate data in the Blockchain or query them. We have followed a common paradigm of handling the request from that frontend that includes:

1. Converting the body of the request into a JSON to easily drill down into the keys and get the values needed readily.
2. Connecting the Blockchain using the identity of a proper entity, which has a presence in the wallet. In this way all our Blockchain-related requests are authorized and valid under the name of the proper user.
3. Checking for the response on this connection request. If the connection is successful, we have opened a channel for the user to manipulate or query the Blockchain. If not, we return an appropriate error.
4. We invoke the proper method to interact with the Blockchain, depending on whether it is a submitting transaction or an evaluating transaction. A submitting transaction is the one that modified the ledger in the Blockchain. An evaluation transaction is the one that is only concerned with querying the chain.
5. On the basis of the response received from the Blockchain, we segregate the server responses. We follow a common guideline for all the responses from the server, i.e we send a JSON object as a response that contains two keys depending on the type of response. The keys are:
   a. Action—It is a boolean depending on whether the response is a success or a failure. Failure cover cases of error while transacting with the Blockchain or server-related issues. We also get a false action when the action being

done was not authorized by the server. Success is the only case which returns a true action.

b. Message—It contains the proper message depending on the type of action. In case of failure, a proper error message is returned from the server. In case of success, we return the message with the appropriate value being queried or the result of that manipulation.

The app.js also contains code for connecting to our MongoDB database. It is used for storing the OTPs for the present session of the patient. Lastly, using the express listen method a server is spun up on the designated port which is by default port number 8000.

12.4.4.3 The network.js File

After importing the necessary methods like FileSystemWallet, Gateway and X509WalletMixin which would be used for creating a wallet for the entity and then connecting to the Blockchain respectively, we move onto accessing our configuration setting mentioned in our config file. The config file contain keys like the app admin, the appAdminSecret, the Certificate Authority (CA) Name and the method of the gateway we will be using to connect to the Blockchain. The CA name is actually the Uniform Resource Locator (URL) on which our CA docker container will be hosted.

When we create a fabric runtime in the Hyperledeger Blockchain, a connection profile is exported from the runtime, which is used in the network.js file for connection purposes. The local_fabric_connection.json file contains all the important fields like the URL of the CA, the timeout for the client connection, the name of our organization and the number of peers along with the URL on which the peer container is hosted. We also get information about the orderer and the timeout associated with it for ordering a transaction.

As we explore the network.js file we come across function named connectToNetwork that is used to create a wallet for a user in our wallet system. The authorization for the creation of the wallet is provided by the admin of our Blockchain. Once the identity for our user has been created in the wallet, a connection to the Blockchain is made and a reference to that network object is returned.

We also find some utility functions that will be used to check the presence of a particular user in the wallet. Once a user is present in the wallet, then only he can connect to the Blockchain network.

Later, we find functions that are implemented to create a wallet for a user, be it doctor or patient. In order to create the identity in the wallet we follow the following guidelines:

1. First of all, we check for the values provided for the user for not being null or invalid.

2. Later, we check if the user is already present in the wallet system. If yes, we return with an error.
3. We then check for the presence of admin in our system. In case the admin is not present, we create an admin using the enrollAdmin.js.
4. We then connect through the gateway to our Certificate Authority. The CA has the privilege of assigning the proper public and private keys to the user that will be used for signing the transactions.
5. Finally, we enroll the user with the CA and create a wallet for them into our file system.
6. If, for any of the steps provided above, we get an error we return it with a proper error message.

12.4.4.4 The Blockchain Server

The core of our application lies with the Blockchain server. The reasons for using Hyperledger as the Blockchain has already been clarified in a previous section. Here we will be looking into the implementation part. First of all, it is important to look at the system requirements that are a must for setting up this chain in the local. Our present system configuration is:

1. VSCode – (1.39.0) – This is a text editor that flaunts the useful IBM Blockchain extension. It is a lightweight, extension-driven text editor that is used for maximizing the development speed.
2. IBM Blockchain Platform VSCode extension – 1.0.31 – This extension is provided by Hyperledger to easily set up and run docker containers on the action of a click.
3. Docker - (19.3.8) – This is the container management and creation software that is being used to set up various identities of the participant of our Blockchain network.
4. Docker-compose – (1.24.1) – It is a framework for docker used defining and running multi-container docker application. Using a simple config file, we can configure all the containers that are used by our system.
5. NodeJs – (10.x) – This is the framework we will be using for setting up the server of our application.
6. Npm – (6.x) – This stands for Node package manager. It is a registry that hosts more than a million packages that are built by the open-source community for node js users.
7. Ubuntu – (18.04) – This is the open-source operating system widely used all over the world for efficient development.

12.4.4.5 The EHR-contract.ts File

A contract, also known as the chaincode, contains the logic related to the modification or querying of the Blockchain. It is the file that is being communicated from our primary backend server and the network.js file. As you could have an observer, the language used for writing this contract is not Javascript but Typescript. Typescript is actually a compile to JS language that helps with beautiful type checking and is an important upgrading over the usual Javascript.

If you look at the source code, you will find an entire folder dedicated to the chaincode-related files. It is important to create a different context for such files as their function and methods of invoking are completely different from the rest of the code. The folder also contains dist/directory where all the ts files are kept are compiling to js. From this directory, the Blockchain extension creates the.cds package that will be later used for the creation of the Blockchain.

The EHR-contract.ts file contains a total of 26 functions that are used to manipulate or query the Blockchain ledger. These functions are comprised of the ones used to create the identities of the various user in the ledger, to manipulate the existence of the EHRs and to manage the correspondence of EHRs and the patients, and also the relationship between patients and doctors. The important functions in this file that we should know about are:

1. getState – on passing the key as the parameter this function queries the chain and returns the value associated with that key.
2. putState – On passing the key and the value as the parameters, these functions update the ledger with the new values.
3. getHistoryByKey – On passing the key to this function, it queries the chain and returns the entire modification history of the value associated.
4. getQueryResult – On passing a selector to this function, it performs a rich text query on the entire ledger and returns an object of the key and values associated with that selector string. It returns all the key and values where the presence of the selector string is found, in the form of an iterator.

We also use some other helper ts (Type-Script) files like the ehr.ts, doctor.ts and patient.ts that are used to easily create the entities on passing them the required values and returning a well-formed object, ready to put into the ledger.

It is important to note that everything that is put into the Blockchain is in the form of a string. All the arrays and all the object needs to be stringified before storing into the ledger.

12.4.5 Implementation

We are using Hyperledger Fabric to create our permissioned Blockchain. The present state of the EHRs does not ensure that the data will not be corrupted over time due to carelessness on the user's part and also do not track changes made to the EHR over time. To tackle these problems we propose introducing a permissioned Blockchain system where all the transactions in the ledger will be append only and the entire history of any patient is saved in the world state once written.

The essential aim of our Blockchain model is to track down the entire medical history of the patient being queried. We plan to achieve this by two approaches:

1. Traversing the entire Blockchain and extract those blocks that correspond to the queried patientID.
2. Using a field that contains the reference to the previous Blockchain. Using this, we can traverse the entire chain in backward direction and gain access to all the relevant blocks and their data. Using this approach should be time-efficient.

The present chain code is written in the composer playground. The main types of files in the folder are:

i. *Model files* – These files have their extension as.cto. These are used by hyperledger to generate the description of all the entities in the chain.
ii. *Chaincode* – These are script files written in Javascript. These manage the logic of the transaction and contain the smart contracts of the chain.
iii. *Access Control file* – These files determine the accesses given to all the peers of the network. They have their extensions as.acl.

12.4.5.1 User Interface

This section describes the user interface for both types of user, viz. doctor and patient.

- Doctor UI: Diagnosis workflow. The red marker surrounding the buttons signifies that button is clicked.
  1. **Doctor Home:** This page is the default home page for every doctor after he/she is logged in. This page contains the profile picture of the doctor, his/her. "DoctorId" and designations. To diagnose an existing patient, the doctor clicks on the username/Patient Ids displayed, which correspond to the patients currently designated to the current doctor. To diagnose a new patient, the patient needs to click on the new patient button and enter the Patient Id of the required patient. After entering the OTP provided by the patient, the doctor can proceed further (**Figure 12.6**).
  2. **Patient Consent:** This page prompts the doctor to enter the "PatientId" of the patient if the patient is not present under the doctor. Once the doctor

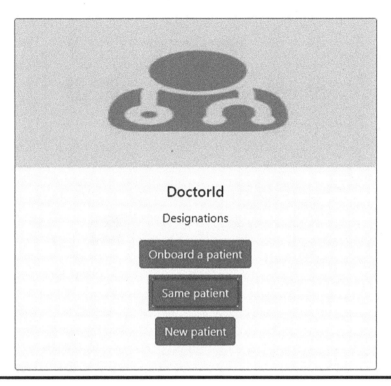

Figure 12.6   Doctor home page: same patient

enters it and clicks "Send code" button, an "OTP" is sent to the patient via the email already provided. The patient then tells this to the doctor and doctor clicks "verify" button to proceed (**Figure 12.7**).

3. **Diagnosis:** This is the generic diagnosis form for the cardiologists. Here the doctor enters the diagnosis data and on clicking "submit" button this is stored into the EHR Blockchain (**Figure 12.8**).

■ Doctor UI: Patient onboarding workflow. The red marker surrounding the buttons signifies that button is clicked.

1. **Doctor Home:** This page is the default home page for every doctor after he/she is logged in. This page contains the profile picture of the doctor, his/her "DoctorId" and designations. To onboard a new patient, the doctor clicks on the "Onboard a patient" button (**Figure 12.9**).

2. **Patient onboarding:** This page asks the doctor to enter basic details about a patient to onboard him/her (**Figure 12.10**).

■ Doctor UI: History Retrieval workflow. In order to retrieve the history details of the patient, the patient first needs to get the consent of the patient via the OTP. We will consider the case of retrieving the history details of an old patient who has been following up the doctor.

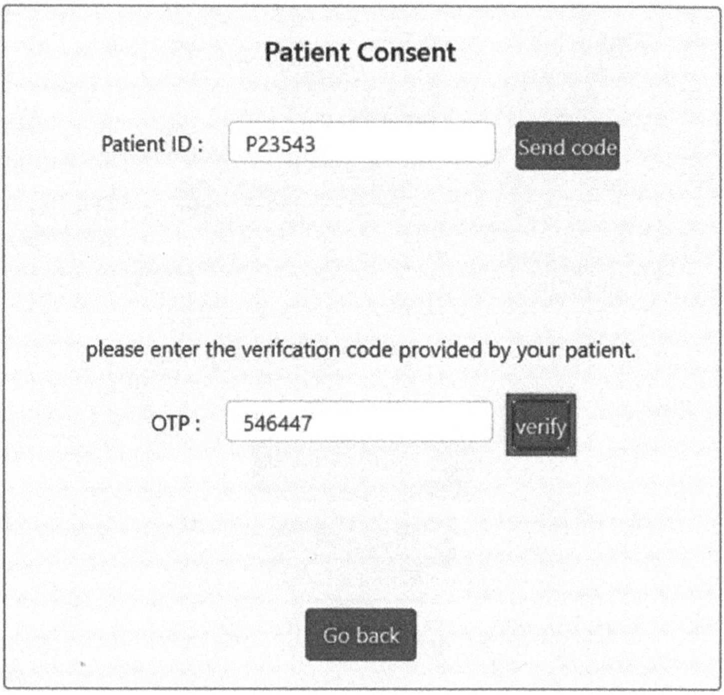

Figure 12.7 Patient consent page

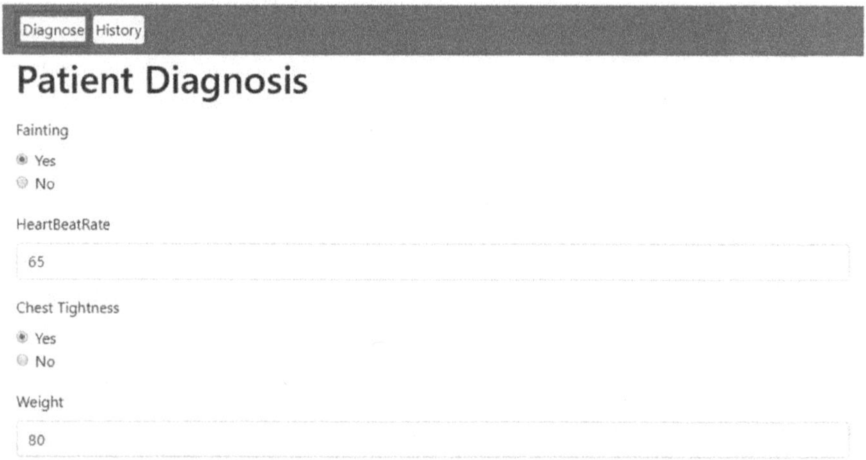

Figure 12.8 Diagnosis form

DoctorId
Designations
Onboard a patient
Same patient
New patient

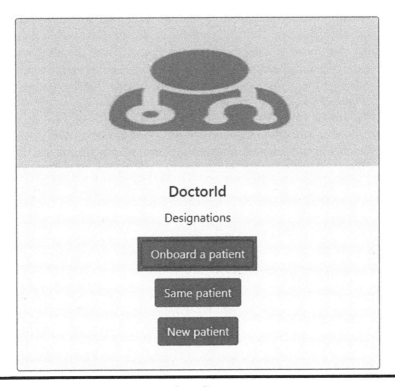

Figure 12.9 Doctor home page: onboarding

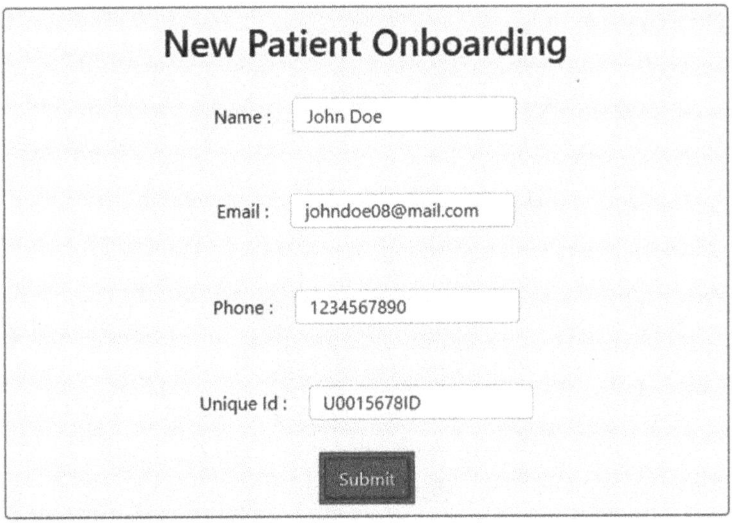

New Patient Onboarding
Name :
John Doe
Email :
johndoe08@mail.com
Phone :
1234567890
Unique Id :
U0015678ID
Submit

Figure 12.10 Patient onboarding form

1. **Doctor Home:** This page is the default home page for every doctor after he/she is logged in. This page contains the profile picture of the doctor, his/her "DoctorId" and designations. The patient IDs of the patients existing under the doctor are also displayed. To get the history details of an already existing patient, the doctor has to click the Patient Id of the required patient (**Figure 12.11**).

2. **Patient Consent:** This page asks for the patient consent, i.e the OTP. The patient provides them; after verifying it, the doctor is led to the page where he/she can add diagnosis or view the patient history (**Figure 12.12**).

3. **History Retrieval:** Here the doctor can click on the history and a structured result will be returned back. This result will be in the form of records entered by different doctors. On clicking the record, we can see the particular details of the record and the doctor can make an analysis of the history of the patient. This is shown in **Figure 12.13**.

◾ Patient UI: Patient history read. The different processes and functionalities of the patient are mentioned here.

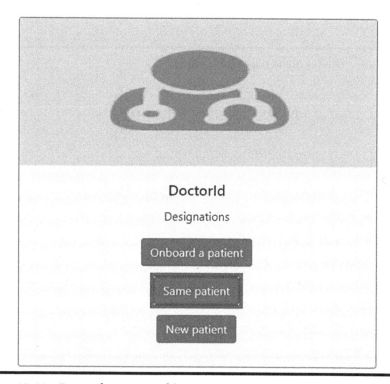

Figure 12.11   Doctor home page: history

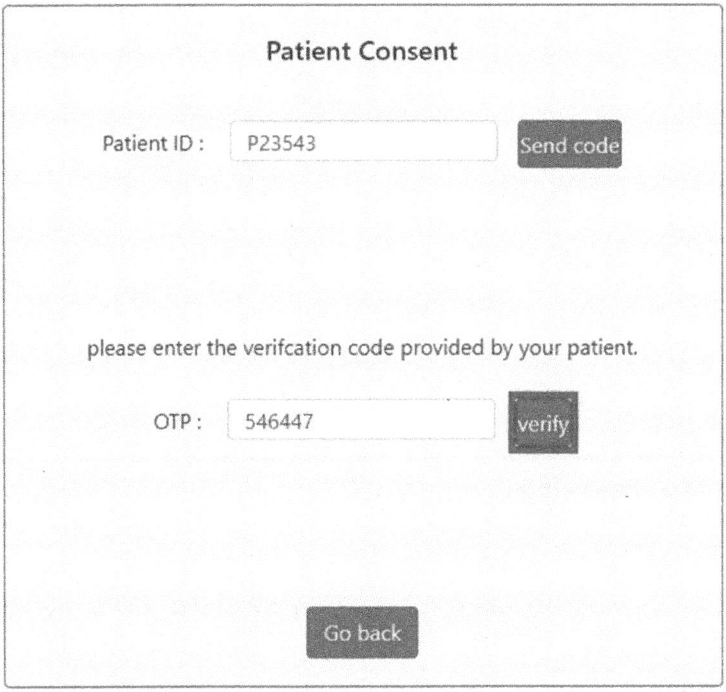

Figure 12.12 Patient consent form

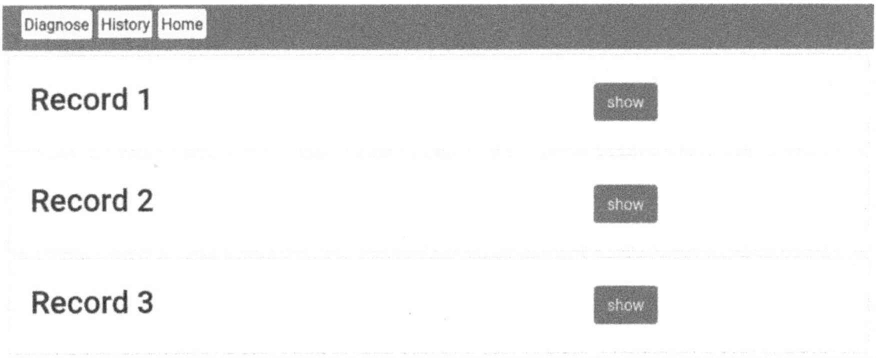

Figure 12.13 Patient history viewed by doctor

1. **Patient Login:** Just as is shown in the figure, there are two options for patient login: the option for OTP and the option for entering the password.

    Since no password is set, the patient can click on the OTP option and after entering the OTP received, the patient is prompted to set a new password as shown in **Figure 12.14**

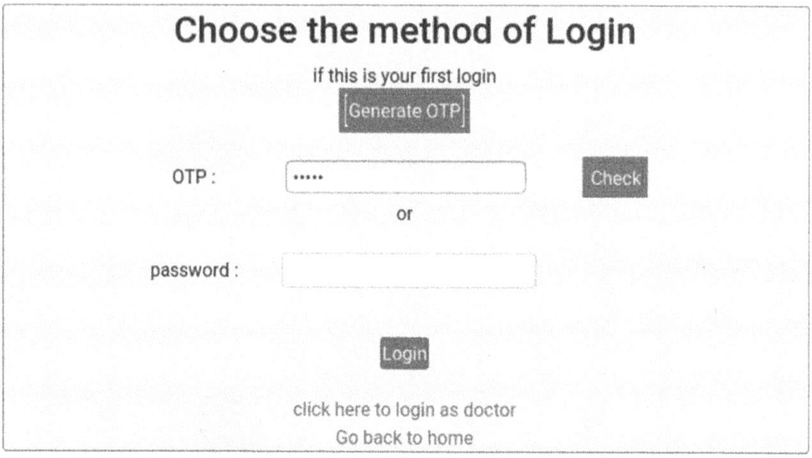

Figure 12.14 Patient login

Figure 12.15 Patient history

2. **History Retrieval:** The patient has the option to click on history which will lead to a detailed history record of the patient, as shown in **Figure 12.15**.
3. **List of Doctors:** Clicking on this, the patient can view the list of doctors the patient visited, as shown in **Figure 12.16**.

Figure 12.16   Patient's current doctors

12.5 Conclusion

The proposed system diminishes the shortcomings in the health sector if the implementation is leveraged to state-of-art efficiency. This system has the potential to make the storage of medical records decentralized so that the monopoly of the medical institutions can be minimized. This can provide seamless accessibility of user data when required. It also achieves the main objective of making the user the controller of his data. Although it has heavy computational requirements and a complex structure, this system is practical enough as it provides the required privacy, interoperability and anonymity by utilizing the best technological frameworks available at the present age.

12.6 Future Work

Further efforts can be made to utilize this system for predicting the probability of chronic disease to a patient [9] or the early prediction of stroke [10] or Alzheimer's [11] by drawing various insights from the data. This can also be used to make valuable contributions to the personalized healthcare for individual patients [12]. The data from the EHRs can be accessed by various academic or medical institutions for research purposes.

References

[1] R. Zhang, R. Xue, and L. Liu, "Security and privacy on blockchain", *ACM Computing Surveys (CSUR)* 2019; 52:1–34.
[2] J. Zarrin, P. Wen, L. B. Saheer, and B. Zarrin, "Blockchain for decentralization of internet: Prospects, trends, and challenges", *Cluster Computing* 2020; abs/2011.01096:1–26.
[3] H. Ullah, S. Aslam, and N. Arjomand, "Blockchain in healthcare and medicine: A contemporary research of applications, challenges, and future perspectives", *arXiv preprint arXiv:2004.06795* 2020; abs/2004.06795:1–12.

[4] R. Epstein, and R. Street Jr. The values and value of patient-centered care. *Ann Fam Med.* 2011;9(2):100–103. doi: 10.1370/afm.1239

[5] M Gerteis, S Edgeman-Levitan, J Daley, and T Delbanco. *Through the Patient's Eyes: Understanding and Promoting Patient-Centered Care.* 1st ed. San Francisco, CA: Jossey-Bass, 1993.

[6] R Epstein, K Fiscella, C Lesser, and K Stange. Why the nation needs a policy push on patient-centered health care. *Health Aff (Millwood).* 2010;29(8):1489–1495

[7] A. Donawa, I. Orukari, and C. E. Baker, "Scaling blockchains to support electronic health records for hospital systems," In *2019 IEEE 10th Annual Ubiquitous Computing, Electronics & Mobile Communication Conference (UEMCON)*, pp. 0550–0556. IEEE, 2020

[8] D. Yaga, P. Mell, N. Roby, and K. Scarfone, "Blockchain technology overview, *arXiv preprint arXiv:1906.11078* Oct 2018. [Online]. doi: 10.6028/NIST.IR.8202

[9] J. Liu, Z. Zhang, and N. Razavian, "Deep EHR: Chronic disease prediction using medical notes," In *Machine Learning for Healthcare Conference*, pp. 440–464. PMLR, 2018.

[10] C. S. Nwosu, S. Dev, P. Bhardwaj, B. Veeravalli, and D. John, "Predicting stroke from electronic health records", In *2019 41st Annual International Conference of the IEEE Engineering in Medicine and Biology Society (EMBC)*, pp. 5704–5707. IEEE, 2019.

[11] H. Li, M. Habes, D. A. Wolk, and Y. Fan, A deep learning model for early prediction of Alzheimer's disease dementia based on hippocampal MRI, *Alzheimer's & Dementia* 2019;*15*:1059–1070.

[12] J. Zhang, K. Kowsari, J. Harrison, J. Lobo, and L. Barnes, "Patient2vec: A personalized interpretable deep representation of the longitudinal electronic health record," *IEEE Access* 2018; vol.6:65333–65346. [Online]. doi: 10.1109/ACCESS.2018.2875677

Chapter 13

Blockchain Impact of Security and Privacy in Digital Identity Management

Smita Bansod
Shah & Anchor Kutchhi Engineering College, India

Lata L. Ragha
Fr. C. Rodrigues Institute of Technology, India

Contents

DOI: 10.1201/9781003129486-13

13.1 Introduction to Digital Identity Management

Identity management (IDM) is the process of identification, authentication and authorization of persons or groups of persons to provide permission to access applications, services or networks by linking user rights and restrictions with established identities using various technologies [1]. For example, in an enterprise, an employee gets access to organizational documents based on the employee number as his identity which also determines the privileges and restrictions to read, write or update the documents.

In the case of governmental and other organizational services, the access is regulated by individual identities like the birth certificate, National ID card or Driving license. With the advent of online delivery of services using the Internet, Digital Identity Management (DIDM) became a critical requirement.

13.1.1 Models of DIDM

There has been a phenomenal increase in the number of digital transactions during the past decade and the DIDM methods [2], starting with the Isolated model, have been improved progressively. In the Isolated model, each user managed the Identity for the different Service Providers for the specific service attributes. The next phase was the Centralized model in which the Identity Management was done centrally for multiple service providers which made the process of Identity Management much easier. The advent of distributed services and multiple service providers demanded new approaches to Identity Management, leading to the Federated model and the User-centered model. The User-centric model was further refined into the Self-Sovereign model to enable the user to provide individual control across many authorities. This model is undergoing continuous upgrading [2]. Figure 13.1 shows the list of different models of Digital Identity Management. Figure 13.2 gives detailed structure of all discussed IDM Models.

1. Isolated IDM Model: This is the oldest model in which the user handles the various identities and credentials related to different service providers. This approach is simple and easy for the service provider, but inconvenient for the user due to the large number of IDs to be managed. Further, it is cumbersome

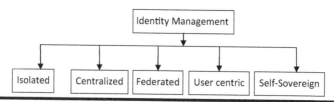

Figure 13.1   DIDM Models

for the user to manage the overload of the upcoming SPs' identities and credentials.

2. Centralized IDM Model: A single authority or hierarchy handles all the management and administrative activities of the IDM system. In this model, every SP uses the unique identity and credentials. The identity provider assumes control over all identity-related processes for the SP, including credential

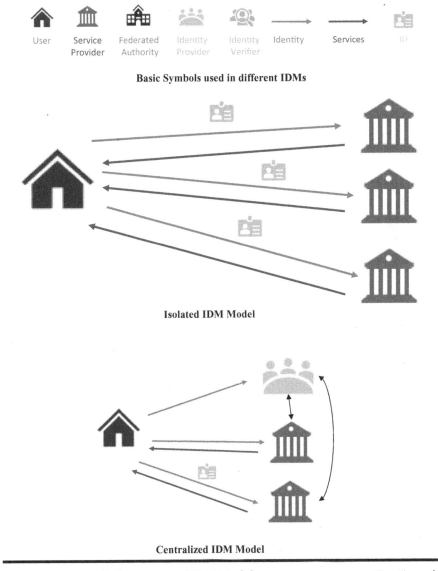

Basic Symbols used in different IDMs

| User | Service Provider | Federated Authority | Identity Provider | Identity Verifier | Identity | Services | ID |

Isolated IDM Model

Centralized IDM Model

Figure 13.2 Detailed structure of IDM Models   (*Continued*)

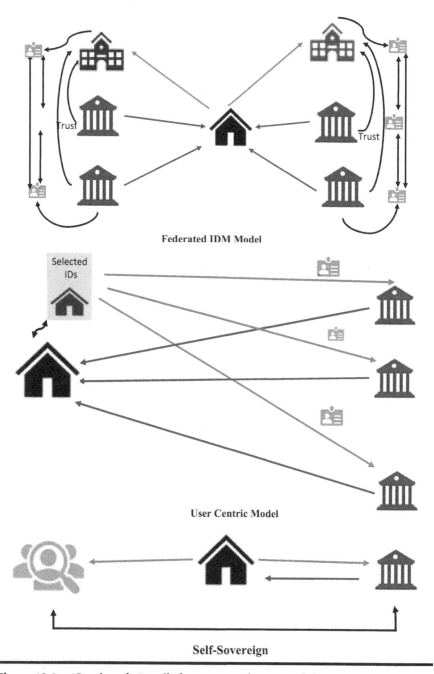

Federated IDM Model

User Centric Model

Self-Sovereign

Figure 13.2 (Continued) Detailed structure of IDM Models

distribution, identification and authentication along with the management of the identity life cycle [3]. All users' identity data is stored in a central database where the service and identity providers reside. So, a Denial of Service (DoS) attack is quite achievable and single source of trust issues also occur on such a centralized system.

3. Federated IDM Model: In this model, IDM is administratively controlled by multiple, federated authorities. Users' identity data are stored over numerous service providers. A common identifier contributes to linking the distributed identity data to a user. Identity management federation need to define the required set of contracts, ideals and technologies that should be permitted by a group of SPs to sanction user identity and privileges and other SPs must agree within the domain. The first product to employ this model is Microsoft's passport, introduced in 1999. It is more powerful than the Centralized model. While the Federated model solved the problem of diversity of SPs, it caused confusion to the users because of the numerous sites under this model. However, each individual site persisted an authority need to handle by group of providers.

4. User-centric IDM Model: Previous models primarily took care of the convenience of the Service Providers. But this model, as the name itself suggests, is user-centric and takes care of the user perspective. User has full control of identity management across service providers. The first invention following this model [4] was the Augmented Social Network ASN in the year 2000. Then **Open ID** and **Facebook connect** emphasize the user managing the ID information and so are considered to be beneficial to the user, but they are vulnerable to multipoint attacks and loss of identity by compromising a single site. The user-centric identity system suffers from many shortcomings such as the minimal exposure of credentials and the elimination of central authority that needs to be fixed before it can be considered truly secure, privacy-compliant and user friendly.

5. Self-sovereign IDM Model: In this model, the individual user is controlling n-number of distributed authorities without the interference of an external authority. The simple User-centric model is shifted into a federated centralized identity control, and identity of the user is shared with others only with some level of consent of the user. It was an important step toward true user control of identity, but just a stage which provided user autonomy. It is basically improving the trust and security while preserving the privacy of the user even in the presence of centralized third parties. Ever since the first reference to this concept in the year 2012, self-sovereign identity management model has become very popular [5, 6]. The industry is continuously working on improving this model of Digital Identity Management [7].

13.1.2 Identity Issues in the Real World

The need for Digital Identity Management arose because of the serious problems faced by the existing paper-based document handling systems. Apart from the time- and space-consuming processes, the paper management system was susceptible to fraud, theft and loss of documents due to fire, flood or damage. To overcome these problems, the Digital Identity Management System was introduced as part of the computerization of business activities and the networking of computers. Digital identity reduces the degree of management and speeds up business activities amongst organizations due to a more prominent interoperability among groups and among different organizations. Over the years, different IDM models were evolved to fur-ther refine the management of identities of the Users and the Service Providers.

But the Digital Identity Management systems introduced new problems, such as hacking of the single server of the Centralized System which stores the identities of many users and service providers leading to Denial of Service (DOS) situations. In 2017, a large number of such servers have been reportedly hacked or penetrated and had their data leaked. The Identity Theft Resource Centre (ITRC), in its report for the year 2020, has mentioned 1472 information breaches during 2019 and 1257 such incidents during 2018. The ITRC report found that hacking accounted for the highest percentage of data breaches, and for 39 percent of incidents. Hacking was also responsible for exposing 81 percent of non-sensitive records. Unauthorized access was noted as the second most common breach, accounting for 36.5 percent of the data breaches.

Different sectors are facing difficulties because of existing identity management systems:

- Personal: User identity is the critical factor in personal applications. The iden-tity damage or theft may spoil the life of the user. Hence the personal data protection laws are also defined by different governments. The IDM system should be designed in such a way that it protects user identity.
- Healthcare: Identity theft is a major issue in the healthcare industry. Leakage of the health data of a person leads to exposure of the data relating to all the stakeholders in the chain, including the patient, doctor, pharmacy and the insurance company, resulting in further complications in the delivery of healthcare.
- Education: A recent survey has indicated that a large number of fake educa-tional certificates are sold in the USA using stolen identities. This has a serious impact on the reputation of the university as well as the companies which recruit such candidates.
- Financial: Loss of money due to compromised identity of the user is very com-mon and multiple identities, such as password, pin and mobile number, are used to minimize such frauds.

- Government: There are several issues related to the coordinated working of the various departments of the government which have a bearing on the time and cost of government operations, particularly while delivering service to common citizens. IDM is an essential requirement for government-level applications with privacy and security becoming critical issues. In addition, government needs to put in place the Identity protection standards and the punitive measures for breach of such standards.
- Businesses: Business houses have to strictly conform to Identity standards in the protection of users' personal data and any violation will cause damage to the brand value of the enterprise.

13.1.3 IDM with Blockchain Technology

Blockchain 3.0 (phase 3) in identity management [8] was introduced to overcome the problems encountered in previous IDMs. Identity management should be designed in such a way that it makes sharing and authenticating an identity more effective, secure and private. Such a system works worldwide integrating with other identity services. This solution is free from maintenance of scattered identity associated with different service providers and without the interference of third-party approval for validation, verification and approval. Identity management has to be constructed based on user privacy. Each identity must be owned by only one person and not anyone else. Digital identity differs from manual identity management. Selection and sharing of a part of various identities is a challenging task. It must provide for selective sharing of identity with the SP. But an IDM model based on the existing technology is not providing complete privacy protection with centralized storage. It can be hacked or used against the user. The emerging Blockchain technology appears to be a solution for these issues. The Bitcoin application has established that for more than a decade Blockchain technology has operated without any breach. Blockchain network, based on World Wide Web infrastructure, has immutable distributed public characteristics with anonymity and persistency, which can support security and privacy with the help of cryptographic encryption, hashing and digital signature functionalities. Although Blockchain technology, along with the related user tools are still maturing, most of the industries and researchers have evinced keen interest to adopt this new IDM model because of the attractive features of this emerging technology. This model assures trust and security of users.

13.1.3.1 IDM Architecture

The generalized architecture of IDM with the Blockchain system is discussed here with three major actors. The first and most important actor is the User, who gains the identity and uses it for accessing the required web-based and application-based

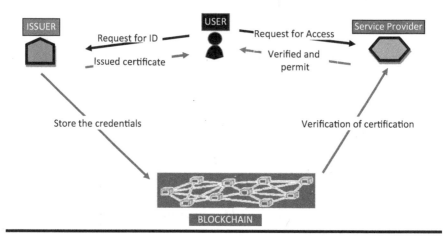

Figure 13.3 IDM architecture with Blockchain technology

services. The next actor is the Issuer, who issues the certificate or credential based on certain identity proof submitted by the User. In addition, the issuer stores the proof and certificate on Blockchain network directly or through hash values. The third actor is the Service provider/Verifier, who responds to a client request and verifies the certificate of the client with the data available in the block of the Blockchain network submitted by the Issuer. If the data are verified, validated and authenticated by the verifier, then the Service Provider permits the User to access the specific website or server. Here the Blockchain plays a major role in improving the security of the IDM system and protecting the privacy of the user. IDM architecture with Blockchain technology is shown in Figure 13.3.

With the use of Smart Contract Code in IDM with Blockchain technology, the system can be made very strong. The government laws/standards can be implemented agreeably with the help of smart contract for providing credentials to service providers.

The IDM using Blockchain becomes highly secure due to the inherent immutability, auditability and persistency characteristics of the Blockchain technology. Authorized Issuer checks the identity proof and provides the identity certificate to the User. Authorization is decided by the key management based on the validity of the Issuer and his capability to provide the certificate. The certificate is issued to the User as well as stored on the Blockchain network in hash format. Block is generated by the Issuer with all the valid information related to the User. The User needs to provide the credential information to the Service Provider to utilize the services. So, the User asks the Service Provider for permission to access the services and SP checks these credentials on featured Blockchain. If the credentials match with the User credentials, the validity of the User is confirmed and the User is enabled to access the services.

13.1.4 Different IDM Systems

Peter Steiner's famous cartoon "On the Internet, nobody knows you're a dog," published by the *New Yorker* on July 5, 1993, reveals the digital identity situation in the real world. Digital identity is one of the oldest and toughest issues from the beginning of the internet era. Digital IDM is a very old concept, but the perfect solution has not yet been devised. There are a number of organizations working on this aspect trying to find a perfect solution for IDM. Researchers are continuously working to overcome the problems of existing systems. DNS-IDM [9] is a Blockchain-based solution which claims that it provides the best feature for privacy and security using Domain Name Server (DNS) concepts. Here is a discussion on the various IDM systems. The first two IDM systems use the cryptographic technique without involving Blockchain technology and others are using Blockchain technology [5, 10–12]. The specific privacy preservation and drawbacks are listed in Table 13.1. Brief details of these IDM systems are as follows:

1. **BlockAuth:** BlockAuth allows users to own and activate their own identity register that permits them to submit their information for verification. It makes use of OpenID which is connected to OAuth family using JSON. It is designed in such a way to provide privacy and security that is fully controlled by the user. BlockAuth provides distributed producer authentication in Information Centric Networking (ICN) [13]. It has protected from various attacks such as prefix hijacking, DoS, replay attack etc.

2. **HYPR:** It was initiated by CEO George and CTO Bojan in 2014. It provides security through biometric using mobile, IOT, Desktop systems. Authentication and security are achieved with HYPR at the same time protect from various cyber-attacks. Fast Identity Online-FIDO alliance is established for authentication which supports different biometric authentication mechanisms.

3. **ShoCard:** It was founded by Armin Ebrahimi in February, 2015. ShoCard is the easiest way to provide digital identity to users and protect their privacy with a simple way as showing driver's license as identity proof. This secure application is accessible through mobile phones for most critical and safe transactions such as banking businesses. ShoCard is mostly a tiny file that only the user of that identity can manipulate. Hence it is a part of self-sovereign IDM. It makes use of QR code for scanning paradigms for all uses with two factors for authentication. ShoCard is in a win-win situation after a tie-up with other organizations, such as banks. It gets identification details and approvals through mobile phones and so the user cannot deny the purchase identity through mobile. The only problem with ShoCard is scalability [14]. It is seen that privacy decreases when scalability is increased. Identity Management is similar to the "chicken-and-egg problem," which should determine whether privacy or scalability is the primary need.

4. **Sovrin:** The Sovrin Foundation [15] is an international non-profit organization which was founded by Timothy Ruff in 2013. It was established to govern the world's first self-sovereign identity (SSI) network. Sovrin develops on Hyperledger Indys, which is an open source Blockchain framework and one of the Hyperledger projects hosted by the Linux Foundation. Hyperledger Indys source code was initially developed and contributed by Evernym. Self-sovereign identity is enhanced with use of highly advanced privacy-enhancing techniques, such as zero-knowledge proofs (for selective disclosure) and anonymous revocation and use for verification so that identity is made accessible to the world. Sovrin works in a decentralized manner to verify user identity using token as an intrinsic component of Blockchain.

5. **UPort:** This was developed by ConsenSys in 2016. UPort is used to develop a secure, usable system. It works as self-sovereign identity to own and control user's identity. UPort collects verification data and users can log in without password. It works on Ethereum applications. It uses third party concept, but third-party selection is done by the user. UPort provides recoverable identity due to persistent uPort ID even after the cryptographic key is lost using a key recovery protocol. UPort does not accomplish any identity proofing, but it provides a framework to gather attributes of identity from users.

6. **Civic:** This is a secure system which protects personal information transfer by identity verification technology. The first token was sold in June 2017. Civic is an open-source and first-of-its-kind marketplace for identity verification services built on Blockchain [16]. Keys are generated by a third-party wallet and encryption uses as firewall between user's keys and civic.

7. **Cryptid:** Masley and partner Dakota Baber invented the CRYPTID, which is also an open-source identity system. Cryptid uses three factor authentications for assuring the identity of the user. Cryptid's current version is in use as Factom which work as its Blockchain backend. Cryptid uses AES-512-CBC for data encryption and RSA-4096 for digital signing and verification. Cryptid utilizes Blockchain characteristics such as immutability and unhackable security in identity storage, making it extremely novel.

8. **Aten Coin:** This is a US-based Anti-Terrorism Digital Currency. It was introduced by the National Aten Coin (NAC) Foundation. This establishment expects to give the Blockchain-based advances and digital currencies utilizing IDM and validation. Identity privacy is not preserved to avoid money laundering. It is a fast and secured digital currency.

9. **Bitnation:** This is also known as cryptonation or voluntary nation. It was founded in July 2014 by Susanne Tarkowski Tempelhof. It captures important records, identity and other authorized actions using Blockchain technology. Bitnation was introduced in 2014 using Ethereum smart contract technology. It's the world's first Decentralized Borderless Voluntary Nation, which organizes Marriage and World Citizenship ID, Blockchain Land Title, Birth Certificate and Refugee Emergency ID. In April 2017, Bitnation's BRER (Bitnation Refugee Emergency Response) program was awarded the Grand Prix 2017 prize co-organized by UNESCO.

10. **KYC-Chain:** Edmund Lowell was the founder as well as the CEO of KYC (Know Your Customer) Chain. It is a Hong Kong-based company. It works like a self-sovereign system, where commercial institutes can manage customer information in a reliable and easy manner using distributed ledger technology, i.e. Blockchain [17]. KYC-Chain uses three factors for identification that are: (i) identity, like passport/government issued card; (ii) residency, means address proof/IP address or protocol; (iii) income/legitimate wealth recommended by the bank/lawyer.

11. **Netki:** This was founded by Justin Newton and Dawn Newton. Netki is a Global Identity Validation solution for the Digital Economy. Netki provides security and scalability using Blockchain technology. Netki's Wallet Network Address (WNS) is intended to permit service providers to easily register Wallet Names on behalf of their customers (such as username.company.com) or for end users to register their own vanity names (such as 'personalname.me'), linking them directly to a wallet address. Netki is a combination of the Namecoin Blockchain and Secure DNS (DNSSEC) for name storage and relating a name with an address.

13.1.4.1 Comparison

The various IDM systems discussed above are summarized in Table 13.1.

Table 13.1 Comparison of Different IDMSs

IDM system	Privacy Preservation Mechanism	Features	Drawbacks
BlockAuth	Multiple level of encryption and decryption of messages with multiple parties	Users can verify with ownership of any site	Work is going on to replace MangoDB to resolve Scalability issues and capture a position in the competitive market place
HYPR	Cryptographic digital key is generated from a biometric	Use Fast Identity Online (FIDO) Authentication	Still intangible and shaky
ShoCard	Two factors authentication and PoA (Age/ Address)	Tie up with other companies to provide identity	Scalability

(Continued)

Table 13.1 (Continued) Comparison of Different IDMSs

IDM system	Privacy Preservation Mechanism	Features	Drawbacks
Sovrin	Zero knowledge proof	Global public utility, self-sovereign	All GDPR compliance issues not resolved
uPort	QR code scanning	Secure, easy-to-use self-sovereign system	Unable to control public profile, use Ethereum, no identity proofing, leakage of attribute data
Civic	Firewall	Simple, cost-efficient, token based and use of smart contract	Unclear anonymity solution and ID Key recovery
Cryptid	Three-way authentication	Open-source, flexible, effectively hack-proof, immutable storage on Blockchain	-
Atencoin	Privacy is not preserved to avoid money laundering	Faster, secure and knows identity.	Source code is not available yet
Bitnation	Not limited Dash, Zcash, Monero	World's first Blockchain IDMS that provides 24*7 service	Regional and cultural adaptation issue
KYC-Chain	Blockchain using cryptographic key concepts	Reliable source and legal framework for IDM, open-source solution	Suffering from the drawbacks of permissioned Blockchain technology
Netki	Not mentioned, follow the rules of personal and data privacy laws	Human-readable wallet address	Open-source API for ID validation

13.1.5 Blockchain Impact of Security and Privacy on IDM

It is evident from the above discussion of the various Identity Management Systems, that each system has some good features and some drawbacks. "Every coin has two sides". The privacy preservation mechanisms in the various IDM systems are continuously being upgraded to make the systems reliable and less complex with good performance and true privacy.

Although Blockchain-based IDM solutions are good in several aspects, they do have limitations due to vulnerability to attacks like hijacking, double spending, DoS, etc. [17]. Some of the Blockchain-related security and privacy issues [13, 18] are as follows:

i. **Data leakage:** Since Blockchain has transparency as its characteristic, data may be disclosed. The use of data encryption algorithms will help overcome this problem to a certain extent, but it may lead to difficulty in verification and validation. If a zero knowledge proof algorithm is used for validation, then privacy can be preserved but there are chances of compromise of private data. However, pattern attacks are possible on metadata.

ii. **Replay:** A replay attack by an unauthenticated user is possible in which a valid block or packet of transaction data is substituted, repeated or delayed leading to loss of data.

iii. **Impersonation/False Reputation**: A malicious user attempting to impersonate a particular authorized user and pretend to be the particular user by increasing reputation is a serious threat. This risk can be mitigated by appropriate challenge response or private key management.

iv. **Private key or wallet address compromise**: A private key is an integral aspect of the Blockchain concept, and its security make-up helps to protect a user from theft and unauthorized access. Key stolen issue, error in key generation, storage leakage or key/wallet address compromise may result in privacy seepage, leading to poor security. Human error while handling keys using tools or secret sharing or key recovery mechanisms [19] also results in key loss.

v. **Data availability issue:** Data should be available 24/7. Blockchain has a distributed architecture and so replicas are available on the network, thereby preventing data loss. But Bitcoin has reported the loss of millions of dollars due to data unavailability or data withholding on account of DOS, DDOS, and Sybil attacks.

vi. **Quantum computing**: Quantum computing could change the world. Apart from breaking encryption, it can revolutionize communications and artificial intelligence. This impacts many areas of information science and computation, where the functionality of a system is established on the difficulty level of some calculation. Quantum computing provides cryptographic algorithms which may throw cryptographic challenges to key management and hashing, resulting in insecure Blockchain systems. The primary and most mature technology that has come out of quantum cryptography is quantum key distribution and similar quantum algorithms.

vii. **Attacks on smart contract:** While developing the smart contract for IDM, a privacy requirement is obfuscating [20]. Due to the byte code analysis tools of smart contract, there is a threat to security and privacy.

viii. **Data protection regulations:** There is country-wise data protection regulation, such as the General Data Protection Regulation (GDPR) of the European Union or the Freedom of Information Act 2000 (FIA) of the United States of America and so on. Apart from the contradictions, gaps and inconsistencies, these regulations have a definite impact on the application of Blockchain technology [3]. Some of the clauses in the regulations, such as 'right to erasure' and 'right to rectification', do not complement the privacy and security characteristics relating to user data of Blockchain technology. Blockchain-based solutions [21] are existing and work is going on to overcome the adverse effects of the Data protection regulation contradictions.

ix. **Peer-reviewed research and bug bounty programs:** When the verification and validation of IDMS happens, secrecy related to code may be compromised.

x. **Social norms:** While developing IDM systems, social norms and user expectations conflict with many factors, including security and privacy.

13.1.6 Benefits and Challenges

Identity management systems with Blockchain technology have overcome many of the drawbacks of other technologies or algorithms. But the inherent limitations of the Blockchain technology have a serious impact on IDMS. IDMS with Blockchain has the following benefits:

1. Distributed system without central control
2. Self-Sovereign Identity (SSI)
3. Overcomes identity theft issue to a large extent
4. Easy way of identity verification
5. Non-custodial login solutions
6. Easy to manage user identity for "Internet of Things" (IoT) systems.

The challenges to be addressed by the IDMS with Blockchain technology are scalability, security and privacy of identity, as explained in Section 13.1.4 of this chapter. User authenticity can be improved with reduced risk by adopting the Personal Identifiable Information method [22]. Privacy and anonymity of user can be improved with different kinds of algorithms such as Zero Knowledge Proof [23].

13.2 Conclusion

The Digital Identity Management field has been employed for many years with a number of models in use, but developing a fool-proof system incorporating accuracy, security and privacy continues to be the biggest challenge in cyberspace. This chapter has highlighted the different IDM models and the various approaches for tackling the IDM issues to make the applications fool proof from distinct attacks. A Self-Sovereign Identity (SSI) system using Blockchain technology with all its benefits appears to meet most of the requirements of an ideal system with minimum limitations. Being an emerging technology, SSI using Blockchain requires careful evaluation of various aspects before it becomes an operative IDM. This chapter analyses the various models to be considered, highlighting their strengths and limitations.

Abbreviations

AES	Advanced Encryption Standard
API	Application Programming Interface
ASN	Augmented Social Network
BRER	Bitnation Refugee Emergency Response
CBC	Cipher Block Chaining
DDOS	Distributed Denial of Service
DIDM	Digital Identity Management
DNS	Domain Name Server
DOS	Denial of Service
FIA	Freedom of Information Act
FIDO	Fast Identity Online
GDPR	General Data Protection Regulation
ICN	Information-Centric Networking
ID	Identity
IoT	Internet of Things
ITRC	Identity Theft Resource Centre
JSON	JavaScript Object Notation
KYC	Know Your Customer
NAC	National Aten Coin
PoA	Proof of Authority
QR code	Quick Response code
RSA	Rivest–Shamir–Adleman (asymmetric cryptographic algorithm)
SP	Service Provider
SSI	Self-Sovereign Identity
USA	United States of America
WNS	Wallet Network Address

References

[1] B.V. Tykn, "Identity Management with Blockchain: The Definitive Guide (2020 Update).html.", Mar. 13, 2019.

[2] T. E. Maliki, and J.-M. Seigneur, "Chapter 71—Online Identity and User Management Services," in *Computer and Information Security Handbook (Third Edition)*, Third Edition, J. R. Vacca, Ed. Boston: Morgan Kaufmann, 2013, pp. 985–1009.

[3] W. L. Sim, H. N. Chua, and M. Tahir, "Blockchain for identity management: The implications to personal data protection," in *2019 IEEE Conference on Application, Information and Network Security (AINS)*, Pulau Pinang, Malaysia, Nov. 2019, pp. 30–35, doi: 10.1109/AINS47559.2019.8968708.

[4] A. Jøsang, and S. Pope, "User centric identity management," in *AusCERT Asia Pacific information technology security conference*, p. 13.

[5] S. E. Haddouti and M. D. Ech-Cherif El Kettani, "Analysis of identity management systems using blockchain technology," in *2019 International Conference on Advanced Communication Technologies and Networking (CommNet)*, Rabat, Morocco, Apr. 2019, pp. 1–7, doi: 10.1109/COMMNET.2019.8742375.

[6] "The Path to Self-Sovereign Identity." http://www.lifewithalacrity.com/2016/04/the-path-to-self-soverereign-identity.html (accessed Aug. 10, 2020).

[7] Q. Stokkink and J. Pouwelse, "Deployment of a blockchain-based self-sovereign identity," in *2018 IEEE International Conference on Internet of Things (iThings) and IEEE Green Computing and Communications (GreenCom) and IEEE Cyber, Physical and Social Computing (CPSCom) and IEEE Smart Data (SmartData)*, Halifax, NS, Canada, Jul. 2018, pp. 1336–1342, doi: 10.1109/Cybermatics_2018.2018.00230.

[8] A. K. Manohar and J. Briggs, "Identity Management in the Age of Blockchain 3.0," *CHI Workshop on HCI for Blockchain: Studying, Critiquing, Designing and Envisioning Distributed Ledger Technologies*, p. 8, 2018.

[9] J. Alsayed Kassem, S. Sayeed, H. Marco-Gisbert, Z. Pervez, and K. Dahal, "DNS-IdM: A Blockchain Identity Management System to Secure Personal Data Sharing in a Network," *Applied Sciences*, vol. 9, no. 15, p. 2953, Jul. 2019, doi: 10.3390/app9152953.

[10] P. Dunphy and F. A. P. Petitcolas, "A First Look at Identity Management Schemes on the Blockchain," *IEEE Security Privacy*, vol. 16, no. 4, pp. 20–29, Jul. 2018, doi: 10.1109/MSP.2018.3111247.

[11] J. Bernal Bernabe, J. L. Canovas, J. L. Hernandez-Ramos, R. Torres Moreno, and A. Skarmeta, "Privacy-Preserving Solutions for Blockchain: Review and Challenges," *IEEE Access*, vol. 7, pp. 164908–164940, 2019, doi: 10.1109/ACCESS.2019.2950872.

[12] Atif Ghulam Nabi, "Comparative Study on Identity Management Methods Using Blockchain," *University of Zurich*, Zurich, Switzerland, 2017. [Online]. https://files.ifi.uzh.ch/CSG/staff/Rafati/ID%20Management%20using%20BC-Atif-VA.pdf

[13] M. Conti, M. Hassan, and C. Lal, "BlockAuth: BlockChain based distributed producer authentication in ICN," *Computer Networks*, vol. 164, p. 106888, Dec. 2019, doi: 10.1016/j.comnet.2019.106888.

[14] A. Ebrahimi, "Identity management verified using the blockchain," *ShoCard, Tech. Rep.*, 2019, (Accessed: mar 4 2019). [Online]. https://shocard.com/wp-content/uploads/2019/02/ShoCard-Whitepaper-2019.pdf

[15] A White Paper from the Sovrin Foundation, "Sovrin™: A Protocol and Token for Self-Sovereign Identity and Decentralized Trust," Jan. 01, 2018. [Online]. https://sovrin.org/wp-content/uploads/Sovrin-Protocol-and-Token-White-Paper.pdf

[16] "White Paper—Civic Token," *Civic Technologies*, 2017. [Online]. https://tokensale.civic.com/CivicTokenSaleWhitePaper.pdf

[17] Edmund Lowell, "kyc-chain.com," *kyc-chain*. https://kyc-chain.com/.

[18] L. Lesavre, "A Taxonomic Approach to Understanding Emerging Blockchain Identity Management Systems," National Institute of Standards and Technology, Jan. 2020, doi: 10.6028/NIST.CSWP.01142020.

[19] R. Soltani, U. T. Nguyen, and A. An, "Practical Key Recovery Model for Self-Sovereign Identity Based Digital Wallets," in *2019 IEEE Intl Conf on Dependable, Autonomic and Secure Computing, Intl Conf on Pervasive Intelligence and Computing, Intl Conf on Cloud and Big Data Computing, Intl Conf on Cyber Science and Technology Congress (DASC/PiCom/CBDCom/CyberSciTech)*, Fukuoka, Japan, Aug. 2019, pp. 320–325, doi: 10.1109/DASC/PiCom/CBDCom/CyberSciTech.2019.00066.

[20] S. Bansod, and L. Ragha, "Blockchain Technology: Applications and Research Challenges," in *2020 International Conference for Emerging Technology (INCET)*, Belgaum, India, Jun. 2020, pp. 1–6, doi: 10.1109/INCET49848.2020.9154065.

[21] N. B. Truong, K. Sun, G. M. Lee, and Y. Guo, "GDPR-Compliant Personal Data Management: A Blockchain-Based Solution," *IEEE Trans. Inform. Forensic Secur.*, vol. 15, pp. 1746–1761, 2020, doi: 10.1109/TIFS.2019.2948287.

[22] R. Rana, R. N. Zaeem, and K. S. Barber, "An Assessment of Blockchain Identity Solutions: Minimizing Risk and Liability of Authentication," in *IEEE/WIC/ACM International Conference on Web Intelligence on - WI '19*, Thessaloniki, Greece, 2019, pp. 26–33, doi: 10.1145/3350546.3352497.

[23] Y. Borse, A. Chawathe, D. Patole, and P. Ahirao, "Anonymity: A Secure Identity Management Using Smart Contracts," *SSRN Journal*, 2019, doi: 10.2139/ssrn.3352370.

Chapter 14

A New Ecosystem for Digital Identity Verification Using Blockchain

Shubham Gupta, Kevin Shah, Aditya Hirapara, Deep Mistry, Ankur Bang, and Udai Pratap Rao
Sardar Vallabhbhai National Institute of Technology, India

Contents

DOI: 10.1201/9781003129486-14

14.1 Introduction

Organizations like banks provide their services in corporate as well as retail sectors. These organizations cannot merely keep their trust in any client without first acquiring some necessary and personal information about them. A verification procedure, usually referred to as the Know Your Customer (KYC) procedure, is conducted to collect information about clients' credibility and authenticity. Although the KYC process is mandatory, it is still a gruesome and tiring process for the client and the banking organization [1]. KYC is not only a prolonged process, but it also incurs immense regulatory and compliance costs. Around 10% of the world's top organizations end up spending at least $100 million annually on this process [2]. On top of being a tiring process, the KYC is an ever-repeating one, where the client has to go through the same KYC process every time for a different banking organization. Due to the lengthened verification process, the business relationship between the customer and financial institution is delayed, which causes both parties to have opportunity costs. The price is also further incurred due to the misconduct concerning Anti-Money-Laundering (AML) and KYC regulations [3].

Along with the issues mentioned above, providing security and privacy to clients' sensitive data is a significant trend. As storing and accessing data stored in a decentralized way provokes attacks to breach a client's privacy and perform identity theft through it. Many researchers have worked in this regard.

In this regard, we aim to propose a novel modification to the traditional KYC verification process. The novel contributions and the highlights of our work are as:

■ Taking into account issues like security, privacy prolonged and repetitive current KYC process, we propose a blockchain-based approach.
■ The proposed solution plans to replace the entire current KYC system with our blockchain-based system that consists of a client-based mobile application and a bank-based website.
■ With the new architecture, when any user wants to register with a new service provider, he/she does not have to provide the same information which was already verified during the previous KYC verification.

The rest of the chapter is organised as follows. Section 14.2 comprises the literature review, giving a brief explanation about the blockchain technology and the recent work in using blockchain for KYC. Section 14.3 explains the proposed algorithm and illustrates the architecture of our Ecosystem. Section 14.4 describes the simulations done to test our Ecosystem. In Section 14.5, we have analysed the results obtained through simulations. Section 14.6 concludes the chapter with a summary and conclusion of our work.

14.2 Background and Related Work

In this section, we give a brief explanation of what blockchain is and how it works. We also discuss some notable and recent works, stating the use of blockchain technology for KYC.

14.2.1 Hashing Algorithm

This chapter will discuss a hashing algorithm, called the MD5 Hashing Algorithm, which is used to obtain data proof.

MD5 transforms messages of arbitrary length into fixed 128 bit message digest. MD5 is widely used as a hash function. MD5 is pre-image-resistant and second pre-image-resistant. MD5 is considered cryptographically secure because it is pre-image-resistant and second pre-image-resistant, which means that producing message having given target message digest or producing two messages having the same message digest is computationally infeasible. MD5 takes five steps to produce a message digest for a given message. Figure 14.1 shows the details.

i. Append Padding Bits: In this step, the message is padded such that the extended length of the message is exactly 64 less than multiple 512. First one set bit ("1") is appended to the message rest all clear bit ("0"). Padding length varies between 1 and 512 inclusive.

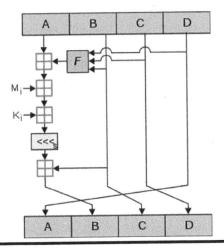

Figure 14.1   MD5 Hashing Algorithm[4]

ii. Append Length: 64 bits are inserted at the end of the first step, which depicts the message's length before the padding bits gets appended.

iii. Initialize MD Buffer: In this step, four buffers named A, B, C, D are used; each of them is a 32-bit register and are initialized in the following manner.
   ■ buffer A: 01 23 45 67
   ■ buffer B: 89 ab cd ef
   ■ buffer C: fe dc ba 98
   ■ buffer D: 76 54 32 10

iv. Process Message in 16-Word Blocks: There are four auxiliary functions which enable MD5 to generate 32-bit numbers from the input of three 32-bit numbers. These functions use logical operators like OR, XOR, NOT.
   ■ $F(X,Y,Z) = (X \wedge Y) \vee (not(X) \wedge Z)$
   ■ $G(X,Y,Z) = (X \wedge Z) \vee (Y \wedge not(Z))$
   ■ $H(X,Y,Z) = X \text{ xor } Y \text{ xor } Z$
   ■ $I(X,Y,Z) = Y \text{ xor } (X \vee not(Z))$

   In this step, messages are processed in a batch of 512 bits, with new buffers for the second batch resulting from the first batch. Processing of this batch of 512 bits consists of 4 rounds. Each round consists of 16 similar operations based on auxiliary function F, modular addition, and left rotation. The figure illustrates one process within the round. Each round has a different auxiliary function.

v. Output: After processing all batches, the final message digest produced is buffer contents of A, B, C and D.

   Advantages of MD5:
   ■ Simple to implement
   ■ Can transform arbitrary length into a message-digest
   ■ Can verify data without necessarily giving the original value

14.2.2 Blockchain and Its Applications

Blockchain was developed as a decentralized ledger pioneer for blockchain Bitcoin by an individual (or group of people) named Satoshi Nakamoto in 2008. Satoshi Nakamoto's existence is undisclosed to date. A blockchain is a timestamped series of unchangeable records of data managed by a group of computers not owned by any single entity ensuring decentralization. The larger the network grows, the more decentralized it becomes thereby, which increases the security [5]. Due to this, Blockchain technology is highly applicable in the areas like cryptocurrency, healthcare applications, maintaining property records, managing smart contracts, supply chain management and e-voting.

A blockchain initially is an increasing number of blocks connected to a chain. A previous block hash, a timestamp and transaction details (usually described as a

Merkle tree) is contained throughout each block. In other words, blockchain stores information that is shared and updated at regular intervals. This networking method has many benefits: data is not stored at a single point, data is kept in public, and data is easily verifiable. The information does not exist at one point, which significantly minimizes the possibility of attacks. The data is accessible to the public on the Internet as it is hosted by innumerable computers simultaneously. The attacker needs to change data at more than 50% of the transaction blocks to manipulate a record, which is not feasible [6].

14.2.3 *Hyperledger Fabric Private vs Public Blockchain*

A blockchain that is considered "Public" is essentially permissionless. Any user can perform actions like reading, writing or participating in the blockchain. A public blockchain is secure so that once validated, it becomes permanent and cannot be changed. A public blockchain is shared, and no one has control over the network, making it a decentralized system.

On the contrary, a private blockchain is a permissioned blockchain. This means that some conditions are placed on who is allowed to participate in the network and its underlying transactions. However, one more critical factor must be taken into consideration to get a better and complete understanding of blockchain technology, that is the idea of an open versus closed blockchain.

The private versus public blockchain considers the permission to be able to write data onto the blockchain. The open versus closed blockchain regards the consent to read data in the blockchain [5].

Use of Hyperledger Fabric as a Private Blockchain

A permission-based blockchain requires an invitation to participate in the blockchain. A private blockchain has its network validated by the network validator or by a set of rules that the network creator itself has created. In a private blockchain, every user does not have equal rights in the participation in the blockchain. Users are granted specific permissions and are allowed to access only certain types of data. Everything else is inaccessible or closed to the user.

The mechanism of access is entirely dependent on the rules that the network creator has set. This differentiation in access gives rise to different types of users and, thus, different roles. The identity management system's blockchain aims to house mainly two types of users:

Service Providers and Verifier. A Verifier is the type of user who must write onto the blockchain after it has verified the user details. A Service Provider is the type of user who can only read data from the blockchain. A Verifier is a type of user that is granted both read and write access. This is why the identity management system requires Hyperledger Fabric as a private blockchain [7].

Components of Hyperledger Fabric Network

1. Ledger

   A ledger consists of all the transactions that have taken place and the current state of the system. The former is known commonly as blockchain, and the latter is known as world state. A ledger stores the details of objects rather than directly storing them.

2. Peer

   The most basic building blocks of a network that host smart contracts and ledgers are called Peers. The ledger is accessed by a simple piece of code, known as chaincode. This technology concept, a chaincode, is used by Hyperledger Fabric to implement Smart Contracts.

3. Membership Service Provider

   An element of the system that lets Peers participate in the Hyperledger Fabric network and gives clients credentials is known as the Membership Service Provider. Multiple MSPs can authorise and control the Hyperledger Fabric network [8].

4. Smart Contract

   Smart contracts are executable programs that create rules between multiple organizations. The transaction logic of the network governs the cycle contained in the world state. Smart contracts are also identified as chaincodes in many cases [9].

5. Ordering Service

   A node that performs the ordering of transactions is called an Orderer, and the other nodes in the network form something is known as the ordering service. Ordering services also keeps a record of all the organizations, which are allowed to create channels. This ordering service orders transactions into a block and works on a first-come-first-served basis, completely independent of the peer processes.

6. Channel

   A channel is a communication path between multiple network members, which gives data isolation and confidentiality. All transactions in a network occur on a channel where each network member must be authenticated and authorized to perform transactions on that channel. The Membership Service Provider (MSP) gives an identity to every peer that joins any channel.

7. Certificate Authority

   This is more commonly known as Hyperledger Fabric, CA. This component is the one that issues PKI-based certificates to network members and organizations [7].

   A network in blockchain comprises nodes called peers that are its building blocks and contain copies of chaincodes and ledgers, as illustrated in Figure 14.2. A peer is a component of the network that hosts the instances of both ledgers and chaincodes. This exact method of storing and hosting the

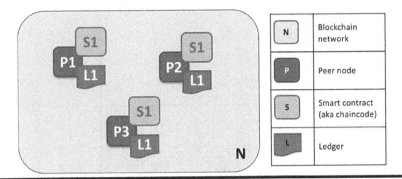

Figure 14.2 A Simple blockchain Network [7]

same instances of chaincodes and ledgers in the peers gives the system a perfect way to avoid a single point of failure. A peer does not always have a single chaincode and ledger; it can have multiple instances in a single peer.

Applications and Peers
When the system tries to do ledger-query interactions, there is a trivial three-step dialogue between the peer and application, as shown in Figure 14.3. In the case of ledger-update interactions, two extra steps are required. The applications always have to connect with peers to access ledgers and chaincodes [10].

Peers and Identity
The Hyperledger Fabric, CA (Certificate Authority) assigns an identity to the peers using a digital certificate. The governing organisation transfers a digital certificate to every individual peer in the network [11].

The channel configuration policy determines the rights of the peer's identity. This happens every time in a blockchain network when a peer uses a channel to connect to the network. The Membership Service Provider (MSP) provides the mapping of identity to an organization.

14.2.4 Related Work regarding Blockchain for KYC

Literature is evident that a very few contributions exist regarding using the blockchain technology for KYC purposes. We here discuss the previous work done and state their potential drawbacks. In [6], Jos'e Parra Moyano and Omri Ross propose KYC optimization using distributed ledger technology. They propose an interface for banks where a customer brings his KYC documents to a bank. The bank verifies the presented documents. This verified information is stored at the bank's local database and a hash of documents for further use by other banks on blockchain. However, the proposed architecture had problems; for example, the local database of banks stores the customer's data, which cannot be considered safe. Customers

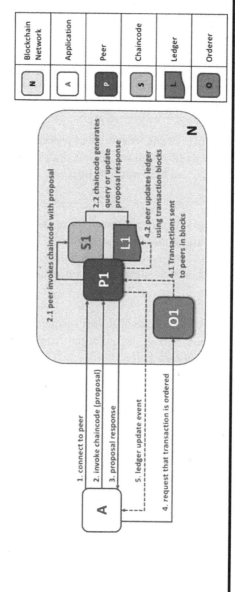

Figure 14.3 Applications and Peers [11]

are not allowed to provide partial access to data to other banks. Customers need to remember the key to reuse their verified information.

Piyush Yadav and Raj Chandak in [12] propose an architecture as an interface for customers and banks to enter his details in the mobile application. These details are stored in the Amazon Web Services (AWS) system, and, after verification, the details are stored on the blockchain. However, some of the identified problems are:—AWS is used to store data until the details are verified, which is central storage, and attack is possible at this point; and blockchain stores the complete data instead of proof of data, which allows other users to read the data. Table 14.1 shows a brief comparison of the related research work.

14.3 Proposed Architecture

This section describes the proposed architecture, Ecosystem and algorithm. We also provide a step by step and the detailed working of the proposed Ecosystem.

Most of the centralized databases are highly probable targets for hackers to attack [5]. A particular identity owner's data is stored in an encrypted format on their device in our system. Thus, our system ensures the privacy of the identity owner's data and makes it harder for attackers to access sensitive data. Additionally, our novel architecture also overcomes the problems in existing work.

The identity system is built on a decentralized model using blockchain. With blockchain and biometrics on a mobile phone, we enable users to share and manage their identity data with the service providers. There are three major components of the system:

i. An application installed on the user's device,
ii. blockchain for Identity verification, and
iii. API server to regulate service providers and verifiers. The Personal Identity Information (PII) of the user is stored on a device in encrypted form with the blockchain's transaction key.

A service provider can use the verified PII of the user directly. If required PII is not verified, the user needs to get the verification from the identity validator once and then provide those details to any service provider. Thus, the system provides a collaborative ecosystem for identity verification to service providers. Figure 14.4 explains the system implementation and communication between all entities: Users, Service providers, Validators, API server, and blockchain.

Steps for the verification of PPI: Figure 14.4 (a) explain the details about the steps for verification of PPT. The detailed step-by-step process and the activity involved in each step is as mentioned below:

Table 14.1 Comparison of Proposed System and Other Research Papers

	Transforming the KYC Process using blockchain [12]	*KYC Optimization Using Distributed Ledger Technology[6]*	*Proposed Implementation*	*Reason for selection*
Data Storage	AWS Server	Bank's local databases	User's phone	User has control over his data.
Blockchain Storage	Data	Proof of Data (Hash)	Proof of Data (Hash)	No service provider should be able to get the details without authorisation.
Data Fields	Fixed defined fields can be requested.	Fixed fields required by banks	Any field the service provider wants	The information required by each service provider varies, So the fixed fields do not work. For example, payment services require a pan card, whereas travel services require passport information.
User's Control Over Data	No option	Permission to data as a whole (Cannot give partial access)	User can choose which details he wants to share with the service provider.	Users should have control over their data and should be allowed to share information only which they want.
Password	User needs to enter the password.	User needs to provide a key.	A mobile client with biometrics as two-factor authentication	Fingerprint and two-factor authentication ensure a high degree of certainty of a user's identity when compared to passwords.
Details Change or Expired	No information provided	No information provided	Can Update the information and can verify again	The details such as passport and driving license expire, so there is a need to build an interface that allows updating the information.

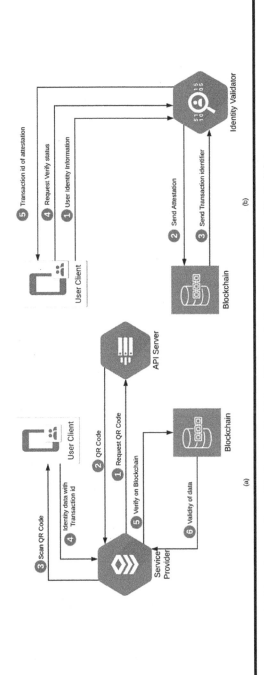

Figure 14.4 (a) User Interaction with Service Provider (b) User Interaction with Identity Validator

Step 1: The user provides his Personal Identity Information (PII) sent to the identity validator. The identity validator verifies the user's information by in-person verification.

Step 2: The validator sends the PPI to attest to the blockchain and stores the transaction identifier. The user can check his PPI verification status, and the transaction identifier is sent back to the user.

Steps for using verified PPI: update expire the steps involved in using the verified PPI. The activities at each step are as below:

Step 1: When a user visits a service provider website, the service provider requests the API server QR code with the requested data type. This QR code is displayed on the user's screen, which has to be scanned by the user.

Step 2: When the user scans the QR code displayed by the service provider, he will be asked to share the provided details, which he can choose to agree or deny. If a user agrees to share the requested details, the user client sends the attested data by validator with a transaction identifier related to the validator's attestation on the blockchain.

Step 3: The service provider compares the attestation of data (hash of data) and the actual data by calculating the hash of data and comparing it. Once the service provider accepts the details, the user may access service as any other authenticated user.

In the proposed system, access to the Blockchain network needs to be private among service providers and verifiers. Permissions are granted based on the role of the entity; Verifiers have both write and read permissions to add verification proofs on the blockchain, and Service Providers have only read permission to be able to verify details.

The API server's primary purpose is to coordinate the details of registered Service Providers and Verifiers on the mobile client's blockchain. It implements the API endpoints to get the list of Verifiers from mobile clients and details about service providers. Also, it serves as the endpoints for establishing socket connection for QR code-based authentication process.

This whole process replaces the traditional registration and login system, where a user needs to fill the form of details and enter a unique password for every service provider. Here, the user will scan the QR code displayed on the service provider's webpage, and all the processes will be handled by the mobile client, API server, and service provider internally. This works as two-factor authentication:

i. Mobile client secured with biometric fingerprint scan ("something user is"), and

ii. Identity data stored in the mobile client ("something user possesses").

14.4 Implementation

This section covers the implementation details of the proposed architecture. In the blockchain network, we have implemented the following functions required for KYC:

- addDetail: To record proof of verification by the verifier.
- queryDetail: To verify proof of user detail by the service provider.
- updateProof: To update proof in case of a change in detail.
- updateExpired: To update expired details of the given field.

We have implemented an Android application as a mobile client. The application is secured with a fingerprint scan on entry. Application has two primary workflows: verification of details and sharing of KYC-verified details with others. Figures 14.5 and 14.6 show the detailed workflow of verification process.

Central API Server

The API server's primary purpose is to coordinate the details of registered service providers and verifiers on the mobile client's blockchain. It implements the API endpoints to get the list of verifiers from mobile clients and details about service providers. Also, it serves as the endpoints for establishing socket connection for QR code-based authentication process. This method is discussed in detail in the following section.

Proposed QR code-based authentication with Service Provider

This method proposes one-step easy authentication for users using their mobile client. The internal process of this method is shown in Figure 14.7.

1. First, the service provider's web client (browser) will initiate socket connection with the API server. Here, a socket connection is used to establish a virtual connection between the user's mobile client and the service provider's client using session-id of the socket. Without it, the mobile client will not identify which browser session is supposed to get the user's data.
2. The API server will generate a QR code with registered details of the service provider and session id on the initiation. QR code has this data in JSON format. Then it will be sent to the web client, which will be displayed to the user who wants to authenticate.
3. Then, the user will scan this QR code with the mobile client. The mobile client will extract the details from the QR code. In the case of registration on a new service provider, it will prompt the user to confirm sharing requested details. Otherwise, it will directly move to the next step.
4. Then, the mobile client will send the HTTP request to the API server with user details and the session-id of browser with the API server.
5. Using the socket session-id, the API server will send those details to the service provider's web client through a socket connection and close the socket connection.

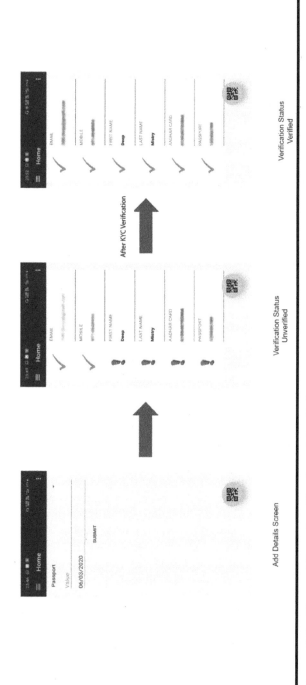

Figure 14.5 The workflow of verification of details for KYC

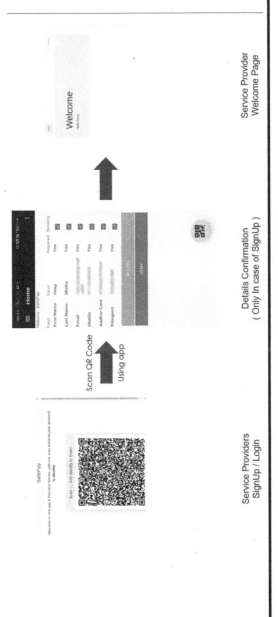

Figure 14.6 The workflow of using KYC verified details at a service provider

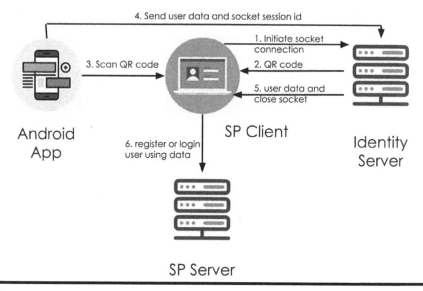

Figure 14.7   The internal process of QR code-based authentication

6. The service provider will verify these details on the blockchain and authenticate the user.

This whole process replaces the traditional registration and login system, where a user needs to fill the form of details and enter a unique password for every service provider. Here, the user will just scan the QR code displayed on the service provider's webpage, and all the process will be handled by the mobile client, API server and service provider internally. This works as two-factor authentication, mobile client secured with biometric fingerprint scan ("something user is") and 2) identity data stored in the mobile client ("something user possesses").

14.5 Results and Discussions

14.5.1 Sample Block of the Hyperledger Blockchain

```
{
"data": {
 "data": [
  {
   "payload": {
    "data": {
     "actions": [
      {
       "payload": {
        "action": {
```

```
"endorsements": <Array of endorsements from
endorser peers>[
<Endorser1 signature>,
<Endorser2 signature>
],
"proposal_response_payload": {
"extension": {
 "chaincode_id": {
  "name": "identity",
  "version": "1.0"
 },
 "response": {
  "message": "",
  "status": 200
 },
 "results": {
  "data_model": "KV",
  "ns_rwset": [{
   "namespace": "identity",
    "rwset": {
     "reads": [{
      "key": "E4BTK46-NM04EGV-JFE7MPB-GW9TKWT",
       "version": {
        "block_num": "13",
        "tx_num": "0"
        }
     }],
      "writes": [{
       "is_delete": false,
       "key": "E4BTK46-NM04EGV-JFE7MPB-GW9TKWT",
       "value": "eyJoYXNoIjoiOGU2ZmMwYmU4Mj1mY2I4MTA
       0OWEiLCJleHBpcnkiOiIxMC8wOS8yMDIwIn0="
      }]
     }
    },
    {
     "rwset": {
      "reads": [{
       "key": "identity",
       "version": {
        "block_num": "3",
        "tx_num": "0"
        }
      }],
      "writes": []
       ...
     },
     "proposal_hash": "11C4jsIytFzyK1RM2bX2c
     ToIV254b0whwisdD8ckKEg="
    }
```

```
      },
      "chaincode_proposal_payload": {
       "input": {
        "chaincode_spec": {
         "chaincode_id": {
          "name": "identity",
          "path": "",
          "version": ""
          },
          "input": {
           "args": [<Input args for chaincode>],
          },
          "type": "GOLANG"
          ....
          ]
          },
        "header": {
         "channel_header": {
         "channel_id": "mychannel",
         "timestamp": "2020-06-13T13:21:49.326Z",
         "tls_cert_hash": "WseZyR2e95aF+iiJuI
          ++2e7uhmIhgNOf2yufN9CzL8w=",
         "tx_id": "912b77738c2d24bacf4033713f7
          0f937bda9aa1a772369cc04beb6e05f8fa421",
         "version": 1
         },
         "signature_header": {
          "creator": {
          "id_bytes": <Creator CERT>,
          "mspid": "Org1MSP"
          },
          "nonce": "0NjrocRO26WiWRPxrcdglHwhfD7+q2r5"
          },
         }
        },
       "signature": "MEUCIQDUjdx57xZyklgFYXhenz0bQcC
        T1Jp6gtKqLEfDh6q21wIgbtMYbzvpHEW+p3tKkBxa
        7Bt2eYo88E1hkDP7zZA="
        }
       ]
      },
     "header": {
      "data_hash": "bsV+/bgVghQKLUJwYU1fkOixwYAjMBth
       r26+HjX8VBY=",
      "number": "14",
      "previous_hash": "+Wv8xGCXhValckZ3bgnaYz3zaf
       VH4nvU0EAKNLU8pD8="
      },
     "metadata": <BlockMetadata obj<has
      metadataSign, validity values>>
}
```

Sample transaction Block of Hyperledger Blockchain

The above shows a sample block which is inserted in Hyperledger blockchain. This is one of the blocks from our blockchain simulation. Each block consists of three fundamental parts: Header, Metadata, Payload data.

The header consists of three values: hash of the current block's data, the hash of the previous block, and block number. These values are represented in the above block as data hash, previous hash, and number, respectively.

Metadata consisted of information about blocks and included transactions inside the block. It has created timestamps, keys, and certificates of block writers, signatures, and validation flag of each transaction.

The Data field consists of an ordered list of transactions. The given block has one transaction. Each transaction has five values: header, signature, proposal, response, and endorsement.

The transaction header has information about a transaction, as in the above block channel id of the blockchain network, timestamp, transaction id, chain code version, etc. Signature is a cryptographic signature of the transaction created by an application by which transaction is proposed. This is to ensure that the transaction has not tampered with and from an authenticated source.

The proposal contains the values required to perform any given chaincode function. It consists of information about which chaincode to use, input parameters to give to chaincode to perform any action. Here, our block's transaction requests to perform an action using the 'Identity' chaincode, and the input field contains all required parameters. Additional field type represents language in which chaincode is written. This is a hyperledger-specific field, as it provides flexibility to use more than one language. In our case, it is the Go language.

The response contains information about the result of the transaction after it is performed. It consists of all actions performed by the transaction as reading/Write (RW) set. In the given block, the transaction has proposed an update request for key 'E4BTK46-NM04EGV-JFE7MPB-GW9TKWT'. So in order to perform this transaction, three entries in a read-write set are needed:

One mandatory read is performed for every transaction. In this, the given chaincode is read. When chaincode is installed on the blockchain network, it creates a transaction block too. Every time that chaincode is requested, it is read from blockchain's history only to ensure authenticity and the latest version is being used. In our case, 'identity' is written as block 3.

Now to perform an update, the read action of key 'E4BTK46-NM04EGV-JFE7MPB- GW9TKWT' is performed. As shown, the key is found and is last updated at block 13. At last, write action with the new value 'eyJoYX... C8wOS8yMDIwIwIn0=' is performed.

An endorsement is the list of signed transaction responses from each required organization to satisfy the endorsement policy. Here, we have two endorsements from peers of two organizations, as our approach requires signatures from two different organizations.

In this section, we discuss the results obtained after the deployment of the proposed architecture. We have also made a discussion about the applicability and utilization of the proposed architecture.

We propose a decentralized ecosystem for the KYC process. The system solves the problem of repetitive and costly independent KYC processes for every different service provider. Users will have to go through the verification process just once, and other service providers can use those verified details without going through the same process. Blockchain provides a transparent, collaborative system between verifiers and service providers.

For flexibility purposes, we have given the decision in the user's hands about which details he wants to verify at a time for any service provider, instead of forcing him to add all the details at once, even if not necessary for a particular service provider. In addition, the user can choose the verifier for verification according to his geographical ease and trust.

The system proposes to give control of data in the user's hands. It stores raw identity details on the user's device only. Blockchain records only proof of verified details for future validation by a service provider. So, the system does not have any raw information about the user other than the mobile client. The user is prompted with confirmation about sharing details with a service provider during registration. He can decide to share details based on his trust. Here due to client-side storage, the concern may rise about user forging fake information after verification. However, he needs to modify proof on the blockchain too, which will not be a single point of failure. So, he needs to have verifier-level authorization to the blockchain.

We also propose the password-less authentication method with our system. It provides a new way to two-factor authentication with effortless user interaction. The system presents QR code scanning as a medium to share details. Scanning QR code with the mobile client will share those details with a service provider without any password. The mobile client will be protected with a biometric fingerprint scan. The system solves the threat of account hijacking using password stealing or guessing. In addition, it saves the user from trouble remembering unique passwords and entering his details on every sign-in process.

14.6 Conclusion and Future Work

The proposed identification system will store data in the user's device in an encrypted form instead of a centralized database, giving mobility to the user to carry his digital identity. Users will be in charge of his data by deciding how much data should be shared and to whom. QR code-based authentication process is proposed as an alternative to traditional authentication processes. All service providers and verifiers will share their verification attestation through a blockchain distributed ledger. Access roles are assigned to service providers and verifiers to maintain privileges to provide secure access to attestation records in the blockchain. The proposed system solves the redundant and costly KYC process, offers a safe alternative to password-based authentication, and provides better user experience with easy sign-in and KYC process.

To create a balanced ecosystem between service providers and verifiers, we can introduce a payment system in which verifiers get paid a fixed amount whenever a service provider uses a detail that a verifier verifies. So this will ensure that verifiers are getting paid for their work; also, as multiple service providers are using the same information, this cost will be a fraction of what would have incurred to the service provider if they were using their verifier—thereby creating an ecosystem of verifiers and service providers.

References

[1] D. Martens, A. V. Tuyll van Serooskerken, and M. Steenhagen, "Exploring the potential of blockchain for KYC," *Journal of Digital Banking*, vol. 2, no. 2, pp. 123–131, 2017.

[2] (2018, July) Know your customer (KYC) will be a great thing when it works. [Online]. Available: https://www.forbes.com/sites/forbestechcouncil/2018/07/10/know-your-customer-KYC-will-be-a-great-thing-when-it-works/#2e8c5d298dbb

[3] (2012, 07) Kyc regulations. [Online]. Available: https://www.rbi.org.in/Scripts/BSViewMasCirculardetails.aspx?id=8179

[4] (2007,01,January) MD5 message-digest algorithm [Online]. Available: https://en.wikipedia.org/wiki/MD5#/media/File:MD5_algorithm.svg

[5] M. Di Pierro, "What is the blockchain?" *Computing in Science & Engineering*, vol. 19, no. 5, pp. 92–95, 2017.

[6] R. Turn, N. Z. Shapiro, and M. L. Juncosa, "Privacy and security in centralised vs decentralised databank systems," *Policy Sciences*, vol. 7, no. 1, pp. 17–29, 1976.

[7] J. P. Moyano and O. Ross, "Kyc optimisation using distributed ledger technology," *Business & Information Systems Engineering*, vol. 59, no. 6, pp. 411–423, 2017.

[8] (2020, 01) Hyperledger fabric documentation. [Online]. Available: https://hyperledger-fabric.readthedocs.io/en/release-1.4

[9] M. Alharby and A. Van Moorsel, "Blockchain-based smart contracts: A systematic mapping study," *arXiv preprint arXiv:1710.06372*, 2017.

[10] C. Ma, X. Kong, Q. Lan, and Z. Zhou, "The privacy protection mechanism of hyperledger fabric and its application in supply chain finance," *Cybersecurity*, vol. 2, no. 1, pp. 1–9, 2019.

[11] C. Cachin et al., "Architecture of the hyperledger blockchain fabric," in *Workshop on distributed cryptocurrencies and consensus ledgers*, vol. 310, 2016, p. 4.

[12] P. Yadav and R. Chandak, "Transforming the know your customer (KYC) process using blockchain," in *2019 International Conference on Advances in Computing, Communication and Control (ICAC3)*. IEEE, 2019, pp. 1–5.

Chapter 15

Blockchain-Based Security and Privacy for Smart Contracts

Vivek Kumar Prasad, Chandan Trivedi, Dhaval Jha, and Madhuri Bhavsar
Nirma University, India

Contents

DOI: 10.1201/9781003129486-15

15.1 Introduction to Blockchain and Smart Contract

Have you ever purchased a vehicle or a house? If so, you have encountered a particular kind of aggravation unique to these complex forms of transactions. Many business leaders have felt similar types of pain and have been researching how it can be alleviated by using Blockchain (BC) and Smart Contracts (SCs) [1]. This chapter is a fine place to begin, irrespective of whether or not you have just heard about both the ideas or you are searching for an in-depth description. SCs are lines of code placed on a BC and are executed automatically when the default contract terms (conditions) are met [2]. At the most fundamental level, they are systems that run as they were set up to run by the people who developed them. The advantages of SCs are most noticeable in business partnerships. They are usually used to implement some sort of agreement such that both parties can be confident of the result without the intervention of the negotiator. BC is a decentralized, distributed ledger on which transactions are digitally registered and connected to provide the asset's complete existence or origin [3]. The transaction is added to the BC only after it has been checked using a consensus protocol, which means that it is the only edition of the reality. Each record is protected, too, to provide an extra layer of protection [4]. Blockchain is said to be "unchangeable" because the records cannot be modified, and transactions are straightforward (or transparent) because all participants in the exchange have access to the same interpretation of the facts [5].

The above paragraph provides a brief introduction about the SC and the BC. Let us dive deep into this and understand it. Bitcoin, a cryptocurrency founded by an anonymous person or party using the pseudonym Nakamoto in 2008 [6], gave birth to BC's concept. BC is a growing set of records known as blocks, which are linked and secured using cryptography. BC uses a Peer-to-Peer (P2P) protocol that can accommodate a single endpoint [7]. The Consensus Mechanism establishes a standard strategy, exact ordering of interactions and blocks, and maintaining the BC's fairness and durability across geographically dispersed nodes. By nature, BC has features such as decentralization, auditability, and integrity. BC will act as a new kind of application bridge and be seen as a potential decentralized alternative to centralized shared information storage. BCs can be categorized into three types based on different access authorization layers: The first category is public BCs (such as Ethereum and Bitcoin). The second category semi-private or Proprietary BCs, and the third is private BCs (such as Hyperledger). The Blockchain is a platform for managing and implementing smart contracts. Smart Contracts are computer programs that run over the BC network and can communicate factors, specifications, and business rules to allow for complex and programmable transfers [8]. In the next section, we will address the Smart Contract Operational Process in detail. The concept and working of the BC are explained, which is also depicted in Figure 15.1.

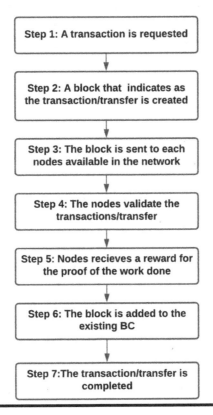

Figure 15.1 Steps in the Blockchain working environment

15.1.1 Smart Contract Operating Process

All parties agree on and sign SCs, which are then applied to the BC network for transfers [9]. These transfers (transactions) are then sent over a P2P network, verified by miners, and deposited in the block of BC, as shown in Figure 15.2.

The returning parameters are provided to the contract creators (e.g., Contract address). Users will then apply contract by submitting the same. This is also called a business transaction or trading. The system's reward feature attracts miners, who will devote their computing resources to verifying the transfer. After obtaining a contract for making or invoking a transaction, miners create a contract or execute contract code in their local environment [10]. Based on input from trusted data feeds (also known as Oracle) and system status, the Contract determines if the current condition meets the control criteria. The response activities must be strictly enforced if the conditions are met. Once a transaction has been authenticated, it is bundled

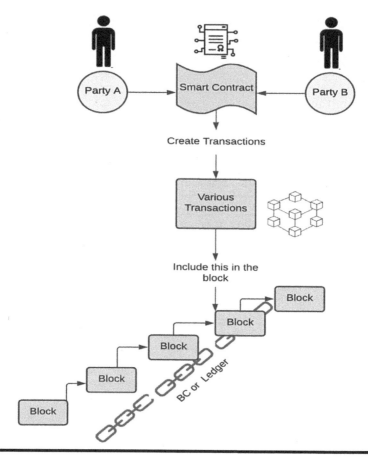

Figure 15.2   Operating Smart Contract in Blockchain

into a new block, and the data update block is added to the Blockchain as soon as the entire network agrees. Next, to introduce the SCs operational process [11], we take Hyperledger Fabric and Ethereum as illustrations. Ethereum is currently the most commonly used framework for creating SCs that can be interpreted as a state machine based on transfers or operations. It starts with an inception state and performs transactions incrementally to transform it into individual final states. These are the ultimate states (conditions) that we acknowledge in the Ethereum world as the standard "version."

Hyperledger Fabric [12] is an adaptation of the BC architecture and one of the Hyperledger projects of the Linux foundation. Hyperledger Fabric is allowed instead of the public BC, such as Ethereum and Bitcoin, where anybody may participate in the network. Since only a selection of organizations related to business can connect through a provider of membership programs and its network, it is safe. The ledger is the sequenced record of transactions in terms of payments or state changes and tamper-resistant. The state transformation is the product of the invocation (transaction) of the chain code. The transaction results in collecting resource key-value pairs generated, modified, or removed by the ledger. Hyperledger Fabric's transaction workflow comprises three stages:

i. **Proposal:** The task that sends a transaction request to the supportive colleagues of various organizations. The proposal calls for using a chain code feature to read or write data to the ledger. The response value, the write set, and the read set included in the transaction outcomes are examples. As a transaction proposal response, the application receives these attributes' collection and the endorsers' signatures.

ii. **Packaging:** The tasks or applications verify the endorsers' signatures and investigate whether the proposal's answers are the same. After that, the program sends the transaction to the ordering service (orderer), which updates the ledger. The customer filters the network transactions and packages them into a block that is ready to be distributed to all peers connected to it.

iii. **Validation:** Each transaction within the block is checked by the associates linked to the purchaser to ensure that appropriate organizations have regularly endorsed as per the endorsement policy. It should be noted that this step does not involve the chaincode to be run, which will only be done in the proposal phase. After validation, each peer adds the block to the chain and verifies the public ledger.

15.1.2 Security in IoT and the Impact of Blockchain-Based Smart Contracts

The Internet of Things (IoT) is a network of connected devices that uses embedded devices, sensors, artificial intelligence, and software to send data across the internet. It is used in a variety of complex systems. Each connecting device will have its own different identity [13].

IoT's primary purpose is to enhance people's living standards by linking objects to humans to make it easier to access the knowledge required across the Internet [14]. IoT presents a new way of communication between objects and humans or between objects themselves. However, besides the IoT having many human comforts, security concerns are emerging from this IoT. The target of different attacks by hackers is to extract confidential data in these IoT devices. This security issue exists in all three IoT layers: the perception layer, the application layer, and the network layer. The origin of this security issue is partly due to the infringement of security policies that makes IoT devices inexpensive, simple, and small. Typically, the term "Blockchain" refers to data structures and occasionally to networks or systems. The Blockchain (BC) is a list of ordered blocks, where transactions are stored in every block. All blocks are related to the previous block in the BC, containing a hash of the last block. Thus, without completely modifying the BC content, the BC's transaction history cannot be updated or removed.

The following points discuss the advantages of the smart contracts (SCs):

i. Risk Reduction: SCs could not be unilaterally changed when they are issued due to BC's immutability. Besides, all stored and duplicated transactions are auditable and traceable across the entire distributed BC system. As a consequence, it is possible to minimize malicious actions such as financial fraud substantially.

ii. Reducing the service and admirations costs: BCs maintain the entire system's trust by distributed consensus processes, bypassing the need for a mediator or central broker. SCs stored in BCs can be activated automatically in a decentralized manner. As a result of the third-party interference, management and operation expenses may be significantly reduced and saved.

iii. Increasing the efficiency of business procedures: The removal of intermediary dependency will dramatically improve the business process's efficiency. In the supply chain system, once the predefined requirement is met, the financial transaction will be immediately concluded in a Peer-to-Peer manner (e.g., the consumer acknowledges the products' receipt). The turnaround time will, as a result, be drastically reduced.

15.2 Challenges and Recent Work Is Done in the Field of BC-Based SC

Before we go ahead with the BC-based SC challenges, we should classify the same with the life cycle of the SCs [15]. The four major phases of the SCs are Creation, Deployment, Execution, and Completion. The same has been depicted in Figure 15.3.

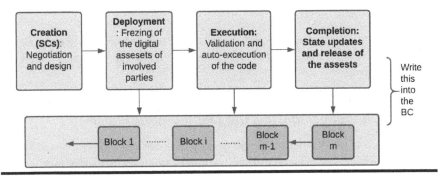

Figure 15.3 Smart Contract life cycle

There is still a range of issues to be solved, but an SC is a promising technology. Based on the four-phase life cycle of SCs, we categorize these significant challenges into four groups as below:

15.2.1 Challenges at the Time of Creating the SCs

Contract development is an essential move for smart contracts to be enforced. Users just have to code and then deploy their respective contracts on different BC platforms. Since BCs are permanent, after being implemented, BC-based SCs cannot be changed. As a result, developers must consider the following issues carefully:

15.2.1.1 Readability

Most SCs are made in computer languages, such as Go, Java, Solidity, and Kotlin. It will then compile and execute source codes. Therefore, systems have distinct types of codes in various periods. A big challenge continues to be how to make programs readable in each shape.

15.2.1.2 Functional Issues

The latest smart contract systems have a variety of technical problems. We face some particular challenges: 1) Re-entrancy implies that it is possible to remember the disrupted function safely again. Fake or malicious users may take advantage of this flaw to steal digital currency. 2) Randomness of the block, i.e., generated blocks, can be used in some SC implementations, such as betting pools and lotteries. Generating pseudo-random numbers in a block or a nonce block timestamp is done to accomplish randomness. On the other hand, nasty miners may build fake blocks to deviate from the pseudo-random generator's output. Attackers can influence the outcomes of probability distribution in this way.

15.2.1.3 Overcharging

Due to the under-optimization of SCs, they can be overcharged. Dead code, expensive loop operations, and repeated calculations are all characteristics of these overcharged patterns.

15.2.2 Challenges during the Deployment Phase

Smart contracts on BC networks will be implemented after development. But to prevent possible bugs, SCs need to be reviewed cautiously. Also, designers of SCs need to be aware of the patterns of interaction of the Contract to minimize possible losses due to malicious actions (such as attacks and frauds).

15.2.2.1 Contract Correctness

It is almost difficult to make any changes once intelligent contracts have been implemented on BCs. It is, therefore, vital to determine the correctness of SCs before formal implementation. However, because of the difficulty of modeling SCs, checking the accuracy of SCs is difficult.

15.2.2.2 The Dynamic Flow of Control

Immutable property of SCs doesn't guarantee SCs control flow's immutability. In general, a smart contract can communicate with other smart contracts (e.g., forming a new contract or transferring funds to the contract). When creating a smart contract, the control flow must be carefully considered. Over time, the interaction of SCs could lead to an increase in the number of interconnected contracts. It is also difficult to foresee the behavior of the contract. Besides, most current approaches focus on identifying possible issues with dynamic control flow in systems, although the operational environment is not always accurate. Therefore, testing whether the execution environment is reliable is also necessary.

15.2.3 Challenges during the Execution

For SCs, the execution stage is critical because it specifies the final state of SCs. During the execution of SCs, a variety of problems must be solved.

15.2.3.1 Trustworthy Oracle

SCs can't work unless they have real-world experience. For instance, Eurobet (a smart football betting contract) is interested in learning the European Cup outcome. On the other hand, a smart contract is designed to run in a sandbox that isolates it from the rest of the Internet. In a smart contract, an Oracle serves as an agent, finding and checking real-world events and transmitting them to the SC. As a consequence, the question of how to select a trustworthy Oracle arises.

15.2.3.2 Dependency on Transaction Order

In an SC, users submit transactions to invoke functions while miners load the transactions into blocks. Owing to the uncertainty of the bisected BC branches, the order of transactions is not deterministic. This confusion may lead to inconsistency in order-dependent transactions.

15.2.4 Completion Challenges

The change to the states in the system will be packaged as a transaction after the SC's execution and transmitted to each node. The emergence of SCs, however, brings more questions.

15.2.4.1 Security and Privacy

Most current SCs and BC platforms lack transactional privacy and lack privacy-preserving mechanisms. In particular, transaction data are distributed over the entire BC network (i.e., the operations' sequence). Therefore, all transactions on the networks are available to all. At the same time, pseudonymous public keys are used by some BC systems to enhance transaction confidentiality. Most transaction information (such as balances) is still publicly available. There are also inherent software bugs in SC systems, which are vulnerable to malicious attacks. Moreover, SCs operate on top of BC networks that are often vulnerable to the framework.

15.2.4.2 Scams

BC and SCs are vulnerable, as a new technology, to malicious attacks launched by scams. Particularly for contract users, the identification of scams is of great importance because it allows them to discontinue their investments early to prevent unnecessary losses.

Intelligent contracts on BC-based platforms have recently been developed. These frameworks provide easy interfaces for developers to build SC applications. Many of them will endorse smart agreements among a variety of incumbent BC platforms. Hyperledger, Ethereum, Stellar, Corda, and Rootstock are examples of smart contract platforms. We chose them primarily because of the popularity of group growth and the implied technical maturity.

15.3 Applications of the SC

Figure 15.4 shows the smart contracts (sc) applications in distributed system security, finance, sharing economy, public sector, the IoT, and data provenance. Let us see each of its applications in detail.

15.3.1 Smart Contract in Distributed System Security

In improving distributed systems' security, smart contracts will carry advantages [16]. One of the leading security threats to computer networks is Distributed Denial-of-Service (DDoS) attacks.

Attackers can flood the targeted device with unwanted overloading requests, causing Internet services to be disabled or suspended [17]. To fight DDoS attacks, a collaborative framework was recently proposed. Compared to traditional solutions, this approach, which focuses on smart contracts, can handle attacks in a fully

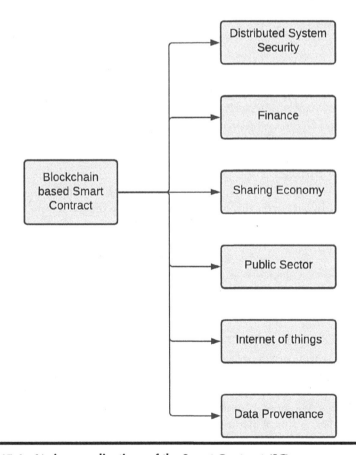

Figure 15.4   Various applications of the Smart Contract (SC)

decentralized manner. In particular, before a server is targeted, attackers' IP addresses will be automatically stored in a smart contract. Other nodes would be aware of the attackers' emails as a result of this. Other security mechanisms, such as the filtering of traffic from malicious users, will be introduced immediately.

Cloud technology is a promising technology allowing users to provide universal access to a shared pool of computational and data services. Users will typically buy services of cloud from trusted Cloud Service Providers (CSPs). However, as CSPs frequently collude to gain more profits, checking CSPs' trustfulness becomes a problem. They suggested a workaround in the paper focused on smart contract and game theory [18]. This approach's basic idea is to allow a client to order two cloud servers to perform the same task. During this process, intelligent contracts create tension, betrayal, and mistrust between the clouds. Users will quickly determine which logical clouds would not clash and cheat in this way. To see whether this idea was feasible or not, tests based on Solidity contracts were run on the authorized Ethereum network.

Moreover, in cloud computing, brokers are usually used—a broker reviews customers' requests to align services from suppliers. However, the broker should be trusted by both customers and service providers. Importantly, to discourage the use of brokers, the paper suggested using smart contracts. Their strategy's fundamental concept is to use shared cloud service-level agreements to define specifications through SCs [19]. Meanwhile, a utility function was designed to address the mismatching problem, which evaluates contracts according to both parties' wants and needs. When a broker is compromised or hijacked, both parties lose confidence.

15.3.2 Smart Contracts in the Public Sector

SCs are now reshaping the public sector's management, along with BC technology. Essentially, BC can avoid data theft and provide public information with transparency [23]. Just take a public offer as an example. BC and SC incorporation will prove both the bidder's and the bidding organization's identity, automate the bidding process, and enable support for reviewing and auditing. There are many barriers to e-voting systems, such as verification of user identity and user privacy protection (or voting anonymity). SCs also offer the solution to e-voting systems. A BC-based e-voting system called Follow My Vote was proposed based on user's identity verification without disclosing user privacy. However, it still relies on a trusted third authority to scramble the voters not to expose consumer/user's privacy.

It is also possible to use SCs to create a personal digital identity and credibility [24]. An online identity management system based on smart contracts is the Tsinghua University User Reputation System (TURS). Three factors are the foundation of a person's TURS profile: professional reputation, personal reputation, and online reputation. Via intelligent contracts that give access permissions to the other participants via programmable clauses, people protect their private information (statements). All transactions documented in BCs, meanwhile, cannot be manipulated or deleted.

15.3.3 Smart Contract in Finance

Smart contracts will theoretically minimize financial risks, reduce management and operation costs, and increase financial services' effectiveness [20]. The advantages of smart contracts in the following traditional financial services are explained next.

Insurance: The use of smart contracts in the insurance sector can reduce processing costs and save money, mainly when dealing with claims. Take motor insurance as an instance. In auto insurance, there are several parties: brokers, drivers, garages, transport providers, and hospitals. By exchanging legal documents in the distributed public ledger, smart contracts will automate lawsuits' settlement, improve performance, decrease the claim's processing time, and control cost.

Commercial and retail banking: The implementation of SCs, concerning capital markets may also carry advantages to the mortgage loan sector [21]. In the stages of origination, lending, and servicing, traditional mortgage loans are usually complex, thereby creating increased costs and delays. By automating the mortgage process with the digitization of legal documents in BCs, smart contracts will lower costs and delays.

Investment banking and capital markets: The long settlement times have hurt conventional capital markets. Smart contracts will considerably shorten the settlement duration from 18 to 22 days to 6 to 10 days, thus increasing consumer attractiveness. As a result, it is expected that it will carry demand growth of 5% to 6% and lead to significant profits in the future.

15.3.4 Smart Contract in IoT

One of the most exciting innovations, the IoT, will support many projects [25], namely inventory tracking systems, supply chain management, libraries, manufacturers, access control, industrial internet, e-healthcare systems, etc. The key IoT effort is to incorporate "smart objects (i.e., things") into the Internet and to provide users with different facilities [26]. IoT has been suggested in an implied manner to simplify different business transactions. The IoT's ability can be unleashed with the incorporation of smart contracts. As an example, take industrial manufacturing. In a centralized way, most existing producers manage their IoT ecosystems. For example, by querying from devices to the server, firmware improvements can only be accessed manually on the central server by multiple IoT devices. Smart contracts offer an automatic solution to this issue. On SCs deployed on BCs distributed across the entire network, manufacturers can position firmware update hashes. Devices will then automatically receive the hashes of firmware from smart contracts. Resources are significantly saved in this way.

Smart agreements may also add advantages to the e-business model of IoT. For instance, to settle the purchase, the conventional e-business paradigm also involves a third party acting as an agent. This centralized payment, however, is expensive and does not make full use of IoT benefits. It was proposed to automate transactions in Distributed Autonomous Corporations (DACs) [27], in which there are no conventional positions, such as governments or companies dealing with payment. DACs can function automatically without human intervention when enforced through SCs. In addition, SCs will also help to accelerate traditional supply chains. For example, the partnership of supply chains with SCs automates contractual rights and obligations during payment and goods distribution. Both parties also have confidence throughout the process.

15.3.5 Smart Contracts in Data Provenance

Smart Contracts (SCs) are also used to guarantee the quality of knowledge in scientific research and clinical health in addition to financial services. In clinical trials in recent years, data have been frequently manipulated or forged. For example, Haruko Obokata contained data on fraud [28], a paper published in *Nature* in 2009. The data generated may either mislead the ongoing research recommendations or delay patient recovery. It can, therefore, severely weaken scientific and public confidence.

To mitigate the problem, data provenance has subsequently been suggested. Data provenance's fundamental concept is to store the data root, derivation, and transformation of metadata knowledge. However, the application of data origin is difficult. In addition to information that is sensitive to privacy (e.g., access time, user ID, and UI roles), the majority of original logging tools, such as the Progger and the Trusted Platform Module (TPM), store information activities [29]. The protection of privacy knowledge is an issue. The data source scheme focused on smart contracts, and Ramachandran and Kantarcioglu proposed Blockchains. Researchers can send their encrypted data to this framework. Smart contracts will monitor the transformations made to the data when there are any changes to the data. Any malicious falsification of knowledge may be recorded in this way.

Also, to secure the intellectual property of innovative digital media, smart contracts may be used. Every digital product (e.g., product identification of the customer and digital wallet address) has a distinctive digital watermark [30]. Suppose there is a violation (for example, without the creator's permission, the buyer sells the digital product to someone). In this case, the law enforcement officer may monitor the illegal file using an extract of the digital watermark and compare the purchaser's digital wallet address with the original file. The violation of property rights can therefore be easily detected. Via smart contracts and Blockchains, the entire procedure can be done.

15.3.6 Smart Contract in Sharing Economy

The sharing economy brings many advantages, such as lowering consumer prices by lending and recycling goods, improving customer service, maximizing capital, reducing the environment's effects [22]. However, most existing shared economy networks suffer from privacy disclosure, high consumer transaction costs, and unreliability of trusted third parties due to centralization. Theoretically, smart contracts will restructure the social economy by decentralizing platforms for economic sharing. They proposed a new system for sharing the economy based on Ethereum's smart postal contracts. This system allows users to exchange and register objects without a reliable third party, in particular. In the meantime, personal data is also kept private. The functional application also confirms the efficiency of the system. Combining the smart contract and the IoT can also develop economy sharing applications.

Meanwhile, the paper for BC-based shared economy implementations suggested a privacy-respecting strategy. Because of the public transparency of BCs, this scheme primarily addresses the privacy leakage issue of BC-based structures. A zero-knowledge approach was, in particular, applied to this method. The feasibility of the proposed process also shows practical implementation.

15.4 A Case Study on Cloud Security Using BC-Based SC

Security and privacy of the IoT continue to be a fundamental challenge, mainly as there are wide-ranging and interconnecting networks. The Blockchain approaches guarantee decentralized privacy and protection. Still, they require considerable energy, delay in terms of communication messages, and overhead computing that is not sufficient for most IoT devices limited by resources. Hence CC can act as a solution for the same. In this case study, cloud and BC-based SC are used for the smart home environment and consist of three basic levels: smart home, overlay, and cloud storage. Each smart home is equipped with an online high resource device known as a miner who handles all communication, both indoors and outdoors [31]. Also, the miner maintains an in-house BC that is used to control and audit communication. A BC intelligent home architecture is secure by thoroughly analyzing its security regarding fundamental security objectives, such as availability, confidentiality, and integrity.

The leading smart home components and their working are discussed below:

i. **Transactions**: As transactions, communications between overlay nodes and local devices are known. There are many transactions, each built for a specific purpose, in the BC-enabled smart home. Data storage devices create the storage transaction. To access cloud storage, and a provider makes access transactions of the cloud or the homeowner. The homeowner or SPs develop a monitoring transaction for the continuous monitoring of system information. A genesis transaction is used to connect a new device to the intelligent home, and a device is removed with a removal process. All of the above transactions use a mutual key to guard communication. Lightweight hashing is used to identify any transaction content changes during transmission, i.e., a private and secure BC in the vicinity stores all transactions to and from the intelligent home.

ii. **The local Blockchain for smart/intelligent home management and its security**: In each smart home, a local private BC tracks transactions and has a policy header for implementing incoming and outgoing transaction policies. Each device's transactions are chained together as an immutable leader, starting with the transaction genesis. There are two headers in each block: the block header and the local BC policy header. The BC has the hash of the previous block to keep the block header immutable. The policy header is used to authorize devices and implement policies of the owner's home control.

The policy header contains four parameters. The parameter "Requester" refers to the PK applicator during the received overlay transaction. The field for local devices is equal to the "device ID" field. The second column in the policy header shows the requested transaction action that can be: locally store data, save cloud data, access to stored device data, and monitor real-time data access from a specific device. The third column in the policy header is the smart home ID of the device. Finally, the last column shows the measures taken to comply with the preceding transaction characteristics.

In addition to the headers, each block has several transactions. For each transaction, five parameters shall be saved in Local BC. In the first two parameters, the transactions on one device are chained, and each transaction is individually identified in the BC. In the third field is inserted the corresponding device ID of the transaction. The transaction type means the type of transaction that may be access, storage, genesis, or monitoring transactions. The transaction will be stored on the 5th field if it comes from the overlay network; else, this file is kept void. The local BC is supported and maintained by a local miner. The same has been depicted in Figure 15.5.

iii. **Intelligent home miner**: An home automation mining system centralizes transactions from smart house input and output. The miner is integrated into the Internet gateway with a separate stand-alone computer. The mining company certifies, allows, and controls transactions. The miner compiles all transactions to a block and attaches the entire block to the BC. The miner keeps a local reservoir for extra power.

iv. **Local storage:** This is a unit for local data storage, such as a backup drive, used by computers. This storage can be combined with the miner, or a separate unit can be used. The storage uses a First in First out system to store data for each device in its original chain.

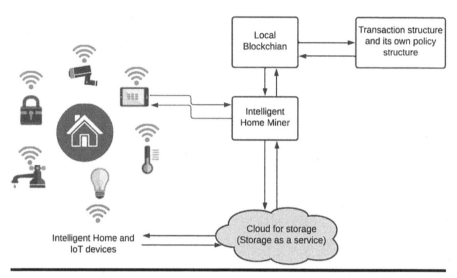

Figure 15.5   BC-based SC for smart homes

The next section of the case study discusses the BC-based intelligent home. The initialization processes, management of transactions, and mutual/shared overlay are described here.

i. **Initialization:** The procedure for adding local BC devices and policy headers is explained here. The miner creates a Genesis transaction by exchanging a key with the device for a smart home device. The mutual key between the miner and the computer can be saved during the Genesis transaction. The home-owner creates his policy on the policy header concept, which adds the policy header to the first block. The miner uses the policy header in the latest BC block so that the owner can change the policy header for the current block to change the policy.

ii. **Handling of the transactions**: Smart devices can directly interact with each other or individuals outside the smart home. Every device within the home can request certain services from another internal device. For instance, e.g., when a person enters the home, the light bulb asks for movement sensor data to automatically turn on lights. For users to control home automation transfers, the miner should provide a mutual key to devices to communicate directly with each other. The miner checks the policy header or asks for permission from the owner to assign the key and then distributes a shared key between devices. Devices communicate immediately after obtaining the key as long as their key is correct. The miner marks the distributed key as invalid by sending a control message to devices to refuse the grant authorization. There are two advantages: on the one hand, the miner (i.e., the owner) has a list of data-sharing devices; on the other, there are shared-key interactions between devices. The additional possible transaction flow within the home is to store data on computers locally. Every computer must be authenticated to store data locally with a shared key. The computer must request the miner to provide the key, and the miner will produce a shared key and send the device key and storage if space is approved. The local storage creates a starting point containing the shared key by obtaining the key. The computer can store data directly in local storage with a shared key. The devices may require data that is known as a store transaction to be held on cloud storage.

For anonymous authentication purposes, the petitioner needs a starting point containing a block number and a hash. The service provider (e.g., Nest thermostat) may own and manage cloud storage, or pay for, the house owner (e.g., Dropbox). In the previous case, the miner requests the starting point by creating a signed transaction with the device key. In the latter case, payment is made through Bitcoin. The storage generates a point of departure in either form and sends it to the miner after receiving a request. It transmits data and the request of the miner if a computer needs data stored in the cloud. By accepting the order, the miner authorizes the cloud storage system to store data. If the computer has been approved and generates a storage transfer and transferred it into the storage and data, the miner extracts the final block and hash from local BC. After saving data for further storage transfers, the cloud storage returns the new block number to the miner.

Other possible transactions include tracking and accessing transactions. The homeowner mainly carries out these transactions for tracking or monitoring devices for custom services outside the home or by the service. The miner tests for local or cloud storage if the requested data have a node access transaction on the overlay. When the data are stored on the local repository, the miner requests and transmits local storage information to the requestor when the data are stored in the cloud; on the contrary, the miner requests cloud storage data and sends it to the requestor or sends the requestor the last number of blocks and hash.

A further scenario allows the requester to read the complete data stored in cloud storage by the device and is suitable when the data stored are for a unique device. Otherwise, as part of a linking attack, the privacy of the user could be endangered. By receiving a monitor transaction, the miner sends current data from the requesting computer to the requester. When the requester is permitted to collect information for a while, the miner sends data regularly so long as the requester sends a request and ends the transaction. The monitor transaction allows homeowners, where regular data are transmitted, to view cameras or other devices. In minutes, the owner can determine a threshold for periodic data to prevent overhead or future attacks. The miner terminates the connection when the miner sends data to the requestor exceeding the threshold.

iii. **Shared overlay:** When a person has more than one house, he needs individual miners and storage for each home. A joint overlay in this instance is defined to lower costs and manage overheads. The common overlay[32] includes at least two smart houses, managed centrally by a shared miner as a single home. The shared overlay is the same as the smart home, but the common BC structure differs from the smart home structure. Every house has a shared BC genesis, and the shared overlay miner chains all of the devices in the transaction of genesis. Another difference in the shared overlay is concerning communications with the miner between the homes. Devices that are in the same home as the miner do not change. Simultaneously, a virtual private network (VPN) [33] is established between the internet gateway and the common overlay mining machine [34], which routes packets to the shared miner [35] for devices located in other houses.

15.5 Conclusion

Emerging smart contracts have become a hot research subject in academic and industrial communities with the growing popularization and deepening of Blockchain technology applications. Without the presence of a trusted authority or a central server, the decentralization, enforceability, and verification features of smart contracts allow contract terms to be enforced between untrusted parties. It is also predicted that smart contracts will revolutionize many conventional industries, such as banking, administration, IoT, etc. Smart Contract based technology is reshaping the processes of traditional industry and sector. Smart Contracts embedded in Blockchain allow the contractual terms of an arrangement to be automatically implemented without a trusted third party's involvement. Due to this, SCs will minimize administrative costs, save service costs, increase business process efficiencies and minimize risks. While the latest wave of innovation in business processes is promising to push SCs, there is a range of challenges to be addressed. We present here the challenges as well as recent technological developments in smart contracts. We also compare traditional smart contract platforms and some representative examples and case studies and categorize smart contract applications.

References

[1] Zhao, J. Leon, Shaokun Fan, and Jiaqi Yan. "Overview of business innovations and research opportunities in blockchain and introduction to the special issue." *Financial Innovation* 2, (2016): 1–7.
[2] Beck, Roman, Michel Avital, Matti Rossi, and Jason Bennett Thatcher. "Blockchain technology in business and information systems research." *Business & Information Systems Engineering* 59, (2017): 381–384.

[3] Morkunas, Vida J., Jeannette Paschen, and Edward Boon. "How blockchain technologies impact your business model." *Business Horizons* 62, no. 3 (2019): 295–306.

[4] Feng, Qi, Debiao He, Sherali Zeadally, Muhammad Khurram Khan, and Neeraj Kumar. "A survey on privacy protection in blockchain system." *Journal of Network and Computer Applications* 126 (2019): 45–58.

[5] Tsai, Wei-Tek, Libo Feng, Hui Zhang, Yue You, Li Wang, and Yao Zhong. "Intellectual-property blockchain-based protection model for microfilms." In *2017 IEEE Symposium on Service-Oriented System Engineering (SOSE)*, pp. 174–178. IEEE, 2017.

[6] Chatterjee, Rishav, and Rajdeep Chatterjee. "An overview of the emerging technology: Blockchain." In *2017 3rd International Conference on Computational Intelligence and Networks (CINE)*, pp. 126–127. IEEE, 2017.

[7] Park, Lee Won, Sanghoon Lee, and Hangbae Chang. "A sustainable home energy prosumer-chain methodology with energy tags over the blockchain." *Sustainability* 10, no. 3 (2018): 658.

[8] Drescher, Daniel. *Blockchain Basics*. Vol. 276. Berkeley, CA: Apress, 2017.

[9] Watanabe, Hiroki, Shigeru Fujimura, Atsushi Nakadaira, Yasuhiko Miyazaki, Akihito Akutsu, and Jay Kishigami. "Blockchain contract: Securing a blockchain applied to smart contracts." In *2016 IEEE international conference on consumer electronics (ICCE)*, pp. 467–468. IEEE, 2016.

[10] McCorry, Patrick, Alexander Hicks, and Sarah Meiklejohn. "Smart contracts for bribing miners." In *International Conference on Financial Cryptography and Data Security*, pp. 3–18. Springer, Berlin, Heidelberg, 2018.

[11] Pan, Xiongfeng, Xianyou Pan, Malin Song, Bowei Ai, and Yang Ming. "Blockchain technology and enterprise operational capabilities: An empirical test." *International Journal of Information Management* 52 (2020): 101946.

[12] Kyoung-Tack, Song, Shee-Ihn Kim, and Seung-Hee Kim. "A design for a hyperledger fabric blockchain-based patch-management system." *Journal of Information Processing Systems* 16, no. 2 (2020): 301–317, DOI: 10.3745/JIPS.03.0136.

[13] Sengupta, Jayasree, Sushmita Ruj, and Sipra Das Bit. "A Comprehensive survey on attacks, security issues, and blockchain solutions for IoT and IIoT." *Journal of Network and Computer Applications* 149 (2020): 102481.

[14] Hakak, Saqib, Wazir Zada Khan, Gulshan Amin Gilkar, Basem Assiri, Mamoun Alazab, Sweta Bhattacharya, and G. Thippa Reddy. "Recent advances in Blockchain Technology: A survey on applications and challenges." *arXiv preprint arXiv* 2009 (2020): 05718.

[15] Sánchez-Gómez, N., L. Morales-Trujillo, J. J. Gutiérrez, and J. Torres-Valderrama. "The importance of testing in the early stages of smart contract development life cycle." *Journal of Web Engineering* 19, no. 2, (2020): 215–242.

[16] Zheng, Zibin, Shaoan Xie, Hong-Ning Dai, Weili Chen, Xiangping Chen, Jian Weng, and Muhammad Imran. "An overview on smart contracts: Challenges, advances, and platforms." *Future Generation Computer Systems* 105 (2020): 475–491.

[17] Chen, Meizhu, Xiangyan Tang, Jieren Cheng, Naixue Xiong, Jun Li, and Dong Fan. "A DDoS attack defense method based on blockchain for IoTs Devices." In *International Conference on Artificial Intelligence and Security*, pp. 685–694. Springer, Singapore, 2020.

[18] Choi, Tsan-Ming, Ata Allah Taleizadeh, and Xiaohang Yue. "Game theory applications in production research in the sharing and circular economy era." *International Journal of Production Research* 58 (2020): 118–127.

[19] Alzubaidi, Ali, Ellis Solaiman, Pankesh Patel, and Karan Mitra. "Blockchain-based SLA management in the context of IoT." *IT Professional* 21, no. 4 (2019): 33–40.

[20] Treleaven, Philip, Richard Gendal Brown, and Danny Yang. "Blockchain technology in finance." *Computer* 50, no. 9 (2017): 14–17.

[21] Gupta, Richa, Vinod Kumar Shukla, Sindhu Suresh Rao, Shaista Anwar, Purushottam Sharma, and Ruchika Bathla. "Enhancing privacy through "Smart Contract" using blockchain-based dynamic access control." In *2020 International Conference on Computation, Automation and Knowledge Management (ICCAKM)*, pp. 338–343. IEEE, 2020.

[22] Islam, Md Nazmul, and Sandip Kundu. "IoT security, privacy and trust in home-sharing economy via blockchain." In Kim-Kwang Raymond Choo, Ali Dehghantanha, Reza M. Parizi (eds.) *Blockchain Cybersecurity, Trust and Privacy*, pp. 33–50. Springer, Cham, 2020.

[23] Zheng, Zibin, Shaoan Xie, Hong-Ning Dai, Weili Chen, Xiangping Chen, Jian Weng, and Muhammad Imran. "An overview on smart contracts: Challenges, advances, and platforms." *Future Generation Computer Systems* 105 (2020): 475–491.

[24] Toapanta, Segundo Moisés, Felix Gustavo Mendoza Quimi, Máximo Geovani Tandazo Espinoza, and Luis Enrique Mafla Gallegos. "Proposal of a model to apply hyperledger in digital identity solutions in a public organization of Ecuador." In *2019 Third World Conference on Smart Trends in Systems Security and Sustainability (WorldS4)*, pp. 21–28. IEEE, 2019.

[25] Zhang, Yuanyu, Shoji Kasahara, Yulong Shen, Xiaohong Jiang, and Jianxiong Wan. "Smart contract-based access control for the internet of things." *IEEE Internet of Things Journal* 6, no. 2 (2018): 1594–1605.

[26] Cha, Shi-Cho, Kuo-Hui Yeh, and Jyun-Fu Chen. "Toward a robust security paradigm for bluetooth low energy-based smart objects in the Internet-of-Things." *Sensors* 17, no. 10 (2017): 2348.

[27] De Filippi, P., and S. Hassan, 2020. "Decentralized autonomous organizations. glossary of distributed technologies." *Journal on Internet Regulation* 10, no. 2. DOI: 10.14763/2021.2.1556.

[28] Ariail, D., and D. Crumbley. "Fraud triangle and ethical leadership perspectives on detecting and preventing academic research misconduct." *Journal of Forensic & Investigative Accounting* 8, no. 3 (2016): 480–500.

[29] Awad, Abir, Sara Kadry, Brian Lee, Gururaj Maddodi, and Eoin O'Meara. "Integrity assurance in the cloud by combined PBA and provenance." In *2016 10th International Conference on Next Generation Mobile Applications, Security and Technologies (NGMAST)*, pp. 127–132. IEEE, 2016.

[30] Li, Zujian, and Zhihong Zhang. "Research and Implementation of Multi-chain Digital Wallet Based on Hash TimeLock." In *International Conference on Blockchain and Trustworthy Systems*, pp. 175–182. Springer, Singapore, 2019.

[31] Dorri, Ali, Salil S. Kanhere, Raja Jurdak, and Praveen Gauravaram. "Blockchain for IoT security and privacy: The case study of a smart home." In *2017 IEEE International Conference on Pervasive Computing and Communications Workshops (PerCom Workshops)*, pp. 618–623. IEEE, 2017.

[32] Zavodovski, Aleksandr, Nitinder Mohan, Suzan Bayhan, Walter Wong, and Jussi Kangasharju. "Icon: Intelligent container overlays." In *Proceedings of the 17th ACM Workshop on Hot Topics in Networks*, pp. 15–21. 2018.

[33] Santosh, S. Venkata Sai, M. Kameswara Rao, P. S. G. Aruna Sri, and C. H. Sai Hemantha. "Decentralized application for two-factor authentication with smart contracts." In *Inventive Communication and Computational Technologies*, pp. 477-486. Springer, Singapore, 2020.

[34] Gleichauf, Paul Harry. "Blockchain mining using trusted nodes." U.S. Patent 10,291,627, issued May 14, 2019.

[35] Sánchez, César, Gerardo Schneider, and Martin Leucker. "Reliable smart contracts: State-of-the-art, applications, challenges and future directions." In *International Symposium on Leveraging Applications of Formal Methods*, pp. 275–279. Springer, Cham, 2018.

Chapter 16

Blockchain Application in Digital Identity Management in Elections

Rajeev Kumar Gupta
Pandit Deendayal Energy University, India

Sweta Gupta
Jagran Lakecity University, India

Rajit Nair
Inurture Education Solutions Private Limited, India

Contents

DOI: 10.1201/9781003129486-16

16.1 Introduction

Blockchain technology was implemented in 2008, when the first cryptocurrency named Bitcoin was developed by Satoshi Nakamoto [1]. The Bitcoin blockchain technology uses a decentered public leader in combination with the stochastic consensus protocol based on Proof-of-Work (PoW) with financial incentives to record a totally ordered blockchain series. In each transaction, the chain is repeated, cryptographically signed, and publicly verifiable so that nobody may disrupt the data written on the blockchain. The blockchain structure is an add-only data structure that allows new blocks of data to be written to it but not altered or removed. The blocks are chained such that each block has a hash that is based on the previous block and guarantees immutability. Although all chain elements are released by Bitcoin blockchain, other forms of blockchain usually focus on the public, private, or consortium. Public blockchain give every user of that network access to read and the ability to make a transaction. This form is used mainly for cryptocurrencies (e.g., Bitcoin, Ethereum, Dogecoin and Auroracoin). Consortium blockchain is a "partly decentralized" blockchain, in which a pre-selected group of nodes controls the consensus phase [2]. Just imagine a consortium of 15 financial institutions, each with a node, 10 of which must sign every block to make the block legitimate. The ability to read the blockchain can be public or just for the participants. Private blockchain restricts not only written access, but also read access for individual members who can internally validate their transactions. That makes the transaction on a private network cheaper since only few trusted nodes with a guaranteed high processing power have to verify them [3]. It can be hoped that nodes are very well connected and defects can be quickly fixed by manual intervention, enabling the use of consensus algorithms that give finality after much shorter block times. Blockchain can be used in different domains for protecting the data such as health sector [4], education [5], banking sector [6], stock market analysis [7] and many more.

We will use a consented blockchain, variation in consortium-based chains that uses the consensus algorithm Proof of Authority(POA) in our proposal. Transactions and blocks are authenticated by authorized accounts known as validators in evidence-of-authority networks. This method is automated and needs no continuous monitoring of the machines by the validators. A licensed blockchain that uses POA consensus algorithm helps us to arbitrarily validate and certify blockchain and censor transactions with their identity and credibility restrictions on a range of select recognized entities. This must be done otherwise by miners on a shared blockchain using the consensus proof-of-work algorithm. Instead of using mining fees as public blockchains, validators are charged for the service they provide by serving as validators in the system. In addition, using a private network restricts an eavesdropper's ability to track traffic or read incoming data. This is important in order to comply with voting rights so that voters can vote without revealing their identification or voting data.

16.2 Security Vulnerabilities during the Election Process

a. Registration database of hacked voters

Voting attacks on registered voters can also undermine the right of people to vote. A close election could effectively swing to exclude voter's parts that would probably favor a candidate. If the identity of an individual has been deleted, they will not sign in at elections. An attack that deletes a whole state registration database can delay or even stop an election [8]. Russian intelligence officers effectively broke voter-recording databases during the 2016 presidential election, according to Special Counsel Robert Mueller's indictments [9]. The charges do not suggest whether Russia's involvement affects the results of the polls.

The indictments resonated with the United States Senate Intelligence Committee's assertion that Russia could at least change or erase the registration data of electors for a limited number of countries. A cyber assault on the elector's database registration is also partially a privacy attack. These databases also contain personal information such as names, addresses, telephone numbers, etc. By selling it online on illegal dark web markets [10], hackers will manipulate PII to target potentially misinformation and propaganda electors.

b. Interests or disuse data on unintentional knowledge

The media people consume help to shape their political beliefs before an election. But the vote could have difficulties finding facts-based sources to inform the voting due to targeted misinformation campaigns correctly. Digital disappointments in the pre-election phases are deeply affecting election results. The democratic process can be stifled by machine propaganda, digitally tracked pictures and images, armed social media, and more.

In the run-up to US mid-term elections, analysts say that homegrown disinformation operations in the US begin to look like Russia's foreign-influence playbook for the 2016 election. Facebook has reportedly found 559 pages and 251 Americans' accounts that allow incorrect content to be amplified and false consensus to be built online. In the meantime, activities with international power do not stop. In August, Facebook revealed that a new Russian network to control the Americans before the mid-term had been detected and removed.

c. Devices suffer from hacked voting

Hackers who exploit vulnerabilities in voting equipment and tabulation systems can manage votes and election results [11]. Each selection component involving some form of electronics device and software (especially when connected to the Internet) is vulnerable to hacking from a cybersecurity perspective. However, security experts believe that the Internet is a highly vulnerable voting machine, tabulation systems, and networks. A significant concern in the case of compromised voting machines is the class breakage of these devices and the safety flaws break up an entire system and a whole class of systems.

Stealing data from one company with software vulnerability is a crime. Still, it is breaking news that hundreds and thousands of companies are found as a common vulnerability in the software. Porous supply chains open widespread electoral security breaks. DEFCON Hackers concentrated on many cases of voting machines with components made external to the US (including the Chinese hardware), showing the ability to exploit vulnerable electoral supply chains through foreign actors [12]. A flaw in the supply chain for election infrastructures allows hackers to find only one entry point to destroy an entire voting machine model or make. Most local councils use software systems from a limited number of elective technology providers and supporters.

There are three powerful corporations of the US electoral sector: Domination, Hart InterCivic, the most significant Vote Systems, and Software companies (ES&S) [13]. In the last decade, 92% of American voters who voted for one of the three firms did on the machine. Attackers targeting one or more such firms could spread malware through thousands of jurisdictions that would simultaneously impact millions of voters on electoral devices.

d. Mutual consent in reporting system

Biased reporting systems may report inaccurate results of the voting. Harvard researchers of Belfer Center expect that attackers will take advantage of these sources to trick the information into reporting the incorrect winner if automated data streams are used to notify news organizations [14]. Hackers might also take over an official social media account and distribute false findings directly.

We may soon see officials making spoofed videos announcing the winners of falsified elections. Using generative adversarial network (GAN), highly realistic fake videos could be created—a type of AI used to perform unchecked machine learning [15]. Generative adversarial network generates increasingly realistic audio, picture, and video material through opposing neural networks.

e. Audit after election

A post-election review can be immediately demanded—a contrast of digital results to print ballots. However, the post-election checks without the correct voting machines are vulnerable to inaccuracy. Experts believe that only a paper trail can be used to ensure accurate post-election audits [16]. That means voting machines that only record electronic votes (often through a contact screen) are not fit for elections' integrity.

A paper ballot system is preferred as the safest voting machines for optical scanning. Under these methods, electors mark with an oval their votes in a paper ballot. The paper ballot is then scanned and scanned by a computer at the polling place for electronic tabulation. No domestic mandates include paper voting systems in the United States today. States like New Jersey, Georgia, Nevada, and many more have no necessary paper history following the elections. The Securing American Votes and Elections Act, the latest bill, proposes that all state and municipal elections guarantee the auditing of paper votes. Risk-limiting audits are regarded as the most accurate and cost-effective post-election audit.

Essentially, the only measure required for evaluating the quality of electoral results is the number of votes. Risk-limiting audits use the hand estimate of the victory margin to determine in proportion the number of options to be audited. Risk-restricted audits are novel, and no implementation in electoral jurisdictions is standard. Only 28 countries currently mandate post-electoral audits.

16.3 Blockchain Solutions

Blockchain's critical features—transparency, immutability, and obligations—highlight the technology's potential to secure elections [17]. Although blockchain advocates claim that technology could increase voter turnout and increase protection, some computer security experts and election specialists say Blockchain unnecessarily complicates and secures election processes like other internet-connected voting systems. While there is no consensus, numerous pilot projects worldwide are beginning to lay the groundwork for a blockchain vote. Below is the technology behind a blockchain-based option that is potentially stable.

a. Media verification through Cryptography

The digital content also comes from a secure and accountable source through cryptographic technologies based on blockchain technology [18]. Essentially, voters only use media with a cryptographic identity that can signify where the media came from as it was cross-referenced in a blockchain with enduring records. Without an identifier, media will be considered less specific. A blockchain system to check media in collaboration with government and non-governmental organizations should be developed in this situation.

b. Apps based on voting process with blockchain

Skeptics note that every vote on the Internet is insecure, and mobile ads complexity levels, further eroding safety, and transparency. Mobile voting campaigners argue that access to elections through mobile devices can increase voting attendance via elections. The blockchain is the missed connection of the entrance to route web voting. West Virginia will provide Overseas Voters from all 55 counties with mobile blockchain votes in mid-choice elections in November [19].

This was initially financed with a $150K grant from risk capitalist Bradley Tusk. The former advisor to Uber wishes to increase voter turnout, especially among active military staff abroad. First Lieutenant Scott Warner said after participating in the pilot program in West Virginia, "I've had to go to perform my civic duty just as long as I could pull up and watch a YouTube video." He is considered one of the first voters to register his vote in a blockchain federal election. Election officers had to copy Warner's votes manually and scan them into a computer. The pilot was using Voatz, a voting company based in Boston, from West Virginia.

The Voatz program uses facial recognition software to validate voters' identities in line with Western Virginia law [20]. Votes on a blockchain are kept inside a cloud called a "digital lockbox." The digital lockbox is secure, stamp-resistant cloud storage with blockchain-immutable ledger technology. County clerks open and collect tabulation votes on the first day.

Other companies that build blockchains are Votem, Obey My Vote, Votebox, and XO.1. In particular, elections on the mobile web could make for a longer digital voting window. For example, Estonia enables voters to log in and vote via its Internet voting infrastructure as much as they wish in the pre-selection period. Since the last vote can be canceled at any new voting point, a voter has the option beforehand.

c. Blockchain voting and Digital Identity

Blockchain may contribute to centralizing voting identity management [21]. An array of identity records, including publicly released IDs and biometric data obtained during online registration, must be compared by Blockchain elections to a voter with their data document in an online voting registry database. Biometrics such as iris and face data are increasingly being used to demonstrate identification along with blockchain voting. A coalition of universities, non-governmental organizations, and the rest, whose agreement confirms the identity and decides the electorate, may be designated by the government or party organizing an election. Blockchain's purists argue that depending on a consortium is contradictory to the central concept of Blockchain—decentering. With the dispensation and revocation of electoral identities by central authorities, a few administrators have determined which votes count, and voters are returned to the mercy of them.

According to approved Josh Benaloh, Microsoft's senior cryptograph, Blockchains is an exciting and useful distributed consensus technology without a central authority [22]. But the paradigm is not in line with elections. Blockchain evangelists have to face a range of technological challenges, restricting the technology's capacity for changing elections if left unresolved. Blockchains could function in an immutable distributed ledger to safely store votes. For voters' identity to be checked effectively, most voting supplier's blockchain requires additional levels of technology to keep voting secret and let voters track and verify votes, although the database is safe.

d. Audits after the election with blockchain

Each voter will be permitted to verify that the recorded votes total is exact in a public blockchain, without disclosing any voter's own identity or vote option. Today, Votem and Voatz blockchain voting companies offer voters systems that allow their votes to be confirmed. Voters have cast voting votes and QR codes for options. By using a new system to check the QR code, voters can rest assured that their vote has been reported correctly. Although the method doesn't make sure voters know that their vote was part of the final election outcome, there is no other guarantee that a form of voting is actually in use. Blockchain voter options say that monitoring and audits can quickly be done by other means, namely to reduce the amount of funds necessary to support the validity of an election.

e. Gold standard for an election process

For an election, the gold standard can be checked by end-to-end (E2E) verification. Three critical components of E2E verifiable elections are:

1. Voters are assured of the careful recording of their decisions.
2. All voters should confirm that the official results have been counted in their votes.
3. The public should ensure that the election results are correct.

In the future, security experts and election officials should come together to build electoral infrastructure and processes which represent the need for a verifiable election for E2E.

16.4 Blockchain-Based E-voting System

Blockchain experiments can be a significant step towards the E2E verifiable objective. Soon, underlying cybersecurity initiatives such as data protection, network and endpoint surveillance, penetration testing, and many other measures will also play a critical role in electoral security.

This chapter discusses and assesses a national e-voting system's feasibility to incorporate existing electronic voting systems based on blockchain. On this basis, we have built an electronic voting framework for blockchain that optimizes the defined needs and considerations. In the following paragraph, we first describe the functions and components for implementing an intelligent e-voting contract and then exploring various blockchain systems to introduce and deploy the smart elections. The nature and architecture of the structure proposed is discussed in the last paragraph.

16.4.1 Election as a Smart Contract

The smart contract involves clarifying the positions that the agreement (in our case, the constituency contract) entails and the different components and alternatives found in this contract process. We first explain the electoral positions and the electoral mechanism.

1. Election roles: The elections in our proposal allow the participation of individuals or organizations and election managers. Several trusted institutions and companies are registered in this role.

   i. The electoral officers determine the type of vote, produce the above polls, configure ballots, register electors, decide how long the election will take, and allocate authorized nodes.
   ii. Voters: Voters can authenticate, load, cast, and track their votes after the election to which they are entitled is completed. Voters can receive a voucher if they vote in a smart city initiative and shortly with tokens.
  iii. District nodes: When election administrators create an election, the smart contract representing each electoral district is used on the blockchain during every vote. When the smart voting contracts are formed, each section node is permitted to communicate with their respective smart voting contract. When an elector casts his vote by his associated intelligent agreement, all the relevant district nodes verify the voting data. When block time is reached, the blockchain is annexed to every poll agreed.
   iv. Bootnodes: any organization hosting a boot node with allowed network access. The District Nodes can be found and communicated by a bootnode. Bootnodes don't hold the blockchain state and have static IPs to identify local nodes more promptly by their peers [23].

16.4.2 Election Method

In our work, every voting process is marked by several intelligent contracts that the blockchain instantiates the election administrators. A smart contract involving several intelligent contracts is created for each constituency. After the user authenticates himself during the voting process, each voter in their linked voting place will sign the smart contract with the corresponding polling district.

   i. Election Creation Managers generate election ballots using a decentralized app:
      The following are the principal activities in the election process: (dApp) [24]. It communicates with an intelligent election contract defining the administrator's list of candidates and voting districts. The smart agreement creates and puts on blockchain for each polling district by several smart polling contracts with candidates. Each electoral district is an indication of any smart vote. Each district node shall communicate with its corresponding smart voting contract when the option has been made (See Figure 16.1).
   ii. Registration of voters: Electoral administrators shall conduct the registration of the electoral point. The election administrators must identify a deterministic list of eligible electors when an election occurs. This calls for a government identity verification service to ensure that qualified persons are authenticated and approved. Each qualified voter should have an electronic ID and PIN and details on which electoral district he or she is based, using these verification services. A suitable wallet will be created for the elector for each qualifying

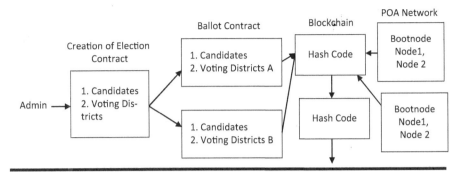

Figure 16.1 Smart Contract for election

elector. Every vote is eligible to have a wallet designed for each voter. The system itself does not know which wallet fits each voter, and a NIKKP can be integrated to generate that wallet.

iii. Vote transaction: When voting in a voting district, the elector communicates with a smart voting arrangement with a given voting district. These smart contracts interact with the blockchain via the appropriate country node, which adds to the vote if a deal is reached among most respective county nodes. Both ballots are stored as a transaction on the blockchain, while each voter is supplied with an ID transaction for verification purpose. Each blockchain transaction includes details about who was elected and where the vote, as mentioned earlier, is located. Each vote is appended by its respective voting smart contract to the blockchain, if and only if all the appropriate local county nodes agree to the vote data verification. When an elector casts their ballot, their wallet's weight is reduced by 1, so that the electors cannot vote more than once. The transaction number, the block on the transaction, the age of transactions, the wallet which sent the transaction and who received it, the total sum that was sent to us and transactions charge, is a single transaction on a public Ethereum blockchain.

iv. All this information is not required for a transaction in our proposed framework. The single transaction has only the transaction ID information on which the transaction is located. The intelligent contract is sent, and this example shows N1SC that a vote has been sent from District N1. Finally, the transaction value is the data were chosen to cast, which means that D reveals that the vote cast in the transaction was party D. Therefore, no information about each voter who cast this particular vote is contained in a transaction in our system.

v. Calculation results: Election is determined on the fly in intelligent contracts. Each smart vote contract makes its record in its storage for its respective venue. When an option is over for each smart contract, the outcome is issued. As stated earlier, each elector receives a transaction identifier of his vote.

vi. Voting verification: Each voter shall go to his/her government officers after being authenticated and present his/her business ID with his/her electronic ID and PIN. The Government official uses the blockchain investigator to locate the blockchain transaction with the necessary transaction ID using the district node access to the blockchain. The voter would then see his vote on the blockchain, showing that he had counted and had correctly counted.

16.5 Assessment of Blockchain as an E-voting Service

The three blockchain systems that we envisage for our smart elections' implementation and deployment are Exonum, Quorum, and Geth. Let's discuss these three blockchain system in detail.

1. Exonum: Looking at the Exonum blockchain, it's complete programming with its Rust language is robust to the end. For private blockchains, an Exonum is created. It has a custom Byzantine algorithm used to achieve network consensus. Exonum supports up to 5000 transactions per second, utilizing this consensus algorithm. Exonum aims to add Java bindings and platform-related interface descriptions to improve Exonum's developer friendliness shortly to address the limitation [25].

2. Quorum: This is an Ethereal-based transaction/contract privacy ledger protocol with new consensus mechanisms. They are the Geth fork, and they are being modified in line with Geth updates. Quorum has modified the consensus mechanism and centered on consortium chain-based consensus algorithms. This consensus enables tens to hundreds of transactions per second [26].

3. Geth: Go-Ethereum or Geth is one of the three initial implementations of the Ethereum Protocol, which runs smart and reliable contract applications with no downtimes, censorship, fraud, or third-party intervention. This system promotes development beyond the Geth protocol and represents the most advanced framework in the frameworks we have evaluated. The transaction per second depends on whether the blockchain is established as a network, whether public or private. Thanks to these skills, Geth was the forum for our work. A blockchain architecture with the same potential as Geth should be considered for these systems [27].

16.6 Design and Implementation

Our proposed system is designed to apply a secure authentication method. This computer uses an RFID scanner and Nexus software. Suppose a user signs with electronic identification, and the user selects a 6-name PIN for the respective identity. Therefore, a user will recognize himself at the voting stand by scanning his ID and providing its corresponding PIN to authenticate himself on the machine.

1. Any instrument in any polling district can be used by eligible voters because the voting district has details. The voter has the right to vote for the requested elector in the pocket. A valid ID and PIN should be given to authenticate successfully in a polling district using a card reader and software.
2. If the authentication is successful, the respective smart contract will be initiated for continuous election. The election above is a smart contract with a list of candidates a voter can opt for.
3. Suppose the voter selected a candidate for the applicant and cast the ballots. In that case, the elector should continue to sign the voting roll with his PIN on a regular voter by adding the corresponding voting PIN of an EPI.
4. After signing it on a ballot, the vote data must also be reviewed through the corresponding district code by which the vote enters smart on the electorate. When the district node above approves the voting data, most of the district node will accept the voting data.
5. Most nodes in the district supported voting data. There was a majority on the particular vote. The user then receives the transaction ID and prints the transaction ID with his vote as an RF code for the corresponding transaction. When the vote is cast and reviewed, one vote in the intelligent agreement will be granted to the party. This feature of the smart contract system is used to assess the outcome in each voting district. Figure 16.2 demonstrates the steps that we have just based on.
6. All transactions obtained and reviewed during the continuous block phase are deployed on the blockchain after the blockchain deadline (see Figure 16.3). With each new block added to the blockchain, each district node updates its copy of the ledger.

16.7 Conclusion

In contemporary society, the concept of adapting automated voting systems to make the democratic election process cheaper, quicker, and simpler is a persuasive one. It normalizes the political process in the electorate's eyes, eliminates a particular barrier to control between voters and elected officials, and puts some pressure on the elected official. It also opens the way for a more direct form of democracy, enabling voters to express their will on particular bills and proposals.

In this chapter, we introduced a unique electronic voting system based on blockchain, which uses smart contracts to ensure safe, cost-effective elections and guarantee voters' privacy. We outlined the architecture of applications, the configuration, and a system security analysis. Compared to previous work, we have shown that

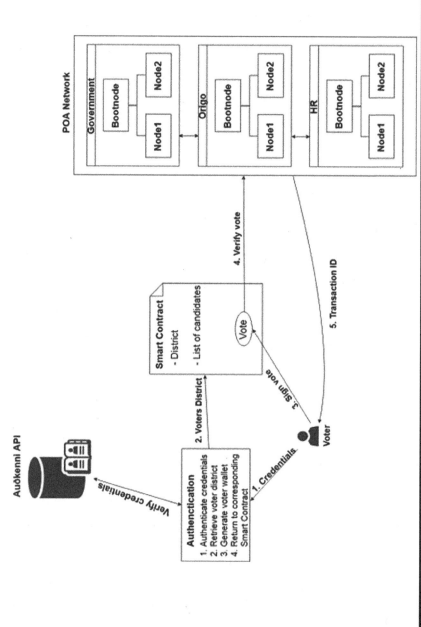

Figure 16.2 Self-authentication and casting of vote by voter[28]

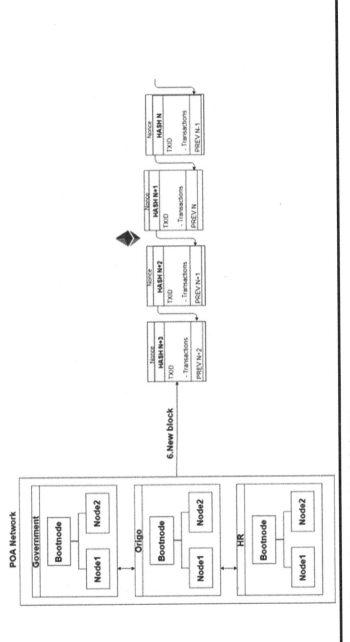

Figure 16.3 Adding of block to the blockchain[28]

blockchain technology provides democratic countries a new opportunity to make their way from a pen and paper election to a more costly and time-efficient voting scheme while improving the current system's safety measures offering new transparency. Using an Ethereum private blockchain, hundreds of transactions can be sent every second to the blockchain, using any smart contract element to load on the blockchain quickly. In larger countries, certain steps have to be taken to avoid more significant transactions per second, such as the parent & child architecture, decreasing the number of transactions stored on the blockchain by 1:100 without jeopardizing the security of the networks. The election scheme requires individual voters to vote in the voting district they prefer and ensures that each vote is counted from the correct district, thus increasing their participation.

References

[1] S. Nakamoto, "Bitcoin: A Peer-to-Peer Electronic Cash System," Satoshi Nakamoto Institute, 2008.

[2] B. Vitalik, "On Public and Private Blockchains," *Ethereum Blog Crypto renaissance salon*, 2015.

[3] R. Nair, S. Gupta, M. Soni, P. Kumar Shukla, and G. Dhiman, "An approach to minimize the energy consumption during blockchain transaction," *Mater. Today Proc.*, 2020,:DOI: 10.1016/j.matpr.2020.10.361.

[4] R. Nair, and A. Bhagat, "Healthcare Information Exchange Through Blockchain-Based Approaches," *Transforming Businesses With Bitcoin Mining and Blockchain Applications*, IGI Global, 234–246, 2019.

[5] M. Turkanović, M. Hölbl, K. Košič, M. Heričko, and A. Kamišalić, "EduCTX: A blockchain-based higher education credit platform," *IEEE Access*, 6, 5112–5127, 2018..

[6] S. Yoo, "Blockchain based financial case analysis and its implications," *Asia Pacific J. Innov. Entrep.*, 11, 312–321, 2017.

[7] R. Nair, and A. Bhagat, "An Application of Blockchain in Stock Market," 103–118, 2019.

[8] J. S. Dean, "Electronic voting with Scantegrity: Analysis and exposing a vulnerability," *Electron. Gov.*, 9, 27–45, 2012.

[9] M. Ramilli, and M. Prandini, "An integrated application of security testing methodologies to e-voting systems," in *Lecture Notes in Computer Science (including subseries Lecture Notes in Artificial Intelligence and Lecture Notes in Bioinformatics)*, 6229, 225–236, 2010.

[10] E. Jardine, "The Dark Web Dilemma: Tor, Anonymity and Online Policing," *SSRN Electron. J.*, 2018. DOI: 10.2139/ssrn.2667711.

[11] F. G. Birleanu, P. Anghelescu, and N. Bizon, "Malicious and deliberate attacks and power system resiliency," in Mahdavi Tabatabaei N., Najafi Ravadanegh S., Bizon N. (eds.) *Power Systems*, Springer, Cham, 223–246, 2019.

[12] L. Constantin, "Hackers found 47 new vulnerabilities in 23 IoT devices at DEF CON," *CIO*, 2016.

[13] C. Z. Acemyan, and P. Kortum, "Assessing the usability of the hart intercivic eslate during the 2016 presidential election," *Proceedings of the Human Factors and Ergonomics Society*, 61, 1404–1408, 2017.

[14] G. Allison, R. D. Blackwill, and A. Wyne, "Belfer Center for Science and International Affairs," in *Lee Kuan Yew*, 2020.

[15] J. Luo, and J. Huang, "Generative adversarial network: An overview," *Yi Qi Yi Biao Xue Bao/Chinese Journal of Scientific Instrument*, 40, 74–84, 2019.

[16] S. N. Goggin, M. D. Byrne, and J. E. Gilbert, "Post-Election Auditing: Effects of Procedure and Ballot Type on Manual Counting Accuracy, Efficiency, and Auditor Satisfaction and Confidence," *Elect. Law J. Rules, Polit. Policy*, 11, 36–51, 2012.

[17] A. Rodríguez-Pérez, P. Valletbó-Montfort, and J. Cucurull, "Bringing transparency and trust to elections: Using blockchains for the transmission and tabulation of results," in *ACM International Conference Proceeding Series*, 46–55, 2019.

[18] A. Lele, "Blockchain," in *Smart Innovation, Systems and Technologies*, 132, Springer, Singapore, 2019.

[19] A. Fowler, "Promises and Perils of Mobile Voting," *Elect. Law J. Rules, Polit. Policy*, 19, 418–431, 2020.

[20] S. Shankar, J. Madarkar, P. Sharma, Securing Face Recognition System Using Blockchain Technology. In: Bhattacharjee A., Borgohain S., Soni B., Verma G., Gao X.Z. (eds) *Machine Learning, Image Processing, Network Security and Data Sciences. MIND 2020. Communications in Computer and Information Science*, 1241, Springer, Singapore, 449–460, 2020.

[21] S. Namasudra, G. C. Deka, P. Johri, M. Hosseinpour, and A. H. Gandomi, "The Revolution of Blockchain: State-of-the-Art and Research Challenges," *Arch. Comput. Methods Eng.*, 28, 1497–1515, 2020.

[22] J. Taskinsoy, "Blockchain: A Misunderstood Digital Revolution. Things You Need to Know about Blockchain," *SSRN Electron. J.*, 1–25, 2019, DOI: 10.2139/ssrn.3466480.

[23] K. Toyoda, K. Machi, Y. Ohtake, and A. N. Zhang, "Function-Level Bottleneck Analysis of Private Proof-of-Authority Ethereum Blockchain," *IEEE Access*, 8, 141611–141621, 2020.

[24] Siraj Raval, *Decentralized Applications—Harnessing Bitcoin's Blockchain Technology*, O'Reilly Media, Sebastopol, CA, 2016.

[25] D. Korepanova, M. Nosyk, A. Ostrovsky, and Y. Yanovich, "Building a private currency service using exonum," in *2019 IEEE International Black Sea Conference on Communications and Networking, BlackSeaCom*, 1–3, 2019.

[26] A. Baliga, I. Subhod, P. Kamat, and S. Chatterjee, "Performance evaluation of the quorum blockchain platform," *arXiv preprint arXiv:1809.03421*, 1809, 2018.

[27] E. Kanimozhi and D. Akila, "Blockchain smart contracts on iot," *Int. J. Recent Technol. Eng.*, 8, 105–110, 2019.

[28] F. P. Hjalmarsson, G. K. Hreioarsson, M. Hamdaqa, and G. Hjalmtysson, "Blockchain-Based E-Voting System," in *IEEE International Conference on Cloud Computing, CLOUD*, 983–986, 2018.

Chapter 17

Leveraging Blockchain Technology for Decentralized Domain Name Broker Service

Sankita Patel, Ujjwal Kumar, Hrishabh Sharma,
Amruta Mulay, and Rishabh Kumar
Sardar Vallabhbhai National Institute of Technology, India

Contents

DOI: 10.1201/9781003129486-17

17.1 Introduction

With the advent of Blockchain technology, the world is shifting towards decentralization. The internet community is striving to move towards decentralized architecture, where users can have real control over their data. Attempts are being made to remove the brokers and centralized entities present in various case studies. One such use-case, which has not been given much attention in recent years but is worthwhile examining, is the secondary market of domain names.

In the current market of domain names, the domain brokers supply the service of buying/selling domain names. Domain name brokers are centralized entities who act as intermediaries in exchanging the ownership of domains and the value associated with it between the buyer and seller. These brokers charge a commission to supply the service to both parties. At the end of the process, the buyer gets the domain name access, and the agreed price is settled with the seller.

Our goal is to supply a service based on Blockchain technology to make the process transparent and reduce the commission charges to minimal. In the proposed service, there is no scope of frauds [refer to Section 17.4.4 of this chapter], which is a substantial concern given the current market scenario. The service (if economically workable) has the potential to create a competitive marketplace for domain selling and to replace completely other domain escrow services provided by the domain name registrars themselves.

17.1.1 Application

A meaningful and appropriate domain name can increase the website's traffic by improving the Search Engine Optimization (SEO) ranking. People might want to sell domain names that are no longer active, and this will help them to receive some money in return. The model aims to connect potential buyers and sellers to transfer domain name ownership. The application scope of the model is not limited solely to companies or organizations; it applied to almost everyone on the Internet.

17.1.2 Motivation

The exponential growth of the secondary market of the domain that motivates us to work on this idea is: With the exponential growth of internet users, domain owner-ship has also grown exponentially, thereby creating a massive demand for domain names. Different categories of domainers (individuals, organizations, etc.) have real-ized the value of attractive and unique domain names, thus creating a competitive secondary marketplace for domain names. There lies a rarity of good and appealing domain names. It even becomes uncommon for these domain names to return to the public domain. Even if it turns out to be so, it is regarded as a casualty or care-lessness on the part of the registrant. With the growth of the secondary market, it has also marked the advent of mediators or negotiators who play a vital role as third parties building favorable situations for transactions. The third parties also stand a chance to scam the buyer/seller involved to make extra profit.

17.1.3 Objective

The proposed work focuses on a growing secondary market of domains and entities involved with legacy **Domain Name Systems (DNS)** architecture. It implements a Blockchain-based service on top of the legacy system to allow domain owners (potential sellers) and their buyers to interact directly without any middlemen.

The aim is to make the process reliable and transparent, and to reduce the com-mission charges to minimal, thereby offering hassle-free service to domain buyers/sellers. In the proposed service, there is no scope for scams, which is a very sub-stantial concern with the current scenario of the market. The proposed service is economically feasible and has the potential to create a competitive marketplace for domain selling. The proposed system is transparent, reliable, and cost-effective, and has the prospective to completely replace other domain escrow services provided by the domain name registrars themselves.

17.1.4 Organization

Section 17.1 gives us a brief introduction to the topic highlighting the objectives, applications, and motivation that have encouraged us to work on the use-case. Section 17.2 contains the background of Domain Name Systems and the terms used in the study. It also provides a theoretical background of all the topics covered to help us get an in-depth understanding of the subject. Section 17.3 is concerned with the concepts and backgrounds of Blockchain technology. Section 17.4 discusses related work done and current implementation in this field. Section 17.5 contains a detailed report about the Blockchain-based proposed implementation methods needed to carry out the project. Section 17.6 discusses the selection of tools. Section 17.7 deals with system analysis and discussion. Finally, Section 17.8 concludes the work and introduces the open challenges.

17.2 Introduction to Domain Name System

This section covers the theoretical background needed to understand the proposed work. It includes a detailed explanation of all the terms of a Blockchain-based system. Additionally, it highlights the terms related to the domain name and its transfer.

17.2.1 Domain Names

Domain names are essentially a combination of letters, digits, and hyphens that are generally chosen so as to convey some meaning, acronyms, or even brand names. A domain name forms the base of **Uniform Resource Locator (URL)**, hence a domain name can also be seen as a component of URL. Further, there are different parts to a domain name; for the sake of convenience, however, we will only look at the top two levels.

A domain name consists of different parts which are called labels, and are concatenated by dots, for example, google.com. From the rightmost side, the first part is called the **top-level domain (TLD)**; in google.com, the TLD is 'com'. The second part/label in the domain name is called second-level domain; in google.com, the second-level domain is 'google'. The parts of the domain name from left to right represent the hierarchical structure of DNS; where each label in the left signifies further subdivision. A TLD has further two categorizations, namely **generic top-level domain (gTLD)** and **country-code top-level domain (ccTLD)**. Initially, there were a total of 7 gTLDs at the time of DNS designing which now has crossed the mark of 1200 gTLDs as of 2018 and 300+ ccTLDs (Figure 17.1).

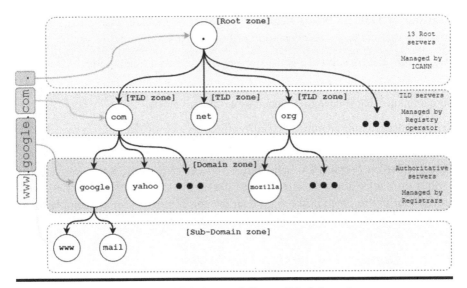

Figure 17.1 **The hierarchy of labels in a fully qualified domain name**

17.2.2 *Terminologies*

Referred from [1]. Throughout the chapter, we use the following terminologies related to the domain name system and domain name transfer.

TLD: Acronym for top-level domain. Examples of TLD include com, org, uk, us, in.

gTLD: Acronym for the generic top-level domain which is a category of TLD. Examples include com, org, net, gov.

ccTLD: Acronym for country code top-level domain which is the second categorization of TLD. It is primarily a two-character territory code of ISO-3166 country abbreviations.

DNS: It is an acronym for Domain Name System, which is a service on the Internet that handles maintaining a mapping of two primary naming systems on the Internet viz. The domain name and **Internet Protocol (IP)** addresses. The system is also responsible for replying to queries for resolving domain names to their corresponding IP addresses.

Certificate Authority (CA): These are trusted entities in the centralized and hierarchical **Public Key Infrastructure (PKI)** which handle approving other certificates on the Internet.

Registry Operator: Registry Operators are entities that manage the registry (database) of a particular TLD (categorized as gTLD and ccTLD) such as VeriSign which runs the '.com' and '.net' (both are gTLDs) registries.

Registrar or Domain Name Registrar: Registrar or Domain Name Registrar is a company that manages the reservation of Internet domain names.

Registrant: A registrant is an entity owning a registered domain name.

Buyer: Buyer in this document refers to an entity that is interested in buying a domain name that is currently owned by a different entity.

Seller: Seller refers to an entity that currently owns a particular domain name and is interested in selling that domain name to some other entity.

Domain Broker Service: Domain Broker Service refers to the service provided by various entities for domain ownership transfer between two interested parties. These are the entities that are in business for their own profit and act as a mediator between buyers and sellers. An entity providing this service is called Domain Broker.

17.2.3 Domain Ownership Verification

When a registrant buys a domain name, it is mandatory to provide required contact details (that include name, postal address, contact number, email address). This information is stored by the registrar, which is shared with the registry holder for the gTLD. Every gTLD database is managed by an organization called a registry holder, which gets information from the registrars.

Verifying domain ownership through the email address is acceptable because it's the primary mode of communication to the registrant. Also, we can easily verify an email address using the **One-Time Password (OTP)** based methods.

17.2.4 Accessing Registry Data

The registrant data (information shared at the time of registration) is stored with the registrar and shared with the registry. Till May 2018, one could find the contact information (name, email address, contact number, postal address) associated with a domain name, using WHOIS [2] protocol service [3]. This was possible because **Internet Corporation for Assigned Names and Numbers (ICANN)** made it mandatory for the registrars and registry to implement this public service (WHOIS) for the sake of identifying and contacting the owner of the domain. But this service has now been modified to bring it in line with the **General Data Protection Regulation (GDPR)** [4] policies (enforced in May 2018). So, WHOIS at its present state does not provide the contact details of the registrants (postal address, email address, contact number), hence we cannot use WHOIS for our verification process.

But WHOIS has now been accompanied by another service, namely **Registration Data Access Protocol (RDAP)** [5] which provides many features over the previous WHOIS protocol. RDAP is a successor to WHOIS, which provides access to information about Internet resources (domain names, IP addresses, and autonomous systems).

Unlike WHOIS, RDAP provides:

- A machine-readable representation of data
- Secure access to data
  - Over HTTPS
- Differentiated access
  - Limited access for anonymous users
  - Full access for authenticated users
- Standardized query, response, and error messages
- Internationalization
- Extensibility
  - Easy to add output elements

Since RDAP provides differentiated access, one can query RDAP service either anonymously or with some authentication. The response to anonymous queries contains redacted information (email addresses are redacted; along with other information). So, for our case study, we need to make authenticated queries to the RDAP service of the respective registry or registrar to verify the domain ownership via email address verification.

To get an authenticated account (for RDAP access), registrars provide an application form (similar to [6]) for access requests and upon successful application, the credentials are shared and authenticated queries will get full access to the required information.

Many RDAP clients have been implemented and some of them have already been deployed such as [7, 8] which can be used to send anonymous queries.

17.3 Background of Blockchain Technology

17.3.1 Blockchain

Blockchain is a distributed database in which data are stored in the form of blocks and each block (except the first block, known as the genesis block) contains the cryptographic hash of the previous block, thus giving it a chain-like structure. The linked structure makes the Blockchain an immutable data structure. The other important property of the Blockchain network architecture is 'Decentralization'. However, the degree of decentralization varies from one Blockchain platform to another, due to obvious trade-offs among characteristics of Blockchain [9].

17.3.1.1 Advantages of Blockchain

Blockchain technology has many inherent advantages over a client server-based approach; we will look at some of its advantages. The main aspect of Blockchain is

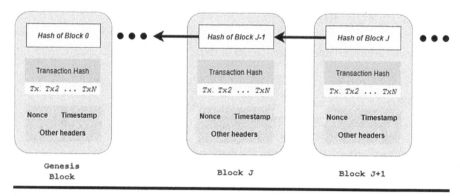

Figure 17.2   Illustration of Blockchain

that it is a decentralized system. This eliminates the central server. The decentralized system distributes the copy of the database to each of its participants on the network, thus making it almost infeasible to hack into the system (except for the "51% attack"). Every participant on the Blockchain network holds the information of the complete chain of blocks in encrypted form. These distributed copies are continuously and periodically synchronized; this removes a single point of failure, thus ensuring availability. The beauty of Blockchain is the transparency that it provides in the system which makes almost any operation to be easily traceable. Each time new information is added into the database, it gets added in the form of new blocks. These new data are collectively agreed upon by each of the other registered nodes on the network, thereby becoming a permanent part of the chain, which makes Blockchain an append-only database. Because of the irreversible nature of transactions, the publicly distributed database is still trusted on the network. The database is ubiquitous in nature—the technology is relevant not only in the financial sector, but also in other fields.

17.3.1.2 Types of Blockchain

Public Blockchain: Public Blockchain networks are open and anyone can join the network anytime and leave without any permission. In public Blockchains, there is no message passing between the participants for reaching the consensus. So, a single person is elected in some way, and incentivized, to decide the next state, and other participants verify. Therefore, a monetary asset is mostly associated with such Blockchains.

Private Blockchain: In private Blockchains, users are able to join or leave if they are authorized to do so. In private networks, consensus can be achieved through various classical algorithms, hence no monetary currency is attached to them.

17.3.1.3 Smart Contract

Smart contracts are basically pieces of code stored inside a Blockchain that serves as a type of agreement. It gets executed when certain pre-written conditions are met. Smart contracts eliminate the risk of any fraudulent activity from the participants.

17.3.1.4 Consensus Protocol

In a Blockchain network, consensus protocols are a way through which distrusted nodes or participants reach a single agreement about the next block to be added in the Blockchain.

In the case of permissioned and private Blockchain networks, participating nodes have valid identities issued by authorities like CA(s) and are known to each other. Such Blockchain networks use classical consensus protocols such as Paxos, Raft, **Practical Byzantine Fault Tolerance (PBFT)**, **Redundant Byzantine Fault Tolerance (RBFT)**, etc. to reach an agreement. On the other hand, the participating nodes are anonymous to each other, in the case of public Blockchain networks. So, to reach an agreement, a leader's election takes place. The leader election can be done in many ways, and that leads to various existing consensus protocols for such networks. The elected leader will be the one to propose a decision for the next block and the rest of the participating nodes validate the new proposed block. Some of the consensus protocols involving leader election, in the scope of our project are discussed below:

Proof of Work (PoW): Proof of Work (PoW) involves a leader election on the basis of solving a complex mathematical problem directly related to hashing. The selected problem is hard to solve, but can be easily verified by the rest of the nodes of the network. High computation power is required to solve the complex problem first, so the probability of getting elected as a leader is directly dependent on the computation power. Bitcoin [10] and Ethereum [11] networks use PoW to reach consensus. However, Ethereum is constantly making a move to shift towards **Proof of Stake (PoS)**. [12]

Proof of Stake (PoS): Proof of Stake (PoS) involves a leader election, in which the probability of being elected directly depends upon the amount of stake (can be the amount of cryptocurrency) the node/participant holds.

Delegated Proof of Stake (dPoS): Delegated Proof of Stake (dPoS) [13] protocol is a variation of the PoS mechanism. In the procedure involved, a fixed number of delegates are voted by the network participants. The delegates, also known as "Witnesses", decide the next block.

17.3.1.5 Comparison of Public Blockchain Network

Bitcoin: This is a **Peer-to-Peer (P2P)** electronic cash system, backed on a widely spread Bitcoin network. All the transactions are made in terms of its cryptocurrency transfer, viz. Bitcoin. It ensures the classical problem of double spending using a P2P network and using a powerful consensus algorithm 'Proof of Work'. It uses special scripts called 'Bitcoin Scripts' to govern transactional activities like sending bitcoins, claiming bitcoins, etc.

Ethereum: It is an open-source public Blockchain network, which, along with a cryptocurrency associated with it, also is able to carry other assets on its backbone Blockchain. The state changes of Ethereum can be easily governed by the Smart Contracts which are executed on **Ethereum Virtual Machine (EVM)**. The transaction on the Ethereum Transactions requires a fee, called Gas, in order to be successfully executed. The higher the gas amount a person is willing to pay for a transaction, the more early his/her transaction is executed on the Ethereum Network.

EOS: This is a public Blockchain network, which allows building decentralized applications on top of it. It also uses Smart Contracts to govern the transaction. But it differs from the existing public Blockchain platforms, in a way that the transactions on EOS are completely free. It uses a hybrid version of Proof of Stake, called Delegated Proof of Stake, to eliminate the transactional fee in the network. But this comes at the cost of a little amount of decentralization.

17.3.2 Detailed Comparison between Ethereum and EOS

Ethereum Platform introduced the concept of smart contracts and introduced the world to decentralized applications (or dApps). Soon after the launch Ethereum started getting more and more attention from the developer community. But the main concern of the Ethereum dApp users is the gas price required to change the state of the smart contract.

To overcome the concern of the users, EOS came into existence, claiming itself to be the dApp suitable platform, in which developers, rather than users, have to pay. So, there is no transaction fee in the EOS platform. They avoid the user transaction fee by claiming the cost through inflation.

Ethereum uses the mining-based consensus protocol, called Proof of Work (PoW). Due to the competition and time required to solve the challenge, the transaction throughput of Ethereum is low. Thus, at the present stage, Ethereum suffers from scalability factors. On the other hand, the decision of the next block is in the hands of 21 Block Producers, which are elected through staking. This lower participation of nodes in the consensus process makes the entire process faster, giving EOS a higher transaction throughput.

EOS always justifies its existence by the fact that it is more decentralized, by expressing the probability of shift of governance into few pool mines in the case of proof of work-based Blockchain platforms. But its own governance lying in the hands of 21 Block Producers, shows that EOS is preferring throughput over the decentralization level in the trade-off involved.

17.3.3 Smart Contract—Security Threats

As explained above, smart contracts are pieces of code that contain the business logic for managing fund transfer and other Blockchain-related transactions. These codes, once deployed, cannot be updated to apply any security patches. Since they are written in a programming language, it is quite obvious to introduce bugs while writing a smart contract and these bugs can lead to a loss of assets from their rightful owners.

17.3.3.1 Major Pitfalls in Smart Contract

Re-entrancy: This is a type of smart contract vulnerability which occurs due to unintended recursive calls within the smart contract by the attacker [14]. Suppose there is a crowdsourcing smart contract 'A', having simple deposit and withdraw functions. If there is a presence of re-entrancy in 'A', then a fallback function from another attacking smart contract 'B' can make recursive calls to the withdraw function of 'A', and withdraw all the crowdsourced funds.

Overflow and Underflow: The variable data types in the languages concerned with smart contracts have a definite maximum size to store the values. The maximum and minimum values are generally cyclic in nature. If the value of a certain variable is increased more than the maximum, then it will end up resulting in a number having a lesser value. This is called overflow. On the contrary, if a value when decreased ends up resulting in a greater value, then this is called underflow. Such types of attacks are common while writing smart contracts. Due to the underflow and overflow, the attacker can exploit the smart contract by giving invalid inputs. Such attacks can easily be handled by putting checks on the inputs accepted.

Short Address attack: This attack is more on the user-interface level rather than the smart contract level. It occurs when the user inputs an invalid address and subsequently the Smart Contract Engine executes it after padding.

Delegate Call: This is a function with a slight difference from the normal CALL method. The DELEGATE CALLS are always executed in the context of the caller environment. The primary use of this type of call is to make upgradable smart contracts. But these advantages can also bring serious vulnerability. If the functional

Table 17.1 Comparison of Public Blockchain Network

	Bitcoin	*Ethereum*	*EOS*
Consensus	PoW	PoW	dPoS
Transaction Fee	Yes	Yes	No
Smart Contract	No	Yes	Yes
TPS	7–8	15–20	4,000
Decentralization Level	High	High	Low

signature of the delegate call and the caller's contract function does not match, then the execution jumps to fallback and can cause many attacks possible.

Apart from the above-mentioned vulnerabilities, there are several more attacks, such as Timestamp Manipulation, Default Visibility, Exception Disorder, Typecast inconsistencies, Stack Size Limit, etc. To know about these vulnerabilities and more in detail refer [15, 16].

17.4 Current Implementation

The current system to transfer domain names consists of a broker which acts as a middleman between the participants. Domain name brokers are centralized entities [17].

17.4.1 Domain Brokers

There are different entities that provide broker services such as hosting providers, a registrar may also provide third-party services to serve as a domain broker. But the mandatory entity that is involved is a Domain Name Registrar, where the final ownership records are modified to complete the ownership transfer process.

Let's take the case of GoDaddy (an organization that provides Hosting Service, Domain Broker Service, and is a Domain Name Registrar itself). Here you can buy a new domain. But let's say we search for "paytm.com" (which is already owned by an entity). In such a case, GoDaddy's interface provides us with an option to take their Domain Broker Service. The "Broker Service Fee" as mentioned there is around > 4000 INR. Now, this fee is for hiring a personal Agent ("Domain Buy Agent" as GoDaddy calls it). Once an entity buys their service, then the negotiation with the current Registrant of "paytm.com" (which may or may not be interested in selling) proceeds. If the negotiation is finalized, then the Buyer will have to pay the final settled price for the domain plus any commission charged by the Service Provider. The GoDaddy's commission for the same is 20% of the settled price. So, in total, the Buyer pays (4000 + 1.2 * (Price of the Domain)) INR to GoDaddy and the original owner of "paytm.com" gets (Price of the Domain) INR.

17.4.2 Domain Transfer from One Registrant to Another

To transfer a domain name to another registrant, the owner can initiate a change of registrant by contacting the current registrar (typically through a web interface). The registrar will then ask for the owner's confirmation via a secure mechanism (which typically will take the form of an email to the registered name holder).

The owner must provide their confirmation within the number of days set by the registrar (not to exceed 60 days) or the transfer will not proceed. Once the registrar receives confirmation from the owner, they will process the transfer and notify the owner and the new registrant once the transfer is completed.

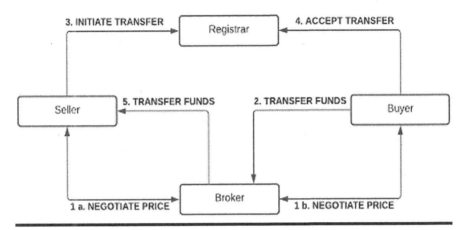

Figure 17.3 Broker's Role in a Centralized Environment

Going through the domain transfer process, it is evident that there is no extra charge involved in ownership transfer between registrants. But the current Domain Broker Services charge a lot.

17.4.3 A Typical (Centralized) Escrow Service

The seller (who is the current owner of the domain name) puts a listing on the broker's list through the interface. An interested buyer may visit the interface and see for different listings, showing his/her interests according to the requirement. Optionally, an interested buyer or potential seller may hire brokers for negotiating the prices in the process. After both the parties agree on a final value of the domain name, the ownership transfer of the domain name fund settlement process starts.

The buyer pays the agreed price + Escrow's commission to the Escrow provider's accounts. Once the funds are received by the Escrow provider, the seller is notified accordingly and provided with further transfer process. The seller has to transfer the ownership of the domain to the Buyer (or the Escrow provider depending on the terms of service). Once the above steps are completed in order, the Escrow provider transfers the funds to the seller's accounts and the domain name ownership to the buyer. All the progress of the process is updated accordingly and any party can view the status at any point of time. The Escrow provider may also put some deadline on the steps involved in the entire process (for example a deadline for the buyer to pay the agreed amount).

17.4.4 Problems with Centralized Approach

The current approach on which the secondary market is working has flaws related to trust between the parties involved. The following problems can easily arise in the current architecture.

Firstly, the buyer transfers the funds to the broker, the seller transfers the ownership of the domain name, but the broker scams and denies the funds transfer to the seller. Secondly, the buyer transfers the funds to the broker, but the seller doesn't complete the ownership transfer of the domain name, and the broker scams with the money received from the buyer. Thirdly, the existence of Brokers introduces the scope of various scams such as phishing attacks, click-baits, masquerade attacks, etc. Finally, due to non-transparency in the system, there is a large scope of overpricing from the broker's end to make more profit. As a result, the buyer may have to pay a greater amount.

17.4.5 Related Work

Currently, in the secondary market of domain names, we can see some major players who have been in the market for a few years now. They have developed strong trust and stability in the market.

Sedo.com [18] is a popular web platform for domain auction, a marketplace for buying and selling, with the option to park domains. Sedo also supplies a domain brokerage service. But it follows a centralized model of operation and the organization is the central entity that facilitates these services.

Another popular platform for domain selling is Escrow.com [19], which does not specialize in the secondary market of the domain, but it is a general platform to facilitate and provide escrow service for buying and selling goods and services online. This is also an established platform since its inception over a decade ago. Escrow.com is also based on a centralized model.

Apart from these consolidated platforms that involve the domain name secondary market, some other popular players are the major organizations around the domain name, such as GoDaddy which provides both Auction platform [20] and Broker Service [21].

Although these common platforms do exist, their mode of operation is centralized and is not very much trusted when we have newer technologies that can be used to design an open and much secure mechanism to carry out these transactions in the domain market. Till now, there are no decentralized platforms for the secondary market of the domain name.

17.5 Blockchain-Based Domain Broker System

A Blockchain-based service will replace the current Broker Services offered by various entities. The service will be replacing some of the costly, fraudulent, semi-transparent practices involved in the process.

17.5.1 Advantages

The middleman plays a vital role in the legacy DNS, but there are high possibilities for any scam to take place. In the new Blockchain-based approach, the elimination of the middleman assures no scope of fraud. Moreover, the Blockchain-based model is a decentralized system. This approach ensures that the brokers do not have a monopoly over the system and extract an unreasonable amount of money from both ends. Along with this, the implementation of the smart contracts in the system encourages trustful ownership transfer between the buyers and sellers.

Another noteworthy thing is that once a transaction concerning a particular buyer and seller has been settled, the ownership details of the same remain in the system, which is unchanged and permanent.

17.5.2 Implementation

In the concerned case study, we want to bring trust between the buyers and sellers for the transactions in the form of digital currency, governed by smart contracts without any need for centralized fiat currency. Keeping in mind all these points, choosing a public Blockchain platform will be more feasible for the selected case study.

The implementation will include a web interface where sellers can list the domain for selling. While making an initial request for listing a domain for sale, the seller has to set a base price for auction on the platform. Interested buyers can put on their bids on the domains which they want to buy. The auction process will be completely governed by a separate smart contract. During bidding the visitors will have to transfer the bid amount at the contract address.

The amount paid by the auction winner will be transferred to the seller's account after ownership transfer of the domain and the rest of the pooled money will be transferred back to the bidder's addresses. All the data related to the listing of the domains will be governed by another smart contract.

17.5.2.1 Value Proposition of Domain Names Using Auction

AFNIC has suggested in one of their Issue Papers [17] that the value of a domain name is determined mostly by factors (like search engine rankings, the meaning of the name, public perception, keyword competition, traffic analysis, etc.) which cannot be formulated easily (at least has not been formulated till date). Moreover, an individual/organization may prioritize these factors differently (based on their opinion), making the valuation even more difficult.

Hence in our opinion, a bidding platform is the most suitable way to determine the value associated with a domain name. For the scenario at hand, we have decided on an English auction type to keep the bidding process intuitive to the bidders. The bidding will be public (i.e. all the bidding made will be publicly visible as the bidding continues). Also, a person can put multiple bids for the same listed domain [22].

17.5.2.2 Components

The entire architecture of our solution comprises the following components: 1) user-facing application, also known as 'dApp', 2) Public Blockchain platform, 3) centralized service to connect with dApp and perform off-chain tasks required, such as email verification, domain name ownership verification, domain name transfer verification, and 4) smart contracts governing the business logic for the auction process and automatic settlement of funds.

17.5.2.3 Detailed Procedure

The entire process starts when a seller lists the domain name owned by him/her on the platform. While listing, the seller is supposed to provide some details through our web interface—contact email, domain name, base price. A domain name submitted for listing is checked for seller's ownership. If the system can confirm that current ownership is found to be with the seller, the domain is successfully listed for bidding (adding it to the Blockchain) otherwise an error is displayed to the seller (through the interface).

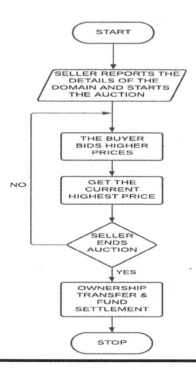

Figure 17.4   Auction Activity

For the ownership verification process, a request is sent to the centralized servers that handle the verification off-chain using information fetched from the registry's RDAP service. A successful verification response is conveyed to the Smart Contract securely. Once a domain name is listed for bidding, the seller has the choice of starting the bidding; if bidding is in progress, he/she can end the bidding too. A potential buyer can bid in ongoing bidding for a domain listing (again through the interface and managed via smart contract). The information related to a domain listing (bid value and bidders) is also displayed on the webpage. To participate in the bidding, the bidder will have to pay the amount that he/she bids with.

Upon the end of the bidding process, the bidder with the highest bid value is the potential buyer. The seller is supposed to (and is informed accordingly by our service) transfer the ownership of the domain name to the highest bidder in a given time duration (downtime period). The service's back-end structure will check for the ownership transfer progress to the rightful owner. If the transfer is successful in the given duration, the fund settlement with the seller takes place and the pooled funds of other bidders are refunded. However, if the ownership transfer doesn't happen in the given span of time, the bidding is revoked and all the pooled funds are refunded to the respective bidders.

17.5.2.4 Actors' Involvement

The different actors involved in interaction with our system are: Seller, Buyer/ Highest Bidder, Bidder and Visitor.

17.6 Selection of Tools

Choosing the right Blockchain platform is necessary as it will also determine what other tools, frameworks, **Software Development Kit (SDK)**, and **Integrated Development Environment (IDE)**, will be used in the process.

From our detailed comparison in Section 17.3.2, we get an idea of trade-offs made by the platform. According to the requirement of the service, we believe that Ethereum would be a good choice for the Blockchain platform as it is a public Blockchain network, provides decentralized application development, has matured itself in terms of both popularity and improvements to its software and protocols. Apart from that the development tools, **Application Programming Interface (API)**, IDEs, programming language, and compiler are all well managed by the community and very popular. In addition, the community support of Ethereum has been growing ever since.

For building a decentralized application, known as dApp on Ethereum, the following tools, libraries, and frameworks are sufficient: Remix IDE, Ganache, Truffle JS, Web3 JS and Metamask.

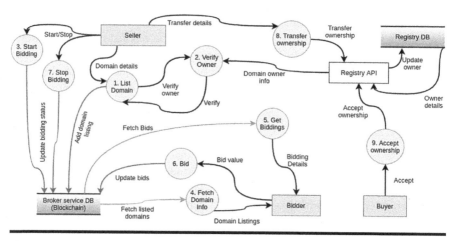

Figure 17.5   Blockchain-based Approach to Transfer Domain Names

Remix IDE is an IDE to write smart contracts for Ethereum. It supports famous languages like Solidity and Vyper. It also allows the efficient debugging of smart contracts.

Ganache is a local implementation of Ethereum, which you can run on your own machine. It allows the local system testing of the dApp.

Truffle JS is a JavaScript library to facilitate the development of dApp on your system. It provides a local solidity compiler to compile the smart contracts. It

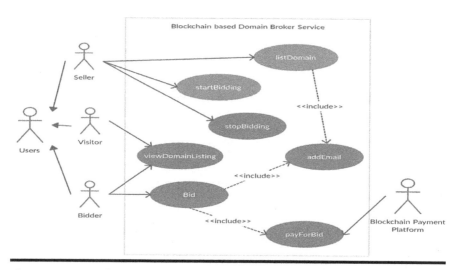

Figure 17.6   Involvement of Various Actors in the System

also allows the deployment of the smart contract to the local ganache network or Ethereum test-nets.

Web3 JS is also a JavaScript library that helps in creating a connection between the Ethereum Blockchain and the web application.

Metamask is a wallet, which helps in signing the transaction and connecting the dApp with the local Ethereum ganache network, test networks, or main networks.

Lastly, we talked about smart contract vulnerabilities in Section 17.3.3 and also mentioned some scenarios where small bugs in contracts led to a huge economic loss to the people involved. It also raises questions about trust issues on Blockchain platforms. To avoid bugs in the smart contract, there are some popular tools (called Fuzzers) available that automate the fuzzing on smart contracts to find potential bugs. Among the tools that provide support for Ethereum and Solidity language are **Echidna** and **SmartCheck.**

17.7 System Analysis and Discussion

Since Blockchain can resist traditional cyberattacks very well, the problems mentioned in Section 17.4.4 of this chapter are easily handled because the core functions of the proposed work processes will be governed by the smart contracts containing the business logic for checking the ownership transfer and funds transfer.

Although the secondary market established on the top of the Blockchain technology provides advantages discussed in Section 17.5.1, the architecture is not foolproof from various attacks as cybercriminals are always developing new approaches specifically for Blockchain technology. Additionally, Blockchain technology has some limitations which can affect the system performance, efficiency, and system resources. In this section, we try to explain possible attacks on the system and the challenges that Blockchain brings with itself which may impact the Blockchain-based system.

The attacks on the proposed architecture can be categorized based on the components involved in the system. At the highest level, the system can face attacks that can be categorized as: attacks on the centralized components/services (that aid the core decentralized components); and attacks on the decentralized components.

17.7.1 Attacks on Decentralized Components

Some of the attacks target the **Blockchain network or the P2P network** of nodes. This is possible because of the existing vulnerabilities in the protocols used by the network for communication, such as **Distributed Denial of Service (DDoS)**, Routing attack (**Border Gateway Protocol (BGP) hijacking**), Timejacking, and Ellipse attack.

There are also attacks that are focused on exploiting loopholes in the **consensus protocols** used by the Blockchain platform; an attack on the heart of the Blockchain platform. Some of the examples are the 51% Attack, the Long-Range Attack, and the Sybil Attack.

There has been an advent of **cryptocurrency wallets** as there has been an increase in the popularity and user base of Blockchain platforms. The architecture of these wallet services is largely centralized and are not Blockchain-based services. Hence cryptocurrency wallets are prone to attacks such as Phishing, Dictionary attack.

The **smart contracts** are a means to perform unbiased transactions (without the involvement of a third party or governing body) to append data to the Blockchain database. Since a smart contract is a piece of a program written by developers there is a high possibility of bugs being introduced in this crucial component of Blockchain technology. These bugs affect a Blockchain platform adversely and also cause huge economic losses. Among the issues that a smart contract is prone to are Short address attack, Integer Overflow/Underflow, Re-entrancy.

The attacks on the first three components are the result of existing faults in the system itself and hence the development of solutions for them are beyond the scope of this case study. Although some of those attacks can be prevented by making a choice of Blockchain network that is resilient to as many network-based attacks as possible. In addition, we can make a selection of a Blockchain network that utilizes a consensus protocol immune to most of the attacks.

Still, special attention is to be given, while writing the pooling contracts for auction which can lead to various Smart Contract Attacks [23] due to Re-entrancy, Underflow, and Overflow, etc. Once deployed on the network smart contracts cannot be updated for security patches. This is because smart contract deployment occurs through a block transaction on the Blockchain network and due to Blockchain's immutability feature nothing can be modified on the network. The famous DAO Attack [24] is a great example of the security attack on a smart contract costing millions of dollars simply as a consequence of bugs in the smart contract code.

Therefore, the analysis to find smart contract vulnerabilities needs to be done through various Smart Contract Analysis and Fuzzing tools. Fuzzing is a software testing technique that consists of finding implementation bugs with the help of malformed/semi-malformed data injection. Fuzzers are software tools that are used to automate the fuzzing process. Among the most popular fuzzing tools are Echidna and SmartCheck.

17.7.2 Limitations of Blockchain

Scalability issue—This is a big limitation of the Blockchain network that is not at all scalable, either horizontally or vertically. This comes as a result of consensus mechanisms that are independent of network capacity as a whole, but depend on the computational capacity of individual nodes that have to solve the mathematically complex problem in PoW. A service such as a broker service may demand a relatively scalable architecture.

Solution: At present, there are two proposed solutions that try to introduce scalability to the Blockchain network: Lightning Network and the Plasma. Both try to increase the TPS of any Blockchain network by creating secure channels between two parties/nodes on the network and thus allowing them to exchange information at a speed not limited by the original Blockchain network.

Inefficiency—A Blockchain network is considered to be highly redundant in terms of storage and computation. The consensus algorithms and mining operations (that make up for the core part of Blockchain) are highly redundant in the sense that every node performs these operations individually on their own copy of the database (distributed ledger). Since there is so much computational redundancy from the computational point of view, it can be said that this is an inefficient system. This is the case with the PoW consensus mechanism.

Solution: (A) New consensus mechanisms are a solution to the current (though secure but) highly inefficient approach of PoW, PoS, dPoS can be a solution to this problem. (B) Lightning Network, as mentioned earlier, can also solve this issue.

Huge database—Blockchain derives part of its strength from a P2P network with distributed databases. Since a Blockchain database is an append-only ledger that is public, its size can grow exponentially. As of Q3 2020, the Bitcoin network has a total of 302 GB [25]. On similar grounds, Ethereum's data amount to 551 GB as of Q3 2020 [26]. Even though for verification purposes, the entire database is not required (Simple Payment Verification allows verification using only the required block), but for the Blockchain network to be more distributed a significant number of nodes should download the entire database. Hence only systems with high resources can participate in the network thus reducing level decentralization.

Solution: (A) One idea is to deploy data servers. (B) The concept of the Merkle tree can reduce the size of the database by approximately 200 times. There can be several approaches to this problem and it is easy to tackle. One of the possible solutions is 'Sharding' [27].

17.8 Conclusion and Open Challenges

We explored the working of the current secondary markets of domain names and their functioning. We also looked at various issues that the current centralized model of operation has and how the inherent features of Blockchain can be utilized to design architecture without such issues. We have also explored how our Blockchain-based implementation can be thought of as a replacement for the current market. Along with the implementation, we discussed our way through what are the best possible choices of architecture for our implementation, various trade-offs made, and the enhancements (to the current model) that the new Blockchain-based service brings to the table. There has been a discussion on the data flow among the various components of the architecture and how they are connected. In conclusion, such a Blockchain-based service is feasible to implement using the current technologies that will provide a trustless platform for the secondary market of domain name buying and selling.

17.8.1 Challenges

The proposed solution discussed here tries to make a decent compromise between scalability, decentralization, consensus, and cost factors which might not be as suitable after a few years given that the current Blockchain technology is still evolving at a fast pace. Along with all the advantages and impact on the fee reduction in the secondary market of domain names through the Blockchain-based approach, one serious challenge is scalability. As discussed, the public Blockchain platform will be more feasible for the case study, but the trade-offs in public Blockchain usually lower down the performance. Overcoming the right solution to meet the high-performance benchmarks for the case study will be a challenge. Layer-2 Blockchain solutions are possible approaches for the same. Another challenge is our system deals with two databases: On-chain database (Blockchain) and Off-chain database (registry database). Connecting these together can pose a lot of security loopholes that can impact the overall system. This will require further testing and thorough analysis of proposed solutions. Currently, Oracles are used whenever smart contracts need to deal with off-chain data; but that may not be a feasible solution considering the scalability and cost factors.

List of Acronyms

AFNIC	Association Française Pour le Nommage Internet en Coopération
BGP	Border Gateway Protocol
CA	Certificate Authority
ccTLD	Country code Top Level Domain
DAO	Decentralized Autonomous Organization
DDoS	Distributed Denial of Service
DNS	Domain Name System
dPoS	Delegated Proof of Stake
EVM	Ethereum Virtual Machine
GDPR	General Data Protection Regulation
gTLD	Generic Top Level Domain
HTTPS	Hypertext Transfer Protocol Secure
ICANN	The Internet Corporation for Assigned Names and Numbers
OTP	One Time Password

P2P   Peer to Peer
PBFT   Practical Byzantine Fault Tolerance
PKI   Public Key Infrastructure
PoS   Proof of Stake
PoW   Proof of Work
RBFT   Redundant Byzantine Fault Tolerance
RDAP   Registration Data Access Protocol
SEO   Search Engine Optimization
TLD   Top Level Domain
TPS   Transactions Per Second
URL   Uniform Resource Locator

References

[1] ICANN, *Resources*, [online] Available: www.icann.org/resources

[2] ICANN, *WHOIS*, [online] Available: https://whois.icann.org/en/about-whois

[3] ICANN, *Temporary Specification for gTLD Registration Data*, [online] Available: https://www.icann.org/en/system/files/files/gtld-registration-data-temp-spec-17may18-en.pdf

[4] GDPR, *What is GDPR*, [online] Available: https://gdpr.eu/what-is-gdpr/

[5] ICANN, *Registration Data Access Protocol (RDAP)*, [online] Available: https://www.icann.org/rdap

[6] RDAP Access, *RDAP Access request form from GoDaddy for.biz domain*, [online] Available: https://rddsrequest.nic.biz/

[7] Tool, RDAP Client, [online] Available: https://client.rdap.org/

[8] ICANN, *RDAP client on ICANN*, [online] Available: https://lookup.icann.org/

[9] Niclas Kannengießer, Sebastian Lins, Tobias Dehling, Ali Sunyaev, "Trade-offs between Distributed Ledger Technology Characteristics", *ACM Computing Surveys*, Vol. 53, No. 2, p. 42, May 2020

[10] Satoshi Nakamoto, "Bitcoin: A peer-to-peer electronic cash system", 2008, [online] Available: https://bitcoin.org/bitcoin.pdf.

[11] Dr. Gavin Wood, "Ethereum: A secure decentralised generalised transaction ledger, EIP-150 revision", 2014, [online] Available: https://gavwood.com/paper.pdf

[12] Ethereum, "Introducing Casper the Friendly Ghost | Ethereum Foundation Blog", [online] Available: https://blog.ethereum.org/2015/08/01/introducing-casper-friendly-ghost/

[13] BitShares, "Delegated Proof of Stake (DPOS) —BitShares Documentation", [online] Available: https://how.bitshares.works/en/master/technology/dpos.html

[14] Chinen, Yuichiro, Yanai, Naoto, Cruz, Jason Paul and Okamura, Shingo, "Hunting for Re-Entrancy Attacks in Ethereum Smart Contracts via Static Analysis", *2020 IEEE International Conference on Blockchain (Blockchain)*, pp. 327–336, doi: 10.1109/Blockchain50366.2020.00048.

[15] Atzei, Nicola, Bartoletti, Massimo and Cimoli, Tiziana, "A survey of attacks on Ethereum smart contracts", [online] Available: https://img.chainnews.com/paper/f8084c122c0dfefd33e6bf03246597e8.pdf

[16] S. Sayeed, H. Marco-Gisbert and T. Caira, "Smart Contract: Attacks and Protections," *IEEE Access*, Vol. 8, pp. 24416–24427, 2020, doi: 10.1109/ACCESS.2020.2970495.

[17] AFNIC, "The secondary market for domain names", 2010, [online] Available: https://www.afnic.fr/medias/documents/afnic-issue-paper-secondary-market-2010-04.pdf.

[18] Sedo, "Sedo company details, the best place for domains is Sedo.com", [online] Available: https://sedo.com/us/about-us/

[19] Escrow, "About Escrow.com, The Online Escrow Service—Escrow.com", [online] Available: https://www.escrow.com/why-escrowcom/about-us

[20] GoDaddy Broker Service, "Domain Broker | Your Domain Buy Service—GoDaddy", [online] Available: https://godaddy.com/domains/domain-broker

[21] GoDaddy Auction, "Domain Auction | Buy & Sell Distinctive Domains—GoDaddy", [online] Available: https://auctions.godaddy.com/

[22] Wikipedia.Org, "Online auction—Wikipedia" [online] Available: https://en.wikipedia.org/wiki/Online_auction

[23] S. Sayeed, H. Marco-Gisbert and T. Caira, "Smart Contract: Attacks and Protections," *IEEE Access*, vol. 8, pp. 24416–24427, 2020, doi: 10.1109/ACCESS.2020.2970495.

[24] X. Zhao, Z. Chen, X. Chen, Y. Wang and C. Tang, "The DAO attack paradoxes in propositional logic," *2017 4th International Conference on Systems and Informatics (ICSAI)*, Hangzhou, 2017, pp. 1743–1746, doi: 10.1109/ICSAI.2017.8248566.

[25] Blockchain.com, "Blockchain Charts", [online] Available: https://www.blockchain.com/charts/blocks-size

[26] Etherscan.io, "Ethereum Full Node Sync (Default) Chart | Etherscan", [online] Available: https://etherscan.io/chartsync/chaindefault

[27] S. S. M. Chow, Z. Lai, C. Liu, E. Lo and Y. Zhao, "Sharding Blockchain," *2018 IEEE International Conference on Internet of Things (iThings) and IEEE Green Computing and Communications (GreenCom) and IEEE Cyber, Physical and Social Computing (CPSCom) and IEEE Smart Data (SmartData)*, Halifax, NS, Canada, 2018, pp. 1665–1665, doi: 10.1109/Cybermatics_2018.2018.00277.

Chapter 18

Using Blockchain for Digital Copyrights Management

Nirmal Kumar Gupta
Manipal University Jaipur, India

Anil Kumar Yadav
IES College of Technology, India

Ashish Jain
Manipal University Jaipur, India

Contents

DOI: 10.1201/9781003129486-18

18.1 Introduction

Copyright is an important part of intellectual property rights and has a natural connection with culture and innovation. Strengthening copyright protection is the key to become culturally powerful for any country. However, with the advent of the social media era, the threshold for digital content creation is gradually lowering, and digital content such as online literature, pictures, audio and video has exploded. The digital content market is welcoming rapid prosperity, while copyright infringement problems have become increasingly serious. Massive digital content is rapidly disseminated through the current Internet ecological environment. The "inherent deficiencies" of digital content, such as "replicability, non-exclusivity, and easy tampering", have led to ubiquitous digital copyright infringements and frequent online copyright lawsuits [1]. Online reprinting, short videos, animation, webcasting, knowledge sharing, audiobooks, online film and television, online literature, online music and other fields, as well as platforms such as e-commerce platforms, application stores, and online cloud storage spaces, are all target areas for piracy and infringement.

Digital content products generally include digital music, digital books, digital videos, digital games, etc. The main links in the full life cycle of their products involve the production, reproduction, circulation and dissemination of digital content products. Blockchain has the advantages of non-tampering and traceability of data, ensuring the authenticity, integrity, openness, transparency, and traceability of data, and overcoming the deficiencies of "replicability and easy tampering" of digital content [2]. It can trace the entire life cycle of digital copyright content.

This chapter aims to focus on the current status and existing problems of digital copyright development and analyse how blockchain technology can better integrate with digital copyright applications. This chapter is divided into seven parts. The first part focuses on the related concepts, connotations and digital copyright industry chain of digital copyright; the second part introduces the current situation of the digital copyright industry and the problems existing in digital copyright protection; the third part mainly analyses blockchain digital copyright application feasibility and application direction; the fourth part analyses the current status of blockchain digital copyright application, blockchain copyright application mode, technical architecture and typical cases; the fifth part focuses on the analysis of blockchain digital copyright application challenges; the sixth part analyses the development trend of blockchain digital copyright applications; the seventh part puts forward the development suggestions of blockchain digital copyright applications.

18.2 The Basic Concepts and Connotation of Digital Copyright

18.2.1 Origin of Copyright

Copyright began in the late Renaissance. The term derives from the English word copyright, the right to copy, which reflects the right created by law to prevent others from copying works without permission and harming the author's economic interests.

Before the advent of printing, copyright concepts and mechanisms did not exist. In the Middle Ages, books were copied by hand, and the cost of piracy was the same as the cost of producing the original book, so there was no motive for piracy. In the middle of the fifteenth century, the invention of printing led to mass production of publishing. In 1709, in order to protect the interests of printers and authors, the United Kingdom promulgated the "Queen Anne's Act", which stipulated that copyright originated from the author and protected the author's exclusive right to print, reprint and publish works for a certain period of time [3]. The "Queen Anne's Act" is considered the world's first copyright law, which makes copyright a common right, and anyone can own a copyright.

18.2.2 Acquisition of Copyright

Acquisition of copyright can be acquired in two ways: automatic acquisition and registration acquisition.

Automatic acquisition is a principle established by the Berne Convention for the Protection of Literary and Artistic Works and also a copyright acquisition principle established by the copyright laws of most countries in the world. In India, the rule allows to get the copyright automatically and for this no formality is required. Copyright appears when a work is made and no convention is needed to be finished for getting copyright. However, certificate of registration of copyright and also the entries created in that function clear proof in an exceedingly court of law with respect to dispute regarding possession of copyright.

Copyright registration is a preliminary proof that the copyright owner enjoys the copyright of the work. The clarification of copyright ownership through copyright registration will help to resolve copyright disputes caused by copyright ownership and provide preliminary evidence for the settlement of copyright disputes (see Figure 18.1).

18.2.3 Digital Copyright

Digital copyright is the enrichment and complement of copyright entering the digital age. It is the right of the author to save, copy, and distribute digital works in a

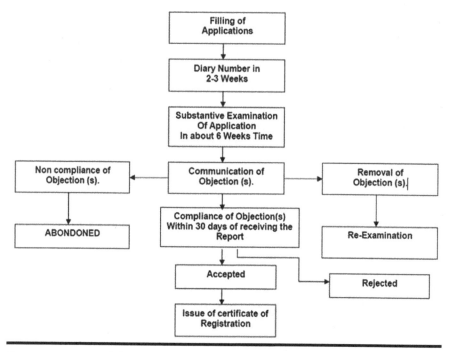

Figure 18.1 Copyright registration process in India

digital way. Digital works are usually solidified in physical media or carriers such as hard disks and optical discs in the form of binary digits, and are transmitted in the form of digital signals through the network.

18.2.3.1 Digital Works

Digital works are the objects of digital copyright protection. The industry's definition of digital works is not uniform. Generally speaking, digital works include two types, one of which is the digitization of traditional works. Fixing traditional works on tangible carriers such as disks or optical discs in the form of digital codes will essentially change the expression and fixed form of the work, and will not have any impact on the "originality" and "reproducibility" of the work. For example, the digitization of traditional publications, such as newspapers, periodicals, books, etc. and the digitization of films; the other is works that naturally exist in digital form for example, computer software, mobile games, etc. (see Table 18.1) [4].

18.2.3.2 Digital Copyright Industry Chain

The digital copyright industry chain can be divided into four parts: upstream, midstream, downstream and digital copyright services [5]. The upstream mainly includes original creators and content providers, including publishing houses, digital periodicals and newspapers, recording companies, game and animation producers, directors, musicians, photographers and other corporate organizations and individuals. Digital content works mainly involve music, movies, TV shows, literary works, etc.

Midstream mainly includes platform service providers such as channel sales platforms. Platform service providers do not produce content themselves, and mainly rely on the advantages of technology, network channels and traffic portals, integrate digital content resources, and provide external retrieval portals and search services. Platform service providers use technological advantages to integrate and operate digital resources, which helps content providers to focus on quality content production.

The downstream mainly includes hardware terminal manufacturers, software terminal developers and digital distributors. Terminal producers and digital distributors are the closest to users and can be considered downstream of publishing. Digital distributors are generally divided into three categories: distributors, retailers and online distribution platforms. Online distribution platforms are currently the most important form.

Digital copyright service is mainly a technology and solution provider that provides a series of services such as copyright registration, copyright transaction, copyright evaluation, and copyright protection for digital content publications. Digital copyright service is an important part of the digital copyright industry chain.

Table 18.1 Covered Areas of Copyrighted Works

Literary works	This can incorporate books, verifiable works, sonnets, articles, papers, essays, speeches, advertisements, discourses, and software programs.
Musical works	This incorporates any mix of melody and harmony. Any of them may be converted to composing or graphically created or replicated.
Dramatic works	Emotional works incorporates plays, screenplays, operas, choreographic shows and any accompanying music. Any work that's meant to be performed dramatically could be a dramatic work.
Choreographic and Pantomimes works	Choreography and pantomimes are also considered as copyrightable dramatic works. Choreography can be called as the composition and planning of dance movements and patterns typically included throughout the music. Distinctly from choreography, pantomime is the art of imitating or acting out things, characters, or alternative events.
Pictorial, graphic and sculptural works	Pictorial, realistic, and sculptural works incorporates two- or three-dimensional work of realistic sketches, drawings, photos, prints, art reproductions, maps, globes, graphs, charts, models, and specialized drawings together with compositional plans.
Motion pictures and other audio-visual works	Films and other varying media works are consisting of a progression of related pictures that are expected to be appeared by the utilization of a machine or gadget, along with going with sounds, if any. It covers a wide scope of cinematographic works included in movies, tapes, video circles, and other media.
Sound recordings	Sound recordings include recorded sounds, it can be either musical and non-musical. Various types of works, such as recorded music, songs, audio books, sound effects, speeches & interviews recordings, audio podcasts, soundtracks etc., are included in this category.
Compilations	You can put together a collection of existing materials and the collection as a whole can be termed as copyrighted.

It focuses on the protection of digital copyright and aims to realize the safe circulation of copyright value. Generally speaking, digital copyright protection includes digital copyright confirmation, digital copyright monitoring, infringement evidence collection, and digital copyright protection [6]. Other digital copyright services also include digital copyright transactions, digital copyright value evaluation, and digital copyright fee settlement.

18.3 Development Status and Problems of Digital Copyright Industry

Copyright is the right to rewrite or copy. Historically, copy technology has experienced three major leaps: printing technology, electronic technology and digital technology. Each leap has brought about a revolution in copy methods. The form of content works will break through the scope of application of copyright law, leading to new challenges for the global copyright legal system. Countries around the world have to respond by revising and improving copyright laws.

As one of the most developed countries in the global publishing industry, the United States has the most complete and mature copyright laws, including the earliest digital copyright protection legislation, detailed and specific legal regulations, strong operability, and frequent revisions [7]. Legal developments, including the "Copyright Law", "Intellectual Property and National Information Infrastructure" and "Millennium Digital Copyright Act", have formed a relatively complete digital copyright legal system in the United States. The United Kingdom, Germany and other western countries have actively revised and introduced a series of digital version-related legal systems to deal with copyright in the digital contents protection issues [8], and actively participating in the formulation of copyright laws and rules, and strive to protect national interests according to international laws.

18.3.1 Digital Copyright Protection

Technical solutions introduce new forms of digital content works and rapid changes in distribution modes have brought challenges to digital copyright protection and forced the continuous evolution of digital copyright protection technology. According to the stage at which copyright protection technology plays a role in the copyright dissemination cycle, copyright protection technical solutions can be divided into three main categories: pre-dissemination, dissemination and post-dissemination stages [9].

With the rapid development of Internet technology, new media based on social media gradually occupy the mainstream of major digital publishing fields. The production cost of digital content has been greatly reduced, and the media revolution and the revolution in communication methods have caused the reproduction and reproduction of digital content works. Dissemination tends to be "zero-cost", and communication channels are diversified. The Internet has increasingly become a high-prone area for infringement and piracy. Internet piracy has brought severe challenges to the copyright industry with innovation as its core.

18.3.2 Problems in Digital Copyright Industry

Digital copyright service is the core of the digital copyright industry, and it focuses on digital copyright protection. In particular, digital copyright protection is an important guarantee for the development of the digital copyright industry. It is of great significance for inspiring the creative enthusiasm of digital copyright creators, promoting the healthy and rapid development of the digital copyright industry, and promoting the cultural prosperity of any country. However, due to the continuous evolution of digital works, the increasing diversity of communication channels, the huge coverage space and scope of influence, the low cost of infringement, the concealment of infringement methods, and the high cost of judicial rights protection, digital copyright protection still faces many difficulties [10].

18.3.3 Copyright Confirmation Difficulties

Work copyright registration is an important means of copyright protection. Copyright registration helps to resolve copyright disputes caused by the ownership of rights, and can provide judicial evidence for the settlement of copyright disputes [11]. However, traditional copyright registration still has the following problems: First, the copyright registration cycle duration is long. Traditional copyright registration relies on offline manual review, and there is a long waiting time. It usually takes 20 to 30 working days from copyright registration to obtaining the certificate Second, the cost of copyright registration of works is relatively high. If the registrant does not entrust an intermediary agency to handle it, due to lack of professional guidance, the registration materials may be returned for modification and perfection, which increases time cost and effort; if an intermediary is entrusted to handle it, an additional processing service fee will be required in addition to the registration fee, which greatly increases the cost; The copyright owner is not very active in registration. The current copyright protection process is low in efficiency, and in anticipation of difficulties in protecting rights, copyright owners are not motivated to register copyright.

18.3.4 Difficulty in Infringement Monitoring

Since the media age, the threshold for digital content creation has been lowered, and there has been an explosion in digital content creation such as online literature, pictures, audio and video. Massive digital content has been used and disseminated by major media platforms and circles of friends, Infringements have also risen. It is difficult to effectively monitor infringements for the following reasons: First, manual monitoring is completely unable to cope with massive data. Only the original creator will pay attention to whether digital content has been infringed. In the situation of massive amounts of data, it is completely impossible to judge whether it has been infringed by the original creator's own monitoring. In addition, evidence of the infringement of digital works may be easily altered and it is difficult for this to be traced. The second is the lack of technical identification capabilities. Limited to the technical level, AI recognition technology cannot yet fully identify infringements performed by tampering [12]. Third, the monitoring scope is small and the monitoring network is single. The scope of the monitoring network is limited to departmental websites, communities and social media, and it is not yet possible for the whole network to be monitored. In addition, most existing infringement monitoring systems can only monitor digital content in a certain field, such as pictures. Fourth, it is difficult to keep track of infringing websites. Infringing websites frequently change their appearances to avoid monitoring and tracing.

18.3.5 Difficulty in Collecting Evidence

Internet application scenarios are complex, with multiple channels and fast circulation. After digital content is processed by pirates, it is almost impossible to trace back. In particular, the methods and channels of infringement are becoming more and more varied, diverse, and concealed, leading to repeated prohibitions on infringements. This is due to the lack of effective protection technology and methods for original works by all parties. On the other hand, the difficulty in safeguarding rights and obtaining evidence also encourages infringement. The difficulty of protecting rights is a chronic problem of copyright protection. The main reasons are: First, it is difficult to obtain evidence in the network environment. The virtuality, concealment and no space and time restrictions of online torts make it more difficult to obtain evidence. In copyright infringement cases, the copyright owner needs to prove the infringement by means of webpage screenshots and other methods when presenting evidence. However, the court does not necessarily accept such evidence, and even requires a notary institution to issue a notarization document and restore the complete process of obtaining such data. In addition, the relatively high cost of notarization and the delay in obtaining evidence may lead to the loss of evidence and other factors that are not conducive to obtaining evidence. Second, there are limited judicial resources, lack of rights protection channels, complicated rights protection procedures, and high rights protection costs. Rights are safeguarded through litigation. The judicial litigation process is complicated and the cycle is long.

18.3.6 Royalty Settlement Is Difficult

In addition to rampant piracy, which infringes on the rights of copyright owners, the difficulty in royalty settlement and low returns also infringe on the rights of copyright owners. The reasons for the difficulty in settlement of royalties and low royalties are as follows: First, the benefit distribution system is not perfect. In the digital publishing industry, digital platform operators and terminal equipment manufacturers control the distribution channels of digital works, and occupy a dominant position in the copyright income distribution system. Content providers or original authors have weak bargaining power and cannot obtain the real work in accordance with the distribution of benefits [13]. The second is the opaque method of calculating revenue. Take the music industry as an example. Distributors have strong channel control. Record production, live music performances, and film and TV series charge for the use of musical works are relatively transparent, and copyright revenue is relatively certain. However, digital publishing channels tend to be diversified. Music original authors authorize copyright to the music platform, and their revenue comes from the calculation of song downloads and click-through rates. However, the above-mentioned data is opaque, easy to tamper with, and difficult to monitor, and the original author and content provider cannot control it, resulting in opaque royalty settlement and lagging income, and it is difficult to protect the interests of original authors.

18.3.7 Difficulty of Restricting Widespread Content

The traditional digital rights management system (DRM) pays too much attention to copyright security and restricts its use in a closed system, ignoring the spread of digital content copyright and the expansion of influence. In the current application of copyright protection and management of digital works, the systems developed by various companies are incompatible with each other, resulting in works that cannot be circulated between systems. Once a certain work supports a certain technology, it must always be used to support the playback of that technology else it results in blocked content distribution.

With the emergence of social media and user-generated content models, the miniaturization and rapid spread of digital content works are notable, the enthusiasm for digital content creation is rising, and the era of creation by everyone has arrived. The works of the majority of original creators not only need copyright protection, but also need to be legally copied, disseminated, and shared to maximize the scope of dissemination and maximize royalties. The contradiction between the closed digital copyright protection system and the openness of digital content copyright has become increasingly prominent, and it is difficult to sustain a purely technical blockade. A more open technical system is urgently needed to support the safe dissemination, fair trading and widespread sharing of digital content copyright.

18.4 Role of Blockchain to Empower Digital Copyright

Blockchain technology has a natural fit with digital copyright protection due to its features such as non-tamperable data, anti-counterfeiting and traceability, and therefore brings opportunities to digital copyright protection.

18.4.1 Establishing Ownership of Data Rights

Blockchain can provide a unique mark for a variety of media data, extract the data "fingerprint" through a hash algorithm, establish a one-to-one mapping relationship between the "data object" and its "fingerprint" (hash value), and determine the data itself through asymmetric encryption technology to ensure the authenticity, integrity and uniqueness of the data object, establish a hard link between the owner of the data private key and the data object, realize the confirmation of data rights, and provide technical means for the copyright ownership of the data content works [14].

In the digital copyright confirmation stage, through blockchain technology, the "fingerprint" information (digital abstract/hash value), author information, creation time and other information of digital content works such as pictures, music, and videos are quickly packaged on the chain, and distributed technologies such as integrated storage, timestamping, consensus algorithm, etc. realize the above-mentioned information and data cannot be tampered with, achieve the role of clarification of copyright ownership and solidification of evidence, and complete the copyright registration and authentication process of original digital works. The use of blockchain can greatly simplify the application of traditional copyright to the regulatory authority for copyright certification.

18.4.2 Anti-tampered, Anti-counterfeiting and Traceability

Blockchain technology realizes distributed storage of data. Each node keeps a copy of data. The loss of a single point of data will not affect data integrity. In addition, a consensus mechanism ensures that it is difficult for a single point to tamper with data. The blockchain extracts the data "fingerprint" through a hash algorithm and establishes a link between the data and the "fingerprint". Any falsification of the data will cause the "fingerprint" to change. Furthermore, the blockchain stores data in a chain, and all data operations and activities can be queried and tracked, providing a means for auditing and tracing the data throughout the life cycle. To sum up, the characteristics of non-tampering, anti-counterfeiting and traceability of blockchain technology ensure the authenticity and traceability of data, and can "verify the true content" of data and realize the solidification of evidence.

Digital copyright services involve multiple stages of digital content copyright registration, trading, and dissemination. Problems in any one link will not only affect copyright protection, but also adversely affect the order and stability of the digital production market. Blockchain has the characteristics of data anti-counterfeiting, openness and transparency, and traceability [15]. It can overcome the "inherent deficiencies" of digital content such as "reproducibility, non-exclusiveness, and easy tampering", making the full life cycle of copyright content traceable, inspectable, and auditable thus promotes the establishment of a full life cycle service system for digital copyright.

18.4.3 Smart Contracts Ensuring Safe Transactions

Blockchain smart contracts can be written into automatically executed contract terms, which helps multiple participants to process transactions and settlement transactions according to pre-agreed rules, thereby completing digital asset delivery and transfer. In addition, the blockchain consensus mechanism and smart contracts have constructed a rule protocol for data generation, transmission, calculation and storage in a decentralized environment, creating conditions for the safe flow of digital content works and asset values using data as a carrier. As a result, a basic agreement for value transfer can be realized, facilitating digital copyright transactions, utilization and circulation.

18.4.4 Infringement Evidence Consolidation

One can utilize the technical features of blockchain data that cannot be tampered with, and use feature value analysis and comparison algorithms to find suspected infringements. Further evidence collection through webpage screenshots, video screen recordings, etc., is reduced and just online one-click forensics and records of suspected infringements and content is required. In the blockchain, judicial evidence collection methods with high credibility and low cost of evidence collection are realized, providing technical support and judicial evidence for subsequent rights protection.

The blockchain stores infringement records on the blockchain, and can be connected to the judicial blockchain of the Internet court through a cross-chain method, or as a member node of the alliance with the Internet court, notary office, judicial authentication centre, arbitration committee, and copyright bureau, etc. Judicial institutions build a blockchain judicial alliance chain to realize the interconnection and intercommunication of electronic evidence and the judicial system [16]. When a user initiates a lawsuit, the court directly extracts relevant information from the third-party blockchain digital copyright platform or judicial blockchain from the third-party blockchain digital copyright platform or judicial blockchain when a user initiates a lawsuit, and makes a decision. The entire process of user proof and rights protection and judge verification is convenient and quick, which improves judicial efficiency.

18.4.5 Transparency of Digital Copyright Transaction Settlement

Digital copyright involves multi-party participation and benefit distribution. Taking digital music as an example, the participants involved music content producers, record companies, online music service platforms, and users. Cross-organization and cross-platform make it difficult to track copyright information, and the complicated transaction process further increases the difficulty of tracking, and the uneven distribution of benefits also leads to copyright disputes.

As an open and transparent distributed ledger, the blockchain can realize multi-party participation, authorization authentication and common governance, making the storage, access, distribution, and transaction of digital content transparent, reshaping the digital copyright value chain, and ensuring and balancing digital copyright is the interest of all parties involved in the value chain. In the distribution and communication of digital content works, based on the immutability and openness and transparency of the blockchain, the number of views, downloads, and transactions of digital content works are effectively recorded on the blockchain network, eliminating the black box operation of centralized platforms, and ensuring that the original creators should gain benefits and enhance the creative enthusiasm of original creators.

In addition, based on the blockchain decentralized network, an incentive mechanism for digital content disseminators can be introduced to reduce the market concentration and channel control capabilities of digital copyright distribution platforms. It provides a certain degree of incentives for consumers and disseminators to support, share, and disseminate the work contents in the form of reposting, likes, comments, investment, etc., so that every communication participant can benefit, thereby enhancing the ability to distribute works through multiple channels, and the exposure of original works to maximize the value of works. In the transaction link, through smart contracts, it can help multiple participants such as original creators, content providers, content platform distributors, digital content disseminators, etc. to realize the automatic distribution of income according to consensus and agreement, balance the interests of all parties, and promote the construction of good digital copyright transaction ecology.

18.5 Blockchain-Based Digital Copyright Protection Service

Blockchain-based digital copyright protection services usually include four parts: copyright storage, copyright monitoring and early warning, infringement evidence collection, and judicial rights protection [17]. They also provide full-link services through storage of certificates, monitoring, early warning to rights protection, and efficiently realize the "full life cycle" management of digital works.

1. **Copyright Storage**

   First, the user's real name is registered on the copyright protection platform and the account is obtained, and the identity authentication process is completed. Second, the user submits the text, pictures, audio and video and other digital content works that need to be recorded to the copyright protection platform. Third, the copyright protection platform will copyright the work information, timestamp and other data are calculated to obtain the hash value of the work, and it is stored on the copyright block chain. Further through the cross-chain operation, the above hash value of the copyright block chain is stored on the judicial blockchain. Then, the judicial blockchain returns the deposit number of the above-mentioned deposit information to the copyright blockchain, and the copyright blockchain returns the information file of the deposit number of the above-mentioned information on the judicial blockchain and the deposit number on the copyright blockchain to the user. Finally, users can download the electronic data deposit certificate issued by the copyright protection platform. Users can also inquire about the ownership, storage time, issuing authority, public key and other information of digital works through the digital copyright protection platform.

2. **Monitoring and Early Warning**

Big Data crawler, Big Data analysis, capture card and other technologies are all used to monitor the infringement of the entire network in real time, analyse and compare the characteristics of the monitored content and the work [18]. If the similarity reaches the threshold, the infringing work and the infringement will be collected for evidence, including collecting relevant infringing webpages, websites, pictures, and audio and video clues, and storing the evidence in the digital copyright blockchain system.

3. **Infringement Evidence Collection**

Infringement clues are found through the monitoring platform, and the infringement clues are stored on the copyright blockchain, and the hash value of the above infringement clues is stored on the judicial blockchain through cross-chain operations. The judicial blockchain returns the deposit address of the above information to the copyright blockchain, and the copyright blockchain returns to the user the deposit address on the judicial blockchain and the deposit address of the copyright blockchain information file.

4. **Judicial Rights Protection**

When an infringement occurs, the user opens an online case on the electronic litigation platform of the Internet Court, and at the same time submits the complaint, user identity verification information, source documents for confirmation of rights, source documents for infringement evidence, and documents containing the blockchain deposit number. The electronic litigation platform verifies the information submitted by the user by calling the judicial blockchain. If the verification result shows that the evidence involved in the case has not been tampered with after it has been stored on the judicial blockchain, it will return the successful verification message. The judge decides whether to file a case based on the information submitted by the judge's work platform and the verification of information.

18.5.1 Technical Architecture

The overall architecture of the general blockchain digital copyright platform technology is mainly divided into: basic layer, core layer, service layer, application layer and management layer [19].

Basic layer: This layer is the basic resource layer of the entire system and provides elastic and flexible computing, storage and network resources for the core technology layer. For example, a large amount of digital rights content information can be stored in this layer of distributed system.

Core layer: This layer is the core technology layer which constitutes the copyright blockchain, covering all important functional modules and components of the blockchain, including consensus algorithms, smart contracts, privacy protection, cryptographic algorithms, digital signatures, timestamps and other technologies. The core layer mainly provides blockchain storage services for the upper layer. The above is achieved by storing the hash information of copyright, infringement and other data information in a blockchain system composed of platform operators, judicial institutions, content institutions, copyright protection, etc. so the copyright information cannot be tampered with.

Service layer: This layer mainly provides basic services such as distributed search, monitoring, identity authentication, evidence comparison, and API interface for the application layer. For example, through Big Data, distributed crawlers and other technologies, search for various digital content such as text, pictures, audio and video on the whole network, and monitor possible infringements in real time; through AI Big Data technology, the text and pictures that may be infringed. The video is compared with the original work to confirm the infringement. Core product functions such as judicial rights protection and copyright transactions include: copyright deposit certification, infringement monitoring, copyright confirmation, copyright transactions and judicial rights protection.

Management layer: This layer first provides authoritative credit endorsements for data in the blockchain system, and stores and authenticates information through copyright certification centres, Internet courts, and arbitration centres to ensure the authenticity of digital copyrights in the circulation process. In addition, this layer also effectively supervises and controls key configurations such as permissions, keys, and certificates, so as to ensure the overall reliability of the blockchain digital copyright system.

18.5.2 Key Technologies and Methods

The key technologies and methods involved in the blockchain-based digital copyright system include consensus algorithms, data on-chain and data storage, smart contracts, and digital content retrieval.

Authentication: Each participant in the digital copyright protection constitutes an alliance chain, and the digital copyright blockchain technology provider is responsible for the operation of the alliance chain. When a new user joins the alliance, it needs to be certified by a third-party CA and approved by the alliance chain before joining. The joining of new members can be decided by voting of the participants in copyright protection, or by the joint discussions of all participants. After the new member obtains the permission, the operator assigns a blockchain identity and node type, generates a public and private key, and obtains the corresponding authority.

Data on the chain and data storage: An important step in digital copyright protection is to register digital copyrights, that is, the copyright information of digital works must be there "on the chain". Considering the performance of the blockchain and the size of the data block, digital content works such as text, audio and video cannot be directly stored on the chain to prevent affecting the efficiency of the blockchain. The chain only retains the lightweight data of the copyright of digital works, including fingerprint information (digital digest hash value) of digital content works, such as pictures, music, and videos, author information, work creation time information, timestamps, etc. Digital copyright on-chain registration information is limited to authorized users to access, and digital content works files are stored in the cloud.

Digital copyright information preservation can be divided into the following steps: First, the digital content work file is divided into several data blocks of equal size. Use an asymmetric encryption algorithm to generate user public key and private key pairs to encrypt data files. Secondly, extract key information from digital content work file data and store them on the chain. Considering the efficiency of blockchain transaction consensus and the operating performance of the blockchain system, a small amount of text information such as digital copyright information, digital work file hash information, and file storage address are stored in the block body [20]. Thirdly, use the Merkle tree to analyse digital content work files and perform verification to ensure completeness.

Smart contract: Blockchain smart contracts can realize credible transactions without a third party, and help the safe circulation of digital copyright value. In the blockchain digital copyright transaction system, the industry has tried to design smart contracts into three types of models: content pre-purchase model, retail model and distributor model [21].

The content pre-purchase model refers to the deployment of smart contracts to enable digital content creators to sell future creations in advance. Before the creation of the work, digital content creators and pre-purchasing users pay a certain amount of deposit and pre-purchase amount to the smart contract respectively. The deposit is used to reduce the risk of default by content creators, and the advance payment is used for users to purchase works at a lower price after the works are listed. After the work is completed, the smart contract automatically distributes the digital content work to users participating in the pre-sale, and transfers the deposit and pre-purchase funds to the content creator. If it is not completed within the scheduled time, the smart contract will pay the creator's deposit to the pre-sale user as compensation At the same time, the pre-paid money will be returned to the pre-purchase user.

The retail model refers to the number of times and time that users are authorized to use digital content works through smart contracts. Once the time limit is exceeded, they will not be authorized. The distributor model means that the creator of a digital work entrusts the right to sell the work to the distributor and agrees on the sharing model through smart contracts. For example, according to the number of times the distributor distributes the content, the income is paid to the content creator in proportion.

Digital content retrieval: Digital content retrieval is an important technology in the monitoring of digital copyright infringement. By extracting the features of the digital content and performing similarity matching, it is possible to identify and detect whether the digital content is pirated and infringed. The basic steps of digital content retrieval mainly include feature extraction, fingerprint generation and similarity matching. For example, in terms of digital graphics and images, the physical features such as the visual information of the image content are extracted, including low-level visual information such as color, texture, shape, and high-level visual information such as objects, spatial relationships, scenes, behaviors, and emotions, and the feature information is combined with the entire network image. The features are compared, and images whose similarity exceeds a certain threshold can be considered as suspected infringement.

In terms of digital music, through the similarity measurement method of melody curve geometric registration and melody feature characterization fuzzy matching, the melody feature is characterized according to the twelve-tone equal temperament law and similar matching is performed on the whole network. The principle of retrieval technology for video and other digital content is similar to that of image retrieval. Feature extraction is carried out by extracting key frames from the video, which is then transformed into an image retrieval problem.

Although the effect of feature value extraction and the accuracy of comparison have been continuously improved in recent years, and the digital content retrieval technology has become increasingly mature, as new forms of infringement such as audio and video mixing, graphics and text washing continue to emerge, how to use deep learning algorithms Identification and solution is still a topic that needs to be explored.

Digital watermark: By embedding a unique identification watermark in a digital work, no matter whether or not the digital work is spread to various new media platforms, it can be identified and traced through the watermark. Once the digital copyright infringement monitoring platform finds infringement, It will immediately collect the evidence [22]. In addition, from the entire life cycle of creation, circulation, and consumption of digital works, every authorization and transfer of digital work copyright can be recorded and tracked. This can not only optimize the management method of digital work creators, but also provide judicial evidence for various disputes.

Privacy protection: Using multiple signatures, a piece of information or data can be signed with multiple private keys, indicating that the information is endorsed, managed, and controlled by multiple people. For multi-signature information, its verification and collaboration require multiple authorizations from the signer to complete. For M/N multi-signature, where $1 \leq M \leq N$, N individuals hold N private keys, and at least M individuals must agree to sign before they can operate on the information. Among them, the most common is the 2/3 combination; that is, at least 2 of the 3 people need to agree to sign to operate the digital asset.

18.6 Challenges Faced by Blockchain Digital Copyright Applications

There are various challenges faced in the application of blockchain digital copyright. Some of them are described below.

18.6.1 Integration of Multiple Departments

Blockchain + digital copyright is a cross-industry application, involving multiple organizations and departments such as blockchain, digital copyright, and judiciary. There are differences in the perceptions of all parties, and the integration of industry resources is difficult. Due to factors such as lack of awareness of new technologies, technical thresholds, and immature business models, many digital copyright agencies and enterprises are still uninformed. In fact, the main driving force for the application of blockchain digital copyright comes from blockchain companies; in the future, however, blockchain companies still face greater challenges in promoting the large-scale commercialization of blockchain digital copyrights. First of all, blockchain companies mostly come from Internet companies, or entrepreneurial teams started with blockchain technology, which are far away from the various links of the digital copyright industry chain, and it is difficult to connect with industry resources. Second, as a technology side, blockchain companies and the judiciary are still in a weak position, and their ability to integrate resources is also relatively weak. Finally, blockchain digital copyright applications have failed to bring predictable benefits to digital copyright companies, and the copyright industry has insufficient motivation to participate.

18.6.2 Interconnection of Blockchain Platforms

Due to existence of various blockchain-based copyright service platforms, the copyright information may not be interoperable. If the copyright information is infringed and plagiarized users register to other copyright platforms, then it may be difficult to discover the infringement and rights protection of original creators. If the real ownership relationship and author identity information of a work cannot be determined, it is easy to cause disputes between platforms and between platforms and the users. Therefore, the inability of information to be interconnected makes copyright confirmation may become a false proposition. In addition, digital copyright infringements have no access to the Internet, and any protection platform cannot achieve real-time and seamless monitoring of copyright infringements across the entire network, resulting in greatly reduced copyright protection effects, poor user experience, and affecting the development of blockchain digital copyright applications.

18.7 The Development Trend of Blockchain Digital Copyright Applications

18.7.1 Greater Scope for Development

Copyright transaction is an important link in the circulation value of digital copyright. It can make all or part of the economic rights in the copyright of digital works realize the economic rights of the copyright owner through copyright licensing or transfer. Based on the trusted network constructed by the blockchain, copyright owners are expected to bypass content platform providers, content distribution platforms and royalty collection associations to independently realize copyright transactions, reduce market information asymmetry, and realize face-to-face transactions between copyright owners and consumers. Based on smart contracts, the copyright transaction process can be automatically triggered and executed according to the conditions agreed by both parties to the transaction [23]. In addition, the blockchain can solve the problems of complicated procedures for accessing, distributing, and profiting copyright content, too many participants, and falsification of data. It prevents opaque transactions and creates a free, fair, and efficient environment for digital copyright transactions. It protects the rights and interests of the original creator, maximizes the original creator's economic benefits, stimulates the original creator's enthusiasm, and prospers the copyright trading market. In the future, digital copyright transactions are expected to usher in more room for development.

18.7.2 Rapid Development of Blockchain Digital Copyright Services

The blockchain digital copyright platform is inseparable from the in-depth application of technologies such as AI and Big Data in the process of serving the copyright industry. In order to discover possible online infringements, in theory, real-time monitoring of all webpage data on the Internet is required. In fact, the general search crawler technology is difficult to deal with, which relies on distributed crawlers and

Big Data analysis technology to automatically crawl and store massive webpage data around the clock. In addition, AI recognition technology can be used to distinguish the similarity of pictures, audio and video, and to identify and analyse the above-mentioned captured data. Once clues of infringement are found, infringement evidence can be immediately conducted. Generally speaking, existing AI technology can identify simple modifications to original digital works, for example, original pictures and pictures modified by retouching software. However, it is still difficult to identify plagiarism in literary manuscripts and picture creativity. In the future, with the continuous upgrading and improvement of AI technology, it is expected to be widely and in-depth applied to realize the identification of the above-mentioned infringements.

Blockchain digital copyright stimulates the production of high-quality content, and the copyright payment atmosphere is expected to form a blockchain-based copyright blockchain platform to realize copyright confirmation, certification and protection of copyright, reducing "infringement losses" and through transparency of copyright. The transaction increases "original income", safeguards the value of digital copyright works and the rights of copyright creators, helps digital copyrights better realize and maximizes copyright owners' income, stimulates copyright creators' creative enthusiasm, and helps them produce better-quality content works. With the increase of copyright owners' awareness of copyright protection and the multi-pronged approach of protection tools and methods, including legal and technical means, an atmosphere of respect for copyright and copyright payment in the whole society is expected to form.

18.8 Steps Required for Improvement

For the improvements of blockchain digital copyright applications we present some suggestions which can be implemented at different levels.

18.8.1 Government level

1. Actively support the development and application of emerging technologies such as blockchain in the field of digital copyright, such as artificial intelligence, Big Data, and blockchain, providing new methods and models for copyright protection in the network environment. At the national level, relevant guidance can be issued to actively promote the deep integration of new technologies such as blockchain with the digital content industry, standardize the order of digital copyright, build a healthy digital copyright ecology, and accelerate the development of our country's digital copyright industry.

2. Promote the establishment of a blockchain digital copyright industry alliance to achieve cross-border resource integration and cooperation. Actively support

the establishment of a cross-industry, multi-organization, and multi-sectoral blockchain digital copyright industry ecological alliance, which is for the blockchain industry and the digital copyright industry. The main body builds a platform for cooperation and exchange to promote the integration of cross-border resources.

3. Promote the pilot demonstration of blockchain digital copyright service application support typical blockchain digital copyright application cases with good application effects and strong demonstration effects, pilot demonstrations in basic and conditional fields, and enhance the application of blockchain in the digital copyright field thoroughly.

18.8.2 Enterprise level

The strengthening of multi-party cooperation and the establishment of a one-stop service platform for the full chain of blockchain copyright is important. Digital copyright protection involves all links in the full life cycle of copyright, including copyright certification, distribution, trading, and infringement rights protection. For blockchain digital copyright service operating companies, only developing blockchain digital copyright certificate services will face greater market competition pressure. In the era of digital economy, platform strategy and ecological strategy have become important business models. Blockchain copyright service companies should actively strengthen cooperation with copyright content parties and judicial institutions, establish a one-stop service platform for the full chain of blockchain copyrights, provide users with convenient blockchain infringement evidence collection and judicial rights protection services, and build a commercial bridge, enhancing its own competitiveness.

18.8.3 Technical level

Here the efforts include: improving digital copyright infringement monitoring capabilities and actively introducing the application of AI and Big Data technology in the monitoring of digital copyright infringement; accelerating the research of AI in the identification of infringement activities such as manuscript washing and creative plagiarism; expanding the breadth and depth of channel monitoring on websites and social media platforms; and improving the discovery of text, images, audio and video infringement capacity.

Another effort could be done by promoting the application of cross-chain technology in the field of blockchain digital copyright. It requires to strengthen blockchain digital copyright platform technology and business cooperation, actively promote cross-chain technology to realize the interconnection of digital copyright information between platforms, break information islands, and jointly promote our country's construction of a healthy copyright protection ecology.

18.9 Conclusion

Today, advances in digital content creation technologies allow anyone to disseminate and share content, but managing the rights to such content remains a vital practice for commercial platforms and for creators themselves, requiring a most efficient way to manage and demonstrate ownership of copyright information in works. In this way, using blockchain technology-based digital rights management system allows authenticating, sharing and managing the rights of digital resources, also being able to process all the information related to the copyright of the product. This system is also specialized in the management of information related to the rights of digital works, with functions that allow to demonstrate the date and time at which the electronic data were created, record any verifiable information in a way that is difficult to falsify, and identify previously registered works, allowing participants to share and verify when and who generated an electronic data transaction. In addition to the creation of electronic data, this system will automatically verify the rights generation of the digital work. The system makes it possible to manage the rights of various types of digital content, including electronic books, educational content, music, movies, and dramatic content.

References

[1] Lichtman, D. and Landes, W.M., 2002. Indirect liability for copyright infringement: an economic perspective. *Harv. JL & Tech.*, *16*, p. 395.

[2] Cao, S., Cao, Y., Wang, X. and Lu, Y., 2017. A review of researches on blockchain. In *Wuhan International Conference on e-Business*. Association For Information Systems.

[3] Loewenstein, J., 2010. *The author's due: Printing and the prehistory of copyright.* University of Chicago Press.

[4] Fabunmi, B.A., Paris, M. and Fabunmi, M., 2009. Digitization of library resources: Challenges and implications for policy and planning. *International Journal of African & African-American Studies*, *5*(2), pp. 23–36.

[5] Holland, M., Nigischer, C. and Stjepandic, J., 2017. Copyright protection in additive manufacturing with blockchain approach. *Transdisciplinary Engineering: A Paradigm Shift*, *5*, pp. 914–921.

[6] Savelyev, A., 2018. Copyright in the blockchain era: Promises and challenges. *Computer law & security review*, *34*(3), pp.550–561.

[7] Bodó, B., Gervais, D. and Quintais, J.P., 2018. Blockchain and smart contracts: the missing link in copyright licensing?. *International Journal of Law and Information Technology*, *26*(4), pp. 311–336.

[8] Heft, A., Mayerhöffer, E., Reinhardt, S. and Knüpfer, C., 2020. Beyond Breitbart: Comparing right-wing digital news infrastructures in six western democracies. *Policy & Internet*, *12*(1), pp. 20–45.

[9] Ginsburg, J. (2001). Copyright and Control over New Technologies of Dissemination. *Columbia Law Review*, *101*(7), pp. 1613–1647. doi: 10.2307/1123809.

[10] Nair, S.B., Digital Piracy in Music Records Industry: An Economic and Legal Analysis on DRM Provisions in India. *International Journal of Research in Engineering, Science and Management*, 1(10), pp. 11–16.

[11] Bodó, B., Gervais, D. and Quintais, J.P., 2018. Blockchain and smart contracts: the missing link in copyright licensing?. *International Journal of Law and Information Technology*, 26(4), pp. 311–336.

[12] Latonero, M., 2018. *Governing artificial intelligence: Upholding human rights & dignity.* Data & Society, New York.

[13] Heilig, L., Schwarze, S. and Voß, S., 2017. An analysis of digital transformation in the history and future of modern ports. *Proceedings of the 50th Hawaii International Conference on System Sciences (HICSS)*, Waikoloa Village, Hawaii.

[14] Van Rijmenam, M. and Ryan, P., 2018. *Blockchain: Transforming your business and our world.* Routledge, London.

[15] Fohlin, E. and Ysberg, J., 2019. *Utilization of Blockchain technologies for enhanced transparency and traceability in the Supply Chain.*

[16] Xiong, Y. and Du, J., 2019, January. Electronic evidence preservation model based on blockchain. In *Proceedings of the 3rd International Conference on Cryptography, Security and Privacy* (pp. 1–5).

[17] Qureshi, A. and Megías Jiménez, D., 2020. Blockchain-Based Multimedia Content Protection: Review and Open Challenges. *Applied Sciences*, 11(1), p.1.

[18] Edelenbos, J., Hirzalla, F., van Zoonen, L., van Dalen, J., Bouma, G., Slob, A. and Woestenburg, A., 2018. Governing the complexity of smart data cities: Setting a research agenda. In *Smart Technologies for Smart Governments* (pp. 35–54). Springer, Cham.

[19] Savelyev, A., 2018. Copyright in the blockchain era: Promises and challenges. *Computer law & security review*, 34(3), pp. 550–561.

[20] Vatsalan, D., Sehili, Z., Christen, P. and Rahm, E., 2017. Privacy-preserving record linkage for big data: Current approaches and research challenges. In *Handbook of Big Data Technologies* (pp. 851–895). Springer, Cham.

[21] Kemmoe, V.Y., Stone, W., Kim, J., Kim, D. and Son, J., 2020. Recent advances in smart contracts: A technical overview and state of the art. *IEEE Access*, 8, pp. 117782–117801.

[22] Saini, L.K. and Shrivastava, V., 2014. A survey of digital watermarking techniques and its applications. *arXiv preprint arXiv:1407.4735.*

[23] Savelyev, A., 2018. Copyright in the blockchain era: Promises and challenges. *Computer law & security review*, 34(3), pp. 550–561.

Index

Page numbers in **bold** indicate tables, page numbers in *italic* indicate figures.